Research Developments in Biometrics and Video Processing Techniques

Rajeev Srivastava
Indian Institute of Technology (BHU), Varanasi, India

S.K. Singh
Indian Institute of Technology (BHU), Varanasi, India

K.K. Shukla
Indian Institute of Technology (BHU), Varanasi, India

T0320588

A volume in the Advances in Information Security, Privacy, and Ethics (AISPE) Book Series

Information Science
REFERENCE
An Imprint of IGI Global

Managing Director:	Lindsay Johnston
Editorial Director:	Myla Merkel
Production Manager:	Jennifer Yoder
Publishing Systems Analyst:	Adrienne Freeland
Development Editor:	Allyson Gard
Acquisitions Editor:	Kayla Wolfe
Typesetter:	John Crodian
Cover Design:	Jason Mull

Published in the United States of America by
Information Science Reference (an imprint of IGI Global)
701 E. Chocolate Avenue
Hershey PA 17033
Tel: 717-533-8845
Fax: 717-533-8661
E-mail: cust@igi-global.com
Web site: http://www.igi-global.com

Library of Congress Cataloging-in-Publication Data

Research developments in biometrics and video processing techniques / Rajeev Srivastava, S.K. Singh and K.K. Shukla, editors.
    pages cm
 Includes bibliographical references and index.
   ISBN 978-1-4666-4868-5 (hardcover) -- ISBN 978-1-4666-4870-8 (print & perpetual access) -- ISBN 978-1-4666-4869-2 (ebook) 1. Biometric identification. 2. Image processing. 3. Digital video. I. Srivastava, Rajeev, 1974- editor of compilation. II. Singh, S. K., 1970- editor of compilation. III. Shukla, K. K., 1958- editor of compilation.
 TK7882.B56R47 2014
 006.4--dc23
                                    2013032974

This book is published in the IGI Global book series Advances in Information Security, Privacy, and Ethics (AISPE) (ISSN: 1948-9730; eISSN: 1948-9749)

British Cataloguing in Publication Data
A Cataloguing in Publication record for this book is available from the British Library.

All work contributed to this book is new, previously-unpublished material. The views expressed in this book are those of the authors, but not necessarily of the publisher. For electronic access to this publication, please contact: eresources@igi-global.com.

Advances in Information Security, Privacy, and Ethics (AISPE) Book Series

ISSN: 1948-9730
EISSN: 1948-9749

MISSION

In the digital age, when everything from municipal power grids to individual mobile telephone locations is all available in electronic form, the implications and protection of this data has never been more important and controversial. As digital technologies become more pervasive in everyday life and the Internet is utilized in ever increasing ways by both private and public entities, the need for more research on securing, regulating, and understanding these areas is growing.

The **Advances in Information Security, Privacy, & Ethics (AISPE) Book Series** is the source for this research, as the series provides only the most cutting-edge research on how information is utilized in the digital age.

COVERAGE

- Access Control
- CIA Triad of Information Security
- Computer Ethics
- Cookies
- Cyberethics
- Data Storage of Minors
- Device Fingerprinting
- Electronic Mail Security
- Global Privacy Concerns
- Information Security Standards
- Internet Governance
- IT Risk
- Network Security Services
- Privacy Issues of Social Networking
- Privacy-Enhancing Technologies
- Risk Management
- Security Classifications
- Security Information Management
- Technoethics
- Telecommunications Regulations
- Tracking Cookies

IGI Global is currently accepting manuscripts for publication within this series. To submit a proposal for a volume in this series, please contact our Acquisition Editors at Acquisitions@igi-global.com or visit: http://www.igi-global.com/publish/.

Titles in this Series

For a list of additional titles in this series, please visit: www.igi-global.com

Research Developments in Biometrics and Video Processing Techniques
Rajeev Srivastava (Indian Institute of Technology (BHU), India) S.K. Singh (Indian Institute of Technology (BHU), India) and K.K. Shukla (Indian Institute of Technology (BHU), India)
Information Science Reference • copyright 2014 • 237pp • H/C (ISBN: 9781466648685) • US $195.00 (our price)

Security, Privacy, Trust, and Resource Management in Mobile and Wireless Communications
Danda B. Rawat (Georgia Southern University, USA) Bhed B. Bista (Iwate Prefectural University, Japan) and Gongjun Yan (University of Southern Indiana, USA)
Information Science Reference • copyright 2014 • 413pp • H/C (ISBN: 9781466646919) • US $195.00 (our price)

Architectures and Protocols for Secure Information Technology Infrastructures
Antonio Ruiz-Martinez (University of Murcia, Spain) Rafael Marin-Lopez (University of Murcia, Spain) and Fernando Pereniguez-Garcia (University of Murcia, Spain)
Information Science Reference • copyright 2014 • 427pp • H/C (ISBN: 9781466645141) • US $195.00 (our price)

Theory and Practice of Cryptography Solutions for Secure Information Systems
Atilla Elçi (Aksaray University, Turkey) Josef Pieprzyk (Macquarie University, Australia) Alexander G. Chefranov (Eastern Mediterranean University, North Cyprus) Mehmet A. Orgun (Macquarie University, Australia) Huaxiong Wang (Nanyang Technological University, Singapore) and Rajan Shankaran (Macquarie University, Australia)
Information Science Reference • copyright 2013 • 351pp • H/C (ISBN: 9781466640306) • US $195.00 (our price)

IT Security Governance Innovations Theory and Research
Daniel Mellado (Spanish Tax Agency, Spain) Luis Enrique Sánchez (University of Castilla-La Mancha, Spain) Eduardo Fernández-Medina (University of Castilla – La Mancha, Spain) and Mario G. Piattini (University of Castilla - La Mancha, Spain)
Information Science Reference • copyright 2013 • 373pp • H/C (ISBN: 9781466620834) • US $195.00 (our price)

Threats, Countermeasures, and Advances in Applied Information Security
Manish Gupta (State University of New York at Buffalo, USA) John Walp (M&T Bank Corporation, USA) and Raj Sharman (State University of New York, USA)
Information Science Reference • copyright 2012 • 319pp • H/C (ISBN: 9781466609785) • US $195.00 (our price)

www.igi-global.com

701 E. Chocolate Ave., Hershey, PA 17033
Order online at www.igi-global.com or call 717-533-8845 x100
To place a standing order for titles released in this series, contact: cust@igi-global.com
Mon-Fri 8:00 am - 5:00 pm (est) or fax 24 hours a day 717-533-8661

Table of Contents

Preface xii

Acknowledgment xvi

Section 1
Biometrics and Security Techniques

Chapter 1
Thermal Human Face Recognition for Biometric Security System 1
Ayan Seal, Jadavpur University, India
Debotosh Bhattacharjee, Jadavpur University, India
Mita Nasipuri, Jadavpur University, India
Dipak Kumar Basu, Jadavpur University, India

Chapter 2
Multimodal Biometrics Recognition for Newborns 25
Shrikant Tiwari, Indian Institute of Technology, India
Sanjay Kumar Singh, Indian Institute of Technology, India

Chapter 3
Biometric Authentication Based on Hand Vein Pattern 52
Munaga V. N. K. Prasad, IDRBT, India
Ilaiah Kavati, IDRBT, India

Chapter 4
Securing Biometrics Using Watermarking 65
Punam Bedi, University of Delhi, India
Roli Bansal, University of Delhi, India
Priti Sehgal, University of Delhi, India

Section 2
Video Processing

Chapter 5
Stereo Vision-Based Object Matching, Detection, and Tracking: A Review... 91
  Mohamed Saifuddin, Sunway University, Malaysia
  Lee Seng Yeong, Sunway University, Malaysia
  Seng Kah Phooi, Sunway University, Malaysia
  Ang Li-Minn, Edith Cowan University, Australia

Chapter 6
Feature-Based Affine Motion Estimation for Superresolution of a Region of Interest 118
  Sung Hyun Kim, Sogang University, Korea
  Rae-Hong Park, Sogang University, Korea
  Seungjoon Yang, Ulsan National Institute of Science and Technology, Korea
  Hwa-Young Kim, Sogang University, Korea

Chapter 7
Daubechies Complex Wavelet-Based Computer Vision Applications 138
  Manish Khare, University of Allahabad, India
  Rajneesh Kumar Srivastava, University of Allahabad, India
  Ashish Khare, University of Allahabad, India

Chapter 8
Application of Computer Vision Techniques for Exploiting New Video Coding Mechanisms 156
  Artur Miguel Arsenio, Nokia Siemens Networks SA, Portugal
    & Universidade Tecnica de Lisboa, Portugal

Chapter 9
Recognition of Humans and Their Activities for Video Surveillance 183
  Alok Kumar Singh Kushwaha, Indian Institute of Technology (BHU), India
  Rajeev Srivastava, Indian Institute of Technology (BHU), India

Chapter 10
Video Authentication: An Intelligent Approach.. 199
  Saurabh Upadhyay, Saffrony Institute of Technology, India
  Shrikant Tiwari, Indian Institute of Technology (BHU), India
  Shalabh Parashar, HCL Technologies, India

Compilation of References 232

About the Contributors 255

Index 260

Detailed Table of Contents

Preface xii

Acknowledgment xvi

Section 1
Biometrics and Security Techniques

Chapter 1
Thermal Human Face Recognition for Biometric Security System 1
Ayan Seal, Jadavpur University, India
Debotosh Bhattacharjee, Jadavpur University, India
Mita Nasipuri, Jadavpur University, India
Dipak Kumar Basu, Jadavpur University, India

This chapter presents an overview of some of the well-known techniques of face recognition using thermal infrared faces. This chapter talks about some of the most recent algorithms developed for this purpose and gives a brief idea of the state of the art of face recognition technology. An approach for evaluating the performance of face recognition algorithms using thermal infrared images is proposed. The results of several classifiers on benchmark dataset (Terravic Facial Infrared Database) are reported.

Chapter 2
Multimodal Biometrics Recognition for Newborns 25
Shrikant Tiwari, Indian Institute of Technology, India
Sanjay Kumar Singh, Indian Institute of Technology, India

Identification of newborns at birth is a critical issue for hospitals, birthing centres, and other institutions where multiple births occur. Mixing, abduction, and illegal adoption of newborns is a global problem, and the research done to solve this problem is minimal. This chapter presents a multimodal biometric framework for the recognition of newborns.

Chapter 3
Biometric Authentication Based on Hand Vein Pattern 52
Munaga V. N. K. Prasad, IDRBT, India
Ilaiah Kavati, IDRBT, India

This chapter discusses vein pattern authentication, which uses the vascular patterns of the back of the hand as personal authentication data. A dynamic ROI extraction algorithm is presented through which more features can be extracted when compared to the fixed ROI. Further, the extracted ROI is enhanced and de-noised. The two key features, bifurcation and ending points, which represent the geometric information of the vein pattern are extracted. A new vein pattern recognition system is introduced by assigning different weights to bifurcation and ending points. The approach is tested on a vein pattern database of 60 different hands. Experimental results show the approach achieves 2.5% of Equal Error Rate (EER) and recognition accuracy of 98.24%.

Chapter 4
Securing Biometrics Using Watermarking 65
Punam Bedi, University of Delhi, India
Roli Bansal, University of Delhi, India
Priti Sehgal, University of Delhi, India

This chapter focuses on the role of watermarking techniques in biometric systems. This work finds application in a number of security implementations based on multimodal biometric authentication. Computationally intelligent techniques can be employed to develop efficient watermarking algorithms in terms of watermarked image quality and distortion tolerance-ability.

Section 2
Video Processing

Chapter 5
Stereo Vision-Based Object Matching, Detection, and Tracking: A Review.. 91
Mohamed Saifuddin, Sunway University, Malaysia
Lee Seng Yeong, Sunway University, Malaysia
Seng Kah Phooi, Sunway University, Malaysia
Ang Li-Minn, Edith Cowan University, Australia

Stereo vision has turned out to be an important research component in the subdivision of computer vision and image processing that deals with the extraction of information from images for the purpose of video surveillance systems, mimicking the human vision for the visually impaired, for robotics to control unmanned vehicles, for security purposes, virtual reality, and 3-Dimensional (3D) televisions, etc. This chapter presents a comprehensive review of recent algorithms for stereo matching, object detection, and tracking techniques for stereo vision.

Chapter 6
Feature-Based Affine Motion Estimation for Superresolution of a Region of Interest 118
Sung Hyun Kim, Sogang University, Korea
Rae-Hong Park, Sogang University, Korea
Seungjoon Yang, Ulsan National Institute of Science and Technology, Korea
Hwa-Young Kim, Sogang University, Korea

This chapter presents an interpolation method of low-computation for a Region Of Interest (ROI) using multiple low-resolution images of the same scene. The proposed Super Resolution (SR) method employs a simple global motion model only to the ROI that contains important information of the scene. The ROIs extracted from multiple images are assumed to have simple global motions. Experimental results show that the feature-based Motion Estimation (ME) is accurate, and reducing the computational load of the ME step is efficient in terms of the computational complexity. It is also shown that the SR results using the proposed method are remarkable even when input images contain complex motions and a large amount of noise. The proposed POCS-based SR algorithm can be applied to digital cameras, portable camcorders, and so on.

Chapter 7

Daubechies Complex Wavelet-Based Computer Vision Applications 138

    Manish Khare, University of Allahabad, India

    Rajneesh Kumar Srivastava, University of Allahabad, India

    Ashish Khare, University of Allahabad, India

In this chapter, the basic concepts of Daubechies complex wavelet transforms, their properties, and capabilities are discussed. Further, two computer vision applications, namely moving object segmentation and moving shadow detection and removal using Daubechies complex wavelet transform, are proposed and discussed. Results obtained show that the Daubechies complex wavelet transform provides better results than other real-valued wavelet transform-based methods for the applications in consideration and have good potential for other applications as well.

Chapter 8

Application of Computer Vision Techniques for Exploiting New Video Coding Mechanisms 156

    Artur Miguel Arsenio, Nokia Siemens Networks SA, Portugal

      & Universidade Tecnica de Lisboa, Portugal

This chapter discusses the concerns related to current multimedia platforms for provisioning of content to end-users that provides them a good quality of experience, which can be achieved through new interactive, personalized content applications, as well by improving the image quality delivered. These issues are addressed by describing mechanisms for changing content consumption. The aim is to give Application Service Providers (ASPs) new ways to allow users to configure contents according to their personal tastes while also improving their quality of experience, and to possibly charge users for such functionalities. The author proposes to employ computer vision techniques to produce extra object information, which further expands the range of video personalization possibilities on the presence of new video coding mechanisms.

Chapter 9

Recognition of Humans and Their Activities for Video Surveillance 183

    Alok Kumar Singh Kushwaha, Indian Institute of Technology (BHU), India

    Rajeev Srivastava, Indian Institute of Technology (BHU), India

This chapter gives a detailed overview and survey of methods for recognition of humans and their activities for video surveillance. Image representations and the subsequent classification process are discussed to focus on the novelties of recent research. The limitations of the state of the art are discussed, and promising directions of research are outlined. Comprehensive comparative analyses of standard existing methods are also presented.

Chapter 10

Video Authentication: An Intelligent Approach... 199

    Saurabh Upadhyay, Saffrony Institute of Technology, India

    Shrikant Tiwari, Indian Institute of Technology (BHU), India

    Shalabh Parashar, HCL Technologies, India

This chapter presents an intelligent video authentication technique for raw videos using a support vector machine-based classifier and its applications. The method discussed covers both types of tampering attacks, spatial and temporal. It uses a database of more than 2000 tampered and non-tampered videos and gives excellent results with 98.38% classification accuracy. A vast diversity of tampering attacks, which are possible for video sequences are also discussed. The proposed method gives good results for almost all kinds of tampering attacks.

Compilation of References 232

About the Contributors 255

Index 260

Preface

This book presents the recent research developments and applications in the areas of Biometrics and Video Processing. The book will serve as a research reference book in the areas of Biometrics and Security Techniques, and Video Processing.

Section 1 of the book presents chapters related to recent research developments in the area of biometrics and security techniques. Biometrics is the science of recognizing people by their physiological and behavioural characteristics. It holds a lot of promise in revolutionizing the way authentication works today. With a very security conscious society, biometrics-based authentication and identification have become the centre of attention for many important applications as it is believed that biometrics can provide the necessary accuracy and reliability. As the objective of biometric systems is to identify individuals based on their physiological or behavioural information, many types of biometric technologies have surfaced in recent years to provide a more secure and user-friendly methods of identification. Physiological characteristics such as face, retina, fingerprints, palm, veins, etc. have been widely researched, and many of these biometric-based products have been commercialized and used in a wide variety of applications. On the other hand, biometric products based on behavioural characteristics such as signature, voice, gait, etc. are less popular, and not as many are commercially available due to their higher rate of error when compared to physiologically based biometric products.

Section 2 of the book presents various chapters related to recent research developments in the field of video processing. The various topics presented in this section include a review on stereo vision-based object matching, detection, and tracking; feature-based affine motion estimation for super resolution of a region of interest; Daubechies complex wavelet-based computer vision applications to video processing; application of computer vision techniques for exploiting new video coding mechanisms; recognition of humans and their activities for video surveillance; and video authentication.

SCHOLARLY VALUE, POTENTIAL CONTRIBUTION/IMPACT, AND PURPOSE

At present most of the books available in the field of biometrics and video processing are tuned to very specific limited research fields. This book intend to serve the purposes of a large audience working in related or allied areas, including students, researchers, professors, practicing engineers, application developers, etc. In addition, this book will be helpful for new as well as experienced researchers to familiarise themselves with the new research areas and their possible applications in the said field. This book incorporates the methodologies to develop algorithms for the related problem in hand and new research trends. In addition, this book also incorporates the chapters related to new challenging application areas. Emphasis has been given to develop each and every chapter incorporating a latest literature review, methods and models, implementation, experimental results, performance analysis, conclusion, future work, and the latest relevant references.

POTENTIAL USES/INTENDED AUDIENCE

Interdisciplinary engineering students at final year UG level, PG level, and doctoral research students, as well as faculty members/trainers/professors, research scientists, and practicing engineers and software application developers will find this book useful.

ORGANIZATION OF THE BOOK

Research Developments in Biometrics and Video Processing Techniques provides an overview, recent research developments in the field of computer vision and image processing, and related applications. This book contains 10 chapters divided in to two sections, namely Section 1: Biometrics and Security Techniques, and Section 2: Video Processing. Section 1 contains 4 chapters from Chapter 1 to Chapter 4, and Section 2 contains 6 chapters from Chapter 5 to Chapter 10.

Section 1: Biometrics and Security Techniques

Chapter 1: "Thermal Human Face Recognition for Biometric Security System"

This chapter presents an overview of some of the well-known techniques of face recognition using thermal infrared faces. This chapter talks about some of the most recent algorithms developed for this purpose and gives a brief idea of the state of the art of face recognition technology. An approach for evaluating the performance of face recognition algorithms using thermal infrared images is proposed. The results of several classifiers on benchmark dataset (Terravic Facial Infrared Database) are reported.

Chapter 2: "Multimodal Biometric Recognition for Newborns"

Identification of newborns at birth is a critical issue for hospitals, birthing centres, and other institutions where multiple births occur. Mixing, abduction, and illegal adoption of newborns is a global problem, and the research done to solve this problem is minimal. This chapter presents a multimodal biometric framework for the recognition of newborns.

Chapter 3: "Biometric Authentication Based on Hand Vein Pattern"

This chapter discusses vein pattern authentication, which uses the vascular patterns of the back of the hand as personal authentication data. A dynamic ROI extraction algorithm is presented through which more features can be extracted when compared to the fixed ROI. Further, the extracted ROI is enhanced and de-noised. The two key features, bifurcation and ending points, which represent the geometric information of the vein pattern are extracted. A new vein pattern recognition system is introduced by assigning different weights to bifurcation and ending points. The approach is tested on a vein pattern database of 60 different hands. Experimental results show the approach achieves 2.5% of Equal Error Rate (EER) and recognition accuracy of 98.24%.

Chapter 4: "Securing Biometrics Using Watermarking"

This chapter focuses on the role of watermarking techniques in biometric systems. This work finds application in a number of security implementations based on multimodal biometric authentication. Computationally intelligent techniques can be employed to develop efficient watermarking algorithms in terms of watermarked image quality and distortion tolerance-ability.

Section 2: Video Processing

Chapter 5: "Stereo Vision-Based Object Matching, Detection, and Tracking: A Review"

Stereo vision has turned out to be an important research component in the subdivision of computer vision and image processing that deals with the extraction of information from images for the purpose of video surveillance systems, mimicking the human vision for the visually impaired, for robotics to control unmanned vehicles, for security purposes, virtual reality, and 3-Dimensional (3D) televisions, etc. This chapter presents a comprehensive review of recent algorithms for stereo matching, object detection, and tracking techniques for stereo vision.

Chapter 6: "Feature-Based Affine Motion Estimation for Super Resolution of a Region of Interest"

This chapter presents an interpolation method of low-computation for a Region Of Interest (ROI) using multiple low-resolution images of the same scene. The proposed Super Resolution (SR) method employs a simple global motion model only to the ROI that contains important information of the scene. The ROIs extracted from multiple images are assumed to have simple global motions. Experimental results show that the feature-based Motion Estimation (ME) is accurate, and reducing the computational load of the ME step is efficient in terms of the computational complexity. It is also shown that the SR results using the proposed method are remarkable even when input images contain complex motions and a large amount of noise. The proposed POCS-based SR algorithm can be applied to digital cameras, portable camcorders, and so on.

Chapter 7: "Daubechies Complex Wavelet-Based Computer Vision Applications"

In this chapter, the basic concepts of Daubechies complex wavelet transforms, their properties, and capabilities are discussed. Further, two computer vision applications, namely moving object segmentation and moving shadow detection and removal using Daubechies complex wavelet transform, are proposed and discussed. Results obtained show that the Daubechies complex wavelet transform provides better results than other real-valued wavelet transform-based methods for the applications in consideration and have good potential for other applications as well.

Chapter 8: "Application of Computer Vision Techniques for Exploiting New Video Coding Mechanisms"

This chapter discusses the concerns related to current multimedia platforms for provisioning of content to end-users that provides them a good quality of experience, which can be achieved through new interactive, personalized content applications, as well by improving the image quality delivered. These issues are addressed by describing mechanisms for changing content consumption. The aim is to give Application Service Providers (ASPs) new ways to allow users to configure contents according to their personal tastes while also improving their quality of experience, and to possibly charge users for such functionalities. The author proposes to employ computer vision techniques to produce extra object information, which further expands the range of video personalization possibilities on the presence of new video coding mechanisms.

Chapter 9: "Recognition of Humans and Their Activities for Video Surveillance"

This chapter gives a detailed overview and survey of methods for recognition of humans and their activities for video surveillance. Image representations and the subsequent classification process are discussed to focus on the novelties of recent research. The limitations of the state of the art are discussed, and promising directions of research are outlined. Comprehensive comparative analyses of standard existing methods are also presented.

Chapter 10: "Video Authentication: An Intelligent Approach"

This chapter presents an intelligent video authentication technique for raw videos using a support vector machine-based classifier and its applications. The method discussed covers both types of tampering attacks, spatial and temporal. It uses a database of more than 2000 tampered and non-tampered videos and gives excellent results with 98.38% classification accuracy. A vast diversity of tampering attacks, which are possible for video sequences are also discussed. The proposed method gives good results for almost all kinds of tampering attacks.

Rajeev Srivastava
Indian Institute of Technology (BHU), Varanasi, India

Sanjay K. Singh
Indian Institute of Technology (BHU), Varanasi, India

K.K. Shukla
Indian Institute of Technology (BHU), Varanasi, India

Acknowledgment

First and foremost, we would like to express our sincere and profound gratitude to our institute (Indian Institute of Technology [Banaras Hindu University], Varanasi, India) for providing all concerned facilities and help in completing this book.

We are very much thankful to all the authors who submitted their manuscripts for consideration and publication and to our editorial advisory board members and reviewers for guiding us during the whole book development process and providing the critical reviews to enhance the quality of the book.

We mention our special thanks to the Director of Intellectual Properties and Contracts, IGI Global, Jan Travers, who considered our proposal and provided us a reputed international platform for publishing our work. We are thankful to Kayla Wolfe (Aquisitions Editor) with whom we interacted in our initial stage of proposal submission. We mention our special thanks to Allyson Gard (Editorial Assistant), who helped us during our final submission stage of the book. We also extend our special thanks to Monica Speca (Editorial Assistant), who helped us at every stage of the development process of the book.

We are thankful to our friends and colleagues at IIT(BHU) for their support, encouragement, and fruitful discussions at various stages to enhance the quality of the book.

We are thankful to our family members who cooperated with us during the whole book development process.

Editor (Rajeev Srivastava) mentions his special thanks to his mother, wife (Deepti Srivastava), daughters (Dishita and Suhani), and brother for their encouragement, help, support, and dedication, which has helped him in completing this book.

Finally, we extend our sincere thanks to our Ph.D. research scholars of the institute, Mr. Subodh Srivastava, Mr. Shailendra Tiwari, Mr. Rajesh Kumar, and Mr. Alok Kumar Singh, for helping us at various stages.

Last but not least, we would like to thank almighty God and everybody who has directly or indirectly helped us in completing this important book.

Rajeev Srivastava
Indian Institute of Technology (BHU), Varanasi, India

Sanjay K. Singh
Indian Institute of Technology (BHU), Varanasi, India

K.K. Shukla
Indian Institute of Technology (BHU), Varanasi, India

Section 1
Biometrics and Security Techniques

Chapter 1
Thermal Human Face Recognition for Biometric Security System

Ayan Seal
Jadavpur University, India

Debotosh Bhattacharjee
Jadavpur University, India

Mita Nasipuri
Jadavpur University, India

Dipak Kumar Basu
Jadavpur University, India

ABSTRACT

Automatic face recognition has been comprehensively studied for more than four decades, since face recognition of individuals has many applications, particularly in human-machine interaction and security. Although face recognition systems have achieved a significant level of maturity with some realistic achievement, face recognition still remains a challenging problem due to large variation in face images. Face recognition techniques can be generally divided into three categories based on the face image acquisition methodology: methods that work on intensity images, those that deal with video sequences, and those that require other sensory (like 3D sensory or infra-red imagery) data. Researchers are using thermal infrared images for face recognition. Since thermal infrared images have some advantages over 2D images. In this chapter, an overview of some of the well-known techniques of face recognition using thermal infrared faces are discussed, and some of the drawbacks and benefits of each of these methods mentioned therein are discussed. This chapter talks about some of the most recent algorithms developed for this purpose, and tries to give a brief idea of the state of the art of face recognition technology. The authors propose one approach for evaluating the performance of face recognition algorithms using thermal infrared images. They also note the results of several classifiers on a benchmark dataset (Terravic Facial Infrared Database).

DOI: 10.4018/978-1-4666-4868-5.ch001

INTRODUCTION

In this modern world, people are worried about the necessity of security, related to the various applications they used in their usual life, from ATMs to attendance maintenance systems. A user-friendly but strongly secured environment is required ubiquitously to protect our privacy and identity without being tampered by any unauthorized means. The traditional security systems generally use password or Personal Identification Number (PIN) and magnetic cards that necessitate the memorization of data to access the system and also bear some drawbacks. It is hard to remember password or PIN and can be stolen or guessed by the intruder; cards, tokens, keys can be lost, forgotten, stolen or duplicated and magnetic cards can be corrupted and unreadable by the card reader device. To overcome these difficulties automated biometric recognition systems can be used as a suitable alternative, which was introduced in earlier centuries. The word 'Biometric' is derived from the ancient Greek words "bios" meaning life and "metron" meaning measure (Toth, 2005; Jain et al., 2007). So, the meaning is "life measurement." Biometric systems use various physical characteristics or behaviors of a person, which is shown in Figure 1 and can be categorized as the name of the part(s) of body involved. Computer vision is one such field with which the visual recognition ability of a person can be achieved in face recognition system, which is comparable to that human by measuring some unique biometric properties or characteristics of a human. The journey was begun with the fingerprint, now several different types

Figure 1. Biometric types

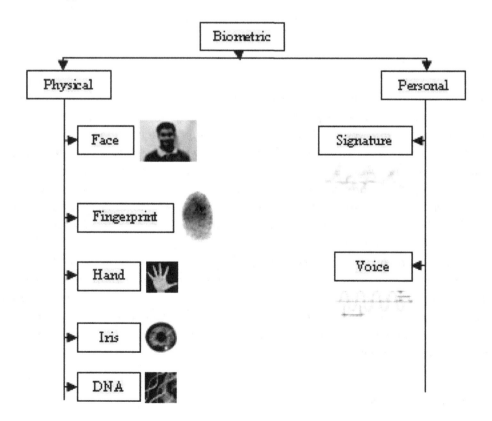

of modalities (face, iris, retina, etc) are available for human identification and verification.

Physical feature is suitable for identity purpose and generally obtained from living human body. Commonly used physical features are fingerprints, facial features, hand geometry, and eye features (iris and retina) etc. The most common used personal traits are signature and voices etc. Nearly all-biometric systems work in the same manner. First, a person is registered into a database using the specified method. Information about a certain characteristic of the human is captured. When the person needs to be identified, the system will take the information about the person again, translates this new information with the algorithm, and then compare the new code with the ones in the database to find out a match and hence, identification. The objective or mission of this chapter is to discuss about different thermal face recognition technique and their categorization based on holistic and feature based approaches. This chapter also includes description of thermal infrared image captured by thermal infrared camera, some critical observations on thermal patterns, benefits and drawbacks of thermal images etc. Comparative study on results of different recent and frequently referred methods along with our own methods also included in this chapter, which will attract to the researchers in the area of computer vision and image processing technology.

FACE RECOGNITION

Face recognition has become one of the most attractive research areas among the computer vision and image processing researchers because of the wide range of commercial and law enforcement applications. Since last four decades, there exist many commercially available systems of face recognition technology to identify human faces; however, face recognition is still a challenging research area due to various facial expressions, poses, non-uniform light illuminations and oc-

clusions. Much work is still needed for design a convenient, accurate, secure and privacy-friendly systems. There is a number of reasons to make face biometric to be superior compared to other biometrics, only some of which are summarized here: face contains anatomical information which is unique to each individual, and no physical interaction is needed. Almost all these technologies require some controlled action by the user, i.e., the user needs to keep his hand on a hand-rest for fingerprinting or hand geometry detection and has to stand in a fixed position in front of a camera for iris or retina identification. So, face is the only biometric that allows you to perform passive detection in different circumstances. The system can recognize the identity of the person without his consent from a distance. This is particularly useful for security and surveillance purposes. Signatures can be modified or forged. Voice recognition is susceptible to noises in civic places and acoustic fluctuations on a phone line or tape recording. So, face recognition is totally non-intrusive in nature. Table 1 summarizes the relative features of various biometric techniques.

There are several application areas in which face recognition can be exploited, a few of which are mentioned below.

- In the areas of security and surveillance (access control to buildings, ATM machines and border checkpoints (Kim et al., 2005; Liu et al., 2005); network security (Moon, 2004); email authentication on multimedia workstations, bank vaults, safety deposit boxes, cash windows and wire transfer areas, nuclear lab, power stations and grid control stations, munitions and hazardous materials storage areas, museums and warehouses storing valuable items,
- Government file archives and computer centers, corporate archives and computer centers, postal distribution centers, government and private carriers, clean rooms in hospitals and in medical and genetic,

Table 1. Comparisons of Biometric Identification Techniques

Biometrics			Unique	Non-Contact	Non- Counterfeit able
Physical feature		Face	√	√	√
		Fingerprint	√		
		Hand	√		
		Iris	√		√
		DNA	√		√
Personal traits		Signature	√		
		Voice	√	√	

engineering labs, blood bank, tissue banks and forensic labs, and research and development facilities),

- Closed Circuit Television (CCTV) control,
- User authentication (passports, driving licenses, employee IDs, electoral registration, banking, electronic commerce, identifying newborns),
- HCI Human Computer Interface (behavior checking at childcare or old people's centers, recognizing a customer and assessing his needs) (Choudhry et al., 1999; Wijaya et al., 2005),
- Intelligent robot,
- Daily attendance register,
- Airport authority for security checks and immigration checks (Airport Cargo, Ticket and Baggage Areas Airport Control Towers, Refueling and Maintenance Areas),
- Police may use for identification of criminals (observed to look for known criminals, drug offenders, etc. and authorities can be informed when one is sited),
- Video indexing (labeling faces in video) (Acosta, et al., 2002; Lee et al., 2004),
- Faces reconstruction (Tredoux, et al., 1999),
- Gender classification (Balci, et al., 2002; Moghaddam, et al., 2002; Brunelli, et al., 1992),

- Expression recognition (Colmenarez, et al., 1999; Shinohara, et al., 2004) – expression recognition can be exploited in the field of medicine for intensive care unit monitoring (Bourel, et al., 2000),
- Facial feature recognition and tracking (Morik, et al., 1999) – facial feature recognition and detection can be exploited for tracking a vehicle driver's eyes and thus monitoring his fatigue (Singh, et al., 1997), as well as for stress detection (Metaxas, et al., 2004),
- Marine port facilities (Prokoski, et al., 1992),

Depending on the facial image acquisition, face recognition techniques can be categorized mainly into two ways: the first methods that operate on intensity images captured by optical camera, the second methods require other sensory data (like infrared sensor). Each method has its own merits and demerits.

Advantages of visual images are as follows:

- Locating and extraction of features can be done easily and
- Optical cameras are not very expensive.
- Face recognition based on visible images suffers from several problems (Kong et al., 2005). If there exist the following differences as single or in combination between the probe image and gallery images.

- Difference in illumination conditions,
- Different viewing directions or poses,
- Various facial expressions,
- Different age group aging, and
- Disguises such as facial hair, glasses, or cosmetics.

To overcome this limitation, several solutions have been designed. One solution is using 3D data obtained from 3D vision device. Such systems are less dependent on illumination changes, but again they have some disadvantages: the cost of such system is high and their processing speed is low. Another solution for the above mentioned problem is to use infrared facial images. Some of the advantages are given below:

- The thermal IR spectrum contains basic anatomical information about face.
- The task of face detection, localization,, and segmentation are comparatively easier and more reliable than those in visible band images.
- Thermal images can be captured under different lighting conditions, even under completely dark environment.

But cost of the system is very high due to the cost of thermal IR camera. The cost of thermal IR camera has been significantly reduced with the development of CCD technology.

CHARACTERISTIC OF THERMAL IMAGES

Before coming to the main part of this chapter, where different thermal face recognition techniques would be explained, we discuss here, about different thermal spectrums and their ranges (wavelength) and thermal emission techniques. The word infra is derived from Latin and meaning of this word is "below," so the infrared means "below red" or "below the visible range." Color of the longest wavelengths of visual spectrum is red. Infrared wave has a longer wavelength (and so a lower frequency) than that of red illumination visible to humans. Objects usually emit infrared radiation across a spectrum of wavelengths, but only a specific region of the spectrum is of interest because sensors are usually designed only to collect radiation within a specific bandwidth.

According to The International Commission on Illumination (CIE), the infrared spectrum is divided into tree bandwidths namely, IR-A that ranges from 700 nm–1400 nm, IR-B that ranges from 1400 nm–3000 nm and IR-C that ranges from 3000 nm–1 mm.

Another commonly used infrared radiation's division (Bhowmik, et al., 2011) scheme is given as follows:

- **Near-Infrared (NIR, IR-A DIN** [Deutsches Institut für Normung is the German national organization for standardization.]**):** The range of the wavelength is in 700 nm to 1000 nm. It is primarily used in fiber optic telecommunication as it is low attenuation losses in the SiO2 glass (silica) medium. In this range of spectrum, image intensifiers are very much sensitive. It is also used in night vision devices such as night vision camera.
- **Short-Wavelength Infrared (SWIR, IR-B DIN):** The range of the wavelength is in 1000 nm to 3000 nm. Water absorption increases significantly at 1,450 nm wavelength. The 1,530 to 1,560 nm wavelength range is the leading spectral region for long-distance telecommunications. SWIR light is reflective light; it bounces off objects much similar to visible light. As a result of its reflective nature, SWIR light has shadows and contrast in its imagery.
- **Mid-Wavelength Infrared (MWIR, IR-C DIN):** It is also known as Intermediate Infrared (IIR). The range of the wavelength is in 3000 nm to 5000 nm. This range of

wavelength is used in guided missile technology for atmospheric window in which the homing heads of passive IR 'heat seeking' missiles are designed to work, homing on to the IR signature of the target aircraft, typically the jet engine exhaust plume. Thermal detectors only show the presence of warm objects against a cooler background.

- **Long-Wavelength Infrared (LWIR, IR-C DIN)**: This infrared radiation band is in 8000 nm to 14000 nm. This is the "thermal imaging" region in which sensors can be obtain a completely passive picture of the outside world based on thermal emissions only and require no external light or thermal source such as the sun, moon or infrared illuminator. Forward-looking infrared (FLIR) camera uses this range of the spectrum. Sometimes it is also known as "far infrared." The sensor elements of microbolometer cameras for LWIR are made up of IR – absorbing conductors or semiconductors, whose radiation - dependent resistance is measured. Because polysilicon is also suitable as an absorber, they can also be made from polysilicon as MEMS and combined with evaluation circuits in CMOS technology.
- **Very Long-Wave Infrared (VLWIR)**: This infrared radiation band is in 14000 nm to 1000000 nm. NIR and SWIR is sometimes known as "reflected infrared" while MWIR and LWIR is sometimes referred to as "thermal infrared." Due to the nature of the blackbody radiation curves, typical 'hot' objects, such as exhaust pipes, often appear brighter in the MW compared to the same object viewed in the LW.

The wavelength ranges of different infrared spectrums are shown in Table 2 and in Figure 2 respectively.

Between the MWIR and LWIR spectrum, a strong atmospheric absorption band lies. Imaging becomes nearly impossible due to nearly complete opaqueness of air in this range of spectrum. The range beyond 14μm is termed the Very Long-Wave Infrared (VLWIR) and although in recent years it has received increased attention.

THERMAL EMISSION

Thermal emission generally comes out from everything having above absolute zero temperature in the form of Electromagnetic waves; likewise everything also absorbs part of Electromagnetic waves, which falls on it. If the radiation that falls on a body, fraction 'r' is reflected, 'a' is absorbed and 't' is transmitted. Therefore,

$$r + a + t = 1 \qquad (1)$$

However, all three terms are independent of wavelength they do vary with it. For example, snow has a high reflectance(r) and very low absorptance (a) in visible light. It has very low reflectance and absorptance approaching unity at about 10 microns. Thus, if our eyes could respond to this wavelength, snow would appear black. The ideal radiator is a black body, which can absorb the entire radiation that falls on it. For such a body, absorptance equals one. At a given wavelength the ratio of infrared energy radiated by an object at a given

Table 2. *Wavelength ranges for different infrared spectrums [22]*

Spectrum	Wavelength range
Near-Infrared (NIR)	0.7-1.0 μm*
Short-wave Infrared (SWIR)	1-3 μm*
Mid-wave Infrared MWIR)	3-5 μm*
Thermal Infrared (TIR)	8-14 μm*
Very Long-wave Infrared (VLWIR)	> 14 (15-1000) μm*

* micro meter / micron

Figure 2. Different infrared sub-bands of the electromagnetic spectrums

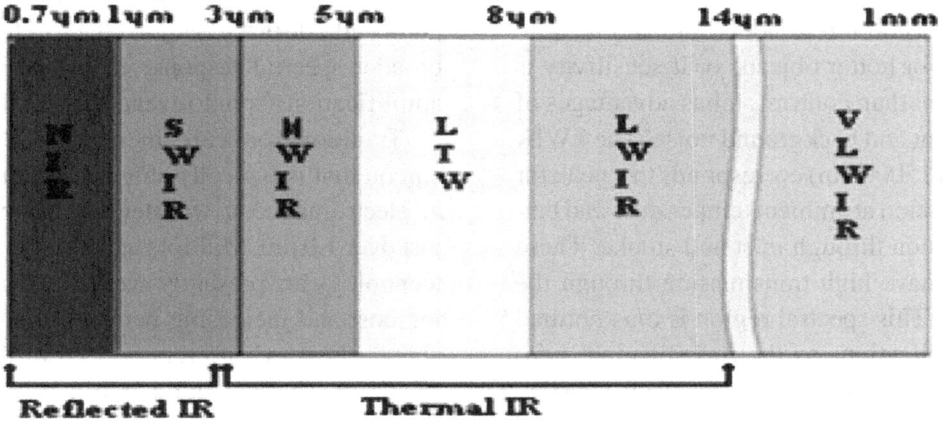

temperature to that emitted by a blackbody at the same temperature is termed as emissivity (usually written ε or e). The emissivity of a blackbody is unity at all wavelengths (ε = 1). Emissivity in the thermal infrared is conversely equivalent to the notion of reflective albedo used in the computer vision literature (Horn, 1997; Horn, et al., 1979).

All objects are composed of continually vibrating atoms, with higher energy atoms vibrating more frequently. The vibration of all charged particles, including these atoms, generates electromagnetic waves. The higher the temperature of an object, the faster the vibration, and thus the higher the spectral radiant energy. As a result, all objects are continually emitting radiation at a rate with a wavelength (λ) distribution that depends upon the temperature of the object and its spectral emissivity, ε (λ).

Radiant emission is usually treated in terms of the concept of a blackbody. A blackbody is an object that absorbs all incident radiation and, conversely according to the Kirchhoff's law, is a perfect radiator. The energy emitted by a blackbody is the maximum theoretically possible for a given temperature. The radiative power (or number of photon emitted) and its wavelength distribution is given by the Planck radiation law given in equation (2) and equation (3).

$$W\left(\lambda,\ T\right) = \frac{2\pi hc^2}{\lambda^5}\left[\exp\left(\frac{hc}{\lambda kT}\right) - 1\right]^{-1} W / \left(cm^2\ \mu m\right),$$

(2)

$$P\left(\lambda,\ T\right) = \frac{2\pi hc^2}{\lambda^4}\left[\exp\left(\frac{hc}{\lambda kT}\right) - 1\right]^{-1} photon\ s / \left(s\ cm^2\ \mu m\right),$$

(3)

Where λ is the wavelength, T is the temperature, h is the Planck's constant, c is the velocity of light, and k is the Boltzmann's constant.

CHOICE OF INFRARED BAND

The spectral allocation of energy emitted by an object is simply the product of the Planck's constant (c) for a given temperature (T), with the emissivity (ε) of the object as function of wavelength (Siegal, et al., 1981). In the spectral range of 780 nm to 3000 nm, IR detectors are used for applications of fiber optic communications, agricultural sorting, environmental monitoring, and chemical analysis.

The IR region of 2000 nm to 5000 nm is used for IR detectors include non-contact temperature sensing, thermal imaging, and gas analysis for pollution control. The 3000 nm to 5000 nm band is more appropriate for hotter objects, or if sensitivity is less important than contrast. It has advantages of lower ambient and background noise. The LWIR (8000 nm to 15000 nm) corresponds to a peak for thermal emission at ambient temperature and better transmission through mist and smoke. These ranges also have high transmission through the atmosphere. This spectral region is thus optimal for such applications as thermal imaging, non-contact temperature sensing, security sensing, and environmental monitoring. Photoconductive MCT detectors provide best performance at these wavelengths. If the surrounding area of the human body temperature (37° C), the Planck's constant has a maximum in the LWIR around 9 μm, and is approximately one sixth (1/6) of this maximum in the MWIR. The emissivity of human skin in the MWIR is at least 0.91, and at least 0.97 in the LWIR. Therefore, face recognition in the thermal infrared favors the LWIR, since LWIR emission is much higher than that in the MWIR. The human visual perception system is optimized to work in daytime illumination conditions. The visual spectrum extends from about 420 nm to 700 nm and the region of greatest sensitivity is near the peak wavelength of sunlight at around 550 nm. However, at night fewer visible light photons are available and only large, high contrast objects are visible. It appears that the photon rate in the region from 800 to 900 nm is five to seven times greater than in visible region around 500 nm. Moreover, the reflectivity of various materials (e.g. green vegetation, because of its chlorophyll content) is higher between 800 nm and 900 nm than at 500 nm. It means that at night more light is available in the NIR than in visual region and that against certain backgrounds more contrast is available. A considerable improvement in night vision capability can be achieved with night viewing equipment, which consists of an objective lens; image intensi-fier and eyepiece. Improved visibility is obtained by gathering more light from the scene with an objective lens than the unaided eye; by use of a photocathode that has higher photosensitivity and broader spectral response than the eye; and by amplification of photo events for visual sensation.

Traditional optical cameras use photosensitive silicon that is typically able to determine energy at electromagnetic wavelengths from 0.4 μm to just over 1.0 μm. Multiple technologies like CCD technology are presently available, with decreasing cost and increasing performance, which are able to measure different regions of the infrared spectrum. The evaluation of infrared camera over the last few decades has opened a new era to the computer vision researchers of imaging options.

SOME OF THE ADVANTAGES OF THERMAL FACE RECOGNITION

- Thermal images can be captured under different lighting conditions, even under completely dark environment.
- Thermal IR face images contain basic anatomical information about faces (Prokoski, et al., 2000).
- The tasks of face detection, localization, and segmentation are comparatively easier and more reliable than those in visible band images (Kong et al., 2005).
- Thermal imaging has better accuracy as it uses facial temperature variations caused by vein structure on facial surface as the distinguishing trait.
- As the heat pattern is emitted from the face surface itself without any source of external radiation these systems can capture images despite low illumination or even in the dark. Humans are homoeothermic and hence capable of maintaining constant temperature under different surrounding temperature.

- The cost of IR cameras has been considerably reduced with the development of CCD technology (Shiqian, et al., 2008).

SOME CRITICAL OBSERVATION ON THERMAL PATTERN

IR imagery are independent of illumination, variations in thermal pattern occur in relation to ambient conditions, subject's metabolism, exhale-inhale effect of subject and so on. It is necessary to know how or when the thermal appearances vary in different situations. Some of the factors affecting thermal distribution are presented in the following subsections.

Core Temperature, Mean-Body Temperature, and Skin Temperature

Aschoff and Wever introduced the terms "thermal core" in 1958. Thermal core means core temperature of a human i.e. the temperature of structures deep within the body, as opposed to peripheral temperature such as that of the skin (Mosby, 2009). The core temperature remains almost fixed, within +/- 0.6 °C, day in and day out. Human are homoeothermic, so it can maintain its constant core temperature throughout the body except when a person suffers a febrile illness (Guyton, et al., 1996). Mean-body temperature (MBT) is the mass-weighted average temperature of body tissues. The skin temperature, in contrast to the core temperature, fluctuates with the temperature of the surroundings (Guyton, et al., 1996; Blatteis, 1998). There is a relationship between core temperature, mean-body temperature and skin temperature $MBT = 0.64 \times T_{core} + 0.36 \times T_{skin}$ (Burton, 1935). The core temperature does not change due to the presence of a closed control loop with negative feedback in the body system which prevents MBT from deviating from this value taken under thermoneutral conditions (Blat-

teis, 1998).. In fact, a rise in core temperature of only 0.5 °C causes extreme peripheral vasodilation (flushing of the skin in humans). This stability implies that the heat produced in the body and that lost from it stay in relative balance, despite the large variations in ambient temperature (Blatteis, 1998). In order to maintain core temperature steady, the rate of heat flow from core to skin is adjusted according to the body's thermal needs and that, as a result, skin temperature varies more widely than core temperature in relation to ambient temperature (Blatteis, 1998).. Under steady-state conditions in a thermoneutral environment, (i.e., one in which neither the mechanism for heat production nor for heat loss is activated nor the perceived thermal comfort is optimal), core temperature thus is higher than skin temperature (Blatteis, 1998). There is no single temperature level that can be considered to be normal because measurements on many normal people have shown a range of normal temperature measured orally, from less than 36.1°C to 37.5°C (Guyton, et al., 1996). When excessive heat is produced in the body by strenuous exercise, temperature can rise temporarily to as high as 38.33-40.0°C. On the other hand, when the body is exposed to cold, the temperature can often fall to values below 96°F (35.56°C) (Guyton, et al., 1996).

Thermal Characteristic Changes According to Surrounding Temperature

Some of the researchers (Chen, et al., 2005; Socolinsky, et al., 2004a; Wu, et al., 2007) have illustrated that the thermal characteristics of faces changes significantly according with variations in ambient temperature. So, the performances of face recognition affects accordingly. Blatteis (Blatteis, 1998) indicated that about three million sweat glands are present within human body, the greatest density being found on the palms, soles and forehead. Thermoregulatory sweating increases with elevation in core temperature (Blatteis, 1998), and therefore the forehead region emits sweat easily when the ambient temperature increases. Evaporation takes place once the sweat reaches the surface, hence causing the skin temperature to lower down.

Body Temperature Variation Due to Metabolism

Temperature and metabolism become directly related in all about every form of living, such as eating, sleeping and through exercise and physical exertion. Ganong (Ganong, 2001) indicates that the body temperature is lowest during sleep, slightly higher in the awake but relaxed state, and rises with activity. Body temperature increases with muscles work or become active, as a result of that action. Any action that takes place within the body needs the metabolism of calories, also known as food energy. More activity that happens in the body, the higher the body temperature will become, which ultimately requires an increase in the metabolism of more calories. Most metabolizing in the body takes place during resting periods, also known as basal metabolism. A cold body temperature or becoming dehydrated decreases the chance of burning more calories. Basal metabolism includes all of the body's natural functions required to sustain life. The basal metabolism of each individual differs because of their bodily functions, their health conditions and their body temperatures. Through physical exercise, more calories become metabolized due to the increase in the body's temperature through working muscle tissue. Calories required for physical activity and exercise account for about half of those needed for basal metabolism. However, the amount of calories metabolized through exercise and muscle exertion increases the body's basal metabolism over time, and temporarily after workout sessions. Through the consumption and digestion of food throughout the day, the body metabolizes another small portion of calories. This natural process, often referred to as the thermic effect, increases

through the process of eating healthy foods and remaining active. Dehydration and excessively decreasing body temperature reduces the body's ability to digest food properly. The human body regulates internal temperature in order to maintain a steady rate in which normal functions occur. As mentioned above, during the winter or in a very cold room, a human will normally shiver. This natural process represents the body fighting in order to keep muscles warm and the body temperature stable. The direct opposite of this situation, when external temperatures become extremely hot or even warm, the body sweats in order to keep the body cool. This process does not increase metabolism and neither does shivering, simply because neither of the two raise or lower body temperature, but rather fight to maintain a stable rate.

Temperature Variation Due to Breathing Patterns

Temperature and breathing become directly related in nearly every animal. The nose or mouth appears cooler as the subject is inhaling and warmer as subject exhales, as exhaled air is at core body temperatures, which are several degrees warmer than skin temperature.

Temperature Variation Due to Alcohol Consumption

The thermal distribution varies, when the subject is under the influence of alcohol consumption. Body temperature is increased with alcohol because it dilates blood vessels in face skin. It can be observed that thermal pattern of the face images changes at different timings after a single session of drinking alcohol. More regions of the face, especially the cheeks and forehead became warm as time passes after consumption. Alcohol consumption can normally affect thermal distribution for each individual differently. It depends on the amount of dosage and how fast the rate of absorption of alcohol takes place in the body.

A BRIEF REVIEW OF LITERATURE ON THERMAL FACE RECOGNITION

In this section, we give a brief review to the significant publications in the literature on thermal face recognition technique and their categorization based on holistic and feature based approaches. Face recognition problems can be classified into two broad categories: feature-base and holistic methods. The analytic or feature-based approaches find a set of geometrical features from the face such as the fore-head, eyes, nose, mouth, cheek, and chin. The holistic or appearance-based methods judge the global properties of the human face pattern. The face is recognized as a whole without using only certain fiducial points obtained from different regions of the face. Feature extraction algorithms aim at finding features from the face that distinguish one face from another. Face patterns can have importantly variable image appearances. Therefore, it is essential to find techniques that introduce low dimensional feature representation of face objects with enhanced discriminatory power.

Firstly, we review the publication based on holistic based approaches.

In 1992, first thermal face recognition work is conducted in Mikos Corporation (Prokoski, et al., 1992). Mikos Corporation first demonstrated that the facial thermograms are unique for each individual. "Elemental shapes" have been identified from any biological sensor data which can be treated as an image. The elemental shapes and their corresponding locations give identification ability. Biosensors, which construct very detailed localized data, such as high-resolution infrared imagers, can result in unique identification of an individual from the determination of elemental shapes and their distribution.

Wilder et al. (1996) have presented one of the first works on thermal face recognition. They have compared the relative performances of three different face recognition techniques namely, Transform Coding of Grey Scale Projections, Eigenface, and Matching Pursuit Filters for visible and thermal IR images of 101 subjects without glasses, each of size 512×450 pixels. They have concluded that the recognition results for one modality were not significantly better than those for the other. They did not consider significant amount of illumination changes for visible images and temperature changes for IR images.

Cutler (1996) is one of the first researchers who have used the eigenface (Turk, et al., 1991) method in the infrared face recognition and applied to a database of 288 hand-aligned low-resolution (160x120) images of 24 subjects taken from 3 viewpoints (frontal, 45 degree and profile). The following recognition rates were reported: 96% for frontal views, 96% for 45 degrees views, and 100% for profile views.

Siddiqui et al. (2004) described in their paper that the face identification using infrared images and eigenfaces. They passed test face through cold effect enhancement and/or sunglasses filtering algorithms and handling facial hair through threshold. Before recognition, they ensured that the test image is a face image or not. If yes, it is passed through an algorithm to check whether the person come from cold and then is projected to eigenspace to find the match. If match is not found then it is passed through another algorithm to ensure whether person has worn sunglasses. They have performed their experiments on 8 subjects having 9 expressions each that makes total of 72 images. In both cases the image is enhanced in order to make recognition more efficient. The results show that their algorithms work quite well and the recognition rate is 100% and do not lead to a false acceptance.

One of the first face recognition system based on thermal face is introduced by Yoshitomi et al. (1997). They focused on the lighting problem in visual face recognition system and suggested infrared face recognition as a solution. For evaluating the identification accuracy of the present method, face-image sequences of man A, man A with glasses, man B, and woman A were collected. The total number of images was 40 for training data, 80 for test data. They have compared the relative performances of three different face recognition techniques namely, Gray-level histogram, Mosaic images, and shape factor. By integrating information from three different techniques, the face was identified with excellent accuracy using voting method.

Socolinsky et al. (2001) presented an illumination invariant face recognition system in Long-Wave Infrared (LWIR) imagery spectrum. They have tested the eigenfaces (Turk, et al., 1991) and the ARENA (Sim, et al., 2000) algorithms on a database of visible and infrared images of 91 distinct subjects each having 320×240 pixels under various illumination conditions, with varying facial expressions, and with or without glasses.

In Socolinsky et al. (2004a), the researchers have used visible imagery and thermal infrared imagery for face recognition in operational scenarios in both indoor and outdoor. They have noticed the performance of the face recognition system for outdoor and face recognition across multiple sessions. The visible imagery is affected by changes in outdoors illumination; thermal imagery is affected both indoors and outdoors by some challenging factors such as physical activity of subjects, weather conditions etc. Their experimental results proved that under controlled lighting conditions, visible imagery has a better recognition rate for indoors. For all of the algorithms that they used, outdoor recognition rate was worse for both visible and thermal images, with a sharper degradation for visible one. They have concluded that face recognition performance with thermal infrared imagery is steady over multiple sessions. IR imagery represents a feasible substitute to visible imaging in the search for a robust and practical face recognition system.

Trujillo et al. (2005) proposed an unsupervised local and global feature extraction paradigm to the problem of facial expression using thermal images. They combined the localization of facial features with the holistic approach. After feature extraction using eigenface, support vector machine is used to classify testing images on IRIS dataset. Each image is 320 x 240 in bitmap RGB format. For their purposed, they have used a gallery set composed of 30 individuals/3 expressions each ("surprised," "happy," and "angry")/3 poses each.

Chen et al. (2003) developed a face recognition technique with PCA. They used PCA to study the comparisons and combination of infrared and visible images to the effects of lighting, facial expression change and the time difference between gallery and probe images. They have paid attention on a very crucial factor in thermal infrared face recognition which is the time difference between training and test images in the galleries. First, they did not consider elapse time for testing the system. They have stated that there is no steady difference between the recognition rate of visible and thermal IR Infrared. Later, they have concentrated on elapse time. They have concluded that visible image is better than thermal IR in time-lapsed recognition. But there is an important clue in their research: The sets of mismatched probes of the two classifiers for the two models did not overlap necessarily. This clue suggested that these two models may have complementary information about the probe. So, the researchers combined the results of the thermal IR and visible based faced recognition systems using some combination rules with three different strategies. Their experimental results indicated that when there was significant time elapse between the gallery and probe images, the visible face recognition outperforms the thermal IR one. Their experimental results also showed that the combination of the two models outperforms both single models.

Buddharaju et al. (2004) presented a two-stage face recognition system based on thermal imaging and statistical modeling. In the first stage, they decrease the search space before arriving at a singular conclusion during the second stage.

Bessel modeling is used for feature extraction on the facial region. The feature set of highly likely matches is fed to a Bayesian classifier to find the exact match. The proposed approach achieves performance rates of 86.4%.

Bhattacharjee et al. (2012) described a comparative study of human thermal face recognition based on Haar wavelet and Local Binary Pattern (LBP). Thermal Infrared (IR) images focus on changes of temperature distribution on facial muscles and blood vessels. These temperature changes can be regarded as texture features of images. In these study two local-matching methods based on Haar wavelet transform and Local Binary Pattern (LBP) are analyzed. Wavelet transform is a good tool to analyze multi-scale, multi-direction changes of texture. Local Binary Patterns (LBP) are a type of feature used for classification in computer vision. Firstly, human thermal IR face image is preprocessed and cropped the face region only from the entire image. Secondly, two different approaches are used to extract the features from the cropped face region. In the first approach, the training images and the test images are processed with Haar wavelet transform and the LL band and the average of LH/HL/HH bands sub-images are created for each face image. Then a total confidence matrix is formed for each face image by taking a weighted sum of the corresponding pixel values of the LL band and average band. For LBP feature extraction, each of the face images in training and test datasets is divided into 161 numbers of sub images, each of size 8×8 pixels. For each such sub images, LBP features are extracted which are concatenated in row wise manner. PCA is performed separately on the individual feature set for dimensionality reeducation. Finally, two different classifiers are used to classify face images. One such classifier multi-layer feed-forward neural network and another classifier is minimum distance classifier. The Experiments have been performed on the database created at our own laboratory and Ter-

ravic Facial IR Database. They have got a good result with 95.09% performance rates.

Jun Li et al. (2008) proposed a learning based framework to address the new problem of hallucinating facial images from thermal infrared images which works locally both in the sense of image spatial domain and on the image manifold. They used a Markov random field model to the predicted normal face to improve the hallucination result. Experimental results show the advantage of our algorithm over the existing methods. Their algorithm can be readily generalized to solve other multi-modal image conversion problems as well. The proposed approach achieves maximum performance rates of 50.06%.

Bhowmik et al. (2008) presented a novel approach for face recognition using thermal images. The proposed approach registers the all (training and testing) thermal face images in polar coordinate, which is scale and rotation invariant. Polar images are projected into eigenspace and finally classified using a multi-layer perceptron. This experiment performed on Object Tracking and Classification Beyond Visible Spectrum (OTCBVS) benchmark thermal face dataset. They performed their experiments on 2000 thermal images of 16 different persons. Out of total 2000 thermal images 1120 IMAGES are used as training set and rest 880 images are taken as testing images. Experimental results show that the proposed approach significantly improves the verification and identification performance and the success rate is 97.05%.

A few holistic based experimental results with thermal images in face recognition are being recorded in Table 3. All the result support the conclusion that face recognition performance with thermal infrared imagery is stable.

Now, the feature based thermal face recognition techniques have been discussed here.

Akhloufi et al. (2008) present an efficient approach of face recognition using infrared spectrum in their work. In their paper, physiological features are extracted from thermal images in order to build a unique thermal faceprint. The obtained physiological features are related to the distribution of blood vessels under the face skin. This blood network is unique to each individual and can be used in infrared face recognition. The obtained results are promising and show that the proposed approach achieves high performance rates of 100%.

Jiang et al. (2005, 2007) presented Facial expression recognition using mathematical morphology, nose min-temperature and temperature histogram through drawing and analyzing the whole geometry characteristics and local characteristics of the interesting area of Infrared Thermal Imaging. The results show that geometry characteristics in the interesting region of different expressions were obviously different. To remove the serious environmental influence on facial temperature, relative change has been considered here for quantitative analysis. Define the rate of change as the ratio of changed amount to initial value.

Martinez et al. (2010) studied the problem of detecting facial components in thermal imagery (specifically eyes, nostrils and mouth). The main objective of this chapter is to enable the automatic registration of facial thermal images. The detection of eyes and nostrils is performed using Haar features and the GentleBoost algorithm. The detection of the mouth is based on the detections of the eyes and the nostrils and is performed using measures of entropy and self similarity. The results demonstrate that reliable facial component detection is feasible using this methodology, getting a correct detection rate for both eyes and nostrils of 0.8. A correct eyes and nostrils detection enables a correct detection of the mouth in 65% of closed-mouth test images and in 73% of open-mouth test images. Their system supports maximum error 0.15.

Hermosilla et al. (2010) proposed a robust thermal face recognition methodology based on the use of local interest points and descriptors. The methodology consists of four steps: face segmen-

tation, vascular network detection, wide-baseline matching using local interest points and descriptors, and classification. They have performed their experiments on the UXX Thermal Faces Database. This database contains 156 320x240 thermal face images that correspond to 6 images per subject and 26 subjects.

Seal et al. (2011a, 2011b, 2012) described an approach for human face recognition based on blood perfusion data from infra-red face images. In their work, blood perfusion data are extracted from face images using different algorithms. Blood perfusion data are related to distribution of blood vessels under the face skin. A distribution of blood vessels are unique for each person and as a set of extracted minutiae points from a blood perfusion data of a human face should be unique for that face. There may be several such minutiae point sets for a single face but all of these correspond to that particular face only. Entire face image is partitioned into equal consequence blocks and the total number of minutiae points from each block is computed to construct final vector. Therefore, the size of the feature vectors is found to be same as total number of blocks considered. For classification, a five layer feed-forward backpropagation neural network has been used. A number of experiments were conducted to evaluate the performance of the proposed face recognition system with varying block size. Experiments have been performed on the database created at our own laboratory. The maximum success of 95.24% recognition has been.

Chen et al. (2002) has used thermogram to do human face recognition. The thermogram of human face has captured from infrared camera. Some of the image processing technologies have used to preprocess the captured thermogram. Then several features have extracted from the processed thermogram. These features incorporated the distribution of temperature statistics, the perimeter of the face, the length/width ratio of the smallest rectangle which contained the face, and the triangle

Table 3. Different holistic based approaches, reported result etc.

Authors	Database Name	Total Number of Images in the Actual Database	Total Number of Images Used	Image Resolution	Recognition Rate	Recognition Technique Used		Classifier Used	Year
Prokoski et al. (20)	Private Database	**NR**	NR	NR	NR	NR		Neural network	1992
Wilder et al. (36)	SMRT II (3)	101 subjects	NR	512x450	96% (Max)	GS Proj.		Weighted sum of the distance metrics	1996
					94% (Max)	Eigenface			
					99% (Max)	Match hrs.			
Cutler (37)	Private Database	288 images (24 subjects)	NR	160x120	96% for frontal views	Eigenface		Euclidian distance	1996
					96% for 45 degrees views				
					100% for profile views				
Siddiqui et al. (39)	Unknown	NR	NR	NR	100%	Eigenface			1996
Yoshitomi et al. (40)	Private Database	NR	120 images	300x300	100% (Max)	Gray-level histogram		Back propagation neural network	1997
					97.5% (Max)	Mosaic image			
					92.5% (Max)	Shape factor		Supervised classification	
Socolinsky et al. (41)	Private Database	91 subjects	NR	NR	96% (Max)	Eigenface		Arena algorithm (9)	2001
					94% (Max)			Nearest neighbor	
					99% (Max	Neural network			
Socolinsky et al. (43)	Private Database	385 subjects	90 subjects	NR	58.89%	Indoor	Outdoor	NR	
					73.93%				
					93.93%	PCA / LDA / Equinox	PCA / LDA / Equinox	Nearest neighbor	2004
					44.29%				
					65.30%				
					83.02%				
Trujillo et.al (33)	IRIS data-set	1529 images (30 subjects)	NR	320x240	71.42% (Surprised)	Eigenface		SVM	2005
					100% (Happy)				
					75% (Angry)				
Chen et al. (44)	Private Database	83 subjects	NR	NR	100%	PCA		Euclidian Distance	2003
Buddharaju et al (45)	Equinox Databse	**NR**	NR	NR	86.4%	NR		Bayesian Classifier	2004
A Seal et al (46)	Terravic Facial IR Databse	20 subjects	20 subjects	320x240	94.11 (Max)	PCA Wavelet, LBP		Multi layer feed forward neural network, minimum distance classifier	2012
	UGC-JU THERMAL FACEDATABASE	Till now 50 subjects	17 subjects		95.09 (Max)				

Continued on following page

Table 3. Continued

Authors	Database Name	Total Number of Images in the Actual Database	Total Number of Images Used	Image Resolution	Recognition Rate		Recognition Technique Used		Classifier Used	Year
Jun Li et al. (47)	Soco-linsky's Database	NR	47 subjects	NR	6.38%	31.91%	CCA/Eigen Transformation	Patch-based LLE	K- Nearest Neighbor	2008
					23.4%	50.0 6%	MRF	Hallucating based approach		
M.K Bhowmik et al. (48)	OTCBVS Dataset	1529 images (30 subjects)	16 subjects	320x240	97.05%		Eigenface		Multi-layer perception network	2008

formed from the three lowest temperature points of the two cheeks and the chin. A three-layer back-propagation neural network was used as the recognition tool. It is shown that the recognition rates for without glasses and with glasses are 95% and 93%, respectively.

Table 4 demonstrates different feature-based methods of infrared images for face recognition, name of the database used, reported result etc. Most of the researchers did not mentioned some of the important features of face recognition like the size of the database they have used in their research articles, False Rejection Rate (FRR), False Acceptance Rate (FAR), Error (ERR), time complexity and response time of their algorithm. These are the areas, where researchers can exploit their idea and share with the research community.

In terms of algorithmic approaches, both appearance and geometry-based methods have been applied in the thermal infrared images. Appearance-based methods like principal component, independent component, and linear discriminant analysis treat the image simply as a matrix of numbers and impose the decision boundary without extracting any geometric features. Even though such approaches are computationally efficient, they do not perform well in challenging conditions such as variable poses and facial expressions. Geometry-based techniques and template matching approaches extract certain features from the

face and then impose probability models (or decision boundaries) on these features. Geometric approaches are usually more robust than appearance based approaches but at an additional computational cost.

AN APPROACH FOR FACE RECOGNITION BASED ON THERMAL INFRARED IMAGES

In this section, we are going to presents a robust approach for face recognition using thermal infrared images. It is a holistic based approach i.e. features extraction methods concentrate on the whole image rather than particular fudicial points. The overall block diagram of the proposed system is shown in Figure 3.

The proposed system can be subdivided into three main parts, namely image preprocessing, extraction of feature, and classifier. So, the system starts with image preprocessing of thermal face image and end with successful classification. Each of the parts has been discussed in detail in subsequent subsections.

Image Preprocessing

The first step of the proposed approach is image preprocessing. In this step, each 24-bits color

Table 4. Different feature based Approaches, reported result etc.

Authors	Database Name	Total number of images in the actual database	Total number of images used	Image resolution	Recognition Rate	Recognition Technique used	Classifier used	Year
Akhloufi et al [49]	Private Database	NR	NR	NR	100%	Medial Axis Transform	Euclidian distance transform	2008
Jiang et al. [50] [51]	Real time facial thermal images	NR	NR	NR	6% (Changing rate) 6.6% (Changing rate)	NR	NR	2007
Martinez et al. [52]	Private Database	22 subjects	22 subjects	NR	65% 73%	Haar wavelet	GentleBoost, SVM	2010
Hermosilla et al. [53]	UXX Thermal Faces Database	26 subjects	26 subjects	320x240	NR	NR	Statistical Classifier	2010
A. Seal et al. [54]	UGC-JU THERMAL FACE DATABASE	Till now 50 subjects	6 subjects	320x240	91.47% (8×8 block)	Minutiae extraction	multi-layer feed forward neural network	2011
A. Seal et al. [55]	UGC-JU THERMAL FACE DATABASE	Till now 50 subjects	7 subjects	320x240	95.24% (Max) with 97.62% accuracy	Minutiae extraction	multi-layer feed forward neural network	2011
A. Seal et al. [56]	UGC-JU THERMAL FACE DATABASE	Till now 50 subjects	6 subjects	320x240	90.25% (8×8 block)	Minutiae extraction	multi-layer feed forward neural network	2012
Chen et al. [57]	Private Database	22 subjects	20 subjects	NR	95% without glass 93% with glass	NR	three-layer back-propagation neural network	2002

NR-> NOT REPORTED (Researchers did not mentioned the relevant information in their literatures)

images have been converted into its binary image through 8-bit grayscale image counterpart. The binary image contents more than one component and it has been seen that the largest component is the face region. So, the largest component (Shinohara et al, 2004) among them has been identified as face skin region and other small components, which are other parts of the image, have been rejected. Then centroid (Shinohara et al, 2004; Bhattacharjee et al., 2012; Morse, 1998-2004) has been calculated from the largest component and

from the centroid, human face has been cropped in elliptical shape using "Bresenham ellipse drawing" (Hearn, 1996) algorithm where, X and Y is x co-ordinate and y-co-ordinate respectively for the centroid which is calculated by equation 1 and 2. Distance between the centroid and the right ear is called the minor axis of the ellipse and distance between the centroid and the forehead is called major axis of the ellipse.

Figure 3. Schematic block diagram of the proposed system

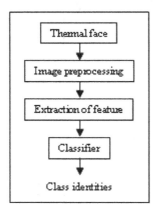

Extraction of Feature

One of the simplest approaches for describing texture or surface of the face is Statistical approach. In this approach, statistical moments of the histogram of an image are being calculated but it doesn't have any information about the relative position of pixels with respect to each other. Co-occurrence matrix defines the position of two pixels relative to each other. So, the first step of feature extraction is to find the co-occurrence (Gonzalez, 2002) from the elliptic shape images. Let f be an 8-bit grayscale image with 256 different intensity values and $[W]_{1 \times 2}$ is a window that tells the relative position of two pixels with respect to each other. This W window has been swept through the whole grayscale image from top-left corner to bottom-right corner and finds the number of times that intensity pairs (z_i, and z_j) appear in f in the position specified by W and store that number in the ith row and the jth column of a separate matrix G is denoted by g_{ij}. The size of the matrix G is 256 by 256. Now, some of the characteristic of co-occurrence matrix has to be find, which, will be treated as features. The characteristics are maximum probability, contrast, and uniformity also known as energy, homogeneity, and entropy.

Maximum probability: the strongest response of a co-occurrence matrix is called maximum probability and denoted by the formula given in equation (4).

$$\max_{i,j} p_{ij} \quad \text{where } p_{ij} = \left(\frac{g_{ij}}{\sum_{i=1}^{i=256} \sum_{j=1}^{j=256} g_{ij}} \right) \quad (4)$$

The values of Maximum probability vary in the range of 0 and 1.

Contrast: A measure of intensity contrast between a pixel and its neighbor over the entire image and it is expressed by the given in equation (5).

$$\sum_{i=1}^{256} \sum_{j=1}^{256} (i - j)^2 p_{ij} \quad (5)$$

The range of the contrast is varying in between 0 to 2552.

Uniformity or Energy: A measure of uniformity in the range 0 to 1. Uniformity is expressed by the given in equation (6).

$$\sum_{i=1}^{256} \sum_{j=1}^{256} p_{ij}^2 \quad (6)$$

Homogeneity: it means spatial closeness of the distribution of elements in G to the diagonal. The range of values between 0 and 1 and is denoted by.

$$\sum_{i=1}^{256} \sum_{j=1}^{256} \frac{p_{ij}}{1 + |i - j|} \quad (7)$$

Entropy: it measures the randomness of the elements of G. The minimum value of entropy is 0 and maximum is 16. Entropy is expressed by the given in equation (8).

$$-\sum_{i=1}^{256}\sum_{j=1}^{256} p_{ij} \, \log_2 p_{ij} \qquad (8)$$

Classifier

ANN classifier has been used to classify each of these vectors (Lin et al., 1996), (Haddadnia et al., 2003). The test images are compared to every training image and the training image that is found to be the closest to the test image is used to identify the training image. The images can be compared using any number of similarity measures. Here a five layer feed-forward back propagation neural network has been used for this purpose. Momentum allows the network to respond to local gradient and to recent trends in the error surface. The momentum is used to backpropagation learning algorithm for making weight changes equal to the sum of a fraction of the last weight change and the new change. The magnitude of the effect that the last weight change is allowed is known as momentum constant (mc). The momentum constant may be any number between 0 and 1. The momentum constant zero means, a weight changes according to the gradient and the momentum constant one means, the new weight change is set to equal the last weight change, and the gradient is not considered here. The gradient is computed by summing the gradients calculated at each training example, and the weights and biases are only updated after all training examples have been presented. Tan- sigmoid transfer functions are used to calculate a layer's output from its net, the first input, and the next three hidden layers and the outer most layer gradient descent with momentum training function is used to update weight and bias values.

Experiment and Result

Experiments have been performed on Terravic facial infrared database (Davis, et al., 2005). It contains total no. of 20 persons (19 men and 1 woman) of 8-bit gray scale JPEG thermal faces. Size of the database is 298MB. The success of 88.89% recognition has been achieved.

FUTURE RESEARCH DIRECTIONS

Face recognition is a forty-year-old problem, but face recognition using thermal infrared images is comparatively newer one. Recently researchers are very much interested towards thermal face images. Since, thermal face images have several advantages over visual face images that we have discussed earlier. There are still many challenges for a thermal face recognition system. New researchers may focus on the following topics. Some of the few topics are real-time face matching recognition with large databases, multiple subjects in scene and with complex backgrounds and variant face poses (half-profile, tilted head or camera).

CONCLUSION

Face recognition is a challenging problem in the field of computer vision and image analysis that has received a great deal of attention over the last few years because of its many applications in various domains. Research has been conducted vigorously in this area for the past four decades or so, and though huge progress has been made, encouraging results have been obtained and current face recognition systems have reached a certain degree of maturity when operating under constrained conditions; however, they are far from achieving the ideal of being able to perform adequately in all the various situations that are commonly encountered by applications utilizing these techniques in practical life.

ACKNOWLEDGMENT

Authors are thankful to a major project entitled "Design and Development of Facial Thermogram Technology for Biometric Security System," funded by University Grants Commission (UGC), India, and "DST-PURSE Programme" at Department of Computer Science and Engineering, Jadavpur University, India, for providing necessary infrastructure to conduct experiments relating to this work. Ayan Seal is grateful to Department of Science & Technology (DST), India, for providing him Junior Research Fellowship-Professional (JRF-Professional) under DST-INSPIRE Fellowship programme [No: IF110591].

REFERENCES

Acosta, E., Torres, L., Albiol, A., & Delp, E. J. (2002). An automatic face detection and recognition system for video indexing applications. In *Proceedings of the IEEE International Conference on Acoustics, Speech and Signal Processing*, (Vol. 4, pp. 3644-3647). Orlando, FL: IEEE.

Akhloufi, M. A., & Bendada, A. (2008). *Infrared face recognition using distance transform*. World Academy of Science, Engineering and Technology.

Balci, K., & Atalay, V. (2002). PCA for gender estimation: Which eigenvectors contribute? In *Proceedings of the Sixteenth International Conference on Pattern Recognition*, (Vol. 3, pp. 363-366). Quebec City, Canada: IEEE.

Bhattacharjee, D. Seal, A. Ganguly, S., Nasipuri, M., & Basu, D. K. (2012). A comparative study of human thermal face recognition based on Haar wavelet transform (HWT) and local binary pattern (LBP). *Computational Intelligence and Neuroscience*. doi: doi:10.1155/2012/261089.

Bhowmik, M. K., Bhattacharjee, D., Nasipuri, M., Basu, D. K., & Kundu, M. (2008). Classification of polar-thermal eigenfaces using multilayer perceptron for human face recognition. In *Proceedings of the 3rd IEEE Conference on Industrial and Information Systems* (ICIIS-2008). IEEE.

Bhowmik, M. K., Saha, K., Majumder, S., Majumder, G., Saha, A., & Sarma, A. N. … Nasipuri, M. (2011). Thermal infrared face recognition – A biometric identification technique for robust security system. In P. M. Corcoran (Ed.), Reviews, refinements and new ideas in face recognition. Vienna, Austria: InTech Open Access Publisher.

Blatteis, C. M. (1998). *Physiology and pathophysiology of temperature regulation*. World Scientific Publishing Co. doi:10.1142/3507.

Bourel, F., Chibelushi, C. C., & Low, A. A. (2000). Robust facial feature tracking. In *Proceedings of the British Machine Vision Conference*, (pp. 232-241). Bristol, UK: IEEE.

Brunelli, R., & Poggio, T. (1992). HyperBF networks for gender classification. In *Proceedings of the DARPA Image Understanding Workshop*, (pp. 311-314). DARPA.

Buddharaju, P., Pavlidis, I., & Kakadiaris, I. (2004). Face recognition in the thermal infrared spectrum. In *Proceedings of the 2004 IEEE Computer Society Conference on Computer Vision and Pattern Recognition Workshops* (CVPRW'04). IEEE.

Burton, A. (1935). Human calorimetry: The average temperature of the tissues of the body. *The Journal of Nutrition*, 9, 261–280.

Chen, X., Flynn, P. J., & Bowyer, K. W. (2003). PCA-based face recognition in infrared imagery: Baseline and comparative studies. In *Proceedings of the IEEE International Workshop on Analysis and Modeling of Faces and Gestures* (AMFG'03). IEEE.

Chen, X., Flynn, P. J., & Bowyer, K. W. (2005). IR and visible light face recognition. *Computer Vision and Image Understanding, 99*(3), 332–358. doi:10.1016/j.cviu.2005.03.001.

Chen, Y., & Wang, M. (2002). Human face recognition using thermal image. *Journal of Medical and Biological Engineering, 22*(2).

Choudhry, T., Clarkson, B., Jebara, T., & Pentland, A. (1999). Multimodal person recognition using unconstrained audio and video. In *Proceedings of the International Conference on Audio and Video-Based Person Authentication*, (pp. 176-181). IEEE.

Colmenarez, A., Frey, B. J., & Huang, T. S. (1999). A probabilistic framework for embedded face and facial expression recognition. In *Proceedings of the IEEE Conference on Computer Vision and Pattern Recognition*, (Vol. 1, pp. 1592-1597). Ft. Collins, CO: IEEE.

Cutler, R. (1996). *Face recognition using infrared images and eigenfaces.* Retrieved from http://citeseer.ist.psu.edu/cutler96face.html

Davis, J., & Keck, M. (2005). A twostage approach to person detection in thermal imagery. In *Proceedings of the Workshop on Applications of Computer Vision*. IEEE.

Ganong, W. F. (2001). *Review of medical physiology* (20th ed.). New York: McGraw-Hill Medical Publishing Division.

Gonzalez, R. C., & Woods, R. E. (2002). *Digital image processing* (3rd ed.). Englewood Cliffs, NJ: Prentice Hall.

Guyton, A. C., & Hall, J. E. (1996). *Textbook of medical physiology* (9th ed.). Philadelphia: W.B. Saunders Company.

Haddadnia, J., Faez, K., & Ahmadi, M. (2003). An effcient human face recognition system using pseudo zernike moment invari- ant and radial basis function neural network. *International Journal of Pattern Recognition and Artificial Intelligence, 17*(1), 41–62. doi:10.1142/S0218001403002265.

Hearn, D., & Baker, M. P. (1996). *Computer graphics C version* (2nd ed.). Englewood Cliffs, NJ: Prentice Hall.

Hermosilla, G., Loncomilla, P., & Ruiz-del-Solar, J. (2010). Thermal face recognition using local interest points and descriptors for HRI applications. In *Proceedings of the Computer Vision and Pattern Recognition Workshops* (CVPRW). IEEE.

Horn, B. (1977). Understanding image intensities. *Artificial Intelligence*, 1–31.

Horn, B., & Sjoberg, R. (1979). Calculating the reflectance map. *Applied Optics, 18*, 1770–1779. doi:10.1364/AO.18.001770 PMID:20212547.

Jain, A. K., Flynn, P., & Ross, A. A. (2007). *Handbook of biometrics.* London: Springer.

Jiang, G., & Kang, L. (2007). Character analysis of facial expression thermal image. In *Proceedings of the IEEE/ICME International Conference on Complex Medical Engineering*. IEEE.

Jiang, G., Song, X., Zheng, F., Wang, P., & Omer, A. M. (2005). Facial expression recognition using thermal. In *Proceedings of the 27th Annual Conference on IEEE Engineering in Medicine and Biology*. IEEE.

Kim, K. (2005). Intelligent immigration control system by using passport recognition and face verification. In *Proceedings of the International Symposium on Neural Networks*, (pp. 147-156). Chongqing, China: IEEE.

Kong, S. G., Heo, J., Abidi, B. R., Paik, J., & Abidi, M. A. (2005). Recent advances in visual and infrared face recognition - A review. *Computer Vision and Image Understanding, 97*(1), 103–135. doi:10.1016/j.cviu.2004.04.001.

Lee, J. H., & Kim, W. Y. (2004). Video summarization and retrieval system using face recognition and MPEG-7 descriptors. [LNCS]. *Proceedings of Image and Video Retrieval, 3115,* 179–188.

Li, J., Hao, P., Zhang, C., & Dou, M. (2008). Hallucinating faces from thermal infrared images. In *Proceedings of Image Processing.* IEEE.

Lin & Lee. (1996). *Neural fuzzy systems.* Beijing, China: Prentice Hall International.

Liu, J. N. K., Wang, M., & Feng, B. (2005). iBotGuard: An internet-based intelligent robot security system using invariant face recognition against intruder. *IEEE Transactions on Systems, Man and Cybernetics. Part C, Applications and Reviews, 35,* 97–105. doi:10.1109/TSMCC.2004.840051.

Martinez, B., Binefa, X., & Pantic, M. (2010). Facial component detection in thermal imagery. In *Proceedings of IEEE Computer Society Conference on Computer Vision and Pattern Recognition workshops* (CVPRW), (pp. 48-52). IEEE.

Metaxas, D. N., Venkataraman, S., & Vogler, C. (2004). Image-based stress recognition using a model- based dynamic face tracking system. In *Proceedings of the International Conference on Computational Science,* (pp. 813-821). IEEE.

Moghaddam, B., & Yang, M. H. (2002). Learning gender with support faces. *IEEE Transactions on Pattern Analysis and Machine Intelligence, 24,* 707–711. doi:10.1109/34.1000244.

Moon, H. (2004). Biometrics person authentication using projection-based face recognition system in verification scenario. In *Proceedings of the International Conference on Bioinformatics and its Applications,* (pp. 207-213). Hong Kong, China: IEEE.

Morik, K., Brockhausen, P., & Joachims, T. (1999). Combining statistical learning with a knowledge-based approach -- A case study in intensive care monitoring. In *Proceedings of the 16th International Conference on Machine Learning* (ICML-99). San Francisco, CA: Morgan Kaufmann.

Morse, B.S. (1998-2004). *Image processing review, neighbors, connected components, and distance.*

Mosby. (2009). *Medical dictionary* (8th Ed.). London: Elsevier.

Prokoski, F. (2000). History, current status, and future of infrared identification. In *Proceedings of the IEEE Workshop Computer Vision Beyond Visible Spectrum: Methods and Applications,* (pp. 5–14). IEEE.

Prokoski, F. J., Riedel, R. B., & Coffin, J. S. (1992). Identification of individuals by means of facial thermography. In *Proceedings of the IEEE International Carnahan Conference on Security Technology: Crime Countermeasures,* (pp. 120-125). Atlanta, GA: IEEE.

Seal, A., Bhattacharjee, D., Nasipuri, M., & Basu, D. K. (2011a). Minutiae based thermal face recognition using blood perfusion data. In *Proceedings of the IEEE International Conference on Image Information Processing.* IEEE.

Seal, A., Bhattacharjee, D., Nasipuri, M., & Basu, D. K. (2011b). Minutiae from bit-plane sliced thermal images for human face recognition. In *Proceedings of the Springer International Conference on Soft Computing for Problem Solving.* Roorkee, India: Springer.

Seal, A., Bhattacharjee, D., Nasipuri, M., & Basu, D. K. (2012). Minutiae based thermal human face recognition using label connected component algorithm. In *Proceedings of the Elsevier International Conference on Computer, Communication, Control and Information Technology*. Elsevier.

Shinohara, Y., & Otsu, N. (2004). Facial expression recognition using Fisher weight maps. In *Proceedings of the IEEE International Conference on Automatic Face and Gesture Recognition*, (Vol. 100, pp. 499-504). IEEE.

Shiqian, W., Fang, Z. J., Xie, Z. H., & Liang, W. (2008). *Blood perfusion models for infrared face recognition*. Jiangxi, China: Jiangxi University of Finance and Economics.

Siddiqui, R., Sher, M., & Rashid, K. (2004). *Face identification based on biological trait using infrared images after cold effect enhancement and sunglasses filtering*. Retrieved from http://wscg.zcu.cz/wscg2004/Papers_2004_Poster/E97.pdf

Siegal, R., & Howell, J. (1981). *Thermal radiation heat transfer*. New York: McGraw-Hill.

Sim, T., Sukthankar, R., Mullin, M., & Baluja, S. (2000). Memory-based face recognition for visitor identification. In *Proceedings of the IEEE International Conference on Automatic Face and Gesture Recognition* (pp. 214-220). IEEE.

Singh, S., & Papanikolopoulos, N. (1997). *Vision-based detection of driver fatigue (technical report)*. Minneapolis, MN: Department of Computer Science, University of Minnesota.

Socolinsky, D., Wolff, L., Neuheisel, J., & Eveland, C. (2001). Illumination invariant face recognition using thermal infrared imagery. In *Proceedings of the IEEE Computer Society International Conference on Computer Vision and Pattern Recognition*, (Vol. 1, pp. 527-534). Kauai, HI: IEEE.

Socolinsky, D. A., & Selinger, A. (2004A). Thermal face recognition in an operational scenario. In *Proceedings of IEEE Conference on Computer Vision and Pattern Recognition*, (pp. 1012-1019). Washington, DC: IEEE.

Toth, B. (2005). *Biometric liveness detection*. Information Security Bulletin.

Tredoux, C. G., Rosenthal, Y., Costa, L. D., & Nunez, D. (1999). Face reconstruction using a configural, eigenface-based composite system. In *Proceedings of the 3rd Biennial Meeting of the Society for Applied Research in Memory and Cognition* (SARMAC). Boulder, CO: SARMAC.

Trujillo, L., Olague, G., Hammoud, R., & Hernandez, B. (2005). Automatic feature localization in thermal images for facial expression recognition. In *Proceedings of the 2005 IEEE Computer Society Conference on Computer Vision and Pattern Recognition* (CVPR'05). IEEE.

Turk, M., & Pentland, A. (1991). Eigenfaces for recognition. *Journal of Cognitive Neuroscience*, *3*, 71–86. doi:10.1162/jocn.1991.3.1.71 PMID:23964806.

Wijaya, S. L., Savvides, M., & Kumar, B. V. K. V. (2005). Illumination-tolerant face verification of low-bitrate JPEG2000 wavelet images with advanced correlation filters for handheld devices. *Applied Optics*, *44*, 655–665. doi:10.1364/AO.44.000655 PMID:15751847.

Wilder, J., Phillips, P., Jiang, C., & Wiener, S. (1996). Comparison of visible and infra-red imagery for face recognition. In *Proceedings of the IEEE International Conference on Automatic Face and Gesture Recognition* (AFGR '96), (pp. 182-187). Killington, VT: IEEE.

Wu, S. Q., Gu, Z. H., Chia, K. A., & Ong, S. H. (2007). Infrared facial recognition using modified blood perfusion. In *Proceedings 6th Int. Conf. Inform., Comm., & Sign*. IEEE.

Yoshitomi, Y., Miyaura, T., Tomita, S., & Kimura, S. (1997). Face identification using thermal image processing. In *Proceedings of the IEEE Int. Workshop Robot Hum. Commun.*, (pp. 374–379). IEEE.

KEY TERMS AND DEFINITIONS

Biometrics: Is the science and technology of measuring and analyzing biological data. In information technology, biometrics refers to technologies that measure and analyze human body characteristics, such as DNA, fingerprints, eye retinas and irises, voice patterns, facial patterns and hand measurements, for authentication purposes.

Classifier: Attempts to assign each input value to one of a given set of classes.

Contrast: Is determined by the difference in the color and brightness of the object and other objects within the same field of view.

Co-Occurrence Matrix: Is defined over an image to identify the distribution of co-occurring values at a given offset. So, it can measure the texture of the image. Because co-occurrence matrices are typically large and sparse, various metrics of the matrix are often used to get a more useful set of features.

Feature Extraction: Is a method of simplifying the amount of resources required to describe a large set of data accurately and efficiently for separating an object from other objects.

A Thermal Image: Is produced by sensing and recording the thermal energy emitted or reflected from the objects which are imaged.

A Visual Image: Is a mental image that arises from the eyes, which is similar to a visual perception.

Chapter 2
Multimodal Biometrics Recognition for Newborns

Shrikant Tiwari
Indian Institute of Technology, India

Sanjay Kumar Singh
Indian Institute of Technology, India

ABSTRACT

Identification of newborns at birth is a critical issue for hospitals, birthing centers, and other institutions where multiple births occur. With approximately 300,000 infants born worldwide each day, a large hospital may experience over one hundred new births every day. Correct identification of infants is essential to ensure that each mother travels home with her own child. Mixing, abduction, and illegal adoption of newborns is a global problem, and the research done to solve this problem is minimal. In this chapter, the authors present a multimodal biometric framework for the recognition of newborns.

INTRODUCTION

The word "biometrics" is derived from the Greek words bio (life) and metric (to measure) and thus Biometrics is the science of measuring biological or behavioural properties of living beings (Jain et al., 2007). Biometrics can be defined as the automatic recognition of a person based on his/her physiological or behavioral properties. A biometric system essentially makes use of behavioral or anatomical characteristics to recognize individuals by means of pattern recognition techniques and statistical methods. Biometric systems are used nowadays in many government and civilian applications, offering greater convenience and several advantages over traditional security methods based on something that you know (normally a secret password or PIN, which can be shared, forgotten, or copied) or something that you have (physical object that is presented to receive ac-

DOI: 10.4018/978-1-4666-4868-5.ch002

cess, such as keys, magnetic cards, identity documents etc., which can be shared, stolen, copied, or lost). Without sophisticated means, biometrics is difficult to share, steal or forge and cannot be forgotten or lost. Therefore, this latter solution provides a higher security level in identity prove. In addition, the combination of possession and knowledge with biometrics makes the identity proof even more secure.

An important issue in designing a practical biometric system is to determine how an individual is identified. Depending on the context, a biometric system can be either a verification (authentication) system or an identification system. Verification involves confirming or denying a person's claimed identity while in identification, one has to establish a person's identity. Biometric systems are divided on the basis of the authentication medium used (Jain et al., 2006). They are broadly divided as recognitions of Hand Geometry, Vein Pattern, Voice Pattern, DNA, Signature Dynamics, Finger Prints, Iris Pattern and Face Detection. These methods are used on the basis of the scope of the testing medium, the accuracy required and speed required. Every medium of authentication has its own advantages and shortcomings. With the advancement of technology and increased use of computers as vehicles of information technology, it is necessary to control unauthorized access to or fraudulent use of personal data. Biometric techniques being potentially able to augment this restriction are enjoying a renewed interest since last two decades.

The rest of the book chapter is organised as follows: The section 2 describes overview of biometrics, multibiometric and why multimodal biometrics is useful for newborn recognition. This section is followed by motivation for multimodal biometric recognition for newborn and related work is described in section 4. The proposed method is explained with results and analysis in section 5, section 6, and section 7, respectively. Finally, section 8 consists of conclusion and future directions.

BIOMETRIC SYSTEM

A biometric system is basically a pattern recognition system that recognizes a person by classifying the binary code of a uniquely specific biological or physical characteristic to the binary code of the stored characteristic. Samples are taken from individuals to see if there is a similarity to biometric references previously taken from known individuals.

Biometric system involves four aspects (Jain et al., 2000, 1999) data acquisition and preprocessing feature extraction, similarity computation and decision making. The digital representation recorded in the system database, which describes the characteristics or features of a physical trait is defines as a template. It is obtained by a feature extraction algorithm and is generated through an enrolment or training process, which is depicted in Figure 1. The recognition process can be performed in two modes by a biometric system (Karthik Nandakumar, 2008).

Figure 1. The core components of a single biometric system

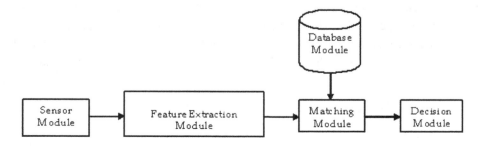

Before considering multi-modal biometrics, it is important to understand the core features of a conventional (uni-modal) biometric system. Brief description about four components is given below:

- **Sensor or Biometric Capture Module:** This is a interface between user and biometric system to capture biometric data, e.g. a fingerprint reader or iris scanner.
- **Feature Extraction Module:** To determine the quality and suitability of biometric data acquired by the sensor in assessed. The acquired data is subjected to a signal enhancement algorithm in order to improve its quality. In order to facilitate matching or comparison of the raw digital representation is usually further processed by feature extractor to generate a compact but expressive representation called feature set. For example the position and orientation of minutiae points in a fingerprint image would be computed in feature extraction module.
- **Matching Module:** The matching (or comparison) stage (also known as a matcher) takes a feature set and an enrollment template as inputs and computes the similarity between them. The matcher module also includes a decision making modules, in which the match scores are used to either validate a claimed identity or provide ranking in order to identify individual. For example, in this module the number of matching minutiae between the query and the template can be computed and treated as matching score.
- **Decision Module:** That provides a degree of confidence in any identity matched against the person providing the biometric sample.

BIOMETRIC TRAITS

Biometric traits can be classified into anatomical and behavioral traits (Jain et al., 2006). Examples of anatomical traits are: iris, fingerprint, hand, retinal scan, DNA etc., and examples of behavioral traits are: speech, signature, handwriting etc. anatomical characteristic can be measured on a part of the body at some point in time (passive), and are always present. On the other hand behavioral characteristic are learned or acquired over time (active) and are produced with a special effort, requiring a "realization" (e.g. a signature realization or a voice utterance). Hence, they are dependent to some degree on the individual's state of mind. Because of that, anatomical traits show less time variability than behavioral traits (Windsor et al., 2007) (see Figure 2).

LIMITATIONS OF UNIMODAL BIOMETRICS

A unimodal biometric system is one that utilizes the information obtained from a single biometric trait in order to authenticate an individual. The unimodal biometric systems present some limitations in their use (Jullan Fierrez Aguilar, 2006) as follows:

- **Noise:** The biometric data collected systematically include some level of noise due to the working environment or quality of sensor.
- **Intra-class variations:** The physical or behavioral traits can vary with time or other reasons.
- **Inter-Class Variations:** All of the biometric features presenting the same capacity to differentiate the individuals is not feasible.
- **Non-Universality:** Some people demonstrate behaviors that are not appropriate to the unimodal systems' needs (inappropriate way of speaking, for instance) or the

Figure 2. Different biometrics traits

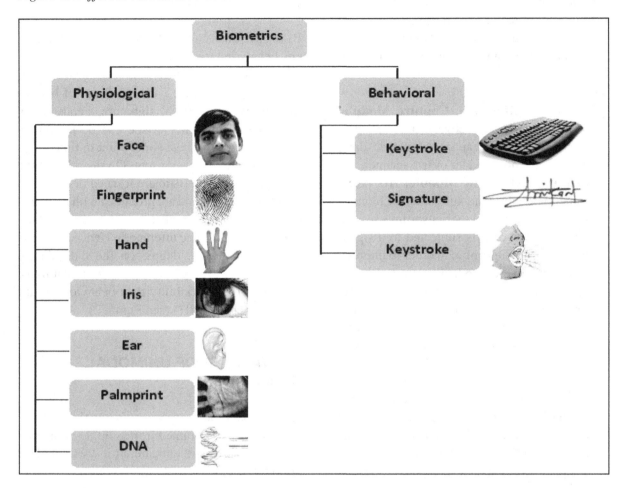

characteristics of the feature chosen for the system are not discriminative enough, or it could even happen that some of the users cannot present their feature due to its lack or to the difficulty of its capture. This problem becomes more noticeable when the user does not collaborate voluntarily.

The ability of the system to perform well (within the limits of its design) is based almost solely upon the quality of the biometric captured. A well captured biometric is rich in distinguishing information, which in turn gives the feature extraction algorithms the best chance of finding a match with existing records.

MULTI-BIOMETRIC

Multibiometric systems represent the fusion of two or more unimodal biometric systems. These systems combine the evidence presented by different body traits for establishing identity. For example, some of the earliest multimodal biometric systems utilized face and voice features to establish the identity of an individual (Brunelli and Falavigna, 1995).

Such systems are expected to be more reliable due to the presence of multiple independent pieces of evidence. The development and application of multi-biometric solutions are a popular, emerging trend on the global biometrics market. In multibiometric systems, humans are identified by two or more biometric identifiers (Jain et al., 2006). Multi-biometric recognition systems are gaining in popularity: for instance, e-passports and e-IDs are supplemented with digital photos and fingerprints of their holders.

MAJOR BENEFITS OF MULTI-BIOMETRICS

- This increases the reliability and recognition quality, while reducing FAR and FRR error rates.
- A variety of identifiers that can be used simultaneously or separately (for instance, the ability to identify a subject by fingerprints in case his/her voice or face is not matched).
- This may speed up the recognition process.

A multibiometric system relies on the evidence presented by multiple sources of biometric information. Based on the nature of these sources, a multibiometric system can be classified into one of the following six categories: multisensor, multialgorithm, multi-instance, multisample, multimodal, and hybrid. A multibiometic system can be based on one or a combination of the following fusion scenarios (Jain et al., 2006):

- **Multiple Sensors:** A single biometric modality is captured by using a multiple sensors. For example using multiple face cameras for creating a 3D input face or for combining the output scores of the different baseline face images.
- **Multiple Algorithms:** In order to create templates with different information content, a single biometric input is processed with different feature extraction algorithms. For example processing fingerprint images according to minutiae and texture based representation.

- **Multiple Instances**: A single biometric modality but multiple parts of the human body are used. One example is the use of multiple fingers in fingerprint verification.
- **Multiple Samples:** The same biometric modality and instance is acquired with the same sensor multiple times. One example is the sequential use of multiple impressions of the same finger in fingerprint verification. This case is sometimes not considered a multibiometric scenario.

WHY MULTIMODAL BIOMETRIC?

Recognition based on multiple biometrics represents an emerging trend. The most compelling reason to combine different biometric modalities is to improve the recognition rate. This can be done when biometric features of different biometrics are statistically independent. There are other reasons to combine two or more biometrics. One is that different biometric modalities might be more appropriate for the different applications and other reason is simply customer preference (Jain et al., 2006).

The terms multimodal or multi-biometric indicates the presence and use of more than one biometric aspect (modality, sensor, instance and/or algorithm) in some form of combined use for making a specific biometric verification/identification decision.

The goal of multimodal is to reduce one or more of the following:

- False Accept Rate (FAR)
- False Reject Rate (FRR)
- Failure To Enroll rate (FTE)
- Susceptibility to artifacts or mimics

Multimodal Biometric systems have following advantage over Unimodal biometric systems:

1. Systems are resistant to intra class similarity of data like facial feature. They combine more than one modality causing reduced intra-class similarity.
2. Multimodal systems are more resistant to noise as compared to Unimodal biometric systems, as they have more than one modality more data is available for matching.
3. Less vulnerable to spoofing, as it is difficult to spoof more than one modality simultaneously.

MOTIVATION

Abduction, swapping and mix-ups are the unfortunate events that could happen to newborn while in hospital premises and medical personnel are finding it difficult to curb this unfortunate incident. Accurate patient Identification (ID) is essential for patient safety, especially with our smallest and most vulnerable pediatric patients. A recent study of misidentification in the Neonatal Intensive Care Unit (NICU) over a 1-year period found "not a single day was free of risk for newborn misidentification" (Gray et al., 2006).

The level of security is very crucial issue in maternity ward and the problem of missing and swapping of newborn is of prime concern to the persons involved and affected. There is a common perception in the society that nothing can be done to prevent this unfortunate tragedy. In comparison to developed nations the developing countries are facing more challenges because of overcrowding and scarcity of medical facilities in the hospital.

Recognition of newborns at birth is a critical issue for hospitals, birthing centers and other institutions where multiple births occur. With approximately 300,000 newborns born worldwide each day, a large hospital may experience over one hundred new births each day. A large hospital may see as many as a hundred new newborns each day. Correct recognition of newborns is essential to ensure that each mother travels home with her own child.

Existing biometric and non-biometric methods fail to provide enough level of security and research done to solve this problem is very minimal. Biometrics is a technology which is expected to replace traditional authentication methods which are easy to be stolen, forgotten and duplicated. The use of biometrics may provide parents the peace of mind knowing that they now have a means of proving that the child, they are carrying home is their own child after the birth. But it is surprising that so little research for newborn recognition is reported, while biometric recognition of adults receives so much funding for research and development. Following are the strong reasons to study biometric technique for newborn personal authentication:

- Every year million newborn come into the world and the total population of newborn and young children at the age of years is around million (Wei et al., 2011). With such a large population, this group cannot be ignored by biometric researchers otherwise whole architecture of biometrics technique is incomplete.
- Recognition of newborn after birth is a critical issue for hospitals, maternity ward and other places where multiple births take place. According to study performed in United States by Gray *et al.* concluded that, out of newborns that are admitted to a neonatal intensive care unit at any given day, there is chance of incorrect recognition (Gray et al., 2006).
- Switching and abduction of newborn babies are global challenges that are faced by hospitals across the world. It has been reported that in United States, every year around newborn babies are switched by mistake (http://www.missingkids.com/enus/documents/infantabductionstats.pdf). Apart from incidental switching, there are instances of abduction of babies and illegal adoption.

RELATED WORK

Hospitals have devised several procedures to ensure that babies are correctly recognized and one of the popular methods is the use of ID bracelets. Soon after the birth ID bracelets are put on babies hands/legs, but this has not been able to provide enough level of security for newborn. The medical technique like Deoxyribonucleic Acid (DNA) typing and Human Leukocyte Antigen (HLA) typing are very efficient and accurate methods for verifying the identity of babies but due to the amount of time it takes to process a DNA or HLA sample and the cost associated with it, these methods for recognition are not feasible for every individual. Further DNA is invasive so it cannot be used each time for recognition of newborn. Another method recommended by Federal Bureau of Investigation is foot and finger printing of the child and mother (Stapleton, 1999). According to survey report of the hospitals in United States perform foot printing of the babies within 2 hours of their birth and hospitals maintain newborn recognition form on which footprint of the child and fingerprint of the mother are collected. The prints are generally collected using ink based methods and then printed on the recognition form.

Although capturing offline newborn's footprint has been exploited in many countries, there exists a big debate on the effectiveness of offline footprint recognition caused by the image quality of offline footprint. In fact, there is no innovation for offline newborn's footprint acquisition in the past 100 years, and nearly most of offline footprint images are illegible due to the following reasons: (1) Use of inadequate materials (ink, paper, cylinder); (2) Untrained personal for footprint acquisition; (3) Baby's skin covered with an oily substance; (4) Reduced thickness of the newborn epidermis easily deforming the ridges upon contact and filling the valleys between ridges with ink; (5) Reduced size of the newborns ridges, which are three to five times smaller than that of adults (Weingaertner et al., 2008).

Medical and computer scientist have explored the efficiency and authenticity of using footprints for newborn recognition and analysis done by Shepard *et al.* using footprints of 51 newborns was examined by fingerprint experts ant they were able to identified only 10 newborn (Shepard et al., 1966; Thompson et al., 1988).

Wierschem (1965) described a study in which footprints collected by Chicago's hospitals (USA) were analysed, concluding that 98% could not be used for recognition. After providing trainment and the right equipment to the medical team, a new analysis of the collected footprints was performed, showing that 99% allowed the newborn's recognition. But this recognition was not based on dactiloscopic ridges. It used the flexion creases of the foot, which change during the first months of life.

Shepard *et al.* (1966) collected footprints of 51 newborns, one at birth and another 5 to 6 weeks after, sending the resulting 102 impressions to the California State Justice Department of Criminal Investigation and Recognition (USA) for analysis. There, expert fingerprint technicians analyzed the sample and were only able to identify 10 babies, resulting in approximately 20% identifiable footprints. However it was felt that the majority of these 20 correctly matched prints would not stand up under legal scrutiny in the courts.

Thompson *et al.* (1981) collected 100 footprints of 20 newborns and verified that only 11% where technically acceptable and only one footprint (1%) had all elements needed for a legal recognition. They also acquired the footprints of 20 premature babies weighting less than 1500*g* at birth. Many prints were obtained from each baby: at birth and then 4 to 8 weeks later, and the best pair of prints were chosen for a matching attempt. Conclusion was that none of these footprints were suitable for recognition purposes.

Pela *et al.* (1975) conducted the study on 1917 foot prints collected by trained staff of hospital in Brazil. Most of the images collected provided insufficient information for recognition of newborn (Pela *et al.*, 1975). The American Academy of Pediatrics and others concluded that individual hospitals may continue the practice of foot printing of newborn and fingerprinting of mother, but universal application of this practice is not recommended.

Apart from footprint, medical and biometric researchers explored the applicability of other biometric modalities such as palmprint, fingerprint and ear for verifying the identity of newborn babies (Galton, 1899). Very few articles referring to the use of fingerprints on newborns were found. Worth mentioning is Sir F. Galton's work (Galton, 1899; Holt, 1973; Cummins et al., 1943; Kucken et al., 2005) where he presented a study of newborn fingerprinting with ink and paper, concluding that fingerprints taken before 17 months after birth are not useful for recognition. Although, fingerprint recognition has been widely and successfully used, it is not feasible for newborns. The main reason is that the finger of newborn is too small and the minutiae points or ridges are not very clear.

Fingerprint and palm print recognition are well-established modalities to recognize adults (over the age of 5 years), but in case of newborn it is not characteristic enough in the first days of life. Further fingerprint, palmprint and hand geometry image is difficult to acquire because newborns usually have their hands closed and keeping all the fingers in the correct position is not easy. Weingaertner et al. (2008) developed a new high resolution sensor for capturing the foot and palm prints of babies. Two images of 106 newborns were collected: one within 24 hours of birth and another at around 48 hours.

The recognition accuracy of 67.7% and 83%were obtained using footprints and palm prints, respectively. Fields et al. (1960) have studied the feasibility of ear recognition on a database of 206 newborns. They manually analysed the samples and concluded that visually ears can be used to distinguish between two children. In all the methods for identifying newborns, no research has evaluated the performance of automatic identification or verification.

Morgan et al. (1939) presented a technique for collecting palm prints of newborns, and stated that they resulted in images good enough to be used for recognition, although no objective analysis of the resulting images were provided, nor did they perform a matching test to support their statement. Palmprint recognition is not suitable for newborns yet since it is often difficult to let a newborn open his hand. The work done by Rubisley P Lemes *et al.* (2011) demonstrates the use of palmprint using high resolution scanner on the database of demonstrates the use of palmprint using high resolution scanner on the database of newborn has the limitation of good quality image, high cost of recognition and highly intrusive.

Although iris recognition for adults yields very high accuracy (Daugman, 2007), for newborns, it is very difficult to capture iris patterns. In case of newborns the use of iris trait as recognition feature is a difficult method, especially the premature. Because newborn hardly open their eyes, they do not have the ability of looking into a scanning device, and touching their eyelids to collect an image could hurt them (Bolle et al., 2003). Apart from this, the iris pattern only stabilizes after two years (Jain et al., 2004). The format of the ear is a biometric feature of easy acquisition, but possesses little discriminatory capacity (Bolle et al., 2003; Victor et al., 2002).

The work done on face recognition of newborn reports the accuracy of 86.9% on the database of 34 babies also suffers from facial expression of newborn as the face database consist of crying or sleeping face because it is very difficult to get the neutral face (Bolle et al., 2003). After doing extensive survey on newborn recognition we have prepared the following table which demonstrates the applicability of different biometric traits to recognize newborn. Comparison of Different modalities for recognition of newborn as shown in Table 1.

Table 1. Comparison of different modalities for recognition of newborn

Biometrics/ Non- Biometrics	Universality	Uniqueness	Permanence	Measurability	Performance	Acceptability	Circumvention
ID-Band	Low	Low	Low	High	High	Low	Low
Barcode	Low	Low	Low	High	High	Low	Low
DNA	High	High	High	Low	High	Low	Low
Fingerprint	(Not possible)	(Not possible)	(Not possible)	(Not possible)	(Not possible)	(Not possible)	(Not possible)
Palmprint	Low	Low	Low	Low	Low	Low	Low
Iris	(Not possible)	(Not possible)	(Not possible)	(Not possible)	(Not possible)	(Not possible)	(Not possible)
Ear	Medium	Medium	Medium	Medium	High	Medium	Medium
Face	Medium	Medium	Low	Medium	High	Medium	Medium
Footprint	Medium	Medium	Medium	Low	High	High	M

RECOGNITION OF NEWBORN USING FACE AND SOFT BIOMETRIC DATA

Among the biometric traits used for computer vision, the face and the ear have gained most of the attention of the research community due to their non-intrusiveness and the ease of data collection. In this section we have tested different face recognition algorithms on newborn and then used multimodal biometrics to increase the recognition accuracy of newborn. For multimodal implementation, we have integrated face and soft biometric data.

To identify the newborn face, five algorithms have been selected for implementation. A brief description about the implementation of PCA, ICA, LDA, LBP and SURF are explained in (Tiwari et al., 2012).

- Principal Component Analysis (PCA) (Belhumeur et al., 1997)
- Independent Component Analysis (ICA) (Bartlett et al., 2002)
- Linear Discriminant Analysis (LDA) (Belhumeur et al., 1997)
- Local Binary Pattern (LBP) (Ojala et al., 2002; Ahonen et al., 2006)

- Speeded Up Robust Features (SURF) (Bay et al., 2008)

We have manually detected faces for solving the face detection errors problem and used geometric normalization (or affine transformation) for face alignment. In our newborn face database most of the time eyes of newborn are closed so that avoiding errors set the distance of inter eye to be 100 pixels. For evaluating performance the newborn database is partitioned into training and testing/ probe. We have collected 10 face images of each newborn, out of 10 images 6 images of each newborn is randomly selected for training/ gallery database (Total of 1680 images) and the remaining 4 images of each newborn is selected for testing/probe database (Total 1120 images).

Evaluation process is performed five times for checking validation and computed Rank-1 identification accuracies. The overall performance evaluation of all the four algorithms is compared which is shown in the Table 2. From the Table 2 and Figure 3, it is observed that the identification accuracy of LBP is 87.76% and SURF is 83.63% at Rank-I.

Table 2. Identification accuracy of the newborn face database

Procedure	PCA	ICA	LDA	LBP	SURF
Identification Accuracy (Rank-1)	74.34%	78.12%	80.15%	82.76%	83.63%

Figure 3. CMC for face recognition algorithm

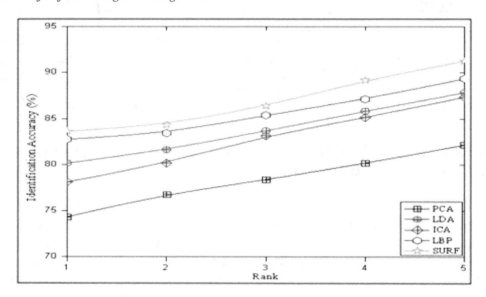

FRAME WORK FOR INTEGRATION OF FACE AND SOFT-BIOMETRIC INFORMATION

In the proposed method, the biometric recognition system is divided into two subsystems (see Figure 4). The two subsystems are the primary biometric system which includes face and the secondary biometric system consisting of soft biometric traits like height, weight, gender and blood-group. Figure 6 shows the architecture of a personal recognition system that makes use of both face and soft biometric measurements (Jain et al., 2004; Jain et al., 2004). Similar to Tiwari et al. (2012) fusion of face and soft biometric is performed.

Let $x = [\omega_1, \omega_2, ..., \omega_n]$ where the total no of newborns enrolled is n and x is the feature vector corresponding to the face. The primary biometric system output is the form of $P(\omega_i|x), i = 1, 2, ..., n$, where $P(\omega_i|x)$ is the probability, x is the feature vector for the test user ω_i. The primary biometric system output is a matching score, which is converted into posteriori probability. For the secondary biometric system, we can consider $P(\omega_i|x)$ as the prior probability for the corresponding test user ω_i.

Let $y = [y_1, y_2, ... y_k, y_{k+1}, y_{k+2}, ..., y_m]$ be the feature vector of soft biometric, where, y_1 through y_k denotes continuous variables and y_{k+1} through y_m are discrete variables. Finally the matching probability of the user ω_i, and the given primary biometric and soft biometrics feature vector is x and y, i.e., $P(\omega_i|x, y)$ can be calculated using the

Figure 4. Framework for fusion of face and soft-biometric information. Here X is the primary (face) feature vector and Y is the soft biometric feature vector.

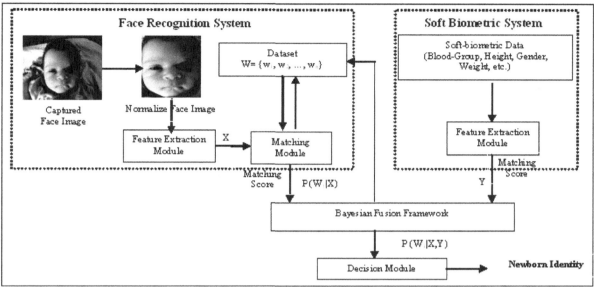

Bayes' rule as (Jain et al., 2004; Jain et al., 2004; Tiwari et al., 2012):

$$P\left(\omega_i | x,\ y\right) = \frac{p\left(y|\omega_i\right)P\left(\omega_i | x\right)}{\sum_{i=1}^{n} p\left(y|\omega_i\right)P\left(\omega_i | x\right)} \quad (1)$$

If the variables are independent then Equation (1) can be rewritten as follows (see Box 1):

In Equation (2), $p\left(y_j | \omega_i\right), j = 1,2,...,k$ represents the conditional probability of the continuous variable y_j for the corresponding user ω_i. This can be evaluated from the conditional density of the variable j for the user ω_i. On the other hand, discrete probabilities $p\left(y_j | \omega_i\right), j = k+1, k+2,...,m$ represents the probability that user ω_i is assigned to the class y_j. This is a measure of the accuracy of the classification module in assigning user ω_i to one of the distinct classes based on biometric indicator y_j.

The logarithm of $P\left(\omega_i | x,\ y\right)$ in Equation (2) can be expressed as shown in Box 2.

The resultant weight in the following discriminant function for newborn ω_i as shown in Box 4 (Jain et al., 2004).

Note: For the soft biometric traits and primary biometric identifier assigned weights are the a_i's, $i = 1,2,...m$ and a_0 respectively.

In our experiments we have selected soft biometric traits such as gender, blood group, weight,

Box 1.

$$P\left(\omega_i | x,\ y\right) = \frac{p\left(y_1 | \omega_i\right)...p\left(y_k | \omega_i\right)P\left(y_{k+1} | \omega_i\right).....p\left(y_m | \omega_i\right)P\left(\omega_i | x\right)}{\sum_{i=1}^{n} p\left(y_1 | \omega_i\right)...p\left(y_k | \omega_i\right)P\left(y_{k+1} | \omega_i\right)......p\left(y_m | \omega_i\right)P\left(\omega_i | x\right)} \quad (2)$$

Box 2.

$$
logP\left(\omega_i \mid x, y\right) = \log p\left(y_1 \mid \omega_i\right) + \ldots + \log p\left(y_k \mid \omega_i\right) + \log P\left(y_{k+1} \mid \omega_i\right)
$$
$$
+ \log P\left(y_m \mid \omega_i\right) + \log P\left(\omega_i \mid x\right) - \log p\left(y\right)
$$
$$
p\left(y\right) = \sum_{i=1}^{n} p\left(y_1 \mid \omega_i\right) \ldots p\left(y_k \mid \omega_i\right) P\left(y_{k+1} \mid \omega_i\right) \ldots p\left(y_m \mid \omega_i\right) P\left(\omega_i \mid x\right) \tag{3}
$$

Box 4.

$$
g_i\left(x, y\right) = a_0 \log P\left(\omega_i \mid x\right) + a_1 \log p\left(y_1 \mid \omega_i\right) + a_k \log p\left(y_k \mid \omega_i\right) + a_{k+1} \log P\left(y_{k+1} \mid \omega_i\right)
$$
$$
+ a_m \log p\left(y_m \mid \omega_i\right) \tag{4}
$$
$$
\text{where } \sum_{i=0}^{m} a_i = 1 \; a_0 \gg a_i, \; i = 1, 2, \ldots m
$$

and height information of the user in addition to the face biometric identifiers. Let $P(\omega_i \mid s)$ be the posterior probability (Face) that the user is newborn ω_i given the primary biometric score 's' of the test user. Let $y_i = (G_i, B_i, W_i, H_i)$ is the soft biometric feature vector corresponding to the identity claimed by the user ω_i, where G_i, B_i, W_i and H_i are the true values of gender, blood group, weight, and height of ω_i. Let $y^* = (G^*; B^*; W^*; H^*)$ is the soft biometric feature vector of the observed test user, where G^* is the observed gender, B^* is the observed blood group, W^* is the observed weight, and H^* is the observed height. Finally the score after considering the observed soft biometric characteristics is computed as

$$
g_i\left(s, y^*\right) = a_0 \log P\left(genuine \mid s\right)
$$
$$
+ a_1 \log p\left(H^* \mid H_i\right) + a_2 \log P\left(W^* \mid W_i\right) \tag{5}
$$
$$
+ a_3 \log P\left(G^* \mid G_i\right) + a_4 \log P\left(B^* \mid B_i\right)
$$

where $a_3 = 0$, if $G^* =$"reject," and $a_4 = 0$ if $B^* =$"reject."

Figure 3 shows the Cumulative Match Characteristic (CMC) of the face biometric system operating in the identification mode, and the improvement in performance achieved after the utilization of soft biometric information. The weights assigned to the primary and soft biometric traits were selected experimentally such that the performance gain is maximized. However, no formal procedure was used and an exhaustive search of all possible sets of weights was not attempted. The use of blood-group, height, weight and gender information along with the face leads to an improvement of 1% in the rank one performance as shown in Figure 5(a), Figure 5(b), Figure 5(c), and Figure 5(d), respectively. From Figure 5(b), Figure 5(c), and Figure 5(d), we can observe that the blood-group information of the newborn is more discriminative than gender and leads to a 1.5% improvement in the rank one performance. The combined use of all the four soft biometric traits results in an improvement of approximately 5.6% over the face biometric system as shown in Figure 5(e).

The gender information did not provide any improvement in the performance of a face recognition system. This may be due to the fact that the gender classifiers and the face recognition system use the same representation. However, the height

Figure 5. Improvement in the performance of a unimodal (face) system after addition of soft biometric traits: (a) face with gender, b) face with height, c) face with weight, d) face with blood-group, and e) face with blood-group, gender, height, and weight

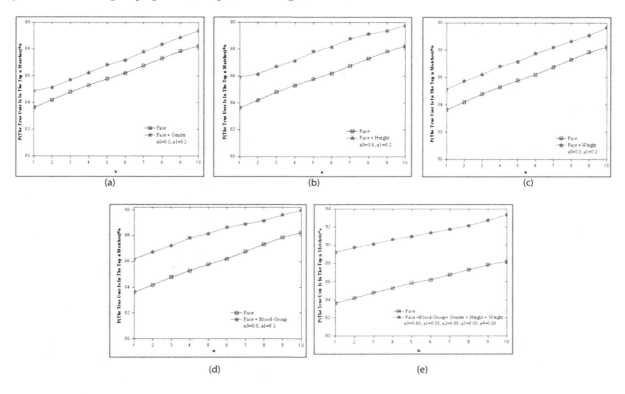

Table 3. Integrating identification accuracy of the newborn face database (F=Face, G=Gender, H=Height, W=Weight, B=Blood-group)

Procedure	F	F + G	F + H	F +W	F+ B	F+G+H+W+B
Identification Accuracy (Rank-1)	83.63%	84.87%	85.92%	85.13%	86.18%	89.23%

and weight information is independent of the facial features and, hence, it leads to an improvement of 2.29%, 1.5% respectively in the recognition performance. The failure of the gender information to improve the face recognition performance establishes that fact that soft biometric traits would help in recognition only if the identity information provided by them is complementary to that of the primary biometric identifier (see Table 3).

RECOGNITION OF NEWBORN USING EAR AND SOFT BIOMETRIC

In this section, we have tried to demonstrate that performance accuracy of newborn can be enhanced by fusion of ear and soft biometrics. In the proposed framework, the biometric recognition system is divided into two subsystems. The two subsystems are the primary biometric system which consist of ear and the secondary biometric system consisting of soft biometric traits like height, weight, gender and blood-group. Figure 10 shows the architecture of a personal recognition system that makes use of both ear and soft biometric measurements (Jain et al., 2004). Similar to (Tiwari et al., 2011, 2012) fusion of ear and soft biometric is performed. We have adopted the same methodology for fusion of ear and soft-biometrics as mentioned in the (Tiwari et al., 2012)

In order to achieve our goal to extract features from ear we evaluate well-known, classical algorithms: PCA, KPCA, FLDA, ICA, GF, and HAAR.

- Principal Component Analysis (PCA) (Belhumeur et al., 1997; Jun Song et al., n.d.; Ping et al., 2005)
- Kernel Principal Component Analysis (KPCA) (Li. 2006)
- Fisher Linear Discriminant Analysis (FLDA) (Kurita et al.; Liu et al., 2004; Chen et al., 2000)
- Independent Component Analysis (ICA) (Bartlett et al., 2002; Nanni et al., 2007)
- Geometrical Feature Extraction (GF) (Choras 2005; Choras et al., 2006)
- HAAR (Pittner et al., 1999; Burrus et al., 1998)

Evaluation process is performed five times for checking validation and computed Rank-1 identification accuracies. The overall performance evaluations of all the six algorithms (PCA, KPCA, FLDA, ICA, GF, and HAAR) are computed on the newborn ear database. The results of this experiment are compiled in following Table 4 and Figure 6, it is observed that the identification accuracy of GF is 83.67% and HAAR is 85.13% at Rank-1.

The key analyses of the ear recognition are explained below:

- The difficulty of ear feature extraction lies in the changes among the same ear caused by head rotation and lighting variation because most of the time newborn are sleeping or crying. The geometry feature extraction depends heavily on the quality of the image preprocessing.
- Due to different lighting conditions the curve segments extraction and the structural extraction will be different even for the same newly born child, which makes the methods unreliable. The rotation discrimination is even more challenging because the angle between the ear and the head is not the same among different babies.

Table 4 shows that among the appearance based algorithms, FLDA provides the best accuracy of 80.57% at the Rank-1 Level. The performance of appearance based PCA, KPCA, FLDA and ICA algorithm increase with decreasing the size of database decreasing the resolution of the image.

For Geometrical Feature Extraction (GF) method works on the concept of finding out the points on the contour and distance between them, so the result is approximated in our algorithm by allowing an error of 2% and accuracy is 83.67%.

- Through experiment, we found that recognition performance of appearance methods (such as PCA, KPCA, FLDA, and ICA) will increase dramatically when the input image contains much less background information around the ear.

Table 4. Identification accuracy of the newborn ear database

Procedure	PCA	KPCA	ICA	FLDA	GF	HAAR
Identification Accuracy (Rank-1)	78.56%	80.03%	71.75%	80.57%	83.67%	85.13%

Figure 6. CMC for ear recognition algorithm

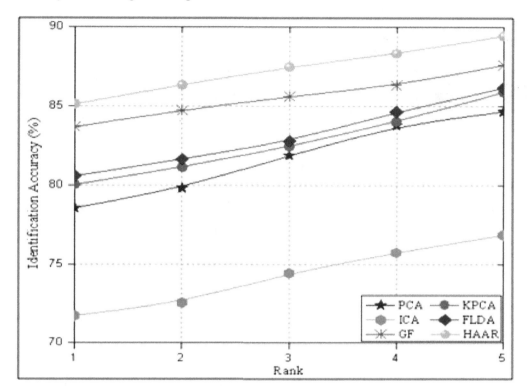

- HAAR wavelet transform is used to decompose the detected image and compute coefficient matrices of the wavelet, which are clustered in the feature template. Decision is made by matching test image with trained image using Hamming distance approach and the result in this algorithm is 85.13%.

FRAME WORK FOR FUSION OF EAR AND SOFT-BIOMETRIC INFORMATION

In this method, we have selected soft biometric traits such as gender, blood group, weight, and height information of the user in addition to the ear biometric identifiers (see Figure 7).

Here $P(\omega_i \mid s)$ is the posterior probability (Ear) that the user is newborn ω_i given the primary biometric score 's' of the test user. Let $y_i = (G_i, B_i, W_i, H_i)$ is the soft biometric feature vector corresponding to the identity claimed by the user ω_i, where G_i, B_i, W_i and H_i are the true values of gender, blood group, weight, and height of ω_i. Let $y^* = (G^*; B^*; W^*; H^*)$ is the soft biometric feature vector of the observed test user, where G^* is the observed gender, B^* is the observed blood group, W^* is the observed weight, and H^* is the observed height. Finally the score after considering the observed soft biometric characteristics is computed as:

$$
\begin{aligned}
g_i\left(s, y^*\right) &= a_0 \log P\left(genuine \mid s\right) \\
&+ a_1 \log p\left(H^* \mid H_i\right) + a_2 \log P\left(W^* \mid W_i\right).. \\
&+ a_3 \log P\left(G^* \mid G_i\right) \\
&+ a_4 \log P\left(B^* \mid B_i\right)
\end{aligned}
\tag{6}
$$

Figure 7. Framework for fusion of primary and soft biometric information (here X is the primary [ear] feature vector and Y is the soft biometric feature vector)

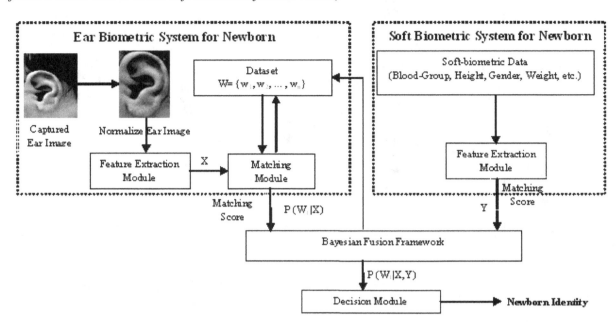

where $a_3 = 0$,. if $G^* =$ "reject," and $a_4 = 0$ if B^* = "reject."

Figure 6 shows the Cumulative Match Characteristic (CMC) of the ear biometric system operating in the identification mode, and the improvement in performance achieved after the utilization of soft biometric information. The weights assigned to the ear (primary) and soft biometric traits were selected experimentally such that the performance gain is maximized. However, no formal procedure was used and an exhaustive search of all possible sets of weights was not attempted. The use of blood-group, height, weight and gender information along with the ear leads to an improvement of 5.6% in the rank one performance as shown in Figure 8(a), Figure 8(b), Figure 8(c) and Figure 8(d), respectively. From Figure 8(b), Figure 8(c) and Figure 10(d), we can observe that the blood-group information of the newborn is more discriminative than gender and leads to a 1.49% improvement in the rank one performance. The combined use of all the four

soft biometric traits results in an improvement of approximately 5.6% over the primary biometric system as shown in Figure 8(e).

RECOGNITION OF NEWBORN USING FACE AND EAR

Face recognition with neutral expressions has reached its maturity with a high degree of accuracy. But changes of face geometry due to the changes of facial expression, use of cosmetics and eye glasses, aging, covering with beard or hair significantly affect the performance of face recognition systems. The ear is considered an alternative to be used separately or in combination with the face as it is comparatively less affected by such changes. However, its smaller size and often the presence of nearby hair and ear-rings make it very challenging to be used for non-interactive biometric applications (Islam et al., 2008).

Figure 8. Improvement in the performance of a unimodal (ear) system after addition of soft biometric traits: (a) ear with gender, b) ear with height, c) ear with weight, d) ear with blood-group, and e) ear with blood-group, gender, height, and weight

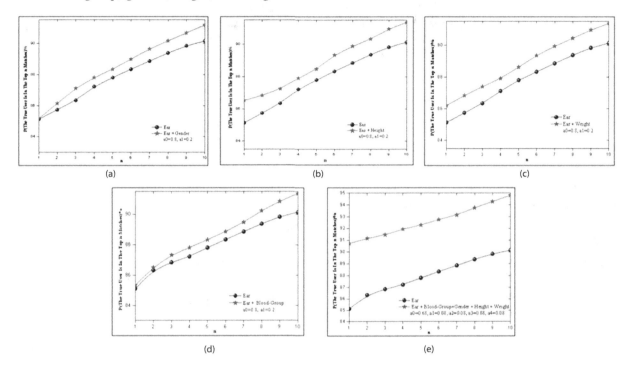

A multibiometric system normally overcomes many of the factors that plague a unimodal biometric system such as noise, variability and error rates (Bubeck et al., 2003). Apart from the benefit of a higher recognition rate, a multimodal biometric system can also help in lowering false rejection error rates. The approach we adopt for our multibiometric system is a multimodal approach (face and ear) with a single algorithm (PCA).

For both face and ear, we used Principal Component Analysis (PCA) for recognition. PCA is a successful method for recognition in images and is largely a statistical method. PCA transforms the image space to a feature space; the feature space is then used for recognition. PCA translates the pixels of an image into principal components. Eigenspace is determined by the eigenvectors of the covariance matrix derived from the images.

The procedure of building newborn face and ear is summarised below:

- Collection of raw images
- Running Viola and Jones (Viola et al., 2004, 2001) and later extended by Lienhart and Maydt (Lienhart et al., 2002) face detector and manual elimination of false detected region.
- Rescaling and labelling the detected faces/ears.
- Grouping the detected faces and ears in different subsets.
- Unimodal Biometrics.

We extracted only the portion of the image, which was detected. For face, the detected portion was further cropped in width to remove some of the unwanted areas not making up the face. The

Figure 9. *An example of a newborn normalized face and ear image*

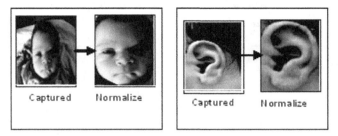

ear was also extracted and further cropped to get a more accurate ear representation. This was all done automatically where the best cropping techniques and parameters were determined experimentally (Darwish et al., 2009). For both face and ear, we used Principal Component Analysis (PCA) for recognition. Brief description about face and ear recognition using PCA is given below:

Let a face/ear image be represented by $N \times N$ matrix $I(x,y)$ and the training database be represented by images $I_1, \ldots, I_M$. Next images are converted to an N^2. The average face Ψ_{train} is

$$\Psi_{train} = \frac{1}{M} \sum_{n=1}^{M} I_n \tag{8}$$

Each face/ear differs from the average face/ear Ψ_{train} by vector

$$\varphi i = I_i - \Psi_{train}$$

Set of vectors is subject to PCA seeking a set of N^2 orthonormal vectors U_n and eigenvalues λ_k.

$$\lambda_k = \frac{1}{M} \sum_{n=1}^{M} \varnothing_n U_n^T \tag{9}$$

where U_k are its eigenvectors and λ_k are its eigenvalues. Let C be a covariance matrix

$$C = \frac{1}{M} \sum_{n=1}^{M} \varnothing_n \varnothing_n^T \tag{10}$$

$$C = A A^T \tag{11}$$

where $A = [\varnothing_1, \varnothing_2, \ldots, \varnothing_M]$.

The mean image ψ of the gallery set is computer (see Figure 9). Each mean-subtracted gallery image, $\varphi i = I_i - \Psi$

Then projected onto the "face space/ ear space" spanned by the M' eigenvectors deriving from the training set. We then use linear combination of M training faces to form eigenfaces U_l

$$U_l = \sum_{n=1}^{M} U_l', \varnothing_n \tag{12}$$

We usually use only a subset of M' eigenfaces/eigenear corresponding to the largest eigenvalues. For classification, an unknown face image I is resolved into weight components by the transformation

$$\omega_k = U_k^T, \varnothing_i, \tag{13}$$

$$k = 1, \ldots, M'$$

This describes a set of point-by-point image multiplication and summations. The weight from the vectors:

$$\Omega = \left[\omega_1, \ldots, \omega_k \right] \tag{14}$$

That describes the contribution of each eigenface or eigenear in representing the input face or

Figure 10. Block-diagram of the multimodal biometric system based on matching score fusion

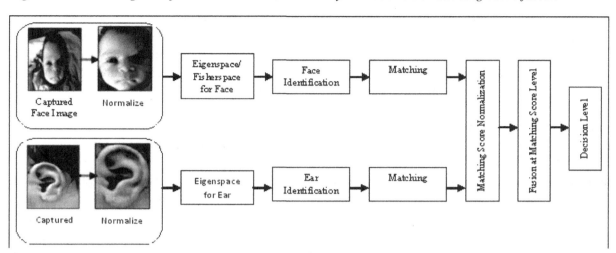

ear image treating the eigenfaces or eigenears as a basis set of face or ear images (Bartlett et al., 2002). Calculating a Euclidian distance is the simplest way to classify the new face or ear class as follows:

$$d_k = \left\| \Omega - \Omega_k \right\| \qquad (15)$$

Where, Ω_k is a vector describing the kth face or ear class.

FUSION OF FACE AND EAR

A multibiometric system normally overcomes many of the factors that plague a unimodal biometric system such as noise, variability and error rates (Bubeck et al., 2003). Apart from the benefit of a higher recognition rate, fusion of face and ear biometric system can also help in lowering false rejection error rates. Match score level fusion is performed for fusion of face and ear of newborn.

Normalization Methods

To properly compare and fuse distances from different modes, there is a need for an accurate normalization technique that can be applied to the distances. *Min-max* is the first normalization technique in our experimental studies. To normalize the distances in our experiments we used the min-max normalization (Middendorf et al., 2008).

More formally, to normalize the distance *x* in the dataset; we get the normalized value x_i' by:

$$X_i' = \frac{(X_i - min_i)}{(max_i - min_i)} \qquad (16)$$

where, *min* and *max* are the minimum and maximum values for each dataset.

Using this normalization technique we get values in the range of [0, 1] for each distance. This will allow us to fuse face and ear values with more accurate comparisons.

The second method used to normalize the matching scores is *median-MAD* (median absolute deviation) method. This normalization scheme is a robust method and has an average efficiency but it does not keep the input distribution and it does not transform the scores into a common numerical range. The normalized scores by this method are given by:

$$X_i' = \frac{(X_i - median)}{MAD}$$

where

$$D = median \ \left(\left|X_i - median\right|\right) \ . \qquad (17)$$

The third normalization technique is *z-score*. This method computed using the arithmetic mean and standard deviation of the data set. Due to sensitivity of both mean and standard deviation to outliers, this method is not robust and it may not transform the scores of our three modalities into a common numerical range, but it has high efficiency. The normalized scores are given by:

$$X_i^{'} = \frac{(X_i - \mu)}{\sigma} \qquad (18)$$

Where σ is the standard deviation and μ is the mean of the data set.

Fusion Methods

In order to combine the scores reported by the three matchers we used two different techniques including weighted sum method and weighted product method.

Weighted Sum

In order to combine the input scores to achieve a final score, one of the simplest fusion methods is weighted sum method. This method has low computational cost and decision in this method is computed by comparing these final scores with a threshold.

Weighted Product

Weighted product is another algorithm that combines the scores using weighted multiplication of each modality scores to obtain a final score. Decision in this method is the same as the previous method that computed by comparing these final scores with a threshold. But the computational cost of this method is more than the previous method.

Figure 13 shows the block-diagram of the proposed multimodal biometric system based on the fusion of face and ear features at the matching score level.

EXPERIMENTAL RESULTS

The size of data base is 2800 (280 Subjects X 10 Images). Each image database used in our research is divided into two training set images, face and ear images and their two corresponding test set images. The first four images per individual will construct the training set and the last six images per individual will be part of the test set. Principal components will be calculated for each individual image separately and the images will be transformed to the PCA space using their corresponding transformation matrix using Eigenfaces technique.

Individual Face and Ear Recognition

Experimental results that were obtained from the proposed face and ear recognition system are given, how we write the code using MATLAB for combined face and ear. At first level face and ear algorithms are tested individually. At this level the individual results are computed and the individual accuracy for face and ear is found to be 78.56% and 74.34% respectively as shown in Table 6.

However in order to increase the accuracy of the biometric system as a whole the individual results are combined at matching score level. At second level of experiment the matching scores from the individual traits are combined and final accuracy graph is plotted as shown in Figure 13. Table 5 shows the accuracy and error rates obtained from the individual system (see Figure 11).

Table 5. Identification accuracy of the newborn ear and soft biometric

Procedure	E	E + G	E + H	E +W	E + B	E+G+H+W+B
Identifica-tion Accuracy (Rank-1)	85.13%	85.18%	86.53%	86.21%	85.26%	90.72%

Figure 11. CMC to show identification accuracies of individual unimodal biometric system

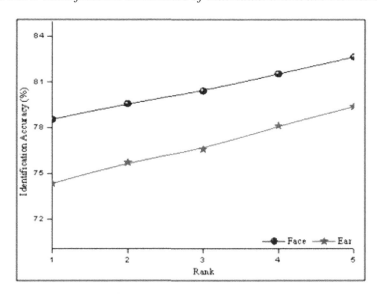

Table 6. Showing individual accuracy for newborn database

Biometric Traits	Algorithm	Accuracy	FAR (%)	FRR (%)
Face	PCA	78.56%	29.2	16.1
Ear	PCA	74.34%	31.3	18.3

Fusion of Face and Ear Recognition

We tested the performance of our approach for ear recognition and face recognition separately and then fused the ear and face match scores using the weighted sum and Weighted Product technique. The results of our experiments are reported in terms of the Cumulative Match Characteristic (CMC) for identification. The results of rank-one identification for the face recognition, ear recognition, and the fusion are presented, and are given as 78.56%, 74.34%, and 94.37%, respectively. As the figure shows, by fusing the face and ear biometric, the performance of the system is increased to 94.37%. We implemented three different normalization techniques (*min-max*, *median-MAD* and *z-score*) and applied two fusion methods (*weighted sum* and *weighted product*).

From Table 7 we observe that *z-score* normalization method outperform other normalization technique in our experimental studies. The weighted product method provides better performance than weighted sum method. Hence, we can conclude that when the scores normalized using

Table 7. Multimodal accuracy for newborn after fusion

Normalization Methods	Fusion Methods	
	Weighted Sum	Weighted Product
Min-Max	88.32%	90.13%
Median-MAD	85.16%	86.72%
Z-Score	92.13%	94.37%

Figure 12. CMC to show identification accuracies after fusion

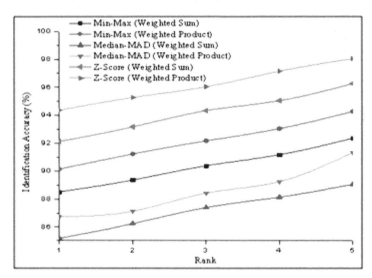

Figure 13. CMC of the multimodal biometric system based on matching score fusion

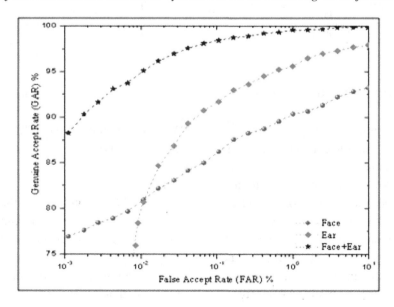

z-score method and combined using weighted product method, the best recognition performance (94.37%) are achieved. However in order to increase the accuracy of the biometric system as a whole the individual results are combined at matching score level. At second level of experiment the matching scores from the individual traits are combined and final accuracy graph is plotted as shown in Figure 12.

CONCLUSION

In this book chapter, we have demonstrated that multimodal biometrics is an effective tool to recognize newborn. For this purpose we fused face with soft biometrics, ear with soft biometrics and face with ear. In the first proposed method, we fused face with soft biometrics identifiers such as height, weight, gender, and blood-group. We are getting the accuracy of 83.63% by implementation of SURF algorithm and after integration with soft biometrics the accuracy is 89.23%. Although the soft biometric characteristics are not as permanent and reliable as the traditional biometric identifiers like face, they provide some information about the identity of the newborn that leads to higher accuracy in establishing the user identity.

In the second proposed method we demonstrated that ear and soft biometric identifiers such as height, weight, gender, and blood-group can be very useful in newborn recognition. In this research we are getting the accuracy of 85.13% by using HAAR algorithm and after fusion with soft biometrics the accuracy is 90.72%.

Our proposed model demonstrated that the utilization of ancillary user information like gender, height, weight and blood group can improve the performance of the traditional biometric system.

The performance of ear recognition in case of newborn is better than face recognition as it does not suffers from facial expression. The proposed algorithm provides the highest identification accuracy of 89.28%.

Finally, we proposed an automated multibiometric system using face and ear. Among several fusion methods a normalized Euclidean weighted product for face/ear of (0.8/0.2), gives the best result for newborn of 94.37%. These results may aid in the development of a passive recognition system where the subject's cooperation is not required.

FUTURE RESEARCH DIRECTIONS

The approach described in this book chapter is relatively successful and promising in recognition of newborn but more research is to be done by the scientist and engineers in the following domain.

- Performance evaluation of face and ear image of newborn after certain interval of time and then analyze the efficiency of recognition in newborn.
- Design and development of pose, Illumination, occlusion and expression invariant based fusion algorithms because newborn are highly non-cooperative user of biometrics.
- Three Dimensional (3D) face recognition can be tested as it is invariant to expression.
- Illumination is also a big challenge because of changing weather condition and the location (indoor or outdoor). So an illumination invariant technique is to be developed for newborn face recognition.
- Covariates based fusion algorithms can be developed, as the values of covariates are to be estimated from the pair of images being compared.

REFERENCES

Aguilar, J. F. (2006). *Adapted fusion schemes for multimodal biometric authentication*. Ph.D. Thesis.

Ahonen, T., Hadid, A., & Pietikainen, M. (2006). Face description with local binary patterns: Application to face recognition. *IEEE Transactions on Pattern Analysis and Machine Intelligence, 28*(12), 2037–2041. doi:10.1109/TPAMI.2006.244 PMID:17108377.

Arun, A., Ross, K., Nandakumar, A., & Jain, K. (2006). *Handbook of multibiometrics*. Berlin: Springer.

Bartlett, M. S., Movellan, J. R., & Sejnowski, T. J. (2002). Face recognition by independent component analysis. *IEEE Transactions on Neural Networks, 13*, 1450–1464. doi:10.1109/TNN.2002.804287 PMID:18244540.

Bay, H., Ess, A., Tuytelaars, T., & Gool, L. V. (2008). Surf: Speeded up robust features. *Computer Vision and Image Understanding, 110*(3), 346–359. doi:10.1016/j.cviu.2007.09.014.

Belhumeur, P. N., Hespanha, J. P., & Kriegman, D. J. (1997). Eigenfaces vs. fisherfaces: Recognition using class specific linear projection. *IEEE TPAMI, 19*, 711–720. doi:10.1109/34.598228.

Bolle, R., Connell, J., Pankanti, S., Ratha, N., & Senior, A. (2003). *Guide to biometrics*. Berlin: Springer Verlag.

Brunelli, R., & Falavigna, D. (1995). Person identification using multiple cues. *IEEE Transactions on Pattern Analysis and Machine Intelligence, 17*(10), 955–966. doi:10.1109/34.464560.

Bubeck, U. M., & Sanchez, D. (2003). *Biometric authentication: Technology and evaluation (Technical Report)*. San Diego, CA: San Diego State University.

Burrus, C., Gopinath, R., & Guo, H. (1998). *Introduction to wavelets and wavelet transforms*. Upper Saddle River, NJ: Prentice Hall.

Chang, K. I., Bowyer, K. W., & Flynn, P. J. (2005). An evaluation of multimodal 2D+3D face biometrics. *IEEE Transactions on Pattern Analysis and Machine Intelligence, 27*(4), 619–624. doi:10.1109/TPAMI.2005.70 PMID:15794165.

Chen, L. F., Mark Liao, H. Y., Ko, M. T., & Yu, G. J. (2000). A new LDA-based face recognition system which can solve the small size problem. *Pattern Recognition, 33*(10), 1713–1726. doi:10.1016/S0031-3203(99)00139-9.

Choras, M. (2005). Ear biometrics based on geometrical features extraction. *Electron. Lett. Comput. Vis. Image Anal., 5*(3), 84–95.

Choras, M., & Choras, R. S. (2006). Geometrical algorithms of ear contour shape representation and feature extraction. In *Proceedings of Intelligent Systems Design and Applications (ISDA)*. IEEE. doi:10.1109/ISDA.2006.253879.

Darwish, A., Abd Elghafar, R., & Fawzi Ali, A. (2009). Multimodal face and ear images. *Journal of Computer Science, 5*(5), 374–379. doi:10.3844/jcssp.2009.374.379.

Daugman, J. (2007). New methods in iris recognition. *IEEE Transactions on Systems. Man and Cybernetics B, 37*(5), 1167–1175. doi:10.1109/TSMCB.2007.903540.

Fernandez, F. A. (2008). *Biometric sample quality and its application to multimodal authentication systems*.

Fields, C., Hugh, C. F., Warren, C. P., & Zimberoff, M. (1960). The ear of the newborn as an identification constant. *Journal of Obstetrics & Gynaecology, 16*, 98–101. PMID:13822693.

Galton, F. (1899). *Finger prints of young children*. London: British Association for the Advancement of Science.

Gray, J. E., Suresh, G., Ursprung, R., Edwards, W. H., Nickerson, J., & Shinno, P. H. (2006). Patient misidentification in the neonatal intensive careunit: Quantification of risk. *Pediatrics*, *117*, e46–e47. doi:10.1542/peds.2005-0291 PMID:16396847.

Holt, S. B. (1973). The significance of dermatoglyphics in medicine. *Clinical Pediatrics*, *12*(8), 471–484. doi:10.1177/000992228730120904 PMID:4579966.

Islam, S. M. S., Davies, R., Mian, A., & Bennamoun, M. (2008). A fast and fully automatic ear recognition approach based on 3D local surface features. [ACIVS]. *Proceedings of Advanced Concepts for Intelligent Vision Systems*, *5259*, 1081–1092. doi:10.1007/978-3-540-88458-3_98.

A. K. Jain, R. Bolle, & S. Pankanti (Eds.). (1999). *Biometrics: Personal identification in networked society* (pp. 87–102). London: Kluwer Academic Publishers.

Jain, A. K., Flynn, P., & Ross, A. (2007). *Handbook of biometrics*. Berlin: Springer.

Jain, A. K., & Lu, X. (2004). Ethnicity identification from face images. In *Proceedings of SPIE International Symposium on Defense and Security: Biometric Technology for Human Identification*. SPIE.

Jain, A. K., Nandakumar, K., Lu, X., & Park, U. (2004). Integrating faces, fingerprints and soft biometric traits for user recognition. In *Proceedings of Biometric Authentication Workshop* (LNCS), (vol. 3087, pp. 259–269). Prague, Czech Republic: Springer.

Jain, A. K., & Pankanti, S. (2000). Fingerprint classification and recognition. In A. Bovik (Ed.), *The Image and Video Processing Handbook*. New York: Academic Press.

Jain, A. K., Ross, A., & Prabhakar, S. (2004). An introduction to biometric recognition. *IEEE Transactions on Circuits and Systems for Video Technology*, *14*(1), 4–20. doi:10.1109/TCS-VT.2003.818349.

Jia, W., Cai, H., Gui, J., et al. (2011). Newborn footprint recognition using orientation feature. *Journal of Neural Computing & Applications*.

Kucken, M., & Newell, A. C. (2005). Fingerprint formation. *Journal of Theoretical Biology*, *235*, 71–83. doi:10.1016/j.jtbi.2004.12.020 PMID:15833314.

Kurita, T., & Taguchi, T. (n.d.). *A modification of kernel-based Fisher discriminant analysis for face detection*.

Li, Y. (2006). *Study on some key issues in ear recognition*. (PhD thesis). University of Science and Technology Beijing, Beijing, China.

Lienhart, R., & Maydt, J. (2002). An extended set of Haar-like features for rapid object detection. In *Proceedings of IEEE International Conference on Image Processing*, (pp. 900–903). IEEE.

Liu, W., Wang, Y., Li, S. Z., & Tan, T. (2004). Space approach of fisher discriminant analysis for face recognition. In *Proceeding of ECCV Workshop on Biometric Authentication*, (pp. 32-44). ECCV.

Middendorf, C., & Bowyer, K. W. (2008). Multibiometrics using face and ear. In *Handbook of Biometrics* (pp. 315–341). Berlin: Springer. doi:10.1007/978-0-387-71041-9_16.

Morgan, L. E., & Pauls, F. (1939). Palm prints for infant identification. *The American Journal of Nursing*, *39*(8), 866–868.

Nandakumar, K. (2008). *Multibiometric systems: Fusion strategies and template security*. (Ph.D. Thesis).

Nanni, L., & Lumini, A. (2007). A multi-matcher for ear authentication. *Pattern Recognition Letters, 28*(16), 2219–2226. doi:10.1016/j.patrec.2007.07.004.

Ojala, T., Pietikainen, M., & Maenpaa, T. (2002). Multiresolution gray-scale and rotation invariant texture classification with local binary patterns. *IEEE Transactions on Pattern Analysis and Machine Intelligence, 24*(7), 971–987. doi:10.1109/TPAMI.2002.1017623.

Pel'a, N. T. R., Mamede, M. V., & Tavares, M. S. G. (1975). Article. *Revista Brasileira de Enfermagem, 29*, 100–105.

Ping, Y., & Bowyer, K. W. (2005). Empirical evaluation of advanced ear biometrics. In *Proceedings of Empirical Evaluation Methods in Computer Vision*. San Diego, CA: IEEE.

Pittner, S., & Kamarthi, S. V. (1999). Feature extraction from wavelet coefficients for pattern recognition tasks. *IEEE Transactions on Pattern Analysis and Machine Intelligence, 21*(1). doi:10.1109/34.745739.

Rubisley, P., Lemes, O. R., Bellon, P., Silva, L., & Jain, A. K. (2011). Biometric recognition of newborns: Identification using palmprints. In *Proceedings of the International Joint Conference on Biometrics*. Washington, DC: IEEE.

Shepard, K. S., Erickson, T., & Fromm, H. (1966). Limitations of footprinting as a means of infant identification. *Pediatrics, 37*(1). PMID:5948147.

Shepard, K. S., Erickson, T., & Fromm, H. (1966). Limitations of footprinting as a means of infant identification. *Pediatrics, 37*(1). PMID:5948147.

Song, Y.-J., Kim, Y.-G., Kim, N., & Ahn, J.-H. (n.d.). Face recognition using both geometric features and PCA/LDA. In *Proceedings of the Sixth International Conference on Advanced Language Processing and Web Information Technology*. IEEE.

Stapleton, M.E. (1999). Best foot forward: Infant footprints for personal identification. *Law Enforcement Bulletin, 63*.

Thompson, J. E., Clark, D. A., Salisbury, B., & Cahill, J. (1981). Footprinting the infant: Not cost-effective. *The Journal of Pediatrics, 99*, 797–798. doi:10.1016/S0022-3476(81)80415-5 PMID:6795326.

Tiwari, S., Singh, A., & Singh, S. K. (2011). Newborn's ear recognition: Can it be done? In *Proceedings of IEEE, International Conference on Image Information Processing*. IEEE.

Tiwari, S., Singh, A., & Singh, S. K. (2012a). Can ear and soft-biometric traits assist in recognition of newborn? In *Proceedings of International Conference on Computer Science, Engineering and Applications*. Berlin: Springer. DOI:10.1007/978-3-642-30157-5

Tiwari, S., Singh, A., & Singh, S. K. (2012b). Can face and soft-biometric traits assist in recognition of newborn? In *Proceedings of IEEE, International Conference on Recent Advanced in Information Technology*. IEEE.

Tiwari, S., Singh, A., & Singh, S. K. (2012c). Fusion of ear and soft-biometrics for recognition of newborn. *Signal & Image Processing: An International Journal, 3*(3), 103–116. doi:10.5121/sipij.2012.3309.

Tiwari, S., Singh, A., & Singh, S. K. (2012d). Integrating faces and soft-biometrics for newborn recognition. *International Journal of Advanced Computer Engineering & Architecture, 2*(2), 201–209.

Victor, B., Bowyer, K., & Sarkar, S. (2002). An evaluation of face and ear biometrics. In *Proceedings of the 16th International Conference on Pattern Recognition*. IEEE.

Viola, P., & Jones, M. (2001). Rapid object detection using boosted cascade of simple features. In *Proceedings of IEEE Computer Vision and Pattern Recognition*. IEEE.

Viola, P., & Jones, M. (2004). Robust real-time face detection. *International Journal of Computer Vision*, *57*(2), 137–154. doi:10.1023/B:VISI.0000013087.49260.fb.

Wayman, J. L., Jain, A. K., Maltoni, D., & Maio, D. (2005). *Biometric systems: Technology, design and performance evaluation*. Berlin: Springer.

Weingaertner, D., Bello, O., & Silva, L. (2008). Newborn's biometric identification: Can it be done? In *Proceedings of the VISAPP*. VISAPP.

Wierschem, J. (1965). Know them by their feet. *Medical Record News*, *168*, 158–160.

Windsor, O. (2007). *A statistical approach towards performance analysis of multimodal biometrics systems*. (Ph.D. Thesis).

KEY TERMS AND DEFINITIONS

Biometrics: Biometrics is a field of science that uses computer technology to identify people based on physical or behavioral characteristics, such as fingerprints or voice scans. The word "biometrics" is derived from the Greek words bio (life) and metric (to measure) and thus Biometrics is the science of measuring biological or behavioural properties of living beings.

Biometric System: A biometric system is basically a pattern recognition system that recognizes a person by classifying the binary code of a uniquely specific biological or physical characteristic to the binary code of the stored characteristic.

Multi-Biometrics: Multi-Biometrics is an authentication technology using different biometric technologies such as fingerprints, facial features, and vein patterns in the identification and verification process. The use of Multi-Biometrics takes advantages of the capabilities of each biometric technology while overcoming the limitations of a single technology.

Multimodal Biometric: Multimodal Biometric System is a system that uses more than one independent or weakly correlated biometric identifier taken from an individual (e.g., fingerprint and face of the same person, or fingerprints from two different fingers of a person).

Newborn/Infant: An infant (from the Latin word *infans*, meaning "unable to speak" or "speechless") is the very young offspring of a human or other mammal. The term *infant* is typically applied to young children between the ages of 1 month and 12 months; however, definitions may vary between birth and 3 years of age. A newborn is an infant who is only hours, days, or up to a few weeks old. In medical contexts, newborn or neonate (from Latin, *neonatus*, newborn) refers to an infant in the first 28 days after birth.

Recognition: Recognition the process of recognizing something or someone by remembering; "a politician whose recall of names was as remarkable as his recognition of faces"; "experimental psychologists measure the elapsed time from the onset of the stimulus to its recognition by the observer."

Template: A biometric template (also called *template*) is a digital reference of distinct characteristics that have been extracted from a biometric sample. Templates are used during the biometric authentication process.

Chapter 3
Biometric Authentication Based on Hand Vein Pattern

Munaga V. N. K. Prasad
IDRBT, India

Ilaiah Kavati
IDRBT, India

ABSTRACT

Recently, a new biometric technology based on human hand vein patterns has attracted the attention of many researchers. This chapter discusses vein pattern authentication, which uses the vascular patterns of the back of the hand as personal authentication data. Vein information is hard to duplicate because veins are internal to the human body. Vein authentication is one of the most accurate and reliable biometric technologies, which is widely employed in mission-critical applications such as banking, etc. A dynamic ROI extraction algorithm was presented through which more features can be extracted when compared to the fixed ROI. The extracted ROI was enhanced, and then the noise content was removed. The key features that represent the geometric information of the vein pattern were extracted; they are the bifurcation and ending points. This chapter presents a new vein pattern recognition system by assigning different weights to bifurcation and ending points. The approach is tested on a vein pattern database of 60 different hands. Experimental results show the approach achieves 2.5% of Equal Error Rate (EER) and recognition accuracy of 98.24%.

INTRODUCTION

There are many real-world applications where security is a strong requirement, and reliable personal authentication is critical to that security. Since September 2001, public awareness about the need for security has been increased considerably. This has lead to a massive rise in demand for the personal identification systems (Wang & Leedham, 2005). Biometrics plays a major role in today's security applications. A biometric system is essentially a pattern recognition system that recognizes a

DOI: 10.4018/978-1-4666-4868-5.ch003

person based on a feature vector derived from specific physiological or behavioral characteristic that the person possesses (Prabhakar, Pankanti & Jain, 2003). Biometric authentication is the most important technology of the 21st century. As we move forward and face the challenges of the 21st century, security of personal information will continue to be foremost in our thoughts (Wilson, 2010). Our lives are already heavily dependent on secure information flow since nearly everything we touch has some connection to information processing. Bank accounts, transportation systems, mobile phones, and computers are all connected to networks, allowing them to serve our needs. The first question that any of these systems asks us is: "Who are you?" The ability to determine our true identity is critical to ensure the protection of both our personal information and the networks that underpin the digital fabric of society. Without Personal Identification Numbers (PINs), passwords, tokens, and now biometrics, such systems would not be able to reliably know who we are and act to protect our interests. The tokens may be lost or passwords may be forgotten, but the people's biology features, such as face, finger mark, iris, palm print and vein, cannot be lost or forgotten.

Biometrics is considered a more natural and reliable solution for personal identification situations. Biometrics offers certain advantages such as negative recognition and non-repudiation that cannot be provided by tokens and passwords (Jain, Flynn, & Ross, 2007). Negative recognition is the process by which a system determines that a certain individual is indeed enrolled in the system although the individual might deny it. This is especially critical in applications such as welfare disbursement where an impostor may attempt to claim multiple benefits under different names. Non-repudiation is a way to guarantee that an individual who accesses a certain facility cannot later deny using it (e.g., a person accesses a certain computer resource and later claims that an impostor must have used it under falsified credentials).

The characteristics that help define a good biometric modality (Jain, Bolle & Pankati, 1999) are:

- **Uniqueness:** How the biometric identifier differentiates the individual from one another.
- **Permanence:** How well does a given biometric attribute resist changes due to aging, injury, disease, and other factors.
- **Universality:** How commonly a biometric is found in an individual and how readily it can be used. A good biometric attribute is one that is found in all human beings, and its usability does not vary significantly.
- **Collectability:** The attribute should be suitable for capture and measurement, and must be convenient for the individual to present to the biometric sensor.
- **Acceptability:** The degree of public acceptance and approval for a given biometric modality. This is a very important criterion because user acceptance is critical to the success of any biometric implementation.
- **Performance:** The accuracy, speed, and general robustness of the biometric in varied environmental circumstances.
- **Resistance to circumvention:** How hard it is to spoof or otherwise defeat a biometric.

Biometrics can be easily deployed to various commercial and government applications like e-commerce, welfare-disbursement, boarder control, criminal investigation, physical access control, etc. As we know, banking system has several leakages such as security threats and transaction frauds in the available system. The use of biometrics is a near perfect solution to such leakages. During the past few decades, many researchers have carried out on utilizing various biometrics for personal recognition. Amongst those biometrics, the most popular ones are Fingerprint, Face, Iris, Palm print, Retina, Hand geometry, Ear for physiological biometrics, as well as Keystroke, Gait, Signature, Voice, DNA, Odor for behavioral one

(Bolle, Connell, Panakanti, Ratha & Senior, 2003). Among the various biometrics that can be used to recognize a person, human veins exhibits some distinct advantages like ease of feature extraction, spoofing resistant, high accuracy, liveness detection and noncontact etc. The human vascular structure is individually distinct and appears to be time invariant (Jain, Bolle & Pankati, 1999). Human blood vessels are formed during the embryo stage with a variety of differentiating features, rendering each pattern unique, and their patterns remain relatively constant over one's lifetime except in the case of injury or decease. A unique network of veins and arteries exists in every hand and finger of each human being. An individual's identity can be authenticated using vein patterns in one's hands, and those patterns are located just under the surface of the skin and are invisible to the human eye, vein patterns are much harder for intruders to copy.

In recent years, personal authentication using vein pattern has gained more and more research attention (Miura, Nagasaka & Miyatake, 2004; Miura, Nagasaka & Miyatake, 2007; Toh, Eng, Choo, Cha, Yau & Low, 2006; Wang, Zhang & Yuan, 2006; Watanabe, Endoh, Shiohara & Sasaki, 2005; Yanagawa, Aoki & Ohyama, 2007; Zhang, Li, You & Battacharya, 2007). It seems, the first known work in the field of hand vein pattern was reported by MacGregor and Welford (1991). Cambridge Consultants Ltd., in collaboration with the British Technology Group (BTG), also studied the hand vein pattern concept with the aim of developing a commercial system which they called Veincheck (Hawkes & Clayden, 1993).

SYSTEM OVERVIEW AND RELATED WORK

A typical vein pattern biometric system consists of five individual processing stages: Image Acquisition, ROI extraction, Image enhancement and Vein Pattern Segmentation, Feature Extraction and Matching, as shown in Figure 1. The acquisition of hand veins is generally done using Infrared (IR) imaging. The IR imaging for veins is of two types namely Near Infrared (NIR) in the range of 0.75µm to 2µm and Far Infrared (FIR) in the range of 6µm to 14µm. In the literature, the NIR (Kumar & Prathyusha, 2009; Cross & Smith, 1995; Ding, Zhuang & Wang, 2005; Tanaka & Kubo, 2004) and FIR (Lin & Fan, 2004; Wang, Leedham & Cho, 2008) sources were used to capture the hand vein images. The NIR cameras are generally used for acquiring the veins as the FIR cameras are highly sensitive and expensive.

To increase the accuracy and reliability of the authentication system, the features of vein patterns extracted should be from the same region in different hands. The region to be extracted from the hand is known as ROI. ROI extraction can be either fixed (Kumar & Prathyusha, 2009; Lin & Fan, 2004) or dynamic. In this chapter a dynamic ROI extraction algorithm was proposed. The advantage of dynamic ROI is that ROI extracted for different hand images varies in size as the size of the hand varies. So, it is possible to extract more features from the larger hand which otherwise is not possible with fixed region of interest extraction.

The most of hand vein pattern techniques are based on structural features like line (Cross and Smith, 1995; Tanaka and Kubo, 2004) and minutiae (Kumar & Prathyusha, 2009; Crisan, Tarnovan & Crisan, 2010; Ding, Zhuang & Wang, 2005; Wang, Leedham & Cho, 2008). Lin & Fan (2004) performed multi-resolution analysis to analyze the palm-dorsa vein patterns and others adopted curvelet (Zhang, Ma & Han, 2006) and Radon Transform (Wu & Ye, 2009) to extract the finger vein features.

Matching technique in a biometric system is an important step because the accuracy of the system alone can determine its effectiveness. To evaluate the similarity between the query image and enrolled images the correlation technique (Cross & Smith, 1995; Tanaka & Kubo, 2004) or some

Figure 1. The block diagram of the typical vein pattern recognition system

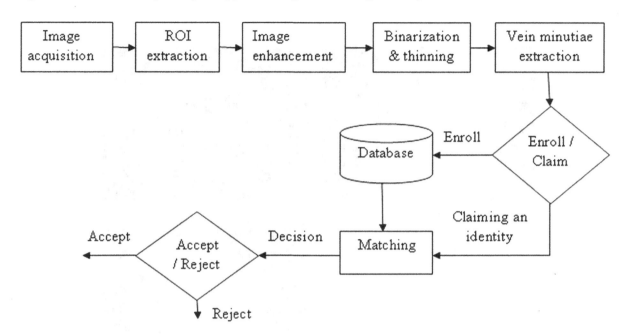

form of distance measures (Kumar & Prathyusha, 2009; Crisan, Tarnovan & Crisan, 2010; Ding, Zhuang & Wang, 2005; Wang, Leedham & Cho, 2008) are used in the literature.

DYNAMIC ROI EXTRACTION

To increase the accuracy of the authentication system the features of vein patterns extracted for different hand images should reference to the same region in the hand image. The region to be extracted from the hand is known as ROI. This chapter presents a dynamic ROI. However, without using the docking device it is difficult to fix the ROI at the same position in different hand images. The two finger Webs (the valley point between the small finger and the ring finger, the valley point between the middle finger and the index finger) can substitute for the docking device. The process of dynamic ROI extraction is shown in Figure 2.

To locate the ROI, the image is binarized using global thresholding algorithm, and then the

hand boundary is extracted using morphological operations (Gonzalez & Woods, 2008) on the binary image. The boundary of the hand β (P) is extracted by first eroding the image P by a suitable structuring element S, and then performing the set difference between P and its erosion. The boundary extraction process is defined in Eq. (1). A 3×3 matrix with element values 1 is used as the structuring element.

$$\beta (P) = P - (P \ominus S) \tag{1}$$

For each boundary pixel, the Euclidean distance from the wrist middle point is calculated. Using these distances, a distance distribution diagram is constructed whose pattern is similar to the geometric shape of the hand as shown in Figure 2c. The four valley points between the fingers can be found which corresponds to the finger Webs (fw_1, fw_2, fw_3, fw_4). The line joining the finger Webs fw_1 and fw_3 is made parallel to the horizontal axis, making the image rotation invariant. The ROI is a rectangular region $R_{P1\ P2\ P3\ P4,}$ and defined using

Figure 2. Defining the ROI: (a) hand vein image, (b) hand boundary, (c) distance profile, (d) extraction of ROI

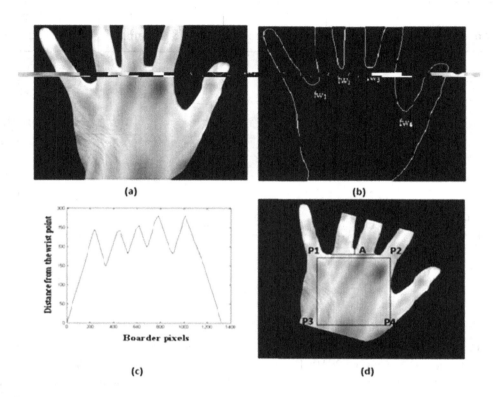

Eq. (2), where *L* represents the length, and *A* is the distance between fw_2 and the line joining $fw_1 fw_3$.

$$L_{P1P2} = L_{fw1fw3} + 2 * A$$
$$L_{P1P3} = L_{fw1fw3} + 3 * A \quad (2)$$

IMAGE ENHANCEMENT AND VEIN PATTERN EXTRACTION

The clearness of vein pattern in the extracted ROI varies from image to image due to sensor's signal-to-noise ratio or lighting conditions, etc. The quality of those images needs to be enhanced before further processing. A contrast enhancing technique is applied on the extracted ROI, to normalize the image. Normalization increases the contrast and reduces the possible imperfections in the image due to the sensor noise and other factors. Let $I(x, y)$ denote the intensity value at position (x, y) in a vein pattern image of size $M \times N$. Then the contrast enhanced image $I'(x, y)$ is obtained using Eq. (3), where I_{max} and I_{min} are the highest and lowest value any pixels in the image and *b* is the contrast coefficient.

$$I'(x, y) = b (I (x, y) - I_{min}),$$
$$\text{where } b = 255 / (I_{max} - I_{min}) \quad (3)$$

After normalization, a 5×5 median filter (Gonzalez &woods, 2008) was used to remove the noise in the image. The median filter is a nonlinear digital filtering technique, often used to remove noise. It preserves edges while removing noise. Then, a 2-D Gaussian low pass filter (Gonzalez &woods, 2008) with standard deviation of σ = 0.8 was applied to suppress the high frequency noise. The Figure 3b shows the image after image enhancement.

After normalization and noise removal, the quality of the image improves. The resultant ROI is subjected to binarization, to separate the vein structure from the image background. Due to the fact that the gray-level intensity values of the vein vary across the image, global thresholding technique does not provide satisfactory results for binarization. A locally adaptive threshold technique (Gonzalez & Woods, 2008) has been applied that will chooses different threshold value for every pixel in the image, based on the mean value of all the pixels in the predefined neighborhood. The authors have experimented with different neighborhood window sizes and selected the value of the window was 31×31. The thresholding process is expressed in Eq. (4), where μ_{xy} is the mean value of the 31×31 neighborhood, for a pixel (x, y). The binary image in Figure 3c shows the extracted vein structure from the background.

$$I(x,y) = \begin{cases} 1 & \text{if } I(x,y) \geq \mu_{xy} \\ 0 & \text{otherwise} \end{cases} \qquad (4)$$

The resulting binary image is subjected to a thinning algorithm (Lam, Lee & Suen, 1992; Yin, Narita, 2002; Zhang, Suen, 1984; Zhou, Quek & Ng, 1994) which generates the vein pattern structure of one pixel thick. However, the resulting binary pattern also contains small unconnected and connected objects. A smart pruning technique

is then applied to eliminate these false segments. The Figure 3d shows the skeleton of the vein pattern after pruning.

FEATURE EXTRACTION

To represent the individuality, the minutiae features (bifurcation points and the ending points) are extracted which are stable and unique from the vein structure. A vein bifurcation point is defined as vein point where vein forks or diverges into branch veins, and the vein ending is the point at which vein ends or disappears abruptly. This disappearance could be due to the abrupt ending of blood vessels or their poor visibility from the imaging system. The minutiae features are extracted from the skeleton image (Maltoni, Maio, Jain & Prabhakar, 2003), by examining the local neighborhood of each vein pixel using a 3×3 window i.e., determining the number of *branches originating from a pixel* (B). The minutiae extraction can be expressed as

$$B = 0.5 \sum_{i=1}^{8} |P_{i+1} - P_i|, \qquad (5)$$

For a pixel P on the vein pattern, its eight neighboring pixels are scanned as follows in Table 1.

Figure 3. Preprocessing and vein extraction: (a) The ROI, (b) after normalization and noise removal, (c) after adaptive thresholding, (d) after thinning and pruning

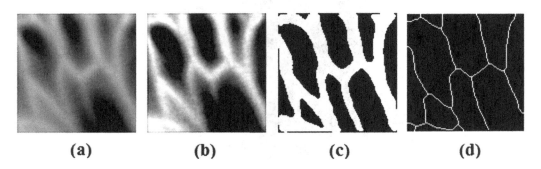

(a)   (b)   (c)   (d)

Table 1.

P$_1$	P$_2$	P$_3$
P$_8$	P	P$_4$
P$_7$	P$_6$	P$_5$

A pixel P is termed as bifurcation point if the value of B for the pixel is three or more. If the value of B is equal to one the pixel P is an end point. However the vein end points are generally not the true endings of the veins and are resided mostly at the edge of the image, due to the cropping of the ROI from the image or their poor visibility from the imaging system. The extracted minutiae from the vein pattern are shown in Figure 4.

A minutiae M_i can be represented by its position, type and orientation, i.e., $M_i = (x_i, y_i, t_i, \Theta_i)$ where (x_i, y_i) denotes the position, t_i is the type (vein bifurcation or ending) and Θ_i is the orientation of the minutiae i.

MATCHING

Matching is the last phase in the vein pattern authentication system. Matching is an important step to determine the effectiveness of the biometric system. Matching is used to authenticate the user, to know whether the user is genuine (already registered) or imposter. Match scores are obtained by comparing the query image with the already registered images. We consider that two minutiae $M_i = (x_i, y_i, t_i, \Theta_i)$ and $M_j = (x_j, y_j, t_j, \Theta_j)$ are matched only if they satisfy the following set of conditions.

i. $\quad t_i = t_j$

ii. $\quad \sqrt{(xi - xj)^2 + (yi - yj)^2} < T_1 \qquad (6)$

iii. $\quad \theta_i - \theta_j < T_\theta$

The thresholds T_1, T_θ are selected empirically.

Match score of a query image against an enrolled image is defined using Eq. (7), where n_m is the number of query image minutiae features matched with the enrolled image and n is the total number of query minutiae features.

Figure 4. Minutiae of the vein pattern (square for bifurcation point; circle for ending point)

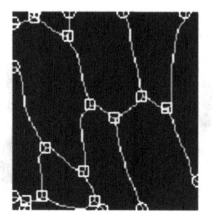

$$\text{Match score} = \frac{n_m}{n} \qquad (7)$$

As the vein end points are generally not the true endings of the veins and mostly they are formed due to poor image quality or poor vein extraction process (Kumar & Prathyusha, 2009), the proposed algorithm for matching gives more weightage to bifurcation points compared to ending points. The bifurcation points are stable and unique compared to ending points. The total match score (m_t) of query image is obtained using Eq. (8), where w_b, w_e are the weights of the bifurcation and ending points respectively, m_b is the match scores with the bifurcation points only i.e., the ratio of how many query image bifurcation points are matched with the enrolled image to the total bifurcation points of the query image, m_e is the match score with the ending points, and $w_b + w_e = 1$.

$$m_t = w_b \times m_b + w_e \times m_e \qquad (8)$$

More the match score (m_t) between two images, greater is the similarity between them. The enrolled image having the highest match score with the query image is considered as the best match.

EXPERIMENTAL RESULTS AND DISCUSSION

Experiments have been carried out on Nanyang Technological University (NTU) Far Infrared (FIR) Vein pattern Database to evaluate the performance of the proposed system. The Vein pattern database consists of 194 gray-scale images 30 users corresponding to 60 different palms. Around 3 images per hand have been collected.

Evaluation Criteria

The accuracy and performance of any biometric recognition system for a particular application can be determined by two criteria namely False Acceptance Rate (FAR) and False Rejection Rate

(FRR). FAR is the frequency that a non authorized person is accepted as authorized while FRR is the frequency that an authorized person is rejected access. It is clear that the system can be adjusted to vary the values of these two criteria for a particular application. However, decreasing one involves increasing the other and vice versa. The system threshold value is obtained using Equal Error Rate (EER) criteria when FAR = FRR. This is based on the rationale that both rates must be as low as possible for the biometric system to work effectively. In order to visually describe the performance of a biometric system, Receiver Operating Characteristics (ROC) curves are usually used. A ROC curve shows how the FAR values are changed relatively to the values of the FRR and vice-versa.

Cumulative Match Curves (CMC) is another method of showing the measured accuracy performance of a biometric system. Enrolled templates are compared with the query template to find the top match, where top match corresponds to the enrolled image in the database with highest matching score. However, it may not be possible always that the top match corresponds to the correct match. Thus, any of top k matches may correspond to the correct match. The identification accuracy at rank k is defined using Eq. (9), where R_k is the number of query images that occurs in top k matches and N is total number of query images in the database. CMC curves represent the identification accuracy (I_k) at various ranks (k).

$$I_k = \frac{R_k}{N} \qquad (9)$$

Performance

To evaluate the performance of the proposed vein patter recognition system and the discrimination power of two types of minutiae, namely bifurcation and ending points in authentication process, we carried out two sets of experiments for identification: Firstly by giving equal weightage to both type of minutiae, and then with assigning high weightage to bifurcation points compared to ending points. In the experiments, we empirically selected the weights as 0.6 and 0.4 for bifurcation and ending points respectively for proposed method 2.

The FAR and FRR of the two approaches at different thresholds are shown in Figure 5. It is observed that FAR reduces as threshold increases and FRR increases with threshold. The equal error rate (EER) of the proposed method 1 is 4% where as for proposed method 2 it is only 2.5%. The Table 2 depicts the value of the EER, at threshold where FAR and FRR curves intersect. It is shown that the proposed method 1 achieves relatively high recognition accuracy; the proposed method 2 further increases the recognition accuracy. The ROC curve for the proposed methods is given in Figure 6.

Figure 5. Equal error rate: (a) proposed method 1, (b) proposed method 2

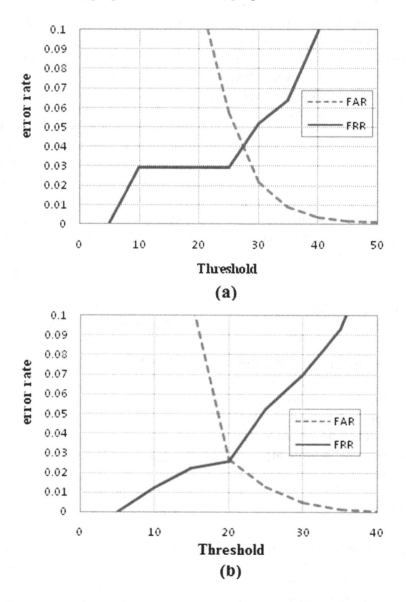

Table 2. Equal error rate (EER) of the proposed methods

Approach	EER (%)	Threshold
Proposed method 1	4	27
Proposed method 2	2.5	20

Figure 6. ROC curve: (a) proposed method 1, (b) proposed method 2

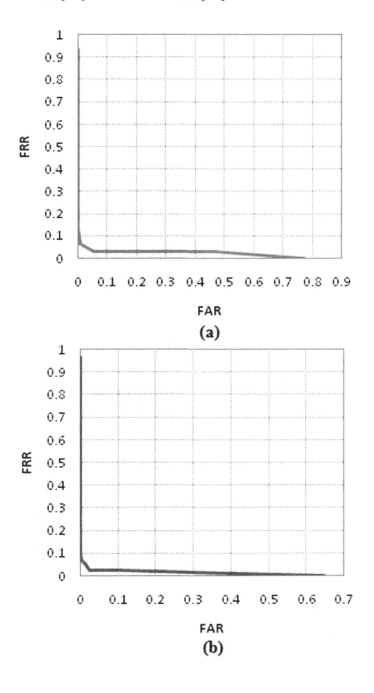

Figure 7. CMC curves of the two methods

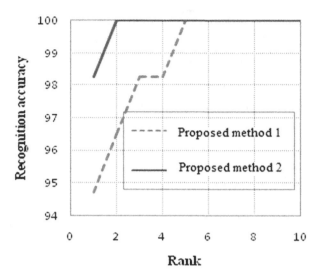

Even though, the two approaches performs equally well in terms of equal error rate, the identification accuracy of the proposed method 2 is relatively high compared to proposed method 1. The CMC curves for the two approaches are shown in Figure 7. It can be inferred that the proposed method 2 achieves an identification accuracy of 98.24% at rank 1 and 100% at rank 2 where as the proposed method 1 achieves only 94.73% at rank 1 and 100% at rank 5. In the experiment, the smallest and largest ROI sizes obtained are 107×111 pixels and 137×141 pixels respectively.

CONCLUSION AND FUTURE WORK

This chapter presents a novel hand vein biometric authentication system. The proposed ROI extraction algorithm made the system almost rotation invariant and it retrieve more minutiae features from the hand. To improve the recognition performance and to show the discriminative power of the minutiae, an efficient matching algorithm was proposed, through which the system achieves an equal error rate of 2.5% and recognition accuracy of 98.24%. The results presented here show the potential of hand vein pattern for personal authentication. However, the response time of the biometric system should be low in authentication process. Therefore, efficient algorithms are needed to facilitate fast search and is suggested for future work.

REFERENCES

Bolle, R. M., Connell, J. H., Panakanti, S., Ratha, N. K., & Senior, A. W. (2003). *Guide to biometrics*. New York: Springer.

Crisan, S., Tarnovan, I. G., & Crisan, T. E. (2010). Radiation optimization and image processing algorithms in the identification of hand vein patterns. *International Journal of Computer Standards and Interfaces*, *32*(3), 130–140. doi:10.1016/j.csi.2009.11.008.

Cross, J. M., & Smith, C. L. (1995). Thermo graphic imaging of the subcutaneous vascular network of the back of the hand for biometric identification. In *Proceedings of the IEEE 29th International Carnahan Conference on Security Technology* (pp. 20–35). IEEE.

Ding, Y., Zhuang, D., & Wang, K. (2005). A study of hand vein recognition method. In *Proceedings of IEEE International Conference on Mechatronics & Automation* (pp. 2106–2110). Niagara Falls, Canada: IEEE.

Gonzalez, R. C., & Woods, R. E. (2008). *Digital image processing*. Upper Saddle River, NJ: Prentice Hall.

Hawkes, P. L., & Clayden, D. O. (1993). Veincheck research for automatic identification of people. In *Proceedings of Seminar on hand and fingerprint*. NPL.

Jain, A. K., Bolle, R. M., & Pankanti, S. (1999). *Biometrics: Personal identification in networked society*. Dordrecht, The Netherlands: Kluwer Academic Publishers.

Jain, A. K., Flynn, P., & Ross, A. (2007). *Handbook of biometrics*. New York: Springer.

Kumar, A., & Prathyusha, K. V. (2009). Personal authentication using hand vein triangulation and knuckle shape. *IEEE Transactions on Image Processing*, *18*(9), 2127–2136. doi:10.1109/TIP.2009.2023153 PMID:19447728.

Lam, L., Lee, S. W., & Suen, C. Y. (1992). Thinning methodologies: A comprehensive survey. *IEEE Transactions on Pattern Analysis and Machine Intelligence*, *14*(9), 869–885. doi:10.1109/34.161346.

Lin, C. L., & Fan, K. C. (2004). Biometric verification using thermal images of palm-dorsa vein patterns. *IEEE Transactions on Circuits and Systems for Video Technology*, *14*(2), 199–213. doi:10.1109/TCSVT.2003.821975.

MacGregor, R., & Welford, R. (1991). Veincheck: Imaging for security and personal identification. *Advanced Imaging (Woodbury, N.Y.)*, *6*(7), 52–56.

Maltoni, D., Maio, D., Jain, A. K., & Prabhakar, S. (2003). *Handbook of fingerprint recognition*. New York: Springer.

Miura, N., Nagasaka, A., & Miyatake, T. (2004). Feature extraction of finger-vein patterns based on repeated line tracking and its application to personal identification. *Machine Vision and Applications*, *15*(4), 194–203. doi:10.1007/s00138-004-0149-2.

Miura, N., Nagasaka, A., & Miyatake, T. (2007). Extraction of finger-vein patterns using maximum curvature points in image profiles. *IEICE Transactions on Information and Systems*, *E90-D*(8), 1185–1194. doi:10.1093/ietisy/e90-d.8.1185.

Prabhakar, S., Pankanti, S., & Jain, A. K. (2003). Biometric recognition: security and privacy concerns. *IEEE Security and Privacy*, *1*(2), 33–42. doi:10.1109/MSECP.2003.1193209.

Tanaka, T., & Kubo, N. (2004). Biometric authentication by hand vein patterns. In *Proceedings of SICE Annual Conference* (pp. 249–253). Okayama, Japan: SICE.

Toh, K., Eng, A. H. L., Choo, Y. S., Cha, Y. L., Yau, W. Y., & Low, K. S. (2006). Identity verification through palm vein and crease texture. In *Proceedings of the IEEE International Conference on Advances in Biometrics* (pp. 546-553). Hong Kong, China: IEEE.

Wang, K., & Zhang, Y. Yuan & Zhuang, D. (2006). Hand vein recognition based on multi supplemental features of multi-classifier fusion decision. In *Proceeding of the IEEE International Conference on Mechatronics and Automation* (pp. 1790-1795). Luoyang, Henan: IEEE.

Wang, L., & Leedham, G. (2005). A thermal hand-vein pattern verification system. In S. Singh, M. Singh, C. Apte, & P. Perner (Eds.), *Pattern Recognition and Image Analysis (LNCS)* (Vol. 3687, pp. 58–65). New York: Springer. doi:10.1007/11552499_7.

Wang, L., Leedham, G., & Cho, D. S. Y. (2008). Minutiae feature analysis for infrared hand vein pattern biometrics. *Pattern Recognition, 41*(3), 920–929. doi:10.1016/j.patcog.2007.07.012.

Watanabe, M., Endoh, T., Shiohara, M., & Sasaki, S. (2005). *Palm vein authentication technology and its applications*. Paper presented at the Biometric Consortium Conference. Arlington, VA.

Wilson, C. (2010). *Vein pattern recognition: A privacy-enhancing biometric*. Boca Raton, FL: CRC Press. doi:10.1201/9781439821381.

Wu, J. D., & Ye, S. H. (2009). Driver identification using finger-vein patterns with Radon transform and neural network. *International Journal on Expert System with Applications, 36*(3), 5793–5799. doi:10.1016/j.eswa.2008.07.042.

Yanagawa, T., Aoki, S., & Ohyama, T. (2007). *Human finger vein images are diverse and its patterns are useful for personal identification*. Kyushu University.

Yin, M., & Narita, S. (2002). *Speedup method for real-time thinning algorithm*. Paper presented at Digital Image Computing Techniques and Applications. Melbourne, Australia.

Zhang, T. Y., & Suen, C. Y. (1984). A fast parallel algorithm for thinning digital patterns. *Communications of the ACM, 27*(3), 236–239. doi:10.1145/357994.358023.

Zhang, Y. B., Li, Q., You, J., & Bhattacharya, P. (2007). Palm vein extraction and matching for personal authentication. In *Proceedings of the 9th International Conference Advances in Visual Information Systems* (pp.154–164). Shanghai, China: IEEE.

Zhang, Z., Ma, S., & Han, X. (2006). Multiscale feature extraction of finger-vein patterns based on curvelets and local interconnection structure neural network. In *Proceedings of the 18th International Conference on Pattern Recognition* (pp. 145 – 148). Hong Kong, China: IEEE.

Zhou, R. W., Quek, C., & Ng, G. S. (1995). A novel single-pass thinning algorithm and an effective set of performance criteria. *Pattern Recognition Letters, 16*(12), 1267–1275. doi:10.1016/0167-8655(95)00078-X.

KEY TERMS AND DEFINITIONS

Binarization: The process of converting an image (gray scale or color) to black and white image.

Finger Webs: The deepest valley points between adjacent fingers of the hand.

Hand Veins: The subcutaneous vascular pattern/network appearing on the back of the hand.

Region of Interest: A rectangular/square region located in the hand vein image.

Vein Bifurcation: Vein bifurcation is a point where the vein forks or diverges into branch veins.

Vein End: Vein end is a point where the vein ends or disappears.

Chapter 4
Securing Biometrics Using Watermarking

Punam Bedi
University of Delhi, India

Roli Bansal
University of Delhi, India

Priti Sehgal
University of Delhi, India

ABSTRACT

This chapter focuses on the role of watermarking techniques in biometric systems. Biometric systems are automated systems of verifying or recognizing the identity of a living person based on a physiological or behavioral characteristic. While biometric-based techniques have inherent advantages over other authentication techniques, ensuring the security and integrity of data is a major concern. Data hiding techniques are thus used in biometric systems for securing biometric data itself. Amongst all the biometric techniques, fingerprint-based identification is the oldest and the most well established method used in numerous applications because fingerprints are unique and they remain unchanged during the human life span. However, fingerprint images should be watermarked without affecting their quality and their minutia matching ability. Moreover, if the watermark embedded in the fingerprint image is the face image of the same individual, the watermarking scheme will have two levels of security such that it will not only protect the cover fingerprint but also provides a more secure system of personal recognition and authentication at the receiver's end. This work finds application in a number of security implementations based on multimodal biometric authentication. Computationally intelligent techniques can be employed to develop efficient watermarking algorithms in terms of watermarked image quality and distortion tolerance ability.

DOI: 10.4018/978-1-4666-4868-5.ch004

INTRODUCTION

Biometric technologies refer to different automated methods for verifying or recognizing the identity of an individual based on one or more of his physical and behavioral characteristics. The word automated refers to methods that are carried out by a machine, generally a computer. Physical characteristics in biometrics typically include fingerprints, eye retinas and irises, facial patterns and hand measurements. Behavioral characteristics typically include signatures, gait, or typing patterns. The primary biometric disciplines include: fingerprints (optical, silicon, ultrasound, touch less), facial recognition (optical and thermal), voice recognition, iris recognition, retina-scan, hand geometry, signature-scan, keystroke-scan, palm-scan (forensic use only) etc. There are some biometric disciplines with reduced commercial viability and some are in exploratory stages such as: DNA, ear shape, odour (human scent), vein-scan (in back of hand or beneath palm), finger geometry (shape and structure of finger or fingers), nail bed identification (ridges in fingernails), gait recognition (manner of walking) etc. The selection of a particular biometric depends on the application where it is going to be used. Jain et al identified seven such factors which can be used for assessing the suitability of any characteristic for use in biometric authentication. They also said that no single biometric will meet all the requirements of every application. (Jain, Bolle, & Pankanti, 1999). These factors include:

1. **Universality:** Every person using the system should possess the selected biometric trait.
2. **Uniqueness:** The biometric trait under study should be different for different people in the population so as to correctly distinguish them from one another.
3. **Permanence:** The trait should be invariant over time with respect to the specific matching algorithm.
4. **Collectability:** The trait should be collectable i.e., the acquisition or measurement of the trait should be practically feasible.
5. **Performance:** The identification accuracy using the selected biometric trait should be acceptable.
6. **Acceptability:** The individuals in the relevant population must be willing to have their biometric trait captured and assessed.
7. **Circumvention:** The trait should not be imitated using an artifact or substitute so as to fool the system using fraudulent techniques.

A Biometric system operates in the following two modes (Jain et al, 2008): *Identification* mode, where the system performs a one-to-many comparison against a biometric database in an attempt to establish the identity of an unknown person. *Verification* mode, where the system performs a one-to-one comparison against a specific template stored in a biometric database to determine if the person under scrutiny is authorized one.

SECURITY AND AUTHENTICATION OF BIOMETRIC DATA

While biometric-based techniques have inherent advantages over other authentication techniques, ensuring the security and integrity of data is a major concern. The tremendous growth in distribution of digital data through the Internet has raised serious authentication issues. Moreover, if biometric datasets fall into criminal hands, they could be used to impersonate individuals, and thereby allow criminals to evade safeguards intended to identify and apprehend them. They can also be used to falsely incriminate an innocent individual in a physical crime.

For a biometrics based verification system to work properly, the verifier system must ensure the legitimate origin of the biometric data at the time of enrollment. In on-line transaction processing systems, transmitting a fingerprint image over the

Internet is not particularly secure. If such an image bit-stream can be freely intercepted it will allow the signal to be saved and fraudulently reused or be tampered by different image processing attacks. All of these attacks aim at decreasing the credibility of a biometric system. Potential candidate solutions are encryption, digital watermarking, and steganography. Data hiding techniques are thus used in biometric systems for securing biometric data itself. Biometric images can be watermarked to protect them against intentional and unintentional attacks and to transmit them securely from central databases to intelligent agencies in order to use them for identification and classification purposes.

Computationally Intelligent watermarking was proposed, to protect fingerprint images and also to authenticate them (Bansal, Sehgal & Bedi, 2012). The idea here was to hide the face image of a person inside his fingerprint image. Such a watermarking scheme with two levels of security not only protects the cover fingerprint but also provides a more secure system of personal recognition and authentication at the receiver's end. As watermarking decreases the quality of the cover image, new strategies were developed which will result in a watermarked image that is good in quality, which will preserve its minutia features completely and which will be robust to numerous image processing attacks. By preserving the minutiae features, the accuracy of fingerprint identification system with the watermarked image remains same as it was before watermarking. Computational Intelligence encompasses elements of learning, adaptation, heuristic and meta-heuristic optimization as well as any of their hybrids and hence their application addresses major concerns in fingerprint image watermarking.

The rest of the chapter is organized as follows: Firstly, fingerprint images are introduced followed by introduction to digital watermarking and particle swarm optimization. Next, the survey of various watermarking techniques available in the literature is presented for both general images as well as fingerprint images. Next, PSO based watermarking for securing fingerprint images in the DCT domain is presented followed by experimental results and analysis. Finally, the chapter ends with the conclusion followed by the references.

INTRODUCTION TO FINGERPRINT IMAGES

Despite claims, there is no best biometric technology. For a particular application, it may be possible to describe the most accurate, easiest to use, easiest to deploy or cheapest biometric for that particular purpose, but no one biometric technology or set of criteria is appropriate for all situations.

By far, amongst all the biometric techniques, fingerprint-based identification is the oldest and a well established method which has been successfully used in numerous applications. The reason behind the popularity of fingerprint-based recognition among the biometrics-based security systems is the invariability of fingerprints during the human life span and their uniqueness (Maltoni et al, 2003). A fingerprint is made of a series of ridges and furrows on the surface of the finger. The uniqueness of a fingerprint can be determined by its overall shape, by the pattern of ridges and furrows as well as the minutiae points. Minutiae points are local ridge characteristics that occur at either a ridge bifurcation or a ridge ending. The traditional use of fingerprint biometrics has been as a forensic criminological technique, to identify criminals by the fingerprints they leave behind them at crime scenes. Forensic experts compare unique features of a latent sample left at a crime scene against a known sample taken from a suspect to establish the identity of the perpetrator. Fingerprint features can be studied in terms of the global ridge pattern and the local ridge pattern.

Global Ridge Pattern

A fingerprint is a pattern of alternating convex skin called ridges and concave skin called valleys with a spiral-curve-like line shape. There are two types of ridge flows: the pseudo-parallel ridge flows and high-curvature ridge flows which are located around the core point (whorl) and/or delta point(s). The commonly used global fingerprint features are shown in Figure 1.

Besides these, the ridge orientation map which represents the local direction of the ridge valley structure is commonly used for fingerprint classification and enhancement.

Local Ridge Pattern

This is the most widely used and studied fingerprint representation. Local ridge details are the discontinuities of local ridge structure referred to as minutiae. They are used by forensic experts to match two fingerprints. There are about 150 different types of minutiae categorized based on their configuration (Jain, hong, Pankati & Bolle, 1997). Among these minutia types, "ridge ending" and "ridge bifurcation" are the most commonly used, since all the other types of minutiae can be seen as combinations of "ridge endings" and "ridge bifurcations." Some minutiae are shown in Figure 2. The American National Standards Institute-National Institute of Standard and Technology (ANSI-NIST) proposed a minutiae-based fingerprint representation. It includes minutiae location and orientation. Minutia orientation is defined as the direction of the underlying ridge at the minutia location.

Fingerprint matching techniques can be placed into two categories: minutiae-based and correlation based. Minutia based techniques represent the fingerprint by its local features, like termina-

Figure 1. Global fingerprint ridge patterns

| Left Loop | Right Loop | Whorl | Arch | Tented Arch or Delta |

Figure 2. Some of the common minutiae types

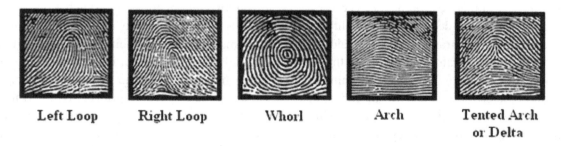

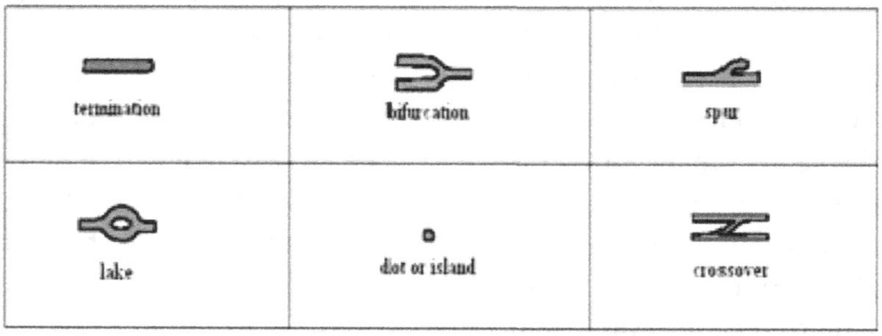

tions and bifurcations. Two fingerprints match if their minutiae points match. This approach has been intensively studied and is also the backbone of the current available fingerprint recognition products. In order to match two fingerprint using correlation based technique, The fingerprint are aligned and the correlation is computed for each corresponding pixe. However, as the displacement and rotation are unknown it is necessary to apply the correlation for all possible alignments.

INTRODUCTION TO DIGITAL WATERMARKING

With the availability of images, audio, video etc. in digital form on the Internet, it has become easy to make perfect copies of multimedia content. This has led to large scale unauthorized copying affecting the music, film, book, and software publishing industries (Katzenbeisser & Petitcolas, 2002). These concerns over protecting copyright have triggered significant research to find ways to hide copyright messages and serial numbers into digital media.

Digital watermarking is the process of computer-aided information hiding in a carrier signal. It is used to verify the authenticity or integrity of the carrier signal and to trace copyright infringements. Like traditional watermarks, digital watermarks are perceptible only after using some algorithm which is known to the intended receiver, and imperceptible anytime else. The term watermark was introduced probably because the marks resemble the effects of water on paper. In 1954, Emil Hembrooke filed a patent of a technology similar to digital watermarking for identifying music works. Komatsu and Tominaga were first to use the term "digital watermarking" in 1988 for their image authentication system (Hartung & Kutter, 1999).

A *digital watermark* is nothing but a pattern of bits inserted into a digital image, audio, video or text file that identifies the file's copyright information (author, rights, etc.) so as to provide copyright protection for intellectual property that's in digital format (Vyaghreswara & Pandit Narahari, 2007).

Digital watermarking is different from watermarking physical objects as it is used for watermarking digital content (Potdar, Han and Chang, 2005). Here, a low-energy signal is imperceptibly embedded in another signal. This low energy signal is called watermark which normally depicts some security or rights information about the main signal. The signal in which the watermark is embedded is referred to as cover signal since it covers the watermark. Generally, the cover signal is a still image, audio clip, video sequence or a text document in digital format.

According to Katzenbeisser et al (2002), watermarking and steganography are the two sub disciplines of *Information Hiding* in which some information content is securely added to a data product using mathematical techniques which work at the primitive level of digital data products, with no perceptual degradation of the data product integrity and no increase in the size of the data.

Both steganography and watermarking describe techniques that are used to imperceptibly convey information by embedding it into the cover-data. However, steganography typically relates to covert point-to-point communication between two parties (Cheddad, Condell, Cullan & Mc. Kevitt, 2010). In steganography, the secret message hidden within the host data may not be related to the cover image at all as the cover image is just a carrier of this secret message to the other party. Thus, steganographic methods are usually not robust against modification of the data, or have only limited robustness. They just protect the embedded information against technical modifications that may occur during transmission and storage, like format conversion, compression, or digital-to-analog conversion. On the other hand in watermarking, the cover message and the hidden secret message are related as the former serves to establish the ownership of the latter. Thus, watermarking has the additional notion of robustness which is the resilience against attempts to remove the hidden data.

Watermarking Framework

A digital watermarking system essentially consists of a watermark embedding module and a watermark detecting module (Cox et al, 2008). The former embeds a watermark into the cover signal and the latter detects and extracts it. A general framework of watermarking a digital image is illustrated in Figure 3. A watermark key is used during the process of embedding and detecting watermarks. This key is private and known only to authorized parties so as to ensure that the watermark is detected only by authorized parties. The communication channel can be noisy and prone to certain image processing attacks and hence the digital watermarking techniques should be resilient to such attacks.

Essential Features

In fact, there are a number of essential features that a digital watermarking system should possess. They are:

1. **Imperceptibility**: The embedded watermark should be imperceptible to the human eye and should not alter the aesthetics or the features of the multimedia content that is watermarked.

2. **Robustness**: This is the most important feature of any watermarking technique. The watermarked content has to be robust to certain quality preserving image processing attacks like quantization, scaling, exposure to noise, compression etc. This means that the watermark should not get degraded or destroyed by these attacks and should still be extractable at the receiver's end, otherwise the overall purpose of watermarking will be defeated. However, when watermarking is used for content authentication, the watermarking technique should be vulnerable to intentional and malicious attacks. In such cases the watermark should get destroyed whenever the content is modified so that any modification to content can be detected.

3. **Inseparability**: Once a watermark is embedded in some digital content, it cannot be separated from it to retrieve the original content.

4. **Security**: The digital watermarking techniques should allow only authorized users from detecting and modifying the watermark embedded in the cover signal by means of watermark keys.

5. **Capacity:** Capacity or payload is also a very important feature of a watermarking technique. Higher the capacity more is the

Figure 3. Digital image watermarking framework

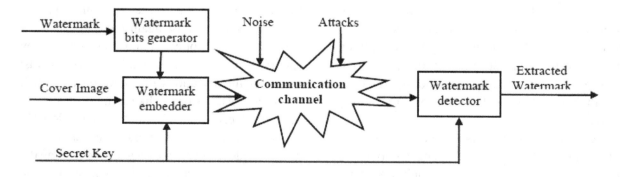

amount of watermark data that can be embedded without degrading the quality of the host signal.

Applications

Watermarking is used for a number of purposes as:

1. **Copyright Protection**: This is the most important application of watermarking today. Watermarking prevents illegal parties from claiming copyright on some data which does not belong to them. The host data is embedded with a watermark which contains some copyright information about the source of the data. Thus, it helps in resolving the rightful ownership of the data.
2. **Traitor Tracking**: Digital watermarks can specify the authorized users of a digital content and can thus be used to track its usage. Such watermarks can be used to identify the users who replicate the content illegally. The watermarking technique used for tracking is also known as fingerprinting.
3. **Copy Protection**: Digital content can be watermarked to indicate that the content cannot be copied. Devices capable of detecting such watermarks do not perform the copy operation.
4. **Data Authentication**: The objective in authenticating applications is to detect alterations and modifications of the data. Watermarks used in such applications are fragile that have low robustness and get destroyed when any kind of modification is made to the cover content.
5. **Broadcast monitoring**: Watermarks embedded in commercial advertisements can be verified by an automated monitoring system to determine whether the advertisements are broadcasted as contracted.

Digital Image Watermarking Techniques

Watermarking techniques can be classified on the basis of a number of criterions. They can be classified on the basis of embedding domain, on the basis of the type of the cover data and on the basis of human perception. Digital images can be watermarked in one of the two domains of images, i.e. the Spatial Domain and the Transform or Frequency Domain. These watermarks can be visible or invisible watermarks depending upon whether they are visible or invisible to the human eye. Combination of visible and invisible watermarks can also be used known as dual watermarks. The proposed work deals with invisible watermarks i.e., the watermarks which are imperceptible to the human eye. Robust watermarking schemes ensure that the output watermarked image is resilient to quality preserving image processing attacks. In fragile watermarking schemes the watermark is lost even if the output watermarked image is exposed to the slightest modification or distortion.

On the basis of the image domain used, image watermarking techniques are classified as follows:

Watermarking in Spatial Domain

A digital image in the spatial domain is represented by a matrix of pixel intensities. Here, the watermark is embedded by modifying the Least Significant Bits (LSBs) of the pixel intensities. Spatial domain techniques are simpler to implement, give good perceptual transparency, but are very fragile. Even the slightest distortion or modification of the watermarked image destroys the watermark. In fact, spatial domain based watermarking algorithms are more robust to geometric attacks (cropping, rotating, resizing etc.) and vulnerable to frequency attacks (JPEG compression, Gaussian noise, median filtering, blurring etc.) as compared to their transform domain counterparts. Following are some of the techniques in the spatial domain:

Simple LSB Substitution

This is the simplest method of watermarking where the watermark bits are embedded in one or more LSBs of the cover image pixels (see Figure 4).

The capacity of this scheme depends on the size of the cover image. Figure 5 shows how LSBs of cover image can be substituted with watermark bits. The pixels are chosen randomly for watermark embedding. The same sequence of pixels is traced during watermark extraction. A number of variations of this technique exist where pixels are chosen adaptively so that the distortion produced in the host image is minimal. However, all the LSB based methods have limited robustness to noise, compression etc. Some variations are:

1. **LSB Matching:** LSB matching (Jarno, 2006; Xialong, Yang, Cheng & Zheng, 2009) also modifies the LSBs of the cover image pixels, but does not simply replace them. Here, secret bits are matched with the LSB's of the cover image. If a match does not occur, one will be randomly added or subtracted from the cover pixel value.

2. **Pixel Value Difference (PVD) based methods:** PVD based methods (Wu & Tsai, 2003; Yang, Weng, Wang & Sun, 2008) provide good imperceptibility by calculating the difference of two consecutive pixels to determine the depth of embedded bits. These methods examine whether two consecutive pixels belong to an edge or smooth area by checking out the difference value between the two consecutive pixels. If the difference value is large, that means the two pixels are located in an edge areas, and more secret data can be hidden here. On the contrary, if the difference value is small, that means the two pixels are located in a smooth area, and less secret data can be embedded.

Patchwork-Based Schemes

Patchwork techniques (Bender, Gruhl & Morimoto, 1995) randomly choose n pairs of cover image pixels, and increase the brightness at one point by 1, while correspondingly decreasing the brightness of another point. In these techniques, a secret key is used to initialize a pseudorandom number generator which outputs the embedding locations in the cover image.

In this technique, if (x_i, y_i) be a randomly selected pair of pixels (according to a secret key K), it is used to hide 1 bit by increasing the x_i by one and decreasing the y_i by one. Then, the modified pair is (x'_i, y'_i). In the extraction process, the n pixel pairs which were used in the encoding step to embed the watermark are retrieved, again using the secret key K and the following sum is computed:

Figure 4. Example of LSB substitution

Cover Image: 11001011   00110101   00011010   00000001 ......

Watermark: 1 0 1 0 ....

Watermarked Image: 11001011   00110100   00011011   00000000 ....

Figure 5. Converting from spatial domain to transform domain via DCT

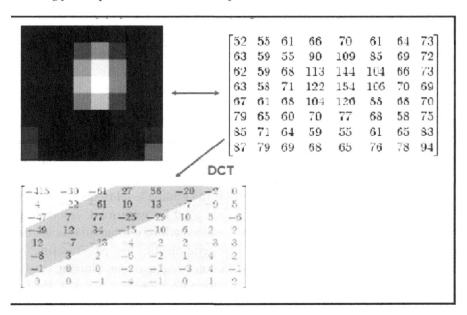

$$S = \sum_{i=1}^{n} x'_i - y'_i \qquad (1)$$

The expected value of the sum of the differences between the x_i's and y_i's of n pixel pairs is given by *2n* if the cover actually contains a watermark otherwise it should be approximately zero. The technique is applied in a way that the image satisfies certain statistical properties.

Texture Block Coding

In this technique (Hartung and Kutter, 1999), the watermark is embedded by copying one image texture block to another area in the image with a similar texture. This technique is robust to distortions since both image areas are distorted in a similar way. Autocorrelation is used to recover each texture region. The problem with this scheme is that it is only appropriate for images that possess large areas of random texture. The scheme could not be used on text images.

Predictive Coding

Predictive coding schemes (Hartung et al., 1999) exploit the correlation between adjacent pixels by coding the prediction error instead of coding the individual pixel intensities. A digital image is scanned in a predefined order to traverse the set of pixels $\{x_i\}$. The set of pixels is then coded using a predictive coding scheme by keeping the first value x_1 and replacing subsequent values by the difference Δ_i between adjacent pixels as: $\Delta_i = x_i - x_{i-1}$. To embed a sequence of watermark bits, a cipher key table (Table 1) is used, which assigns a corresponding bit c_i to all possible differences Δ_i. The secret key comprises of the correspondence between bit values and the differences. To embed a watermark bit b, a pixel x_i is selected with corresponding difference Δ_i. If the bit value c_i corresponding to Δ_i has the same value as bit b, proceed to the next bit; otherwise select the closest value in the cipher table that has the appropriate bit value.

Table 1. Cipher key table

Δ_i	......	-4	-3	-2	-1	0	1	2	3	4	......
c_i	......	1	0	0	1	0	0	0	1	1	......

Watermarking in Transform Domain

In the transform domain an image is represented by its frequency content. Thus on application of some functions/transforms like the Fast Fourier Transform (FFT) or the Discrete Cosine Transform (DCT) or the Discrete Wavelet Transform (DWT) on a digital image, it gets converted to a matrix of transform domain coefficients which represent the overall energy distribution of the image. The watermark is embedded by modifying these transform coefficients. After embedding the watermark, the inverse transform is applied to get the watermarked image. Transform domain techniques offer superior robustness to frequency based image processing attacks. The reason behind the resiliency of transform domain techniques towards frequency based attacks is that the distortions introduced by the watermarks into the transform coefficients will spread over all the pixels in the spatial domain. As a result, the changes introduced in these pixel values are visually less significant.

DCT Domain-Based Image Watermarking

The DCT is a signal decomposition that separates an image into high, middle and low frequency components as shown in Figure 5. The spatial domain matrix of pixel intensities gets transformed to matrix of DCT coefficients that occur in each term when the discrete cosine transform is applied onto a spatial image. The top left corner of the DCT matrix contains the low frequency components which contain most of the image information. Embedding the watermark in these components is perceptible to human eye as the human visual system is able to perceive changes in low frequency signal components. The bottom right corner represents the high frequency components which are normally truncated during compression. Hence, it is the middle level frequency components which are used for watermark embedding. DCT based watermarking is robust to simple image processing operations like low pass filtering, brightness and contrast adjustment, blurring etc. but are computationally more expensive. At the same time, they are weak against geometric attacks like cropping, rotation, scaling etc.

Equation (2) gives the forward DCT of an image block of size N × N (Gonzalez et al, 2005). $DCT(i, j)$ represents the coefficient at coordinate (i, j) and $gray\_value(x, y)$ represents the gray scale value of the pixel at location (x, y) in the original block.

$$DCT(i, j) = C(i) * C(j) * \sum_{x=0}^{N-1}\sum_{y=0}^{N-1} gray\_value(x, y)$$
$$* \cos\left[\frac{(2x+1)i\pi}{2N}\right] \cos\left[\frac{(2y+1)j\pi}{2N}\right]$$

$$(2)$$

where

$$C(i), C(j) = \begin{cases} \sqrt{\dfrac{1}{N}} & for\, i, j = 0 \\ \sqrt{\dfrac{2}{N}} & for\, i, j = 1, 2 \ldots N-1 \end{cases}$$

Equation (3) performs the inverse DCT to transform the image back to the spatial domain.

$$gray\_value(x,y) = \sum_{x=0}^{N-1}\sum_{y=0}^{N-1} C\left(i\right) \times C\left(j\right) \times DCT\left(i,j\right)$$
$$\times \cos\left[\frac{\left(2x+1\right)i\pi}{2N}\right]\cos\left[\frac{\left(2y+1\right)j\pi}{2N}\right]$$

$$(3)$$

where, $C\left(i\right), C\left(j\right)$ remain the same as above.

One of the earliest watermarking techniques in this category was presented in 1997 (Cox et al, 1997). They used the perceptually significant portion of the DCT with respect to the Human Visual System (HVS) for embedding the watermark. The embedding algorithm consisted of the following steps:

1. Divide the cover image into 8×8 blocks.
2. Apply forward DCT (Equation 2) to each of these blocks.
3. Apply some block selection criterion (e.g. HVS).
4. Apply some coefficient selection criterion (e.g. highest).
5. Embed watermark by modifying the selected coefficients.
6. Apply inverse DCT (Equation 3) to each block to get the watermarked image.

Many other variations of this approach were later introduced by researchers where the algorithms differed either in the block selection or the coefficient selection criterion.

INTRODUCTION TO PARTICLE SWARM OPTIMIZATION

Particle Swarm Optimization (PSO) is originally attributed to Kennedy and Eberhart (1996) and was first intended for simulating social behaviour. Kennedy and Eberhart, 2001 describes many philosophical aspects of PSO and swarm intelligence. PSO is a computational method that optimizes a problem by iteratively trying to improve a candidate solution with regard to a given measure of quality. Here, a problem is optimized by having a population of candidate solutions called particles which move around in the search-space according to simple mathematical formulae over the particle's position and velocity. It is a population based stochastic optimization technique (Engelbrecht, 2005), inspired by social behavior of bird flocking or fish schooling. Each particle's movement is influenced by its local best known position and is also guided toward the best known positions in the search-space, which are updated as better positions are found by other particles. This is expected to move the swarm towards the best solution.

A PSO algorithm maintains a swarm of particles, where each particle represents a potential solution. A swarm is similar to a population, while a particle is similar to an individual. The particles are "flown" through a multidimensional search space, where the position of each particle is adjusted according to its own experience and that of its neighbors. Let $x_i\left(t\right)$ denote the position of particle i in the search space at time step t. The position of the particle is changed by adding a velocity $v_i\left(t+1\right)$ to the current position, i.e.

$$x_i\left(t+1\right) = x_i\left(t\right) + v_i\left(t+1\right) \qquad (4)$$

It is the velocity vector that drives the optimization process, and reflects both the experiential knowledge of the particle and socially exchanged information from the particle's neighborhood. The experiential knowledge of a particle is generally referred to as the cognitive component, which is proportional to the distance of the particle from its own best position found since the first time step. The socially exchanged information is referred to as the social component of the velocity equation.

In global best PSO, or gbest PSO, the neighborhood for each particle is the entire swarm. The social network employed by the gbest PSO reflects the star topology. For star neighborhood topology, all particles are interconnected and each particle can therefore communicate with every other particle. The social component of the particle velocity update reflects information obtained from all the particles in the swarm. In this case, the social information is the best position found by the swarm, referred to as $\hat{y}(t)$. Each particle is attracted towards the best solution found by the entire swarm. For gbest PSO, the velocity of particle i is calculated as (Equation 5):

$$v_{ij}(t+1) = v_{ij}(t) + c_1 r_{1j}(t)\left[y_{ij}(t) - x_{ij}(t)\right] + c_2 r_{2j}(t)\left[\hat{y}_j(t) - x_{ij}(t)\right]$$

(5)

where $v_{ij}(t)$ is the velocity of particle i in dimension $j = 1,\ldots,n_x$ at time step t. $x_{ij}(t)$ is the position of particle i in dimension j at time step t, c_1 and c_2 are positive acceleration constants used to scale the contribution of cognitive and social components respectively. $r_{1j}(t)$, $r_{2j}(t) \sim U(0,1)$ are random values in the range [0,1], sampled from a uniform distribution. The personal best position y_i associated with particle i is the best position the particle has visited since the first time step. Considering minimization problems, the personal best position at the next time step $t+1$ is calculated as (Equation 6):

$$y_i(t+1) = \begin{cases} y_i(t) & if \quad f(x_i(t+1)) \geq f(y_i(t)) \\ x_i(t+1) & if \quad f(x_i(t+1)) < f(y_i(t)) \end{cases}$$

(6)

where f is the fitness function which measures how close the corresponding solution is to the optimum, i.e. it quantifies the performance, or quality of a particle (or solution). The global best position $\hat{y}(t)$ at time step t, is given by Equation (7) as:

$$\hat{y}(t) \in \left\{ y_0(t),\ldots y_{ns}(t) | f(\hat{y}(t)) = min\left\{ f(y_0(t)),\ldots f(y_{ns}(t)) \right\} \right\}.$$

(7)

where, n_s is the total no. of particles in the swarm. The basic concept of PSO lies in accelerating each particle toward its personal best and the global best locations, with a random weighted acceleration at each time step. Another important feature to be considered in a PSO algorithm is the stopping condition, i.e. criteria used to terminate the iterative search process. The following stopping conditions can be used:

1. Terminate when a maximum number of iterations has been exceeded.
2. Terminate when an acceptable solution has been found.
3. Terminate when no improvement is observed over a number of iterations.

When selecting a termination criterion, two important aspects have to be considered: The stopping condition should not cause the PSO to prematurely converge, otherwise suboptimal solutions will be obtained and the stopping condition should protect against oversampling of the fitness.

LITERATURE SURVEY

A number of watermarking techniques are available in the literature for embedding information securely in an image (Katzenbeisser & Petitcolas, 2002; Cheddad et al, 2010). Here, we begin with some of those transform domain techniques which were proposed for watermarking fingerprint images. Vatsa, Singh et al (2006) presented robust watermarking of fingerprint images using a combination of the wavelet and LSB based watermarking techniques. However, since the method used the entire image for embedding, the watermark may be lost if the watermarked image was exposed to segmentation of the ridge and border regions. Also, since the watermark was hidden in LSB's of wavelet coefficients, the robustness of the method was low. Further, Zebbiche, Ghouti, Khelifi, and Bouridane (2006, 2008) proposed watermarking schemes in the DCT as well as DWT domains to protect the fingerprint images by watermarking them with their minutiae data itself. The method was robust to some extent but data hiding capacity was low. Recently, Naik, and Holambe (2010) proposed a blind DCT domain image watermarking scheme which hides DCT coefficients of a face image in the lower order DCT coefficients of sub blocks of a fingerprint image.

Next, we discuss some of the transform domain techniques which were proposed for watermarking any kind of images. Parameswaran and Anbumani (2007) used the Discrete Wavelet Transform for watermarking of digital images, where content based watermark was constructed using relationship between neighbouring wavelet coefficients in each band. However, this is not possible in our case where the watermark is predefined. Wang and Pearman (2004) proposed a data hiding technique based on the estimation of DCT AC coefficients. Further, Shinfeng, Shie, and Guo (2010) proposed a DCT based watermarking method particularly robust against JPEG compression. However, the low frequency DCT coefficients used in watermarking are chosen randomly.

In recent years, Singular Value Decomposition (SVD) has been used as a new transform for watermarking (Chang, Tsai & Lin, 2005; Li, Yuan & Zong, 2007). It has been shown experimentally that significant improvement in computational time is achieved through eigen value analysis over truncated SVD based methods (Ashwani & Srinivas, 2006). Most of the SVD based methods are non blind and require the original image for watermark extraction. Bhatnagar & Balasubramanian (2009) proposed a semi blind reference watermarking scheme based on DWT-SVD where the original image is not required but the original reference image is required for watermark extraction. Li, He-Huan, Chin-Chen, and Ying-Ying (2011) introduced watermarking in redistributed invariant wavelet domain to enhance robustness with respect to geometric distortions. However, if the watermarked image is exposed to various image processing attacks, the extracted watermark is low in quality.

Watermarking techniques lately have been used in conjunction with evolutionary computation (Wang, Sun & Zhang, 2007; Aslantas, Ozer & Ozturk, 2008 & 2009; Rohani & Avanaki, 2009; Amiri & Jamzad, 2009; Rafigh & Moghaddam, 2010; Kishore, Sivasankar, Ramashri & Harikrishnan, 2010; Wang, Lin & Yang, 2011; Vellasques, Sabourin & Granger, 2011; Bansal, Sehgal & Bedi, 2012). Wang et al. (2007) have embedded the watermark in the wavelet domain and used PSO only in the watermark extraction phase. Aslantas et al. (2008) have proposed a fragile watermarking scheme where the watermark is embedded by modifying LSBs of the PSO selected DCT coefficients of the image. Hence, as the name suggests, the watermark is lost if the image is subjected to certain image processing attacks. They (Aslantas et al, 2009) further evaluated the performance of the same technique using different intelligent optimization algorithms like Genetic Algorithms (GA), Differential Evolution algorithm (DE) etc. Their results show that GA and PSO based watermarking gave similar results, with PSO performing marginally better in some cases. Rohani et al (2009) proposed a watermarking scheme in the DCT domain by optimizing SSIM index using PSO, but the embedding procedure is such that the original image is required for watermark extraction. Amiri et al (2009) proposed a wavelet domain watermarking technique based on GA, but the technique was effective for very small watermarks. Rafigh et al (2010) and Wang et al (2011) proposed techniques that were robust to various image processing attacks when the amount of hidden data was less and therefore used binary images as watermarks. Vellasques et al (2011) proposed intelligent watermarking of document images which are bi-tonal in nature, whereas the present work deals with gray scale images. Bansal et al, 2012 proposed a technique in the DCT domain to authenticate a gray scale fingerprint image by watermarking it with its corresponding gray scale facial image. In contrast to other PSO based techniques, their work focuses on fingerprint images and hence considers the fingerprint ridge orientation certainty together with SSIM index in the objective function for PSO. As a result, the quality and the matching ability of the watermarked fingerprint are retained. Recently, Tiwary & Sahoo (2011), proposed a method to hide data in PDF files through the replacement of trash spaces or by appending at the end of the file.

PSO BASED WATERMARKING FOR SECURING FINGERPRINT IMAGES

This section presents a watermarking technique for securing fingerprint images in the DCT domain. This technique uses Particle Swarm Optimization (PSO) to find the best DCT coefficients for the embedding of the watermark.

The highlights of this technique are as follows:

1. The DCT coefficients used for data embedding are optimized using SSIM index and OCL index. As a result, the PSO function looks for an optimal solution with respect to watermarked image quality and its matching ability.
2. Data embedding is done block wise rather than in the whole image. Only those blocks are selected which contain the ridge area of the fingerprint and not the noisy area at the borders. This ensures that the watermark is not lost even if the ridge area is segmented from the noisy borders in the background.
3. The original image is not required for watermark extraction.
4. The methods are robust to numerous image processing attacks.

This technique aims at watermarking a gray scale fingerprint image with its corresponding gray scale facial image of a smaller size. In this process, there are three key issues which are addressed:

1. The watermarked image must be of good quality so that the watermark is imperceptible.
2. The algorithm must be robust so that extraction of the watermark is possible even after the watermarked image is exposed to various image processing attacks.
3. Finally, insertion of the watermark should not alter features of the input fingerprint image which are used for fingerprint recognition by fingerprint based identification systems.

The following subsections discuss the objective function to be used by PSO in the presented technique and the algorithms for watermark embedding and extraction.

Formulation of Objective Function for PSO

In order to formulate the objective function for PSO, both the watermarked image's quality and minutia prediction capability are considered. The objective function is formulated as a combination of the quality metrics structural similarity index (SSIM) and the Orientation certainty level index (OCL). As a result, the selected coefficients generated by optimizing the proposed objective function result in minimum distortion of the host image after the facial image data is embedded.

Structural Similarity Index (SSIM) is the generalized form of the Universal Image Quality Index (UQI) defined as follows (Wang & Bovik, 2003):

$$Q = \frac{4\sigma_{ow}\hat{o}\hat{w}}{\left(\hat{o}^2 + \hat{w}^2\right)\left(\sigma_o^2 + \sigma_w^2\right)} \tag{8}$$

where, o and w are corresponding windows of the same size of the original and watermarked images and $\hat{o}$ and $\hat{w}$ are the corresponding averages of o and w respectively. σ_o^2 and σ_w^2 are the corresponding variances of o and w and σ_{ow} is the covariance of o and w. The quality index takes the Human Visual System (HVS) into consideration which has a remarkable ability to detect the high frequency signals (edges) in an image. This quality metric evaluates image degradation as a combination of three different factors: the loss of correlation, the luminance distortion and the contrast distortion. Its definition can be rewritten as a product of three components, each measuring the above factors:

$$Q = \frac{2\sigma_{ow}}{\sigma_o \sigma_w} * \frac{2\hat{o}\hat{w}}{\left(\hat{o}^2 + \hat{w}^2\right)} * \frac{\sigma_o \sigma_w}{\left(\sigma_o^2 + \sigma_w^2\right)} \qquad (9)$$

The first component measures the degree of linear correlation between o and *w*. The second component measures how close the mean luminance is between o and *w* and the last component measures the similarity of the image contrasts. The dynamic range of is [-1, 1] with the best value of 1 and the worst value of -1. The UQI is generalized to Structural Similarity Index (SSIM) as the former produces unstable results when either of the terms in the denominator is very close to zero. Thus, *SSIM* measures the similarity between two images and is defined as:

$$SSIM\left(o, w\right) = \frac{\left(2\hat{o}\hat{w} + d_1\right)\left(2\sigma_{ow} + d_2\right)}{\left(\hat{o}^2 + \hat{w}^2 + 1\right)\left(\sigma_o^2 + \sigma_w^2 + d_2\right)}$$

$$(10)$$

where, d_1 and d_2 are appropriate constants.

The OCL index (Lim, Jiang & Yau, 2002; Zhao, Liu, Zhang & Zhang, 2010) is a local feature based fingerprint image quality index which measures the energy concentration along the dominant ridge orientation on a local block in a fingerprint image. The gray level gradient (*dx, dy*) at a pixel exhibits the orientation and the orientation strength of the image at this pixel. The orthogonal basis for an image block can be formed by finding its eigen values and eigen vectors. The covariance matrix *C* of the gradient vector for an image block is given by:

$$C = \frac{1}{|w|} \sum_{i \in w} \left\{ \begin{bmatrix} dx \\ dy \end{bmatrix} \begin{bmatrix} dx & dy \end{bmatrix} \right\} \qquad (11)$$

Let λ_1 and λ_2 be two eigen values of the covariance matrix in Equation (15), where $\lambda_1 <<< \lambda_2$. Then, for the above watermarked fingerprint image block w the OCL index is defined as:

$$OCL(w) = \lambda_1 / \lambda_2 (12)$$

It gives an indication of how strong the energy is concentrated along the ridge-valley orientation. The lower the OCL index the stronger it is. Its value lies between 0 and 1.

Hence the PSO module which locates optimized coefficients for watermark embedding will minimize the following objective function:

$$OF = (1 - \gamma)\left(1 - SSIM\left(o, w\right)\right) + \gamma(OCL(w))$$

$$(13)$$

where, γ is a weighting constant.

Watermark Embedding

Figure 6 shows the steps of the watermarking algorithm. The steps in detail are as follows:

1. **Reading images:** Read the cover fingerprint image I (m × n) and the watermark facial image F (u × v) to be hidden.
2. **Create watermark array:** Convert the watermark image F to a sequence of binary digits that can be hidden in the cover image. For this purpose extract four MSB's of each pixel in F and concatenate them to obtain a sequence of bits W to be hidden in I. The proposed algorithm uses this approach. The sequence of bits in W can be permuted for security. Let the length of W be *len*.
3. **Extraction of Region of Interest (ROI):** Divide the input fingerprint image I into a number of blocks of size N × N. Any cap-

Figure 6. Block diagram of the Watermarking Algorithm

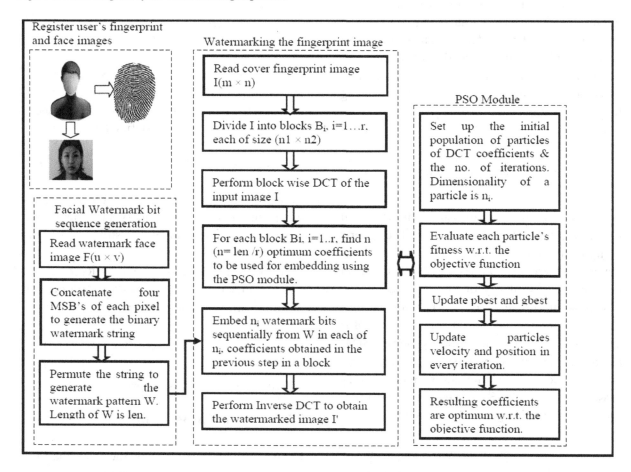

tured fingerprint image usually consists of two areas: the foreground (ridge area that originates from the contact of the fingertip with the sensor) and the background (the noisy area at the borders). The watermark is embedded only in the blocks classified as ridge blocks. Let the number of ridge blocks be r. Calculate the number of watermark bits to be hidden in each ridge block as $n = len/r$.

4. **Compute block wise DCT:** For each block of the input image I, compute its forward DCT (Equation 2). DCT is a kind of signal decomposition that converts images from spatial domain to frequency domain. DCT (i,j) represents the coefficient at coordinate

(i,j) and *gray_value*(x,y) represents the gray scale value of the pixel at location (x,y) in the original block.

5. **Using PSO:** In order to obtain the best coefficients' locations for each ridge block, certain parameters for the PSO function are set. The number of iterations *iters* are set according to the level of accuracy required. Each particle in the swarm has a dimensionality equal to n as that is the number of coefficients required as the solution in each ridge block. Hence, the initial population is constructed by randomly taking combinations of n coefficients from all the low frequency coefficients of the block. Next, the objective function to be used by the PSO module is set based on the

SSIM index and the OCL index as discussed in the previous subsection by Equation (13). In every iteration, the watermarked image is computed using the coefficients of each particle and the fitness of the particle is then calculated with respect to the objective function. The position of every particle is updated depending upon its personal best *pbest* and the best particle obtained so far in the entire population i.e. *gbest* using Equations (6) and (7) respectively. The resulting PSO selected particle represents the optimum solution which when used for embedding, will result in better image quality. The output of the PSO module will be the positions of *n* best coefficients for each ridge block B_i, i=1...r, which are to be used for embedding *n* bits in the same block in the embedding step.

6. Watermark embedding: Next, the *n* bits from the watermark pattern W are sequentially embedded by quantizing the *n* best coefficients (computed using PSO) in each ridge block B_i, i=1...r as follows:

Let *D* be the value of the DCT coefficient and *M* be the modulus, the remainder *rem* and the quotient *q* respectively are given by Equation (14) and Equation (15)

$$q = \frac{|D|}{M} \tag{14}$$

$$rem = |D| \bmod M \tag{15}$$

The initial value *D* of the coefficient is changed to *D'* to embed the binary information of the watermark pattern as follows: If the current input watermark bit is 0:

$$rem' = M / 4$$
$$D_{min} = q \times M + rem'$$
$$D_{max} = (q + 1) \times rem'$$

Let D_{min} and D_{max} be of the same sign as *D*. Now, modify *D* to *D'* as:

$$D' = \begin{cases} D_{min}, if \left| D_{min} - D \right| \leq \left| D_{max} - D \right| \\ D_{max}, if \left| D_{min} - D \right| > \left| D_{max} - D \right| \end{cases} \tag{16}$$

Equation (19) assigns to *D'* a value out of D_{min} and D_{max} that is closer to it. However, If $|D'| \bmod M \geq M / 2$ then $D' = D_{min}$ Similarly, if the current input watermark bit is 1:

$$rem' = 3 \times M / 4$$
$$D_{min} = (q - 1) \times M + rem'$$
$$D_{max} = q \times M + rem'$$

Let D_{min} and D_{max} be of the same sign as *D*. Now again modify *D* to *D'* according to

Figure 7. Host fingerprints: (a) I1, (b) I2, (c) I3, (d) I4

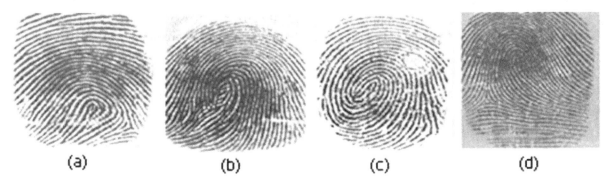

(a)   (b)   (c)   (d)

Figure 8. Facial images to be embedded: (a) F1, (b) F2, (c) F3, (d) F4

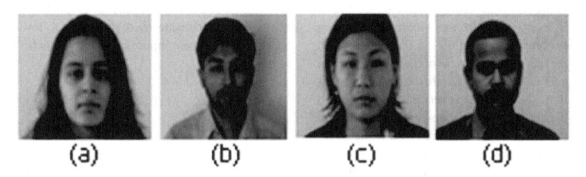

Equation (19). However, If $|D'| mod M \leq M / 2$ then $D' = D_{max}$

The value of M is a predefined constant and is used as a reference threshold. Higher is the value of M, the robustness of the method increases, but the quality of the watermarked image decreases. Hence M is chosen so as to obtain a balance between robustness and image quality.

7. Compute block wise inverse DCT: After embedding all watermark bits in the extracted ridge blocks, inverse DCT is applied on each image block independently, using Equation (3), to give the watermarked image I'.

Watermark Extraction

The hidden watermark facial image can be extracted by the reverse process. This process uses the positions found with PSO and the modulus M in the embedding phase as extraction key. The watermark pattern is extracted with the help of the key and Equation (17). First compute the forward block wise DCT (Equation 2) of the watermarked fingerprint image. For each ridge block B_i, i=1...r, extract the coefficients depending on the key. For each such coefficient D, let the extracted watermark bit be w as:

$$w = \begin{cases} 0, if \left(|D| \, mod \, M \right) < M / 2 \\ 1, if \left(|D| \, mod \, M \right) \geq M / 2 \end{cases} \qquad (17)$$

All the bits are concatenated and the inverse permutation transformation is applied. Once the watermark pattern is obtained, the facial image is constructed.

EXPERIMENTAL RESULTS AND ANALYSIS

For experimental purposes, the results have been tabulated for four standard fingerprint images of size 512 × 512 as shown in Figure 7 and the corresponding facial images as shown in Figure 8 (Jain & Mukherjee, 2002). The facial watermarks are taken in two sizes, i.e., 45 × 45 and size 64 × 64. The experimental results have been tabulated for some existing DCT- PSO based techniques (Rohani et al, 2009; Kishore et al, 2010; Bansal et al, 2012) and existing DCT but non-PSO based techniques (Shingfeng et al, 2010; Naik et al, 2010). The objective quantitative measures used for comparison between the original and the watermarked images of dimension $m \times n$ are as follows:-

Peak Signal Noise Ratio (PSNR) defined as:

Table 2. Comparative values of the quality measure PSNR obtained after embedding the facial image in two sizes (45 × 45 and 64 × 64) in the host fingerprint images using existing and proposed DCT based approaches

Host Image	Watermark image size	Rohani et al Method	Kishore et al Method	Shinfeng et al Method	Naik et al Method	Bansal et al Method
I1	45 × 45 64 × 64	38.62 33.95	44.23 43.17	35.66 31.92	42.55 39.72	46.35 43.64
I2	45 × 45 64 × 64	39.44 34.67	45.24 43.56	34.38 31.54	43.14 39.03	46.94 44.59
I3	45 × 45 64 × 64	36.70 31.32	45.19 41.75	34.01 30.91	42.15 38.89	46.81 42.89
I4	45 × 45 64 × 64	42.25 38.13	48.72 47.65	37.82 35.32	46.26 43.15	50.89 48.52

Table 3. Comparative values of the quality measure MSSIM obtained after embedding the facial image in two sizes (45 × 45 and 64 × 64) in the host fingerprint images using existing and proposed DCT based approaches

Host Image	Watermark image size	Rohani et al Method	Kishore et al Method	Shinfeng et al Method	Naik et al Method	Bansal et al Method
I1	45 × 45 64 × 64	0.948 0.926	0.982 0.978	0.943 0.931	0.985 0.972	0.996 0.993
I2	45 × 45 64 × 64	0.947 0.935	0.991 0.994	0.952 0.938	0.987 0.974	0.997 0.994
I3	45 × 45 64 × 64	0.941 0.904	0.988 0.970	0.944 0.911	0.985 0.971	0.995 0.992
I4	45 × 45 64 × 64	0.932 0.916	0.990 0.983	0.925 0.914	0.978 0.962	0.998 0.992

$$PSNR = 10 * \log_{10} \left\{ \frac{\sum_{i=0}^{M-1} \sum_{j=0}^{N-1} 255^2}{\sum_{i=0}^{M-1} \sum_{j=0}^{N-1} \left[I(i,j) - I'(i,j) \right]^2} \right\}$$

(18)

Mean Structural Similarity Index (MSSIM) defined as:

$$MSSIM = \frac{1}{M} \sum_{j=1}^{M} SSIM\left(x_j, y_j\right)$$

(19)

where, x_j and y_j are the image contents at the jth local window; and M is the number of local windows in the image. $SSIM\left(x_j, y_j\right)$ is calculated as defined in Equation (10) in the previous section.

Normalized Correlation (NC) is used as the objective quantitative measure to compare the original and the extracted watermarks. It is defined as:

$$NC = \frac{\sum_i w_i w_i'}{w_i^2}$$

(20)

where, w represents the inserted watermark and w' represents the extracted watermark. The NC value can be anywhere between 0 and 1. The closer the NC value is to 1, the higher the accuracy is for the recovered watermark.

Table 4. Values of PSNR, SSIM and NC obtained after attacking the watermarked image with various image-processing attacks. The results are obtained after watermarking I1 with F1 (45×45)

Attacks	Non PSO based Method in DCT		PSO based Method in DCT	
	PSNR	NC	PSNR	NC
Unattacked	36.289	1	46.357	1
JPEG Comp(Q:10)	36.220	0.9758	37.435	0.9889
JPEG Comp(Q:8)	35.793	0.7246	36.856	0.9615
JPEG Comp(Q:5)	34.747	0.6347	35.567	0.9572
JPEG Comp(Q:3)	33.238	0.6060	34.665	0.9431
Sharpen	28.252	0.9866	29.867	0.9865
Sharpen Edges	29.997	0.9849	30.145	0.9874
Diffuse glow	17.844	0.9407	17.854	0.9414
Despeckle	34.537	0.7510	34.986	0.8460
Median filter	31.016	0.5905	31.913	0.7713
Unsharp mask	36.279	0.9913	30.876	0.9952
Blur	34.772	0.7880	34.776	0.8785
5% Impulse Noise	27.031	0.9748	27.567	0.9755
5% Gaussian Noise	26.553	0.7425	26.799	0.8109
Auto Levels	13.120	0.9788	13.765	0.9885
Equalize	12.852	0.9383	12.853	0.9445
Crop	12.170	0.9383	12.776	0.9554

Table 5. Matching performance of the watermarked fingerprint images generated by the non-PSO-based method and the proposed methods

Cover fingerprint images	Size of watermark	Matching Score		
		Original fingerprint	Watermarked fingerprint by Shinfeng et al Method (non PSO)	Watermarked fingerprint by Bansal et al method (PSO)
I1	45×45	1257	1110	1185
I2		1569	1398	1440
I3		1695	1245	1413
I4		1464	1050	1128
I1	64×64	1257	951	995
I2		1569	1262	1352
I3		1695	1142	1302
I4		1464	713	1007

Watermarked Fingerprint Quality

Table 2 and 3 list the comparative PSNR and MSSIM values respectively, between cover and watermarked images for existing together with the presented watermarking techniques in the Discrete Cosine Transform Domain. The input fingerprint image is divided into 8 × 8 sized blocks and PSO is run block wise to obtain best DCT coefficients' locations in each ridge block. Each block of a cover image is used to hide 3-6 bits of the input watermark bit pattern depending on the size of the facial image to be hidden.

Vulnerability to Image Processing Attacks

Table 4 lists the comparative PSNR and MSSIM values between cover and watermarked images and the corresponding NC values between original and extracted watermarks for the non PSO based method, the DCT-PSO based method (Bansal et al, 2012). The non PSO based method is the method which uses the same embedding strategy but the coefficients used for embedding are chosen randomly and not through PSO. The listed values in Table 4 are tabulated after the watermarked image has been exposed to various image processing attacks. These results clearly show that the PSO based methods are more efficient as they give much better results than the non PSO based method for all the three metrics used, especially for JPEG compression (four quality levels Q are considered) and median filtering.

Matching Performance

Table 5 lists the matching performance of the watermarked fingerprint images generated by the non PSO and the PSO based methods. The matching performance has been measured in terms of minutia score (Jain, Ross & Prabhakar, 2001) calculated through a fingerprint recognition system. Minutia scores of the PSO based method for all images are higher than the non PSO based method, thereby indicating the effectiveness of the proposed methods in retaining features of the original fingerprint.

CONCLUSION

Securing biometric data in large biometric systems has always been a major area of concern. The role of watermarking techniques for securing fingerprint images is discussed in this chapter. The chapter also presented a computationally intelligent watermarking scheme for securing fingerprint images in the Discrete Transform Domain. For this purpose, fingerprint images were watermarked with corresponding facial images in order to protect them as well as authenticate them. As fingerprint matching is based on minutiae points present on the fingerprint image, the watermarking techniques should be developed in such a way that these minutiae are not disturbed and the matching ability of the fingerprint is retained. It can be seen that the PSO based watermarking techniques was robust to a number of frequency attacks on the watermarked image and was able to retain the feature set of the original fingerprint. Thus, without affecting its matching ability, the watermarked fingerprint is not only secured, it can also be authenticated by extracting the embedded data.

FUTURE RESEARCH DIRECTIONS

This work can be extended to other biometric images also like iris images, face images, palm images etc. Although the present chapter has focused on DCT domain watermarking, this work can be extended to other image watermarking domains like Discrete Wavelet Domain (DWT), etc. The presented work can be extended to colored images. As the hiding capacity of a colored image is more than that of a gray scale image, colored images of one biometric can be employed to hide other biometric data of the same individual for the purpose of multimodal biometric authentication. More computationally intelligent techniques can be used to determine the capacity of each block of the host image before determining the optimum coefficients by PSO to be used for embedding. Neural Networks and Fuzzy techniques can also be used in conjunction with PSO for the same.

REFERENCES

Amiri, S. H., & Jamzad, M. (2009). A robust image watermarking method in wavelet domain using genetic algorithm. In *Proceedings of the International Conference on Availability, Reliability and Security* (ARES, 2009), (pp. 612-617). ARES.

Aslantas, V., Ozer, S., & Ozturk, S. (2008). A novel fragile watermarking based on particle swarm optimization. In *Proceedings of the International Conference on Multimedia and Expo* (ICME 2008), (pp. 268-272). ICME.

Aslantas, V., Ozer, S., & Ozturk, S. (2009). Improving the performance of DCT based fragile watermarking using intelligent optimization algorithms. *Optics Communications*, *282*, 2806–2817. doi:10.1016/j.optcom.2009.04.034.

Aswani Kumar, C., & Srinivas, S. (2006). Latent semantic indexing using eigen value analysis for efficient information retrieval. *International Journal of Applied Mathematics and Computer Science*, *16*(4), 551–558.

Bansal, R., Sehgal, P., & Bedi, P. (2012). Securing fingerprint images through PSO based robust facial watermarking. *International Journal of Information Security and Privacy*, *6*(2), 34–52. doi:10.4018/jisp.2012040103.

Bender, W., Gruhl, D., & Morimoto, N. (1996). Techniques for data hiding. *IBM Systems Journal*, *45*(3-4), 313–336. doi:10.1147/sj.353.0313.

Bhatnagar, G., & Balasubramanian, R. (2009). A new robust reference watermarking schemebsed on DWT-SVD. *Computer Standards & Interfaces*, *31*, 1002–1013. doi:10.1016/j.csi.2008.09.031.

Chang, C. C., Tsai, P., & Lin, C. C. (2005). SVD based digital watermarking scheme. *Pattern Recognition Letters*, *26*, 1577–1586. doi:10.1016/j.patrec.2005.01.004.

Cheddad, A., Condell, J., Curran, K., & Mc Kevitt, P. (2010). Digital image steganography - Survey and analysis of current methods. *J Signal Processing*, *90*(3), 752–776.

Cox, I. J., Kilian, J., Leighton, F. T., & Shamoon, T. (1997). Secure spread spectrum watermarking for multimedia. *IEEE Transactions on Image Processing*, *6*(12), 1673–1687. doi:10.1109/83.650120 PMID:18285237.

Engelbrecht, A. P. (2005). *Fundamentals of computational swarm intelligence*. Hoboken, NJ: John Wiley & Sons.

Gonzalez, R., & Woods, R. (2005). *Digital image processing*. PHI.

Harris, C., & Stephens, M. (1988). A combined corner and edge detector. In *Proceedings of the Fourth Alvey Vision Conference*, (pp. 146-151). IEEE.

Hartung, F., & Kutter, M. (1999). Multimedia watermarking techniques. *Proceedings of the IEEE*, *87*(7), 1085–1103. doi:10.1109/5.771066.

Jain, A. K., Bolle, R., & Pankanti, S. (1999). *Biometrics: Personal identification in networked society*. Boston: Kluwer Academic Publications.

Jain, A. K., Hong, L., Pankati, S., & Bolle, R. (1997). An identity authentication system using fingerprints. *Proceedings of the IEEE*, *85*(9), 1365–1388. doi:10.1109/5.628674.

Jain, A. K., Ross, A., & Prabhakar, S. (2001). Fingerprint matching using minutiae and texture features. In *Proceedings of the International Conference on Image Processing* (ICIP 2001), (pp. 282-285). ICIP.

Jain, V., & Mukherjee, A. (2002). *The Indian face database*. Retrieved from http://vis-www. cs.umass.edu/~vidit/ IndianFaceDatabase/

Jarno, M. (2006). LSB matching revisited. *IEEE Signal Processing Letters*, *13*(5), 285–287. doi:10.1109/LSP.2006.870357.

Katzenbeisser, S., & Petitcolas, F. A. P. (2002). *Information hiding techniques for steganography and digital watermarking*. New York: Artech House.

Kishore, V., Sivasankar, A., & Ramashri, T., & HariKrishna, K. (2010). Robust image watermarking using particle swarm optimization. *Advances in Computational Sciences and Technology*, *3*(3), 397–406.

Li, L., He-Huan, X., Chin-Chen, C., & Ying-Ying, M. (2011). A novel image watermarking in redistributed invariant wavelet domain. *Journal of Systems and Software*, *84*, 923–929. doi:10.1016/j. jss.2011.01.025.

Li, Q., Yuan, C., & Zong, Y. Z. (2007). Adaptive DWT-SVD domain image watermarking using human visual model. In *Proceedings of ICACT*, (pp. 1947-1951). ICACT.

Lim, E., Jiang, X., & Yau, W. (2002). Fingerprint quality and validity analysis. In *Proceedings of the International Conference on Image Processing* (ICIP, 2002), (pp. 469-472). ICIP.

Naik, A. K., & Holambe, R. S. (2010). A blind DCT domain digital watermarking for biometric authentication. *International Journal of Computers and Applications*, *1*(16), 11–15.

Parameswaran, L., & Anbumani, K. (2007). A semi-fragile image watermarking using wavelet inter coefficient relations. *International Journal of Information Security and Privacy*, *1*(3), 61–75. doi:10.4018/jisp.2007070105.

Potdar, V. M., Han, S., & Chang, E. (2005). A survey of digital image watermarking techniques. In *Proceedings of the 3rd International Conference on Industrial Informatics*, (pp. 709-716). IEEE.

Rafigh, M., & Moghaddam, M. E. (2010). A robust evolutionary based digital image watermarking technique in DCT domain. In *Proceedings of the Seventh International Conference on Computer Graphics, Imaging and Visualization (CGIV) 2010*, (pp. 105-109). CGIV.

Rohani, M., & Avanaki, A. N. (2009). A watermarking method based on optimizing SSIM index using PSO in DCT domain. [CSICC.]. *Proceedings of CSICC*, *2009*, 418–422.

Shinfeng, D. L., Shie, S. C., & Guo, J. Y. (2010). Improving the robustness of DCT-based image watermarking against JPEG compression. *Computer Standards & Interfaces*, *32*, 60–66.

Tiwary, R. K., & Sahoo, G. (2011). A novel methodology for data hiding in PDF files. *Information Security Journal: A Global Perspective*, *20*(1), 45-57.

Vatsa, M., Singh, R., Noore, A., Houck, M. M., & Morris, K. (2006). Robust biometric image watermarking for fingerprint and face template protection. *IEICE Electronics Express*, *3*(2), 23–28. doi:10.1587/elex.3.23.

Vellasques, E., Sabourin, R., & Granger, E. (2011). A high throughput system for intelligent watermarking of bi-tonal images. *Applied Soft Computing*, *11*, 5215–5229. doi:10.1016/j. asoc.2011.05.038.

Vyaghreswara, R. N., & Pandit Narahari, S. N. (2007). Multimedia digital rights protection using watermarking techniques. *Information Security Journal: A Global Perspective, 16*(2), 93-99.

Wang, Y., Lin, W., & Yang, L. (2011). An intelligent watermarking method based on particle swarm optimization. *Expert Systems with Applications, 38*, 8024–8029. doi:10.1016/j.eswa.2010.12.129.

Wang, Y., & Pearmain, A. (2004). Blind image data hiding based on self reference. *Pattern Recognition Letters, 25*, 1689–1697. doi:10.1016/j.patrec.2004.06.012.

Wang, Z., & Bovik, A. C. (2004). A universal image quality index. *IEEE Signal Processing Letters, 9*(3), 81–84. doi:10.1109/97.995823.

Wang, Z., Sun, X., & Zhang, D. (2007). A novel watermarking scheme based on PSO algorithm. *LNCS, 4688*, 309–314.

Wu, D. C., & Tsai, W. H. (2003). A steganographic method for images by pixel-value differencing. *J Pattern Recognition Letters, 24*, 1626–1639.

Xiaolong, L., Yang, B., Cheng, D., & Zheng, T. (2009). A generalization of LSB matching. *IEEE Signal Processing Letters, 16*(2), 69–72. doi:10.1109/LSP.2008.2008947.

Yang, C. H., Weng, C. Y., Wang, S. J., & Sun, H. M. (2008). Adaptive data hiding in edge areas of pixels with spatial LSB domain systems. *IEEE Transactions on Information Forensics and Security, 3*(3), 488–497. doi:10.1109/TIFS.2008.926097.

Zebbiche, K., Ghouti, L., Khelifi, F., & Bouridane, A. (2006). Protecting fingerprint data using watermarking. In *Proceedings of the First NASA/ESA Conference on Adaptive Hardware and Systems (AHS)*, (pp. 451-456). NASA/ESA.

Zebbiche, K., Khelifi, F., & Bouridane, A. (2008). An efficient watermarking technique for the protection of fingerprint images. *EURASIP Journal on Information Security*. Article Id 918601.

Zhao, Q., Liu, F., Zhang, L., & Zhang, D. (2010). A comparative study on quality assessment of high resolution fingerprint images. In *Proceedings of the International Conference on Image Processing* (ICIP, 2010), (pp. 3089-3092). ICIP.

ADDITIONAL READING

Cox, I. J. (2008). *Digital watermarking and steganography*. Burlington, MA: Morgan Kaufmann.

Engelbrecht, A. P. (2007). *Computational intelligence: An introduction* (2nd ed.). Hoboken, NJ: John Wiley & Sons. doi:10.1002/9780470512517.

Greenberg, S., Aladjem, M., Kogan, D., & Dimitrov, I. (2000). Fingerprint image enhancement using filtering techniques. *Real–Time Imaging, 8*, 227–236.

Gunsel, B., Uludag, U., & Tekalp, A. M. (2002). Robust watermarking of fingerprint images. *Pattern Recognition, 35*(12), 2738–2747. doi:10.1016/S0031-3203(01)00250-3.

Hong, L., Wan, Y., & Jain, A. (1998). Fingerprint image enhancement: Algorithm and performance evaluation. *IEEE Transactions on Pattern Analysis and Machine Intelligence, 20*(8), 777–789. doi:10.1109/34.709565.

Jain, A. K., Patrick, F., & Arun, A. (2008). *Handbook of biometrics*. Berlin: Springer. doi:10.1007/978-0-387-71041-9.

Kennedy, J., & Eberhart, R. (2001). *Swarm intelligence*. New York: Morgan Kaufmann.

Lin, C. (2011). An information hiding scheme with minimal image distortion. *Computer Standards & Interfaces, 33*, 477–484. doi:10.1016/j.csi.2011.02.003.

Maity, S. P., & Kundu, M. K. (2002). Robust and blind spatial watermarking in digital image. In *Proceedings of the Indian Conference on Computer Vision, Graphics and Image Processing* (ICVGIP' 2002), (pp. 1-6). ICVGIP.

Maltoni, D., Maio, D., Jain, A. K., & Prabhakar, S. (2003). *Handbook of fingerprint recognition* (2nd ed.). Berlin: Springer.

Shih, F. Y. (2008). *Digital watermarking and steganography: Fundamentals and techniques*. Boca Raton, FL: Taylor & Francis. doi:10.1007/978-3-540-92238-4.

Vatsa, M., Singh, R., & Noore, A. (2009). Feature based RDWT watermarking for multimodal biometric system. *J. Image and Vision Computing, 27*(3), 293–304. doi:10.1016/j.imavis.2007.05.003.

KEY TERMS AND DEFINITIONS

Biometrics: Biometrics is the name given to the various methods of capturing, storing and utilizing biometric data.

Biometric Data: Biometric data refers to records used to identify people uniquely, for e.g. fingerprints, palmprints, retina scans, etc.

Discrete Cosine Transform Domain: A Discrete Cosine Transform (DCT) expresses a sequence of finitely many data points in terms of a sum of cosine functions oscillating at different frequencies. Like any Fourier-related transform, DCTs express a function or a signal in terms of a sum of sinusoids with different frequencies and amplitudes. The distinction between a DCT and a DFT is that the former uses only cosine functions, while the latter uses both cosines and sines.

Digital Watermark: A digital watermark is a kind of marker covertly embedded in a noise-tolerant signal such as audio or image data. It is typically used to identify ownership of the copyright of such signal.

Fingerprint Matching: Fingerprint matching refers to the computation of match score between two fingerprints, which should be high for fingerprints from the same finger and low for those from different fingers. Fingerprint matching is a difficult pattern-recognition problem due to large variations in fingerprint images of the same finger and large similarity between fingerprint images from different fingers.

Minutiae Points: Minutiae points are local ridge characteristics that occur on the surface of a finger as either a ridge bifurcation or a ridge ending.

Particle Swarm Optimization: Particle Swarm Optimization (PSO) is a computational method that optimizes a problem by iteratively trying to improve a candidate solution with regard to a given measure of quality.

Section 2
Video Processing

Chapter 5
Stereo Vision–Based Object Matching, Detection, and Tracking:
A Review

Mohamed Saifuddin
Sunway University, Malaysia

Lee Seng Yeong
Sunway University, Malaysia

Seng Kah Phooi
Sunway University, Malaysia

Ang Li-Minn
Edith Cowan University, Australia

ABSTRACT

Computer vision has become very important in recent years. It is no longer restricted to a single camera that is only capable of capturing a single image at any given time. In its place, stereo vision systems have been introduced that not only make use of dual cameras to capture multiple images at once, but they also simulate the exact same nature of the human eye vision. Stereo vision has turned out to be an important research component in the subdivision of computer vision and image processing that deals with the extraction of information from images for the purpose of video surveillance systems, mimicking the human vision for the visually impaired, for robotics, to control unmanned vehicles, for security purposes, virtual reality and 3 Dimensional (3D) televisions, etc. In this chapter, a comprehensive review of all recent algorithms such as stereo matching, object detection, tracking techniques for stereo vision are presented.

DOI: 10.4018/978-1-4666-4868-5.ch005

INTRODUCTION

Computer vision is a subject, which attempts to recreate the human vision by fabricating models which seem to have related properties to visual observation. It also tried to develop models which seem to have related characteristics to graphical perceptions. Stereo vision is an essential component of computer vision. It is the extraction of 3D information from digital images by examining the relative positions of the objects captured by the dual cameras. With the help of stereo vision, it is possible to reconstruct, either partially or fully, a 3D scene from two or more images that have been captured under marginally dissimilar angles. There are two main categories of computer vision: plane and stereo vision. The most notable difference between them is the depth information i.e. distance of the objects from the cameras. This is not possible to be detected by a single camera as it requires the use of dual cameras. Each lens captures its own view and then two independent images are sent to the system for processing. The system compares the images while shifting the two images together over top of each other to find the parts that match. The shifted amount is called disparity. The disparity at which objects in the image best match is used by the system to calculate their distance. When both the images are processed by the system, they are combined into a single image by matching up the similarities and then adding in the minor differences. These minor differences between the captured images combine to give out a relatively bigger difference in the resultant image. This combined image is greater than the aggregate of its parts. It is a 3D stereo image.

Innovative work in the field of Computer Vision began in the early 60's when Robert from MIT had successfully finalized a 3D scene analysis project(Weiss, 1999). In his project, in order to achieve the 3D scene analysis, 2D image processing had been employed. This particular project had long been considered to be the origin of the stereo vision technique. Nowadays, a comprehensive stereo vision system could be created by concealing the initial steps from capturing images to the final step of recreating the visual surface of the objects. The concept of 'computation stereo' was first proposed by Barnard and Fisher(Arnaud, 2004) who explained that it covered the topics of image matching, depth information, image acquisition and also feature extraction. This has led to the conclusion that a stereo vision system with dual cameras can be utilized at the same time to capture the left & right images effectively so as to obtain the required depth information to be used in a range of applications such as a video surveillance system, mimicking the human vision for the visually impaired, for robotics, to control unmanned vehicles, for security purposes, virtual reality and 3D TV etc.

In a stereo vision process, the primitives extracted from the images that are being matched such as segments, pixels, regions etc. is found to be the most significant phase. There are two extensive types of matching methods (Banks, Bennamoun, Kubik, & Corke, 1997) .The first one makes use of pixel neighborhood correlation method, which generates a dense disparity map, whereas the other method makes use of matching based on characteristics, in this case, generating a disparity map that is comparatively sparse. In any case, the stereo matching based on edge points utilizing linear images is given more importance.

Figure 1 illustrates the general processes of stereo vision based object detection and tracking. In comparison to single camera systems, a stereo vision system is able to overcome the main problems associated with the reconstruction and correspondence issues (TKanade & Okutomi, 1993). Initially, the images are acquired from the left and right cameras which then undergo three stages of processing: stereo-matching, object detection and object tracking. Each camera seems to capture its own perception of the image and the two separate images are then transferred to the acquisition state for further processing. During

Figure 1. General flow of stereo vision based matching, detection, tracking

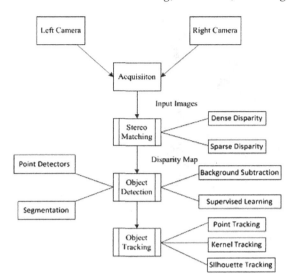

the stereo matching processing, the two input images are compared with each other in order to find the parts that match. These images are then merged into a single image by pairing the similarities and combining the marginal differences together. This difference between the two images is known as disparity and it is used to identify the distance between the two images. There are two main types of stereo matching algorithm called dense and sparse disparity algorithms (Nalpantidis, Georgios, & Antonios, 2008). The generated disparity map is filtered with the depth-based background modeling process in order to remove shadows. With the depth information, the objects are detected on the plan-view map. The stereo frames and the depth information are used to detect the 3D points cloud. Then, the 3D localized histograms are computed for each of the detected objects. In this book chapter, four object detection techniques, namely, point detectors, background subtraction, segmentation and supervised learning (Yilmaz, Javed, & Shah, 2006) are reviewed. Object tracking is defined as the estimation of the trajectory of a detected object in the image plane as it shifts about in the scene. Three main groups of object tracking algorithms are reviewed in this

chapter. They are Point, Kernel and Silhouette tracking (Yilmaz, Javed, & Shah, 2006).

BACKGROUND

Dual Camera Stereo Vision

The main goal of Stereo Vision is recovering the 3D structure of a scene with the help of several images from the 3D scene, where each of the images has been obtained from distinct viewpoints. These images could be acquired from either a single moving camera or multiple cameras.

When taking into account the 3D positions of the objects that are viewed simultaneously by 2 or more cameras from distinctive positions, the most commonly used technique for assuming this is stereovision. Linear stereo vision relates to the usage of direct cameras that provide line-images of the scene (Burie, Bruyelle, & Postaire, 1995; Bruyelle, 1994; Ruichek, Hariti, & Issa, 2007). The Figure 2 provided shall explain how the field of view in such cameras is condensed to a plane.

When compared to traditional video cameras, the data to be processed is considerably cut down.

Figure 2. Fields of view in a linear camera

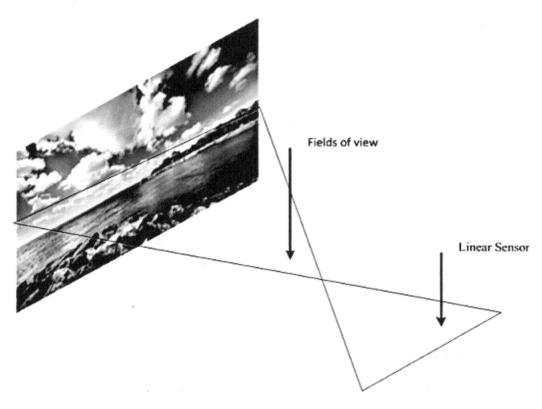

However, linear cameras possess superior horizontal resolution in comparison to video cameras. Such a trait is deemed to be very imperative for precise observation of the scene in front of the camera.

A linear stereo vision system is developed in such a way that their optical axes are found to be parallel and divided by distance E as shown in Figure 3. Also, these lenses have a similar focal length f. In order for the cameras to capture the same scene, their fields of view are combined in the matching plane known as optical plane. A particular adjustment technique is which considers the point that the line-scan cameras are not able to provide the vertical information is shown in (Bruyelle, 1994).

The fundamental principle that brings about stereo vision is 'Triangulation'. This theory states that the location of any visible 3D object in space has been confined to a straight line which goes through the object's projection and also through the center of projection. With the help of Binocular stereo vision, the position of a point can be determined by obtaining the intersecting point where the two lines pass through the object's projection as well as the center of projection. This is explained in Figure 4.

There are two main issues concerning stereo vision (Kanade & Okutomi, 1993). They are:

- The correspondence issue: to find a set of matching points so that each point in the pair is found to be the projection of the equivalent 3D point. Here, the concept of triangulation relies on the result of the correspondence issue. Also, uncertain correspondence amongst the points in the two images leads to several coherent versions of the scene.

Figure 3. Geometry of the linear stereoscope

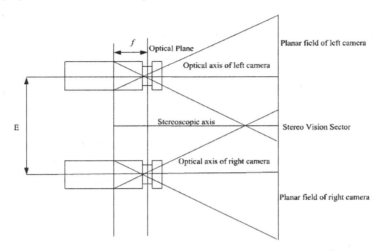

Figure 4. Triangulation theory explained

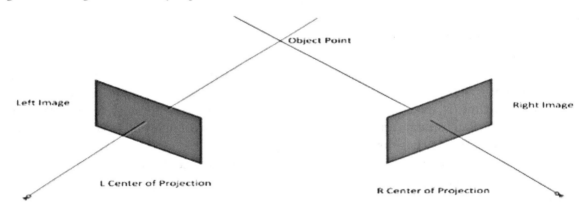

• The reconstruction issue: the disparity map can be computed from the given corresponding points and in case the stereo geometry is known, then it can be converted to a 3D map of the scene.

Feature Extraction

For extracting the features from the targeted images, the initial step is to obtain the primitives that are to be matched from each image. Various kinds of primitives can be obtained from tradi-

tional video images. However, when linear images are taken into account, a restriction is placed on the choices due to the one-dimensional quality of their profile. This leaves us with only one option to look for the edge points that match up to the boundaries of the various objects found in an image. The low-level dispensation of a group of dual stereo-based linear images produces the features that are essential in the equivalence stage. The one-dimensional signals that emerge in the sample images i.e. edges play a prominent role in the matching process due to the fact that significant discrepancies in the grey-level functions relate to the boundaries of the objects that are being monitored in a scene.

Here, Deriche's operator is utilized to carry out the task of edge extraction and also with the help of a technique which chooses appropriate local extrema after separating the gradient level signal into neighboring intervals in which the sign of the operator stays incessant. The maximum amplitude relates to the point of a distinctive edge that is correlated to each interval with a constant sign only when this amplitude is found to be higher than a small threshold value.

STEREO VISION-BASED OBJECT MATCHING

The purpose of the edge-stereo matching activity is to propose an explanation for which the matches can be seen as consistent as possible with regards to particular constraints. However, this is found to be a constant satisfaction issue. In order to solve the stereo correspondence problem, two sorts of constraints are taken into account: - local constraints (position & slope) that are utilised to get rid of improbable matches so as to take into account only appropriate pairs of edges as contenders. The other ones are global constraints (smoothness, uniqueness & ordering constraints) that are put on to the probable matches so as to emphasize the finest ones and they are expressed by an objective function that is expressed so that the top matches relate to its least value. In order to map the enhancement process, a Hopfield neural network is utilised (Ruichek, Hariti, & Issa, 2007)

A simple geometric triangulation process acquires a 2D point described by its horizontal position and depth for each marked pair once the matching process has been achieved. If the base line linking the perspective centres O_l and O_r is defined as X-axis and the Z-axis remains parallel in relation to the optical axes in the optical plane, then the source of the {X, Z} coordinate system is found flanked by the centres of the lenses (as shown in Figure 5).If we take into account a point P (x_p, z_p) of coordinates x_p and z_p from the optical plane.

The coordinates of the image, x_l and x_r signify the forecasts of point P in the left and right image sensor respectively. These set of points are denoted as an analogous pair. With the help of the *pinhole lens model*, the coordinates of point P located in the optical plane can be expressed as:

$$Z_p = \frac{E.f}{d} \tag{1}$$

$$X_p = \frac{x_l . z_p}{f} - \frac{E}{2} = \frac{x_r . z_p}{f} + \frac{E}{2} \tag{2}$$

Where the focal length of the lenses is denoted by f, E is the width of the base line and $d = |x_p - x_r|$ is given as the disparity amongst the left & right forecasts of the point P on the dual sensors.

Review of Stereo Matching Algorithms

One of the most significant tasks in the field of computer vision is estimating the gap between several points or further primitives in a scene that is comparative to the location of the camera lens. With the help of a set of synchronised camera signals that are obtained from a stereo rig, its depth information can be extracted from the intensity image available. The disparity maps (Faugeras, 1993) or depth images can be obtained by point-to-point matching amongst both the images in the stereo set-up. If the corrected stereo pairs from the horizontal scan lines belong to the identical epi-polar line as assumed, then the matching process is accurately carried out as one directional search.

Figure 5. Pinhole model

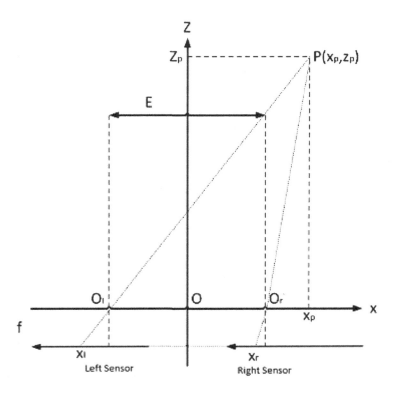

Review of Dense Disparity Algorithms

The dense disparity algorithms can be classified into two main categories, in relation to the way in which the disparities are allocated to pixels. In the first group, according to the data that is being provided by its local neighbouring pixels, the disparity of each pixel in the algorithm is decided upon. In the algorithms from the other category, the disparity values are assigned to every pixel based on the information that is obtained from the entire image. Thus, the former group of algorithms are known as local methods and the latter group is called as global methods. The chief characteristics of the local procedures (Nalpantidis, Georgios, & Antonios, 2008) have been discussed and summarized in the Table 1.

SAD: Sum of Absolute Differences, ZNCC: Zero Mean Normalized Correlation, NCC: Nor-

malized Cross-Correlation, SSD: Sum of Squared Differences, D: Disparity

The most prominent characteristics of the global procedures which utilize both global optimization and dynamic programming are discussed and summarized in Table 2.

Review of Algorithms for Sparse Disparity

Since majority of the modern day applications demand denser inconsistency information, algorithms, which result in comparatively sparser or even semi-dense disparity maps have a tendency to be less appealing. Although they are found to be quite beneficial when rapid depth evaluation is mandatory at similar time interval, as a complete picture, they are deemed to be unimportant. These categories of algorithms have a tendency to concentrate on the most important features of the

Table 1. Features of the local methods under dense disparity algorithms

Authors	Technique	Characteristics	Speed (fps)	Image Size	Inconsistency Levels
Muhlmann et al. (2002)	SAD	• Colour usage • Handles occlusion • Left to right consistency • Unique constraints	20	160 x 120	
Zach, Karner & Bishof (2004)	SAD	• Implemented on GPU • Handles occlusion • Bidirectional matching	50	256 x 256	88
Di Stefano, Mattoccia & Marchionni (2004)	SAD	• Unique constraints • Handles occlusion	39.59	320 x 240	16
Binaghi et al. (2004)	ZNCC	• Varying windows depending on neural networks	0.024	284 x 216	30
Kotoulas et al. (2005)	SAD	• Cellular automata	40	1000 x 1000	
Yoon et al. (2005)	SAD	• Left to Right consistency check • Handles occlusion • Variable windows	7	320 x 240	32
Ogale & Aloimonos (2005a)	SAD	• Unique Interval constraint • Handles occlusion	1	384 x 288	16
Mordohai & Medioni (2006)	NCC	• Handles occlusion • Colour usage • Tensor voting	0.002	384 x 288	20
Yoon & Kweon (2006a)	SAD	• Varying support – weights • Colour usage	0.016	384 x 288	16
Yoon & Kweon (2006b)	SAD	• Specular reflection compensation • Colour usage • Varying support weights	0.016	384 x 288	16

images, thus resulting in occlusion and scantily textured unmatched areas. Subsequently higher processing speeds, precise results can be expected but with limited density. Even though a lot of ideas prosper in this direction, only a small quantity of indicatory algorithms have been discussed here due to the growing interest in relatively denser disparity maps.

An algorithm proposed by Veksler (Veksler, 2002) could detect and then match dense qualities amongst both the sides of the images in a stereo set thus resulting in a semi-dense inconsistency map. A dense trait is one where an interconnected pair of pixels from the image on the left and an equivalent pair of pixels from the image on the right in a manner that the edge intensity on their

periphery sets is found to be more robust than the matching error. All of this achieved during the process of matching. This algorithm is found to compute 14 inconsistency levels with 1fps for the Tsukuba pair, thus resulting in 66% of density and an avg error of 0.06% in the regions of non-occlusion.

In Veksler (Veksler, 2003) a different method centred on the same basic ideas of the previous one. The most notable difference is that this method makes use of graph cuts algorithm in order to achieve a dense extraction of features. As a result, this algorithm is found to produce a semi-dense output with substantial precision in the regions where the features have been identified. The subsequent outcomes are found to be better

Table 2. Characteristics of the global methods that use global optimization and dynamic programming

Writer	Technique	Characteristics	Speed (fps)	Image Size	Inconsistency Levels
Gutierrez & Marroquin (2004)	Gauss – Markov random field	• Continuity • Handles occlusion • Coherence • Occlusion • Adjacency	< 0.017	256 x 255	32
Hong & Chen (2004)	Graph cuts	• Handles occlusion • Colour segmentation	0.33	384 x 288	16
Bleyer & Gelautz (2004)	Global cost function	• Colour segmentation • Handles occlusion			
Zitnick et al. (2004)	Global cost function	• Handles occlusion • Colour segmentation			
Brockers et al. (2005)	Cost relaxation	• 3D support regions • Handles occlusion			
Kim & Sohn (2005)	Vector field regular-ization	• Canny edge detector • Handles occlusion	0.15	384 x 288	16
Hirschmuller (2005)	Global cost function	• Mutual information • Handles occlusion	0.77	450 x 375	60
Bleyer & Gelautz (2005)	Global cost function	• Colour segmentation • Handles occlusion	0.05	384 x 288	16
Ogale & Aloimonos (2005)	Left-Right diffusion process	• Phase-based matching • Handles occlusion	0.5	384 x 288	16
Sun et al. (2005)	Belief propagation	• Colour segmentation • Handles occlusion • Symmetrical treatment	0.02	384 x 288	16
Hirschmuller (2006)	Global cost function	• Mutual information • Handles occlusion • Bidirectional match	<1	450 x 375	64
Veksler (2006)	Graph cuts	• Prior local stereo algorithm	1.04	434 x 383	20
Klaus et al. (2006)	Belief propagation	• Colour segmentation	0.07	384 x 288	16
Yang et al. (2006a)	Hierarchical belief propagation	• GPU utilization	16	320 x 240	16
Yang et al. (2006b)	Hierarchical belief propagation	• Colour segmentation • Handles occlusion			
Strecha et al. (2006)	Hidden Markov random field	• Handles occlusion • Expectation maximization algorithm			
Zitnick & Kang (n.d.)	Propagation belief inside a MRF frame-work	• Colour segmentation • Handles occlusion			
Torra & Criminisi (2004)	DP	• Handles occlusion • Prior feature matching			
Veksler (2005)	DP	• Applied to pixel tree structure	~2		
Kim et al. (2005)	DP	• Handles occlusion • Prior inconsistency candidate assignment • Dual pass inter scan line enhancement	0.23	384 x 288	16
Lei et al. (2002)	DP	• Handles occlusion • Colour usage • Could affect the region tree structure	0.1	384 x 288	16
Wang et al. (2006)	DP	• Inter scan line consistency • Adaptive aggregation • Colour usage	43.5	320 x 240	16

in terms of density and error percentage; however they necessitate longer computational time. It is found to attain a density of up to 75% with a running speed of 0.17fps and overall error of 0.36% in the occluded regions. The corresponding results for the sawtooth pair are as follows: 87%, 0.08fps and 0.54%.

In contrast, a 'DP' (Dynamic Programing) algorithm known as Reliability Based Dynamic Programming (RDP) was proposed by Gong & Yang (Gong & Yee-Hong, 2005a) which made use of a separate measure in order to assess the reliabilities of the matches. The outcome is semi-dense unequivocal inconsistency map with a density of 76%, 16fps and error rate of 0.32% for the Tsukuba model and 72%, 7fps and 0.23% respectively for the sawtooth pair of images. Subsequently, the findings for the Venus and Map pairs are 73%, 6.4fps and 0.18% and 86%, 12.8fps and 0.7% respectively. From the gathered results of the reported computational rates, they are found to be suitable for a real time procedure if the semi dense disparity map is satisfactory.

A real-time stereo matching procedure was proposed by Gong and Yang (Gong & Yee-Hong, 2005b) which is comparable to the previously suggested one based on the RDP algorithm. Semi-dense disparity maps are found to be generated by this algorithm. The outcomes are as follows: 85% dense disparity map, 23.8fps and error rate of 0.3% for Tsukuba pair, 93% density, 12.3fps and 0.24% error rate for sawtooth pair, 86% density, 9.2fps and 0.21% error rate for the Venus set and

88% density, 20.8fps and 0.05% error rate for the Map image set. Depending on the execution speed, this technique could be used to create denser disparity maps. The Table 3 given will summarize the features (Nalpantidis, Georgios, & Antonios, 2008) of this discussed algorithm.

STEREO VISION-BASED OBJECT DETECTION

Object detection is seen as the basic step for further video analysis steps such as tracking. Each tracking algorithm necessitates an object detection mechanism either when the entity emerges in the video for the first time or in each frame of the video. Making use of information in a single frame is the most commonly used approach for detecting objects. However, so as to cut down the amount of erroneous detections, the temporal information that is calculated from an order of frames is used by some object detection techniques. This temporal data is utilised in the case of frame differencing that focuses on the sequential frames for the changing regions. Provided that the object areas in the image are known, it is then up to the tracking mechanism to carry out the task of performing object correlation from one frame to another to produce the image tracks.

Though stereo vision based object detection techniques calls for a book chapter of its own due to the various algorithms that have been proposed over the years, for the purpose of completeness,

Table 3. Characteristics of the sparse density algorithms

Writer	Technique	Concentration	Speed (fps)	Image Size	Inconsistency Levels
Veksler (2002)	Local	66	1	384 x 288	14
Veksler (2003)	Graph cuts	75	0.17	384 x 288	16
Gong & Yang (2005a)	RDP	76	16	384 x 288	16
Gong & Yang (2005b)	RDP	85	23.8	384 x 288	16

Table 4. Categories of object detection techniques

Classifications	Demonstrative Work
Point Detectors	Moravec's detector (Moravec, 1979) Harris detector (Harris & Stephens, 1988) Affine Invariant Point Detector (Mikolajczyk & Schmid, 2003) Scale Invariant Feature Transform (Lowe, 2004)
Segmentation	Active Contours (Caselles, Kimmel, & Sapiro, 1995) Mean-Shift (Comaniciu & Meer, 2002) Graph-cut (Shi & Malik, 2000)
Background Modelling	Wall flower (Toyoma, Krumm, & Meyers, 1999) Eigen background (Oliver, Rosario, & Pentland, 2000) Mixture of Gaussians (Stauffer & Grimson, 2000) Dynamic texture background (Monnet, Mittal, Paragios, & Ramesh, 2003)
Supervised Classifiers	Neural Networks (Rowley, Baluja, & Andkanade, 1998) Support Vector Machines (Papageorgiou, Oren, & Poggio, 1998) Adaptive Boosting (Viola, Jones, & Snow, 2003)

only the most popular methods have been discussed in the background of object tracking. The Table 4 highlights the several object detection techniques (Nalpantidis, Georgios, & Antonios, 2008) that have been considered here

Point Detectors

Points of interest have been widely made use of in the setting of stereo, motion and tracking issues. One of the most desirable features of any point of interest is its invariance to modification in camera viewpoint and also illumination. Some of the most commonly used point detectors of interest are Moravec's interest operator (Moravec, 1979), Harris interest point detector (Harris & Stephens, 1988), KLT detector (Hayashi, Hashimoto, Sumi, & Sasakawa, 2004) and SIFT detector (Shi & Tomasi, 1994). For a more detailed comparative assessment of the point detectors of interest, it is explained in detail in the survey by Mikolajcyk and Schmid (Mikolajczyk & Schmid, 2003).

In order to find the points of interest, Moravec's operator calculates the difference in the image strengths in a 4 x 4 patch in the diagonal, horizontal, vertical and anti-diagonal directions and then chooses the least of all the four discrepancies as demonstrative values for the window. If the

intensity deviation is found to be a local maximum in a 12 X 12 path, then that point is affirmed as interesting.

The Harris detector calculates the 1st order derivatives of the images, (I_x, I_y), in the x and y directions to focus on the directional discrepancies in the intensity and then to encode this difference, a second moment matrix is computed for every pixel in the neighbourhood:

$$M = \begin{pmatrix} \Sigma I_x^2 & \Sigma I_x I_y \\ \Sigma I_x I_y & \Sigma I_y^2 \end{pmatrix} \qquad (3)$$

This matrix M is utilised in the point of interest detection step for the KLT tracking technique. The Figure 6 shows the points of interest after the application of the various point detectors.

It has been noted that both the Harris and KLT seem to focus more on the variations in the intensity by making use of similar measures. In practice, both these techniques seem to locate the same points of interest. The only dissimilarity is that the extra KLT benchmark which administers a pre-defined spatial distance amongst the points of interest.

Lowe (2004) proposed the SIFT (Scale Invariant Feature Transform) technique so as to present

Figure 6. Points of interest after the application of the various point detectors: (a) Harris detector, (b) KLT detector, and (c) SIFT operator (Nalpantidis, Georgios, & Antonios, 2008)

  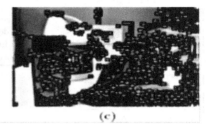

(a)   (c)   (c)

dense detection of the points of interest under various alterations. This method is comprised of 4 basic steps. Firstly, a scale based space is created by treating the image with Gaussian filters at various scales. Then these convolved images are utilised to create Difference-of-Gaussians (DoG) images. Then the minima and maxima from the scales across the DoG images are used to select the points of interests. Secondly, by interpolating the colour values with the help of the neighbouring pixels, the location of each candidate is updated. In the next step, the candidates along the edges as well as the low contrast ones are then eliminated. In the final step, depending on the crests of the histograms of the gradient guidelines in small vicinity surrounding a contender point, the remaining points of interest are allotted orientations. It is an important point to note that the SIFT detector produces a higher amount of points of interest in relation to other point interest detectors. It is based on the circumstance that the points of interest are accumulated at different resolutions and scales. It not only surpasses most detectors but is also more resistant to distortions in the images.

Background Subtraction

The process of detecting objects can be accomplished by creating an illustration of the scene known as the background model and the aberrations for each incoming frame from the model are found. In the background model, any substantial change in the image region indicates an object in motion. The pixels which constitute the region under a change and are noted for further processing. Usually, in order to obtain a connected region which corresponds to the objects, a connected component is applied. This whole process is known as background subtraction.

Frame differencing among temporally flanking frames have been well documented since Jain and Nagel (Jain & Nagel, 1979). However, it is the work of Wren et al (Wren, Azarbayejani, & Pentland, 1997). It is noted that a single Gaussian model is deemed to be unfit for outdoor scenes (Gao, Boult, Coetzee, & Ramesh, 2000) since several colours could be observed at specific locations due to the recurrent motion of the objects, reflectance or even shadows. For example, a combination of Gaussians was used to represent the pixel colour by Stauffer and Grimson (Stauffer & Grimson, 2000). In this technique, a matching Gaussian is found when a pixel in the present frame is tested alongside the background model by evaluating it with ever Gaussian in the model. Instead of using colour-based data only, region-based scene information is integrated by a different approach. Elgammal and Davis(Elgammal, Hardwood, & Davis, 2000) used a non-parametric kernel density assessment to represent the per-pixel background. In order to perform background subtraction, the texture and colour features are fused over a block of 5 x 5 pixels by Li & Leung (Liyuan & Maylor, 2002).This method is found to be less sensitive to illumination since the texture doesn't fluctuate greatly with changes in illumination. A three-tiered algorithm was proposed by Toyoma et al. (Toyoma, Krumm, & Meyers, 1999) to deal with the issue related to background subtraction. Those authors made use of frame-level and region information additionally to the pixel level subtraction.

A different technique for the process of background subtraction is to denote the strength of the deviations in the pixels of an image classification as isolated states equivalent to the proceedings in the surrounding. For example, while monitoring cars on a highway, the image pixels could be in a shadow, background or foreground state. To categorize the small blocks in an image as ones belonging to those states, Rittscher et al. proposed the Hidden Markov Models (Rittscher, Kato, Joga, & Blake, 2000). In the context of detecting lights on or off for proceedings in a room, Stenger et al. (Stenger, Ramesh, Paragois, Coetzee, & Buhmann, 2001) utilised the HMMs to perform background subtraction.

Rather than modelling the disparity of individual pixels, a holistic technique making use of the eigenspace decomposition was proposed by Oliver et al. (Oliver, Rosario, & Pentland, 2000) which is found to be less sensitive to illumination. This is shown in the Figure 7.

One of the drawbacks of these techniques is that they necessitate a static background. This inadequacy is explained by Zhong and Sclaroff (Zhong & Sclaroff, 2003) and Monnet et al. (Monnet, Mittal, Paragios, & Ramesh, 2003). Both

these techniques are found to be capable of dealing with a time-varying background.

Summarising, majority of the advanced tracking methods for stationary cameras make use of background subtraction to find the areas of interest like Haritaouglu et al. (Haritaoglu, Harwood, & Davis, 2000) and Collins et al. (Collins, Lipton, Fujiyoshi, & Kanade, 2001). This is due to the fact that the latest background subtraction techniques have the ability to model the changes in illumination, sporadic motion of the background textures, noise and hence they can precisely identify the objects in a range of conditions. By redeveloping the background models for smaller temporal windows, these methods could be applied to video obtained from mobile cameras, for example, three frames, from the start, Kanade et al (Kanade, Collins, Lipton, Burt, & Wixson, 1998) or by balancing the sensor motion, for example, producing background mosaics like Rowe and Blake (Rowe & Blake, 1996) and Irani and Anandan (Irani & Anandan, 1998). However, postulations of planar scenes and small motions in consecutive frames are required for both of these solutions.

Segmentation

The main objective of this procedure is to separate the target image into perceptually identical regions. Each segmentation technique deals with two main issues, the norms for a decent partition and then the technique for attaining competent separation,

Figure 7. Background subtraction based Eigenspace disintegration: (a) the input image with no objects, (b) recreated image, (c) the differential image (Nalpantidis, Georgios, & Antonios, 2008)

Shi and Malik (Shi & Malik, 2000). However, only the current segmentation practises that are appropriate for object tracking are discussed.

Mean-Shift Clustering

For dealing with the issue related to segmentation, the mean shift technique was proposed by Comaniciu and Meer (Comaniciu & Meer, 2002) to look for clusters in the combined spatial + colour space [l, u, v, x, y], where [l, u, v] stands for the colour and [x, y] stands for the spatial position. Mean Shift clustering is ascendable to several supplementary applications like detecting edges, image regularization [60] and tracking by Comaniciu et al. (Comaniciu, Ramesh, & Andmeer, 2003). This type of segmentation also necessitates fine tuning of several restrictions to attain improved segmentation, for example, selecting the colour and spatial kernel bandwidths and hence the threshold for the least size of the texture relatively affects the resultant segmentation.

Segmenting Images with the Help of Graph-Cuts

Segmentation of images could also be expressed as a graph partitioning issue by running the partisan edges in the graph. Here, the entire weight of the trimmed edges amongst the two sub graphs is known as a cut. Wu and Leahy (Wu & Leahy, 1993) made use of the least cut criterion, in which the objective is to locate those dividers, which minimize a cut. Shi and Malik (Shi & Malik, 2000) introduced the normalized cut to conquer the issue related to over segmentation. In this approach, the cut also depends on the relation of the entire connected weights of nodes in every partition for all nodes in the graph. However, this method only requires only those few parameters which are selected manually in comparison to mean-shift segmentation. Normalized cuts are also found to be used in the framework of object silhouettes being tracked, Xu and Ahuja (Xu & Ahuja, 2002).

Active Contours

In the context of active contours, the process of segmenting objects is attained by developing a closed outline for the object's boundary in a manner that the outline encompasses the object area tightly. A significant issue related to contour-based techniques is the initialization of the outlines. In image gradient based techniques, the outline is usually positioned external to the object's area and shrivelled until the object's periphery is met, Kass et al (Kass, Witkin, & Terzopoulos, 1988) and Caselles et al (Caselles, Kimmel, & Sapiro, 1995). However, these procedures necessitate previous background or object information, Paragois and Deriche (Paragois & Deriche, 2002). With the help of several frames or a single reference frame, initialization could be performed without creating prior regions. For example, the authors Paragois and Deriche (Paragois & Deriche, 2000) used background subtraction for initializing the outline.

Supervised Learning

With the help of a supervised learning technique, the process of detecting objects could be achieved by studying various views of the object spontaneously from a given set of instances. These learning techniques include decision trees, Grewe and Kak (Grewe & Kak, 1995), support vector machines Papageorgiou et al. (Papageorgiou, Oren, & Poggio, 1998), neural networks, Rowley et al. (Rowley, Baluja, & Andkanade, 1998), adaptive boosting, Viola et al. (Viola, Jones, & Snow, 2003). A probable method for reducing the quantity of data that has been labelled manually is to support co-training with supervised learning, Blum and Mitchell (Blum & Mitchell, 1998). Co training has been found to successfully lower the quantity of manual interaction that is essential for training in the framework of Adaboost, Levin et al. (Levin, Viola, & Fruend, 2003) and support vector machines, Kockelkorn et al (Kockelkorn, Luneburg, & Scheffer, 2003).

STEREO VISION-BASED OBJECT TRACKING

This section classifies the various tracking procedures into comprehensive categories. This review is focused more on the different techniques of tracking objects based on stereo vision in general and not those methods used only for tracking specific objects.

The main aim of any object tracking algorithm is to estimate the path of an object with time by tracing its relative location in each frame in the video. It also postulates the entire area of the image which has been engaged by an object during each time period. The duty of identifying the objects and to establish connection amongst the object cases across the frames could either be achieved together or distinctly. In the first instance, the object areas in each frame are attained through a detection procedure and the objects through the frames correspond to the tracker. In the second case, the correlation and the object's region is collectively appraised by updating the location of the objects repeatedly and also the region information that has been acquired from preceding frames. In both tracking methods, the appearance and shape models are utilised to represent the objects. A classification of the tracking methods is shown in Figure 8 and its corresponding demonstrative work is shown in Table 5 (Nalpantidis, Georgios, & Antonios, 2008).

The three main tracking categories are explained below:

Point Tracking

The detected objects from the successive are characterized as points and the correlation of these points depends on the state of the previous object which includes the object's position and motion. In order to identify the objects in each frame, an external procedure is required. The process of tracking can be expressed as the relation between the perceived objects which are represented across the frames as points. They are be classified into two main groups, *deterministic* & *statistical* methods. The former makes use of *qualitative motion heuristics* as proposed by Veenham et al. (Veenman, Reinders, & Backer, 2001) in order to restrict the issue of correspondence. While the latter makes use of object's measurement and takes ambiguities into consideration in order to establish correlations.

Deterministic Techniques for Correlation

The cost for correlating each object is defined in frame *t-1* to a solitary object in frame t with the help of a pair of motion constraints. Reduction of the correlation cost is expressed as a combination of the optimization issue. An explanation, which comprises of one-to-one correlations amongst

Figure 8. Classification of the tracking methods

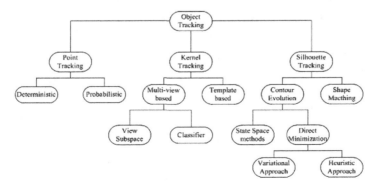

Table 5. Different categories of object tracking

Classifications	Demonstrative Work
Point Tracking	
• Deterministic methods • Statistical methods	MGE tracker (Salari & Sethi, 1990) GOA tracker (Veenman, Reinders, & Backer, 2001)
	Kalman filter (Broida & Chellappa 1986) JPDAF (Bar-Shalom & Foreman 1988) PMHT (Streit & Luginbuhl 1994)
Kernel Tracking	
• Density and Template based appearance models • Multi-view appearance models	KLT (Shi & Tomasi, 1994) Layering (Tao, Sawhney, & Kumar, 2002) Mean-shift (Comaniciu, Ramesh, & Andmeer, 2003)
	Eigentracking (Black & Jepson, 1998) SVM tracker (Avidan 2001)
Silhouette Tracking	
• Contour evolution • Matching shapes	State space models (Isard & Blake, 1998) Heuristic methods (Ronfard, 1994) Variational methods (Bertalmio et al. 2000)
	Hausdorff (Huttenlocher, Noh, & Rucklidge, 1993) Histogram (Kang, Cohen, & Medioni, 2004) Hough transform (Sato & Aggarwal 2004)

all the probable associations, is acquired by ideal methods for allocation such as Kuhn (Kuhn, 1955) or greedy search algorithms. The cost of correlation is normally expressed with the help of a permutation of the following constraints: *maximum velocity, proximity, common motion constraints and small velocity change, proximal uniformity* and *rigidity.*

By using a greedy approach depending on the rigidity and proximity constraints, Sethi and Jain (Sethi & Jain, 1987) solved the correlation issue. This algorithm takes two successive frames into account and is adjusted by the criterion of the nearest neighbour. A method proposed by Salari and Sethi (Salari & Sethi, 1990) solves this issue, by determining the correlations for the perceived points first and then extends the tracking process of the neglected objects by appending several imaginary points. Another greedy approach was proposed by Rangarajan and Shah (Rangarajan & Shah, 1991) which is hampered by proximal uniformity. Here, the preliminary correlations are acquired by calculating the optical flow from the first two frames. The occlusion is processed by determining the correlation for the points that are detected in the present frame. In the work proposed by Intille et al. (Intille, Davis, & Andbobicka, 1997), the objects are first detected with the help of background subtraction. Veenman et al. (Veenman.C., Reinders, & Backer, 2001) prolonged the work of Sethi and Jain (Sethi & Jain, 1987) and Rangarajan and Shah (Rangarajan & Shah, 1991) by presenting the *common motion* constraint for correlation. This approach is also found to handle the issues related to misdetection and occlusion. Shafique and Shah (Shafique & Shah, 2003) proposed a multi frame technique which formulated the correlation as a graph theoretic issue. They utilised a window of frames throughout point correlation in order to supervise occlusions whose periods are shorter as compared to the temporal window that is being utilised so as to perform efficient matching.

Statistical Techniques for Correlation

The magnitudes acquired from video sensors contain noise unvaryingly. Additionally the motions of the objects could also undergo random distresses such as moving vehicles. Statistical correlation methods resolve the issues related to tracking by taking into account the model uncertainties and the magnitude during the estimation of the initial object state. These methods make use of the state space methods in order to develop the object features such as velocity, location and acceleration. Such methods have been comprehensively utilised for tracking outlines, Isard and Blake (Isard & Blake, 1998), recognition of activities, Vaswani et al. (Vaswani, Roychowdhury, & Chellappa, 2003), motion structure, Matthies et al. (Matthies, Szeliski, & Kanade, 1989) and object identification, Zhou et al. (Zhou, Chellapa, & Moghadam, 2003).

Kalman Filters

Kalman filters are arithmetic approaches termed after Rudolf E. Kalman. Its main objective is to make use of measurements that have been monitored over time which comprise of noise (arbitrary variations) and additional errors, and generate values which tend to be nearer to the accurate values of the measurements and also their related calculated values (Kalman filter on Wikipedia). Over the years, it has been noted that Kalman filter has become the popular choice for solving the issues related to object tracking in computer vision, due to its predictor – collector nature. In order to track people depending on their velocity and location information, Beymer had employed a Kalman filter technique (Beymer, 2000). In his real time stereo based pose recognition and human tracking algorithm; Harville et al (Harville, 2004), both location information and occupancy were used. In this stereo based HMI (Munoz-Slinas, Aguirre, & Miguel, 2007), Munoz-Salinas had employed a Kalman filter approach to achieve object detection and tracking depending on the colour and location information.

Condensation Algorithm

It has been noted that object tracking is usually a prerequisite for object recognition and it is one of the most straightforward but difficult features of computer vision. It is seen as a non-trivial issue to categorize which pixels in an image structure the silhouette of an object. Condensation is seen as a probabilistic algorithm which helps to solve this issue. The conditional density propagation (condensation algorithm) is a computer vision technique as explained in (Condensation Algo-

rithm on Wikipedia). Its main objective is to detect and then track the outline of the moving objects in a disorderly environment. Isaard and Blake have described this algorithm in (Isard & Blake, 1998). One of the most thought-provoking aspects of this algorithm is that it doesn't seem to compute every pixel in the image. Instead, the pixels to be processed are selected at random and only their subsets are used for processing. Several theories regarding the probabilistic quality of this approach are naturally supported about what is moving where. Hyashi et al. (Hayashi, Hashimoto, Sumi, & Sasakawa, 2004) had used the condensation algorithm in their stereo based multiple human tracking scheme.

Particle Filter

The particle filters also known as the Sequential Monte Carlo methods (SMC) and they're complicated simulation techniques based on model estimation (Yilmaz, Javed, & Shah, 2006). They are usually viewed as a substitute to the Extended Kalman Filter (EKF) or Unscented Kalman filter (UKF) with the theory that with adequate illustrations, they can be able to move towards the Bayesian optimal approximation, so that they are found to be more precise than EKF and UKF.

A joint particle filter is found to experience exponential complexity while tracking several objects as the quantity of targets increase (Vermaak, Godsill, & Perez, 2005). The problem had been resolved with the help of Multiple Particle Filters (MPFs) (Vermaak, Doucet, & Perez, 2003). A MPF comprises of utilising an autonomous particle filter for each target along with an iteration factor that is able to modify the weight of the particles so as to avoid the coalescence issue. Munoz-Salinas et al. had also employed the MPF for their stereo-based object detection and tracking methods in [69 & 72]. In order to track several humans at the same time, multiple independent particle filters were utilised. The Table 6 given offers a qualitative analysis (Nalpantidis, Georgios, & Antonios, 2008).

Table 6. Qualitative analysis of the point trackers

Demonstrative work	#	Entry	Exit	Occlusion	Optimal
GE (Sethi & Jain, 1987)	M	X	X	X	X
JPDAF (Bar-Shalom & Foreman 1988)	M	X	X	X	X
Kalman (Bar-Shalom & Foreman 1988)	S	X	X	X	√
MGE (Salari & Sethi, 1990)	M	√	√	√	X
MHT (Cox & Hingorani 1996)	M	√	√	√	√
GOA (Veenman, Reinders, & Backer, 2001)	M	X	X	√	√
MFT (Shafique & Shah, 2003)	M	√	√	√	X

\# - Number of objects, S – Single object, M – Multiple objects, √ - Tracker can handle occlusions, X – Tracker can't handle occlusions

Kernel Tracking

Kernel based tracking is usually carried out by estimating the object's motion, which is signified by a simple object area, since one frame to another. The motion of the object is usually in the type of parametric motion or thick flow field processed from the consequent frames. These methods are found to differ in terms of the number of tracked object's, appearance depiction utilised and the method utilised to calculate the object's motion. Depending on the appearance depiction used, these tracking methods have been classified into two subcategories specifically templates and density based appearance models and multi view appearance models.

Tracking with the Help of Template and Density-Based Appearance Models

As the image concentration is very susceptible to changes in illumination, image gradients proposed by Birchfield (Birchfield, 1998) can also be used as features. Also, more effective techniques for template matching have been brought forward by Schweitzer et al. (Schweitzer, Bell, & Wu, 2002). By uncovering the mean colour of the pixels within the rectangular object region, Fieguth and Terzopoulos (Fieguth & Terzoupoulos, 1997) generated the object models to reduce the computational complexity. An object tracking procedure de-

pending on modelling the entire image as a set of layers was proposed by Tao et al. (Tao, Sawhney, & Kumar, 2002). A combined modelling of the foreground and background regions for tracking has been proposed by Isard and MacCormick (Isard & MacCormick, 2001) is which a combination of Gaussians is used for background appearance. A subspace-based technique to estimate the affine transformation i.e. eigenspace from the present image of the object to the image that is recreated utilising eigenvectors was proposed by Black and Jepson (Black & Jepson, 1998). Avidan (Avidan 2001) made use of a Support Vector Machine (SVM) classifier for the purpose of tracking. In this method, SVM classification score over the areas in the image are maximised and the position of the object is estimated. One high point of this method is that the information regarding the object's background is incorporated within the tracker. The Table 7 discussed offers a qualitative assessment of the trackers (Nalpantidis, Georgios, & Antonios, 2008) based on the Geometric models.

Silhouette Tracking

The objects to be tracked might have complicated shapes, for instance, head, hands, torso etc. which can't be described well by geometric shapes. Techniques based on silhouette tracking offer a precise description of their shape for such objects. Its main purpose is to discover the object area from every

Table 7. Qualitative analysis of trackers based on the geometric model

Demonstrative work	#	Motion	Training	Occlusion	Initialization
Simple template matching	S	T	X	P	√
KLT (Shi & Tomasi, 1994)	S	T + S	X	P	√
EigenTracker (Black & Jepson, 1998)	S	A	√	P	√
Bramble (Isard & MacCormick, 2001)	M	T + S + R	√	F	√
SVM (Adrian 2001)	S	T	√	P	√
Layering (Tao, Sawhney, & Kumar, 2002)	M	T + S + R	X	F	X
Mean-Shift (Comaniciu, Ramesh, & Andmeer, 2003)	S	T + S	X	P	√
Appearance tracking (Jepson et al. 2003)	S	T + S + R	X	P	√

\# - number of objects, S – single object, M – multiple objects, respectively, A – affine, T – translational motion, R – rotation, S – scaling, P – partial occlusion, F – full occlusion, Init – Initialization, √ - tracker requires initialization, X – tracker doesn't require initialization

frame with the help of an object model that has been obtained using the preceding frames. They could be classified as a colour histogram, object outline or edges. Silhouette based tracking methods have been categorised into two main groups: shape matching and contour tracking. The former looks for the object's outline in the present frame, while the latter develops a preliminary outline to its recent location in the present frame either with the help of state space model or undeviating minimization of the functional energy.

Shape matching with the help of an edge based representation was performed by Huttenlocher et al. (Huttenlocher, Noh, & Rucklidge, 1993) in which the Hausdorff distance had been utilised. Similarly, the Hausdorff distance was utilised by Li et al. (Li, Chellappa, Zheng, & Der, 2001) for authentication of the trajectories and the issue of the pose approximation. Here, tracking is accomplished by computing the optical flow vector that is computed within the postulated outline in a way that the avg flow offers the new object's location. Kang et al (Kang, Cohen, & Medioni, 2004) utilised the colour histograms and edges as object models. In comparison to conventional histograms, the authors suggested creating histograms from concentric circles with several radii positioned on a pair of control points in a reference circle.

The object state was defined by Terzopoulos and Szeliski (Terzopoulos & Szeliski, 1992). The changing aspects of the control points have been exhibited in terms of the *spring model* that shifts the control points depending on the parameters of the spring firmness. A contour tracker was proposed by Chen et al. (Chen, Rui, & Huang.T, 2001) in which the contour was parameterised as an ellipse. Every node in the contour had an HMM associated to it and each of its states was outlined by the point placed along the lines normal to the control points of the contour. Similarly, Mansouri (Mansouri, 2002) achieved contour tracking by using the optical flow constraint. Cremers and Schnorr (Cremers & Schnorr, 2005) also made use of optical flow for outline development and constraint in a manner that an object could only contain uniform flow vectors within the region. In the same context, Ronfrad (Ronfard, 1994) defined the functional energy administrating the outline evolution depending on the immobile image models expressed as Ward distances, which is the measure of the image contrast, Beaulieu and Goldberg (Beaulieu & Goldberg, 1989). The Figure 9 given shall explain the results of contour tracking (Nalpantidis, Georgios, & Antonios, 2008). Figure 9(a) shows the contour tracking of a tennis player and Figure 9(b) shows the process of contour tracking with the existence of occlusion.

Figure 9. Results of contour tracking (Nalpantidis, Georgios, & Antonios, 2008)

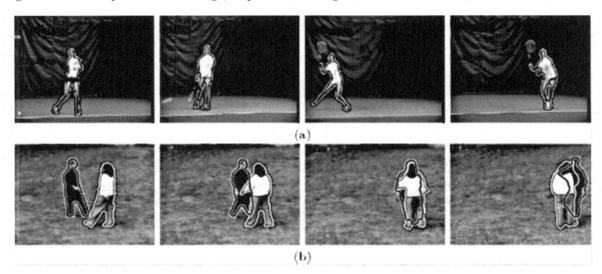

(a)

(b)

Table 8 shall offer a qualitative analysis of the various Silhouette trackers.

FUTURE RESEARCH DIRECTIONS

In the context of stereo vision based local-matching algorithms, developing a temporal seeding technique for time-consuming algorithms like graph cuts would help in reducing the computation time, hence causing the algorithm to function in real time. Since these techniques are utilized in limited context, it might be useful for applications like motion estimation. They might also result in a must faster algorithm. The main issue related with temporal seeding is error propagation and this problem can be overcome by carrying out the process for a certain number of frames and then utilizing the stereo algorithm to establish newer start-up disparities. This would result in closely packed results for temporal seeding.

For stereo vision based human object detection, developing a cheap high performance system is still the main challenge. The crucial step could be the usage of only stereovision sensors and also to implement several viable algorithms which con-

firm one another. The first algorithm could yield a set of targets which would be tracked in time and then confirmed by the remaining algorithms. Some of the confirmation criteria are presented as follows. A sub-pixel analysis is utilized to achieve appropriate accuracy. Auto-calibration methods are also needed. Since stereo vision algorithms involve considerable amount of computations, real-time performance could only be achieved with the help of powerful dedicated chipset.

Regarding stereo vision based object tracking; the future research should be focused on combining the information from several cues such as body parts, clothes etc. in order to decrease the amount of false primitives and also by incorporating the semantic map with *priori* data regarding the possible location of the people. In order to improve the human tracking process, the integration of appearance, motion models and also a Kalman filter should be considered.

The future work must also make an attempt to increase the field of view and also the range of the stereo vision system. The most effective and simple way of achieving this is to include more cameras and they should be positioned in a way that they're able to capture the data from various

Table 8. Qualitative analysis of the various silhouette tracking methods

Demonstrative Work	#	Occlusion Handling	Training	Characteristics	Method
Shape Matching					
Huttenlocher et al. (1993)	S	X	X	Edge template	Template matching
Li et al. (2002)	S	X	√	Edge template	Template matching
Sato & Aggarwal (2004)	S	√	X	Silhouette	Hough Transform
Kang et al. (2004)	S	X	X	Colour histogram	Histogram matching
Contour Evolution Making use of State Space Models					
Terzopoulos & Szeliski (1992)	S	X	√	Gradient mag	Kalman filtering
Isard & Blake (1998)	S	X	√	Gradient mag	Particle filtering
MacCormick & Blake (2000)	M	F	√	Gradient mag	Particle filtering
Chen et al. (2001)	S	X	√	Gradient mag	JPDAF
Contour Evolution Making use of Direct Minimization					
Bertalmio et al. (2000)	S	X	X	Temporal gradient	Gradient descent
Cremers et al. (2005)	S	.P	√	Region Statistics	Gradient descent
Mansouri (2002)	S	X	X	Temporal gradient	Gradient descent
Paragois & Deriche (2002)	S	X	X	Temporal gradient	Gradient descent
Yilmaz et al. (2004)	M	F	X	Region statistics	Gradient descent

\# - number of objects, S – single object, M – multiple objects, P – partial occlusion, F – full occlusion, √ - tracker can handle occlusions, X – tracker can't handle occlusions

regions around the target object. With the usage of several cameras with diverse focal lengths and baselines, the range could be further increased. Also, with the addition of more cameras, the false matching brought about by the correlation stage can be eliminated. It also leads to a more robust perception of depth.

CONCLUSION

The topics concerning stereo vision based matching; object detection and its tracking have been discussed here. Also, some of the most prominent algorithms have been addressed in all those subtopics. The concept of dual – camera stereo vision has been discussed, followed by the two main issues that surround stereo vision, namely, *correspondence* and the *reconstruction* issue. Under stereo-based object matching, the two prominent categories *dense* and *sparse* have been

explained along with the prominent algorithms for each of them. Under the category of stereo-based object detection, the concepts of *point detectors*, *background subtraction*, *segmentation* and *supervised learning* have been discussed along with the current algorithms under each group. Finally, under stereo-based object tracking, the three main subcategories namely *Point, Kernel & Silhouette* tracking have been discussed along with their current algorithms. They are further classified into *Deterministic* and *Probabilistic*, *Multi-view* and *Template based*, and *Contour evolution* and *Shape matching*.

REFERENCES

Arnaud, E. (2004). *PhD Thesis: Methods de filtrage pour du Suivi des sequences d'images - application au suivi de Points Caracteristiques*. France: Universite de Rennes I.

Banks, J. E., Bennamoun, M., Kubik, K., & Corke, P. (1997). *A Taxonomy of image matching techniques for Stere Vision*. Brisbane: Queensland University of Technology.

Beaulieu, J., & Goldberg, M. (1989). Hierarchy in picture image segmentation. [IEEE.]. *IEEE Transactions on Pattern Analysis and Machine Intelligence, 11,* 150–163. doi:10.1109/34.16711.

Beymer, D. (2000). Person Counting using Stereo. *Proceedings of Workshop on Human Motion,* (pp. 628 - 635).

Birchfield, S. (1998). Elliptical head tracking using intensity gradients and color histograms. *IEEE Conference on Computer Vision and Pattern Recognition (CVPR)* (pp. 232 - 237). IEEE.

Black, M., & Jepson, A. (1998). Eigentracking: Robust matching and tracking of articulated objects using a view-based representation. *International Journal of Computer Vision, 26*(1), 63–84. doi:10.1023/A:1007939232436.

Blum, A., & Mitchell, T. (1998). Combining labeled and unlabeled data with co-training. *11th Annual Conference on Computational Learning Theory,* (pp. 92 - 100).

Bruyelle, J. (1994). *PhD Thesis:Conception et Realisation d'un Dispotif de prise de vue Stereoscopique Lineaire - application a la Detection d' obstacles a l'avant des vehicles Routiers*. France: universite des sciences et technologies de Lille.

Burie, J., Bruyelle, J., & Postaire, J. (1995). Detecting and localising Obstacles in front of a moving Vehicle using linear Stereo Vision. *Mathematical and Computer Modelling, 22*(4-7), 235–246. doi:10.1016/0895-7177(95)00135-O.

Caselles, V., Kimmel, R., & Sapiro, G. (1995). Geodesic active contours. *IEEE International Conference on Computer Vision (ICCV)* (pp. 694 - 699). IEEE ICCV.

Chen, Y., Rui, Y., & Huang, T. (2001). Jpdaf based HMM for real - time contour tracking. *IEEE Conference on Computer Vision and Pattern Recognition (CVPR)* (pp. 543 - 550). IEEE.

Collins, R., Lipton, A., Fujiyoshi, H., & Kanade, T. (2001). Algorithms for cooperative multisensor surveillance. [IEEE.]. *Proceedings of the IEEE,* 1456–1477. doi:10.1109/5.959341.

Comaniciu, D., & Meer, P. (2002). Mean shift: A robust approach toward feature space analysis. [IEEE.]. *IEEE Transactions on Pattern Analysis and Machine Intelligence,* 603–619. doi:10.1109/34.1000236.

Comaniciu, D., Ramesh, V., & Andmeer, P. (2003). Kernel based object tracking. [IEEE.]. *IEEE Transactions on Pattern Analysis and Machine Intelligence, 25,* 564–575. doi:10.1109/TPAMI.2003.1195991.

Condensation Algorithm on Wikipedia. (n.d.). Retrieved from Wikipedia: http://en.wikipedia.org/wiki/condensationalgorithm

Cremers, D., & Schnorr, C. (2005). Statistical shape knowledge in variational motion segmentation I.Srael Nent. Cap. J. 21. *International Journal of Computer Vision, 54:2003.2005. ICCV 2005,* 1492 - 1499.

Elgammal, A., Hardwood, D., & Davis, L. (2000). Non - parametric model for background subtraction. *European Conference on Computer Vision (ECCV)* (pp. 751 - 767). ECCV.

Faugeras, O. (1993). Three-dimensional computer vision: a geometric viewpoint. MA, USA: Cambridge.

Fieguth, P., & Terzoupoulos, D. (1997). Color-based tracking of heads and other mobile objects at video frame rates. *IEEE Conference on Computer Vision and Pattern Recognition (CVPR)* (pp. 21 - 27). IEEE.

Forsyth, D. A., & Ponce, J. (2002). *Computer Vision: A Modern Approach*. Upper Saddle River, NJ, USA: Prentice Hall.

Gao, X., Boult, T., Coetzee, F., & Ramesh, V. (2000). Error analysis of background adaption. *IEEE Conference on Computer Vision and Pattern Recognition (CVPR)* (pp. 503 - 510). IEEE CVPR.

Gong, M., & Yee-Hong, Y. (2005a). Fast unambiguous stereo matching using reliability-based dynamic programming. [IEEE.]. *IEEE Transactions on Pattern Analysis and Machine Intelligence, 27*(6), 998–1003. doi:10.1109/TPAMI.2005.120 PMID:15943431.

Gong, M., & Yee-Hong, Y. (2005b). Near real-time reliable stereo matching using programmable graphics hardware. *Proceedings of IEEE Computer Society Conference on Computer Vision and Pattern Recognition* (pp. 924 - 931). IEEE.

Grewe, L., & Kak, A. (1995). Interactive learning of a multi-attribute hash table classfier for fast object recogniiton. *Computer Vision Image UNderstand., 61*, 3.

Haritaoglu, I., Harwood, D., & Davis, L. (2000). W4: real-time surveillance of people and their activities. *IEEE Transactions Pattern Analysis Mach. Intell. 22, 8* (pp. 809 - 830). IEEE.

Harris, C., & Stephens, M. (1988). A combined corner and edge detector. *In 4th Alvey Vision Conference*, (pp. 147 - 151).

Harville, M. (2004). Stereo person tracking with adaptive plan-view templates of height and occupancy statistics. IVC, 22(2).

Hayashi, K., Hashimoto, M., Sumi, K., & Sasakawa, K. (2004). Multiple-person tracker with a fixed slanting stereo camera. *Proceedings of the Sixth IEEE International Conference on Automatic Face and Gesture Recognition (FGR' 04)* (pp. 681 - 686). IEEE.

Huttenlocher, D., Noh, J., & Rucklidge, W. (1993). Tracking non - rigid objects in complex scenes. *IEEE International Conference on Computer Vision (ICCv)* (pp. 93 - 101). IEEE ICCV.

Iain, M., Takahiro, I., & Baker, S. (2003). The template update problem. [IEEE.]. *IEEE Transactions on Pattern Analysis and Machine Intelligence, 26*, 810–815. PMID:18579941.

Intille, S., Davis, J., & Andbobicka, A. (1997). Real-time closed-world tracking. *IEEE Conference on Computer Vision and Pattern Recognition (CVPR)* (pp. 697 - 703). IEEE CVPR.

Irani, M., & Anandan, P. (1998). Video indexing based on mosaic representations. *IEEE Transactions Pattern Analysis Mach. Intell. 20, 6* (pp. 577 - 589). IEEE.

Isard, M., & Blake, A. (1998). Condensation conditional density propagation for visual tracking. *International Journal of Computer Vision,* 5–28. doi:10.1023/A:1008078328650.

Isard, M., & MacCormick, J. (2001). Bramble: A bayesian multiple-blob tracker. *IEEE International Conference on Computer Vision (ICCv)* (pp. 34 - 41). IEEE.

Jain, R., & Nagel, H. (1979). On the analysis of accumulative difference pictures from image sequences of real world scenes. *IEEE Trans. Pattern Analysis Mach. Intell.1, 2* (pp. 206 - 214). IEEE.

Kalman filter on Wikipedia. (n.d.). Retrieved from Wikipedia: http://en.wikipedia.org/wiki/kalmanfilter

Kanade, T., Collins, R., Lipton, A., Burt, P., & Wixson, L. (1998). Advances in cooperative multi - sensor video surveillance. *Darpa IU Workshop* (pp. 3 - 24). Darpa IU.

Kang, J., Cohen, I., & Medioni, G. (2004). Object reacquisition using geometric invariant apperance model. *International Conference on Pattern Recognition (ICPR)* (pp. 759 - 762). ICPR.

Kass, M., Witkin, A., & Terzopoulos, D. (1988). Snakes: active contour models. *International Journal of Computer Vision, 1*, 321–332. doi:10.1007/BF00133570.

Kockelkorn, M., Luneburg, A., & Scheffer, T. (2003). Using transduction and multiview learning to answer emails. *European Conference on Principle and Practise of Knowledge Discovery in Databases*, (pp. 266 - 277).

Kuhn, H. (1955). The Hungarian method for solving the assignment problem. *Naval Research Logistics Quart., 2*, 83–97. doi:10.1002/nav.3800020109.

Levin, A., Viola, P., & Fruend, Y. (2003). Unsupervised improvement of visual detectors using co-training. *IEEE International Conference on Computer Vision (ICCV)* (pp. 626 - 633). IEEE ICCV.

Li, B., Chellappa, R., Zheng, Q., & Der, S. (2001). Model - based temporal object verification using video. [IEEE.]. *IEEE Transactions on Image Processing*, 897–908.

Liyuan, L., & Maylor, L. (2002). Integrating intensity and texture differences for robust change detection. *IEEE Transactions Image Process. 11, 2* (pp. 105 - 112). IEEE.

Lowe, D. (2004). Distinctive image features from scale-invariant keypoints. *International Journal of Computer Vision, 60*(2), 91–110. doi:10.1023/B:VISI.0000029664.99615.94.

Mansouri, A. (2002). Region tracking via level set pdes without motion computation. *IEEE Trans. Patt. Analy. Mach. Intell. 24, 7* (pp. 947 - 961). 947 - 961.

Matthies, L., Szeliski, R., & Kanade, T. (1989). Kalman filter based algorithms for estimating depth from image sequences. *International Journal of Computer Vision, 3*(3), 209–238. doi:10.1007/BF00133032.

Mikolajczyk, K., & Schmid, C. (2003). A performance evaluation of local descriptors. *IEEE Conference on Computer Vision and Pattern Recognition (CVPR)* (pp. 1615 - 1630). IEEE.

Monnet, A., Mittal, A., Paragios, N., & Ramesh, V. (2003). Background modeling and subtraction of dynamic scenes. *IEEE International Conference on Computer Vision (ICCV)* (pp. 1305 - 1312). IEEE ICCV.

Moravec, H. (1979). Visual mapping by a robot rover. *In Proceedings of the International Joint Conference on Artificial Intelligence* (pp. 598 - 600). IJCAI.

Munoz-Slinas, R., Aguirre, E., & Miguel, G.-S. (2007). People detection and tracking using stereo vision and color. *Image and Vision Computing, 25*(6), 995–1007. doi:10.1016/j.imavis.2006.07.012.

Nalpantidis, L., Georgios, C., & Antonios, G. (2008). Review of Stereo Vision Algorithms: From Software to Hardware. *International Journal of Optomechatronics, 2*, 435–462. doi:10.1080/15599610802438680.

Oliver, N., Rosario, B., & Pentland, A. (2000). A bayesian computer vision system for modeling human interactions. *IEEE Transactions Pattern Analysis Mach. Intell 22, 8* (pp. 831 - 843). IEEE.

Papageorgiou, C., Oren, M., & Poggio, T. (1998). A general framework for object detection. *IEEE International Conference on Computer Vision (ICCV)* (pp. 555 - 562). IEEE ICCV.

Paragois, N., & Deriche, R. (2000). Geodesic active contours and level sets for the detection and tracking of moving objects. *IEEE Transactions. Pattern Analysis Mach. Intell. 22, 3* (pp. 266 - 280). IEEE.

Paragois, N., & Deriche, R. (2002). Geodesic active regions and level set methods for supervised yexture segmentation. *International Journal of Computer Vision, 46*(3), 223–247. doi:10.1023/A:1014080923068.

Rangarajan, K., & Shah, M. (1991). Establishing motion correspondence. [IEEE.]. *Conference Vision Graphics Image Process, 54*, 56–73.

Rittscher, J., Kato, J., Joga, S., & Blake, A. (2000). A probabilistic background model for tracking. *European Conference on Computer Vision (ECCV) Vol.2* (pp. 336 - 350). ECCV.

Ronfard, R. (1994). Region based strategies for active contour models. *International Journal of Computer Vision, 13*(2), 229–251. doi:10.1007/BF01427153.

Rowe, S., & Blake, A. (1996). Statistical mosaics for tracking. *Israel Verj. Cap. j. 14*, 549 - 564.

Rowley, H., Baluja, S., & Andkanade, T. (1998). Neural network-based face detection. *IEEE Transactions. Pattern Analysis Mach. Intell. 20, 1* (pp. 23 - 38). IEEE.

Ruichek, Y., Hariti, M., & Issa, H. (2007). Global techniques for Edge based Stereo Matching. In R. S. (Ed), Scene reconstruction pose estimation and tracking (pp. 383-410). Austria: I-tech education and publishing.

Salari, V., & Sethi, I. K. (1990). Feature point correspondence in the presence of occlusion. [IEEE.]. *IEEE Transactions on Pattern Analysis and Machine Intelligence*, 87–91. doi:10.1109/34.41387.

Schweitzer, H., Bell, J., & Wu, F. (2002). Very fast template matching. *European Conference on Computer Vision (ECCV)* (pp. 358 - 372). IEEE.

Sethi, I., & Jain, R. (1987). Finding trajectories of feature points in a monocular image sequence. [IEEE.]. *IEEE Transactions on Pattern Analysis and Machine Intelligence*, 56–73. doi:10.1109/TPAMI.1987.4767872 PMID:21869377.

Shafique, K., & Shah, M. (2003). A non-iterative greedy algorithm for multi-frame point correspondence. *IEEE International Conference on Computer Vision (ICCV)* (pp. 110 - 115). IEEE.

Shi, J., & Malik, J. (2000). Normalized cuts and image segmentation. *IEEE Transactions Pattern Analysis Mach. Intell. 22, 8* (pp. 888 - 905). IEEE.

Shi, J., & Tomasi, C. (1994). Good features to track. *IEEE Conference on Computer Vision and Pattern Recognition* (pp. 593 - 600). IEEE CVPR.

Stauffer, C., & Grimson, W. (2000). Learning patterns of activity using real time tracking. *IEEE Transactions Pattern Analysis Mach. Intell. 22, 8* (pp. 747 - 767). IEEE.

Stenger, B., Ramesh, V., Paragois, N., Coetzee, F., & Buhmann, J. (2001). Topology free hidden markov models: Application to background modeling. *IEEE International Conference on Computer Vision (ICCV)* (pp. 294 - 301). IEEE ICCV.

Tao, H., Sawhney, H., & Kumar, R. (2002). Object Tracking with Bayesian estimation of dynamic layer representations. *IEEE Trans. Patt. Analy. Mach. Intell. 24, 1* (pp. 75 - 89). IEEE.

Terzopoulos, D., & Szeliski, R. (1992). Tracking with kalman snakes. In A. V. Yuille (Ed.), *A. Blake, & A*. MIT Press.

Toyoma, K., Krumm, J., & Meyers, B. (1999). Wallflower: Principles and practices of background maintenance. *IEEE International Conference on Computer Vision (ICCV)* (pp. 255 - 261). IEEE ICCV.

Vaswani, N., Roychowdhury, A., & Chellappa, R. (2003). Activity recognition using the dynamics of the configuration of interacting objects. *IEEE Conference on Computer Vision and Pattern Recognition (CVPR)* (pp. 633 - 640). IEEE.

Veenman, C., Reinders, M., & Backer, E. (2001). Resolving motion correspondence for densely moving points. [IEEE]. *IEEE Transactions on Pattern Analysis and Machine Intelligence*, 54–72. doi:10.1109/34.899946.

Veksler, O. (2002). Dense features for semi-dense stereo correspondence. *International Journal of Computer Vision 47(1 - 3)*, 247 - 260.

Veksler, O. (2003). Extracting dense features for visual correspondence with graph cuts. *Proceedings of IEEE Computer Society Conference on Computer Vision and Pattern Recognition* (pp. 689 - 694). IEEE.

Vermaak, J., Doucet, A., & Perez, P. (2003). Maintaining multimodality thorugh mixture tracking. *Ninth IEEE International Conference on Computer Vision* (pp. 1110 - 1116). IEEE.

Vermaak, J., Godsill, S., & Perez, P. (2005). Monte Carlo filtering for multi-target tracking and data association. [IEEE.]. *IEEE Transactions on Aerospace and Electronic Systems*, *41*, 309–332. doi:10.1109/TAES.2005.1413764.

Viola, P., Jones, M., & Snow, D. (2003). Detecting pedestrians using patterns of motion and appearance. *IEEE International Conference on Computer Vision (ICCV)* (pp. 734 - 741). IEEE ICCV.

Weiss, Y. (1999). Segmentation using Eigenvectors: a unifying view. *Proc. IEEE Internatinal Conference on Computer Vision* (pp. 975-982). IEEE Newspapers & Conf.

Wren, C., Azarbayejani, A., & Pentland, A. (1997). Pfinder: Real-time tracking of the human body. *IEEE Transactions Pattern Analysis Mach. Intell. 19, 7* (pp. 780 - 785). IEEE.

Wu, Z., & Leahy, R. (1993). An optimal graph theoretic approach to data clustering: Theory and its applications to image segmentation. [IEEE.]. *IEEE Transactions on Pattern Analysis and Machine Intelligence*, *11*, 1101–1113. doi:10.1109/34.244673.

Xu, N., & Ahuja, N. (2002). Object contour tracking using graph cuts based active contours. *IEEE International Conference on Image Processing (ICIP)* (pp. 277 - 280). IEEE ICIP.

Yilmaz, A., Javed, O., & Shah, M. (2006). Object Tracking. *Survey (London, England)*.

Zhong, J., & Sclaroff, S. (2003). Segmenting foreground objects from a dynamic textured background via a robust kalman filter. *IEEE International Conference on Computer Vision (ICCV)* (pp. 44 - 50). IEEE ICCV.

Zhou, S., Chellapa, R., & Moghadam, B. (2003). Adaptive visual tracking and recognition using particle filters. *IEEE International Conference on Multimedia and Expo (ICME)* (pp. 349 - 352). IEEE.

ADDITIONAL READING

Black, M., & Jepson, A. (1998). Eigentracking: Robust matching and tracking of articulated objects using a view-based representation. *International Journal of Computer Vision*, *26*(1), 63–84. doi:10.1023/A:1007939232436.

Collins, R., Lipton, A., Fujiyoshi, H., & Kanade, T. (2001). Algorithms for cooperative multisensor surveillance. *Proceedings of the IEEE*, 1456–1477. doi:10.1109/5.959341.

Forsyth, D. A., & Ponce, J. (2002). *Computer vision: A modern approach*. Upper Saddle River, NJ: Prentice Hall.

Haritaoglu, I., Harwood, D., & Davis, L. (2000). W4: Real-time surveillance of people and their activities. *IEEE Transactions on Pattern Analysis and Machine Intelligence*, 22(8), 809–830. doi:10.1109/34.868683.

Isard, M., & Blake, A. (1998). Condensation conditional density propagation for visual tracking. *International Journal of Computer Vision*, 5–28. doi:10.1023/A:1008078328650.

Kanade, T., Collins, R., Lipton, A., Burt, P., & Wixson, L. (1998). Advances in cooperative multi - sensor video surveillance. In *Proceedings of the Darpa IU Workshop* (pp. 3 - 24). Darpa IU.

Monnet, A., Mittal, A., Paragios, N., & Ramesh, V. (2003). Background modeling and subtraction of dynamic scenes. In *Proceedings of the IEEE International Conference on Computer Vision (ICCV)* (pp. 1305 - 1312). IEEE.

Papageorgiou, C., Oren, M., & Poggio, T. (1998). A general framework for object detection. In *Proceedings of the IEEE International Conference on Computer Vision (ICCV)* (pp. 555 - 562). IEEE.

Ronfard, R. (1994). Region based strategies for active contour models. *International Journal of Computer Vision*, 13(2), 229–251. doi:10.1007/BF01427153.

Shi, J., & Tomasi, C. (1994). Good features to track. In *Proceedings of the IEEE Conference on Computer Vision and Pattern Recognition* (pp. 593 - 600). IEEE.

Veksler, O. (2002). Dense features for semi-dense stereo correspondence. *International Journal of Computer Vision, 47*(1 - 3), 247 - 260.

Wu, Z., & Leahy, R. (1993). An optimal graph theoretic approach to data clustering: Theory and its applications to image segmentation. *IEEE Transactions on Pattern Analysis and Machine Intelligence, 11*, 1101–1113. doi:10.1109/34.244673.

KEY TERMS AND DEFINITIONS

Background Subtraction: It is a procedure utilised in image processing techniques to deduct unrelenting noise patterns which are generated in the optical system.

Disparity: Each lens captures its own view and then two independent images are sent to the system for processing. The system compares the images while shifting the two images together over top of each other to find the parts that match. The shifted amount is called disparity.

Feature Extraction: A group of operations in digital image processing in which certain features like boundaries of objects, shapes, areas etc. are enhanced selectively for image analysis or pattern recognition.

Object Detection: Object tracking is defined as a procedure where a significant object contained by an image would then be tracked while the object shifts about in the image.

Object Tracking: The process of estimating the path of an object with time by tracing its relative location in each frame in the video.

Segmentation: The main objective of this procedure is to separate the target image into perceptually identical regions.

Stereo Matching: The purpose of any stereo matching activity is to propose an explanation for which the matches can be seen as consistent as possible with regards to particular constraints, such as local constraints (position and slope) and global constraints (smoothness, uniqueness, and ordering).

Stereo Vision: It is the extraction of 3D information from digital images by examining the relative positions of the objects captured by the dual cameras.

Chapter 6
Feature–Based Affine Motion Estimation for Superresolution of a Region of Interest

Sung Hyun Kim
Sogang University, Korea

Rae-Hong Park
Sogang University, Korea

Seungjoon Yang
Ulsan National Institute of Science and Technology, Korea

Hwa-Young Kim
Sogang University, Korea

ABSTRACT

This chapter presents an interpolation method of low-computation for a Region Of Interest (ROI) using multiple low-resolution images of the same scene. Interpolation methods using multiple images require the accurate motion information between the reference image of interpolation and the other images. Sometimes complex local motions applied to the entire images are estimated incorrectly, yielding seriously degraded interpolation results. The authors apply the proposed Superresolution (SR) method, which employs a simple global motion model, only to the ROI that contains important information of the scene. The ROIs extracted from multiple images are assumed to have simple global motions. At first, using a mean absolute difference measure, they extract the regions from the multiple images that are similar to the selected ROI in the reference image of interpolation and use feature points to estimate the affine motion parameters. The authors apply the Projection Onto Convex Sets (POCS)-based method to the ROI using the estimated motion, simplify the iterative computation of the whole system, and use an edge-preserving smoothing filter to reduce the distortion caused by additive noise. In experiments, they acquire test image sets with a hand-held digital camera and use a Gaussian noise model. Experimental results show that the feature-based Motion Estimation (ME) is accurate and reducing the computational load of the ME step is efficient in terms of the computational complexity. It is also shown that the SR results using the proposed method are remarkable even when input images contain complex motions and a large amount of noise. The proposed POCS-based SR algorithm can be applied to digital cameras, portable camcorders, and so on.

DOI: 10.4018/978-1-4666-4868-5.ch006

INTRODUCTION

In digital multimedia and consumer applications, Resolution Enhancement (RE) of images or video with image details is desired. For example, a high-quality digital image is obtained from a single or multiple Low-Resolution (LR) images or video (Park, et al., 2003; Islam, et al., 2010). Also, digital zooming of the Region Of Interest (ROI) is one of important multimedia or surveillance applications. RE can be achieved by denoising, deblurring, or reconstruction of image details. Digital images are magnified with some image quality degradation. Image interpolation using a single image usually gives image degradation such as blurring of edges and image details. Techniques to achieve higher RE of an image or video in imaging system, using a single or multiple images, are called Superresolution (SR). SR has various applications such as digital television, medical imaging, remote sensing, and so on (Meijering, 2002). Success of SR depends on image interpolation.

Simple linear interpolation methods such as nearest neighbor, bilinear, and bicubic interpolation, based on space-invariant models, are generally used for the computational simplicity, with low-quality image containing some blurred edges and blocking artifacts. For better subjective performance, many interpolation methods have been proposed; including an edge-guided interpolation method via directional filtering and data fusion (Zhang & Wu, 2006), an image magnification method based on similarity analogy (Chen, et al., 2009), a ramp edge model to maintain both the continuity and sharpness of edges (Leu, 2001), a directional interpolation based on the estimated orientation of edges and ridges (Wang & Ward, 2003), a RE method based on Laplacian pyramid representation (Takahashi & Taguchi, 2003; Jeon, et al., 2006), a frequency domain based method (Islam, et al., 2012), a wavelet-based interpolation method (Chang, et al., 2006), training based methods (Freeman, et al., 2002; Sun, et al., 2003), and an interpolative classified vector quantization

method (Hong, et al., 2008). Recently, a sparsity-based patch-based SR method using dictionaries is proposed (Jianchao, et al., 2010). Also a SR reconstruction of multispectral data is presented to improve the clustering and classification efficiency (Li, et al., 2009). A performance evaluation of various interpolation and SR algorithms is presented for various gray level and color images by using both objective measures and subjective evaluation (Ye & Lu, 2011).

SR methods using multiple LR images of the same scene produce the HR image by utilizing sub-pixel information of LR images (Park, et al., 2003; Van Eekeren, et al., 2010). These SR methods generally assume the degradation models and find the solutions, in which motion information between the LR images is needed. Motion Estimation (ME) is very important for obtaining sub-pixel information from multiple LR images. Also, a scene-based video SR using minimum mean square error estimation is presented (Cao, et al., 2011). A joint method for multiframe demosaicing and SR of color images is presented (Farsiu, et al., 2006).

A large number of SR techniques have been investigated with different degradation models for image restoration (Park, et al., 2003). SR methods using multiple images include non-uniform interpolation (Maymon & Oppenheim, 2011), SR reconstruction of compressed video using transform domain statistics (Gunturk et al., 2004), Iterative Back Projection (IBP) (Song, et al., 2010), regularization approach (Tom & Katsaggelos, 2001), and Projection Onto Convex Sets (POCS) (Patti, et al., 1997; Tang, et al., 2011). Because the SR method in the frequency domain is restricted to assume a simple motion model, the spatial domain approaches have been commonly used. In conventional SR methods using multiple images, different ME approaches have been adopted: block matching algorithms (BMAs) for translational models (Tom & Katsaggelos, 2001; Molina, et al., 2003; Cetin & Ari, 2012), gradient descent methods for affine models (Patti, et al., 1997; Tang, et al., 2011;

Bergen, et al., 1992; Paragios & Deriche, 2005), and object-based ME for complex motion models and local motions (Eren, et al., 1997). BMAs are suitable only for translational motions and ME by the affine motion model is limited to global motions. The object-based method is robust to complex motions but needs a high computational complexity since it requires object segmentation and ME of foreground and background layers. Also, a joint POCS SR method combined with compressive sensing theory is proposed (Liu & Wu, 2011).

The performance of the conventional SR methods using multiple LR images is remarkable and ME used in these algorithms is very accurate. However, they do not have proper application examples, because they have a too high computational load to be applied to commercial application devices. Thus, a low computational algorithm is needed for easy and practical implementations. The SR methods using multiple images estimate the accurate sub-pixel information, which will be effective especially when input images include regions such as text to be recognized. In that case, we do not need to interpolate an entire image that may contain a number of regions with different local motions. Thus, we propose a method to interpolate only the ROI (Gonzalez & Woods, 2010; Seong & Park, 2008). The motion between ROIs can be simpler than that between full images and thus we can solve problems by directly applying simple ME methods to the ROIs. With a single motion model, accurate ME of the entire LR image, which contains several objects with complex, nonlinear, or nonuniform motions, can be very difficult (Chung, et al., 2006). Inaccurate ME leads to degradation of the reconstructed image. In order to eliminate this drawback, we simply propose an ME method of an ROI by assuming a simple motion model.

This chapter is an extended and updated version of the paper (Kim, et al., 2008), in which the proposed algorithm is described and analyzed in more detail. Also, experimental results of the proposed and existing algorithms are compared with more test images. In the proposed algorithm, the region of the rectangular shape, which is similar to the region or object in the reference image of interpolation, is detected from each of multiple images except for the reference image. Its computational load is lower than the conventional method (Eren, et al., 1997) that requires complicated algorithms for object segmentation and ME of the foreground and background. We use a simple region matching algorithm for detection of similar ROIs from multiple images and apply the global ME method under the assumption that detected ROIs undergo simple global motions (Shi & Tomasi, 1994; Chai & Shi, 2011; Hartley & Zisserman, 2004). To reduce a computational load of ME, we employ the feature-based affine parameter estimation, which extracts only once the motion information between LR images. For SR, we apply motion information to the POCS-based SR method. For noisy images, the performance of the SR techniques is degraded due to the sensitivity of a feature extraction scheme to small intensity variations or noise. Thus, we employ the bilateral filter as a preprocessing step (Tomasi & Manduchi, 1998). Simulation results show that the ROI context in the proposed method makes complex ME problems simple and the presented feature-based ME is efficient in terms of a computational load. Also the bilateral filter is useful for SR of noisy images.

The rest of the chapter is organized as follows. In the second section, we describe previous SR methods using multiple images and in the third section, we propose the POCS-based SR algorithm for interpolating an ROI. Next, experimental results are presented, showing the effectiveness of the feature-based ME method, in terms of the ME accuracy and the computational load. Also, the performance of the proposed POCS-based SR method using multiple frames and the bilateral filter is shown. Finally, we conclude the chapter.

SR Techniques Using Multiple LR images

Each of LR images of the same scene has the similar objects or regions with different relative motions and thus contains the sub-pixel information of a HR image, for which SR using multiple LR images is useful.

The SR method using multiple LR images is a generalization of the restoration technique using a single image. The degradation model is generally expressed in vector-matrix form as

$$\mathbf{y}_k = \mathbf{DB}_k\mathbf{M}_k\mathbf{x} + \mathbf{n}_k \qquad (1)$$

where $\mathbf{x}$ and $\mathbf{y}_k$ are the original HR image and the k-th degraded LR image, respectively, and $\mathbf{n}_k$ represents the noise in the k-th image (Park, et al., 2003), all being expressed as one-dimensional (1-D) vectors. $\mathbf{M}_k$, $\mathbf{B}_k$, and $\mathbf{D}$ are the k-th motion, k-th blurring, and downsampling matrices, respectively. The HR image $\mathbf{x}$ is transformed into the k-th LR image by motion $\mathbf{M}_k$, blurring $\mathbf{B}_k$, and then downsampling $\mathbf{D}$. Finally the k-th LR image $\mathbf{y}_k$ is obtained after a noise term $\mathbf{n}_k$ is added. To solve the ill-posed problem of (1), a number of techniques have been proposed, for example, the regularization approach (Tom & Katsaggelos, 2001), POCS (Patti, et al., 1997; Tang, et al., 2011), and so on.

The regularization-based SR approach (Tom & Katsaggelos, 2001; Suo, et al., 2011) is expressed as:

$$\hat{\mathbf{x}}^{n+1} =$$
$$\hat{\mathbf{x}}^n + \beta\left[\sum_{k=1}^{P}(\mathbf{DB}_k\mathbf{M}_k)^T(\mathbf{y}_k - \mathbf{DB}_k\mathbf{M}_k\hat{\mathbf{x}}^n) - \alpha\mathbf{C}^T\mathbf{C}\hat{\mathbf{x}}^n\right]$$
$$(2)$$

where $\mathbf{C}$ represents a highpass filter, P is the total number of LR images employed, α denotes a regularization parameter, β signifies a convergence control parameter, the superscript n is the iteration index, and the superscript T denotes the transpose operation. $\hat{\mathbf{x}}^n$ is updated by the residual term that is defined by the difference between the LR pixel value and the value projected onto LR grid (as expressed by $\sum_{k=1}^{P}(\mathbf{DB}_k\mathbf{M}_k)^T(\mathbf{y}_k - \mathbf{DB}_k\mathbf{M}_k\hat{\mathbf{x}}^n)$). The regularization parameter α regulates adaptively the data, updating the HR sub-pixel values and smoothing the updated pixels with a lowpass filter. The regularization term $\mathbf{C}^T\mathbf{C}\hat{\mathbf{x}}^n$ reduces the influences of the noise and the distortion caused by incorrect ME. If ME is accurate and noise is not added, α is small. Otherwise, α is large. The image after passing $\hat{\mathbf{x}}^n$ through a highpass filter (weighted by $\alpha\beta$) is subtracted from $\hat{\mathbf{x}}^n$, which corresponds to lowpass filtering. In summary, the regularization approach interpolates an image using the regularized IBP.

POCS is expressed as:

$$\mathbf{x}_{k+1} = \mathbf{P}_m\mathbf{P}_{m-1}\cdots\mathbf{P}_1\mathbf{x}_k, \qquad k = 0, 1, \cdots \qquad (3)$$

where $\mathbf{P}_i$, $1 \le i \le m$, denotes the operator to project $\mathbf{x}_k$ onto the i-th convex constraint set. A signal $\mathbf{x}$ in the Hilbert domain reaches an intersection between constraint sets by repeatedly projecting the signal onto each convex set (Patti, et al., 1997; Tang, et al., 2011; Panda, et al., 2011). POCS can also be applied to SR using multiple images. In the image domain, constraint sets consist of a set of LR images of similar objects with different motions. Projection is accomplished by the motion warping, blur filtering, and downsampling. Thus, by projecting any sub-pixel value onto the intersection of constraint sets, we can find the solution. In POCS-based SR performed as a non-linear method, the constraint sets can be expressed as

$$C_{t_r}(m_1, m_2, k) = \left\{ x(n_1, n_2, t_r) \,\middle|\, \left|r^{(x)}(m_1, m_2, k)\right| \le \delta_0(m_1, m_2, k) \right\} \qquad (4)$$

with the residual $r^{(x)}(m_1,m_2,k)$ represented by:

$$r^{(x)}(m_1,m_2,k) = \\ y(m_1,m_2,k) - \sum_{(n_1,n_2)} x(n_1,n_2,t_r)h_{t_r}(n_1,n_2;m_1,m_2,k) \quad (5)$$

where (m_1,m_2) $((n_1,n_2))$ denotes the LR (HR) grid. $x(n_1,n_2,t_r)$ signifies a desired HR pixel value at time reference t_r, $y(m_1,m_2,k)$ represents an observed LR pixel data at frame k, and $h_{t_r}(n_1,n_2;m_1,m_2,k)$ is a blur function. In (4), $\delta_0(m_1,m_2,k)$ is a bound that determines the solution to be updated, in proportion to the standard deviation of the noise.

The projection operator of POCS is expressed as presented in Box 1 where $P_{t_r}(m_1,m_2,k)\left[x(n_1,n_2,t_r)\right]$ represents that

$x(n_1,n_2,t)$ is updated by the projection operator $P_{t_r}(m_1,m_2,k)$. $\delta_0(m_1,m_2;k)$ decides whether or not the sub-pixel value at the HR grid is to be updated, in which selection of $\delta_0(m_1,m_2;k)$ value plays an important role in noise reduction.

As previously stated, the performance of the SR methods using multiple images is better than that of the SR methods using a single image, under the assumption that the motion operator $\mathbf{M}_k$ yields the accurate motion field. But if the motion field is estimated incorrectly, the motion information yields the noticeable error in the interpolated image (Eren, et al., 1997; Suo, et al., 2011). Especially, if a motion model is complex or there exist a number of local motions, serious performance degradation occurs, requiring a higher computational load.

Table 1. Comparison of the feature-based and conventional motion estimation methods in terms of the processing time (unit: sec) on Pentium-IV (2.3 GHz)

Test images		Feature-based	Conventional
Box	1st, 2nd	0.28	4.81
	1st, 3rd	0.25	4.68
	1st, 4th	0.23	4.61
Books	1st, 2nd	0.28	4.92
	1st, 3rd	0.27	4.79
	1st, 4th	0.25	5.11
License plate	1st, 2nd	0.09	1.46
	1st, 3rd	0.06	1.46
	1st, 4th	0.06	1.50
Calendar	1st, 2nd	0.08	1.42
	1st, 3rd	0.08	1.54
	1st, 4th	0.08	1.42

Box 1.

$$P_{t_r}(m_1, m_2, k)\left[x(n_1, n_2, t_r)\right] = x(n_1, n_2, t)$$

$$+ \begin{cases} \dfrac{(r^{(x)}(m_1, m_2; k) - \delta_0(m_1, m_2; k))h_{t_r}(n_1, n_2; m_1, m_2; k)}{\displaystyle\sum_{o_1}\sum_{o_2} h_{t_r}^2(o_1, o_2; m_1, m_2; k)}, & r^{(x)}(m_1, m_2; k) > \delta_0(m_1, m_2; k) \\[1em] 0, & r^{(x)}(m_1, m_2; k) \le \left|\delta_0(m_1, m_2; k)\right| \\[1em] \dfrac{(r^{(x)}(m_1, m_2; k) + \delta_0(m_1, m_2; k))h_{t_r}(n_1, n_2; m_1, m_2; k)}{\displaystyle\sum_{o_1}\sum_{o_2} h_{t_r}^2(o_1, o_2; m_1, m_2; k)} & r^{(x)}(m_1, m_2; k) < -\delta_0(m_1, m_2; k) \end{cases} \quad (6)$$

PROPOSED POCS-BASED SR ALGORITHM OF AN ROI

Motivation of the Proposed Algorithm

The conventional ME methods employed in SR include local ME methods: block-based BMAs or pixel-based optical flow techniques. There are also global ME methods, for example, affine and perspective models. Estimation of the simple translational motion by BMAs with two translation parameters is too restrictive for general description of motions whereas the global ME methods with more than two parameters (Molina, et al., 2003; Bergen, et al., 1992; Paragios & Deriche, 2005) require a high computational load. The computation-intensive method (Eren, et al., 1997) was presented, in which an image is segmented into several objects and the local motion of each object is estimated.

At this time, we must consider the objective of these SR techniques. We may want an entire image to be interpolated and enhanced. However, if we want to restore accurately only a small portion of the image that contains alphanumerics and to reduce the computational load, we do not need to interpolate the whole image. Then, we can convert the complicated ME problem of a whole

image into the simplified global ME problem of the ROI. In this context, we make an attempt to interpolate only an ROI using multiple images. At first, we select an ROI from any of LR images (reference image of interpolation) and extract the similar regions from the other LR images. In the case of noisy images, an edge-preserving filter is used to reduce the noise and the ME error. After estimating the motions between the similar regions in multiple images, finally we interpolate these ROIs using the iterative POCS method (Patti, et al., 1997; Tang, et al., 2011).

Figure 1 shows an example of the application using the SR technique of an ROI. Our proposed algorithm can be employed in the device such as a digital camcorder. If a user selects the region that the user wants to see in detail, the algorithm finds the similar regions from temporally adjacent frames in the acquired video data, and carries out the image SR of the ROI. This interpolated, vivid image also can be used in the optical character recognition system as a pre-processing step.

Figure 2 shows the block diagram of the proposed SR algorithm of an ROI that consists of four steps: 1) ROI extraction by the region matching algorithm, 2) noise reduction, 3) feature-based affine ME, and 4) SR by the iterative POCS method.

Figure 1. An example of interpolation of an ROI using multiple LR images

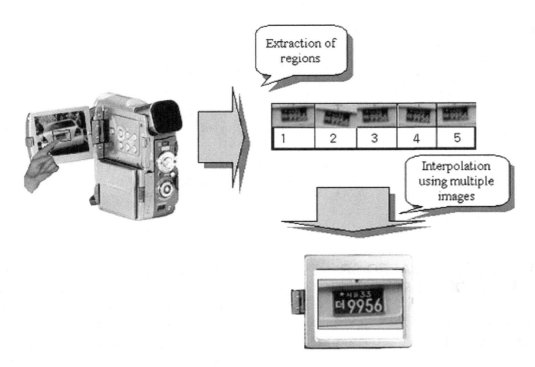

Figure 2. Block diagram of the proposed POCS-based interpolation algorithm of an ROI using multiple LR images

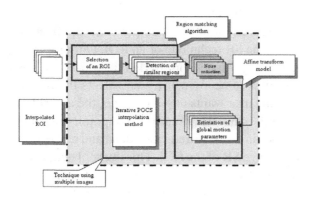

Extraction of an ROI

Accurate extraction of the ROIs from the multiple images is not required, because the goal of this process is to simplify the ME procedure that will

be performed in the next stage. Let $I(m_1, m_2, k)$ denote the LR intensity image at (m_1, m_2) at frame k. We employ the mean absolute difference (MAD) as a matching measure to detect the ROI (Gonzalez & Woods, 2010), which is expressed as:

$$MAD(d_1, d_2) = \frac{1}{MN} \sum_{m_1=P_1}^{P_1+M-1} \sum_{m_2=P_2}^{P_2+N-1} \left| I(m_1, m_2, t_r) - I(m_1+d_1, m_2+d_2, k) \right|,$$
$$|d_1| \leq S_1, \quad |d_2| \leq S_2$$

(7)

where (P_1, P_2) represents the coordinate value of the top left corner of the rectangular ROI that a user selects, $M \times N$ signifies the size of the ROI, t_r denotes the time reference, and $(2S_1 + 1) \times (2S_2 + 1)$ is the search area size. The MAD criterion detects the optimal (d_1, d_2) that yields the smallest value. With ROIs detected roughly from other images, in the next step accurate ME is performed. Figure 3 shows the example of the ROI extraction, in which the global motions such as translation and rotation exist between two frames.

Feature-Based ME

For accurate ME, motion information in a more general motion model is needed. For ME, the motion model should be s elected in advance. A low-complexity image registration method for global ME was proposed, in which a gradient descent based method with an affine motion model is presented (Haque, et al., 2012).

We assume the affine motion model as a motion model. To obtain the affine motion parameters, the conventional SR techniques using multiple images have employed the gradient descent method. A gradient descent method is robust to the video sequence with the global motion, since the outliers such as local motions can be eliminated by iteration until the residual error becomes small. The extracted ROI does not contain local motions, and thus the gradient descent method robust to outliers is not required. To reduce a computational load,

we apply a feature-based global ME method to SR using multiple images.

At first, in a single image, we find feature points using the eigenvalues for x-, y-, and xy-directional gradients, in which more than three pairs of feature points are needed for estimation of six affine motion parameters. To find the corresponding feature points, a Kanade-Lucas-Tomasi (KLT) feature tracker is used (Shi & Tomasi, 1994; Chai & Shi, 2011), in which the gradient descent method is employed with a small number of feature points.

POCS-Based SR

As the final step of the proposed SR of an ROI, POCS is used. As an initial interpolator, we use a cubic spline method. Feature-based ME is performed once between extracted LR ROIs for reducing the computational load, and the detected motion information is applied to the iterative POCS. The pixel-based global ME used in the conventional SR technique is performed iteratively in the POCS algorithm until the motion error becomes the minimum. On the other hand, ME of the proposed algorithm is not carried out in the

Figure 3. ROI specified by a user in the reference image of interpolation

ROI in a reference image

Detected region in the other image

iterative POCS stage, so the processing time can be reduced remarkably.

Pre-Filtering by a Bilateral Filter

The performance of ME and image enhancement is greatly dependent on noise, thus pre-filtering has been used for noise reduction in a video codec that utilizes wavelet-based ME, in which a novel motion field filtering step for video denoising was used (Pizurica, et al., 2007). The conventional SR methods using multiple images also have considered the noise. Note that the more the amount of noise is, the lower the performance of SR is. We use a noise reduction filter as the pre-processing stage in our algorithm.

The regularization algorithm in (2) reduces the noise by controlling the regularization parameter. If the amount of noise is large, lowpass filtering is required, however the fine details of the interpolated image will be lost as well. The POCS method also reduces the noise by employing the constraint sets. If the Gaussian noise with the standard deviation σ is added to the image, δ_0 is set to $c\sigma$, where c is set to 3 when the statistical confidence of 99% is assumed (Panda, et al., 2011). Thus, in (6), the noise can be decreased by increasing δ_0 value. However, this method also has the limitation on the performance of noise reduction. Therefore, to efficiently reduce the noise, a noise reduction stage is needed as a preprocessing step. To prevent the edge blurring by lowpass filtering, a nonlinear edge preserving smoothing filter is required.

Figure 4 shows the bilateral filter used in this chapter as an edge-preserving filter (Tomasi & Manduchi, 1998). This filter also has been employed as the regularization method in the SR algorithm using multiple images (Farsiu, et al., 2004), however, in this chapter, the filter is used once for reducing the noise and ME error in the input stage of the whole system, as shown in Figure 2. For a noisy input image, the Gaussian lowpass

filter and the edge stop function are used, in which an input parameter, the pixel gradient value of the input, is used. With small (large) Gaussian weights, the edge is preserved (smoothed). The bilateral filter is expressed as

$$y'(n_1, n_2) =$$
$$\frac{1}{w(n_1, n_2)} \sum_{m_1} \sum_{m_2} G(m_1, m_2) l(y(n_1 - m_1, n_2 - m_2) - y(n_1, n_2)) y(n_1 - m_1, n_2 - m_2)$$

$$(8)$$

where y represents an input noisy image, G signifies the Gaussian function, l denotes the edge stop function, w is a normalization term represented by:

$$w(n_1, n_2) =$$
$$\sum_{m_1} \sum_{m_2} G(m_1, m_2) l(y(n_1 - m_1, n_2 - m_2), y(n_1, n_2))$$

$$(9)$$

and y' denotes the final filtered image. l as an edge stop function is expressed as:

$$l(i) = e^{-\frac{1}{2}\left(\frac{i}{\sigma_b}\right)^2} \tag{10}$$

where the weight is controlled by σ_b value. Simulation results with noisy images show that POCS combined with the bilateral filter as a preprocessing is very effective for noise reduction.

EXPERIMENTAL RESULTS AND DISCUSSIONS

In this section, we present the experimental results of the proposed algorithm for SR of the ROI and show the performance of noise reduction by the bilateral filter. In the first experiment, we extract the regions from input frames that are similar to the ROI, selected by a user from the reference frame of interpolation (note that a set

Figure 4. Bilateral filtering for noise reduction

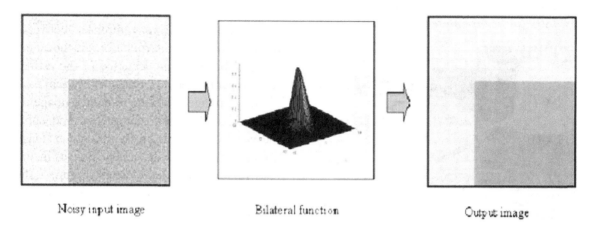

Noisy input image   Bilateral function   Output image

of test images consists of four frames of the same scene with the reference image of interpolation specified, in which a user selects the ROI). Each reference image is arbitrarily selected from four test images. The second experiment shows the accuracy of the estimated motion parameters in terms of the difference image. Also we compare the computation time of the feature-based ME method with the pixel-based method. The third experiment shows the SR result of the ROI using the POCS method. The last experiment shows that noise is reduced greatly by the proposed SR method compared with the bilateral filter.

Test LR Input Images

Generally, to compare quantitatively the SR performance, researchers decimate an original image, interpolate the decimated image using their algorithms, and compute a Peak Signal to Noise Ratio (PSNR) between the original image and the interpolated image. In this chapter, we just interpolate the original image, since we are interested in more practical situations where real images containing local motions are obtained by a digital camera. Without original HR images, we cannot compute quantitative measures such as the PSNR. The performance of the proposed method can be evaluated visually.

We use test images as shown in Figure 5; three test sets of 640×480 input images (of the same scene) in Figures 5(a), 5(b), and 5(c) are acquired by a digital camera. Figure 5(a) shows the reference Box image, one of four Box images that contain simple translations as a global motion. Figure 5(b) shows the reference Books image, one of four Books images that have translational and rotational motions. Figure 5(c) shows the reference License plate image, one of four license plate images that also contain translational and rotational motions.

Extraction of the ROI Using a Region Matching Algorithm

When selecting the ROI, we find the regions that include the important information such as texts in the Box and Books images, and the numbers in License plate. Note that the size of the ROI is set to 200×200 (Box and Books images) or 100×100 pixels (License plate). Figure 6 shows the ROIs extracted from input images, in which the reference images of SR are shown in the leftmost column. In Figure 6(a), since Box images contain only translations, similar regions are detected correctly using (7) with the smallest MAD. In Figures 6(b) and 6(c) containing translations and rotations, the detected ROIs still contain the ro-

(a)

(b)

(c)

tational motion, so the registration step for a rotation model is necessary.

Affine ME Using Feature Points

Figure 7 shows the experimental result of the global motion parameter estimation, in which the inverted

difference image is shown with the dark (white) region representing the large (small) difference. In experiments, ME is accomplished between the reference image of interpolation and the other test images. To show the accuracy of the estimated motion parameters, we transform (warp) each of three test images onto the reference image using the estimated motion parameters and subtract the warped image from the reference image to obtain the inverted difference image, in which dark regions show large errors. Figure 7 shows that ME is performed correctly on the whole. The pixels that are not transformed in warping are replaced by the linearly interpolated value using the neighboring pixels, thus the transformed image is blurred, resulting in errors near edges. Also the border pixels of the transformed image do not have pixel information, thus intensity differences between those pixels and the pixels in the reference image are large.

Table 1 shows the comparison of the feature-based method and the pixel-based method in terms of the computation time on PC (Pentium-IV, 2.3 GHz CPU). As shown in Table 1, the computational load of the feature-based method is lower than that of the conventional method (by a factor of 14 on the average), since the latter requires the gradient computations over all the pixels in the image whereas the former carries out the operations at only a small number of detected feature points.

SR of the ROI

This experiment shows the SR results of the ROI by the proposed method in which feature-based ME is combined with POCS. In this experiment, we compare the interpolated image by the proposed POCS-based method with those of other methods; bi-linear, POCS methods using an incremental motion estimator (Bergen, et al., 1992; Paragios & Deriche, 2005). In experiments, we use the BMA, in which the block size is 16×16, the search range is from -11 to 11, and the MAD is used as

Figure 6. Extracted ROIs from input images. The leftmost ROIs are selected by a user from the reference images of interpolation: (a) box (200×200), (b) books (200×200), (c) license plate (100×100)

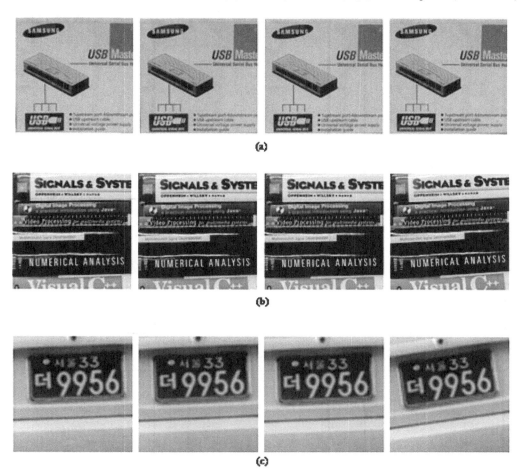

a matching function. In both POCS methods, a Gaussian model (Gaussian standard deviation: 1) is used as the blur operator and we set δ_0 to 1 assuming noise-free conditions and set the number of iterations to 5.

Figure 8 shows the SR results of the test images by three methods scaled up horizontally and vertically by a factor of two: 400×400 in Figure 8(a), and 200×200 in Figures 8(b) and 8(c), in which for easy comparison, we cut and magnify portions of the SR results. Images in Figure 8 are arranged from left to right as the images reconstructed by the bi-linear, conventional POCS, and proposed POCS-based methods.

In Figure 8(a), the resulting image of the bi-linear method is blurred on the whole and we cannot recognize texts correctly. Interpolated images by the POCS using an incremental motion estimator and the proposed POCS-based algorithm are remarkable, so we can recognize clearly characters. The image interpolated by the proposed POCS-based method with the low computational complexity for ME is similar to that of the conventional POCS. In Figure 8(b), the images interpolated by conventional POCS and the proposed method are also good. In Figure 8(c), the image interpolated by the bi-linear method is blurred on the whole, especially texts over numbers and the

Figure 7. Inverted difference images between the ROI in the reference image and the transformed ROIs: (a) box (200×200), (b) books (200×200), (c) license plate (100×100)

horizontal lines under numbers are not clear. The conventional POCS and the proposed POCS-based method yield sharp and vivid results with small motion errors.

Noise Reduction by the Bilateral Filter

In this experiment, we demonstrate that the proposed POCS-based method using the bilateral filter yields better performance than the conven-

tional POCS method when the noise is severe. For noisy cases, we add the Gaussian noise with standard deviation 10. Figure 9 shows, from left to right, the result of the bi-cubic interpolation method without noise reduction, the conventional POCS method, and the proposed POCS-based method using a bilateral filter. For easy comparison, we cut and magnify portions of the interpolated results: 400×400 in Figures 9(a) and 9(b), and 200×200 in Figure 9(c). In Figure 9(a), the resulting image by the bi-cubic interpolation

Figure 8. Performance comparison of SR techniques (bi-linear, conventional POCS [δ_0 =1, 5 iterations], and the proposed POCS-based method [δ_0 = 1, 5 iterations]): (a) box (400×400), (b) books (400×400), (c) license plate (200×200)

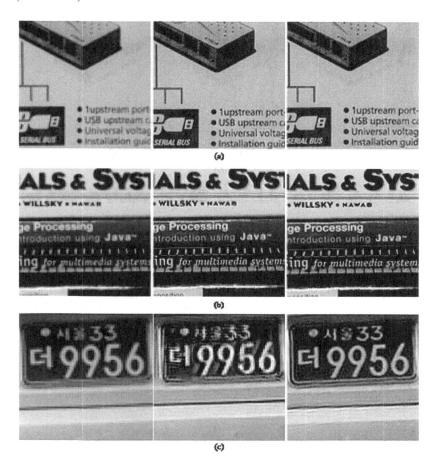

without noise reduction is severely degraded by the noise. On the other hand, the image interpolated by the conventional POCS method shows that the noise is reduced by controlling δ_0 of (6) (δ_0 =15, 25 iterations), however the noise still remains. By applying the bilateral filter to the POCS method, the noise is reduced significantly and edges are preserved well with less blurring and motion errors are smaller in the proposed POCS-based method, as shown in Figure 9(c). Figures 9(a) and 9(b) also show the similar tendency that the proposed POCS-based method using a bilateral filter is effective for noise reduction.

FUTURE RESEARCH DIRECTIONS

Automatic detection of the ROI is to be investigated for applications such as remote sensing and surveillance. Reliable feature extraction is also to be fully developed for robust systems. Also further reduction of the computational load of the POCS algorithm while maintaining the HR image quality is to be studied.

Figure 9. Performance comparison of SR techniques (bi-cubic, conventional POCS [δ_0 =15, 25 iterations], and POCS using the bilateral filter [δ_0 =5, 5 iterations] for noisy images with additive white Gaussian noise [standard deviation =10]): (a) box (400×400), (b) books (400×400), (c) license plate (200×200)

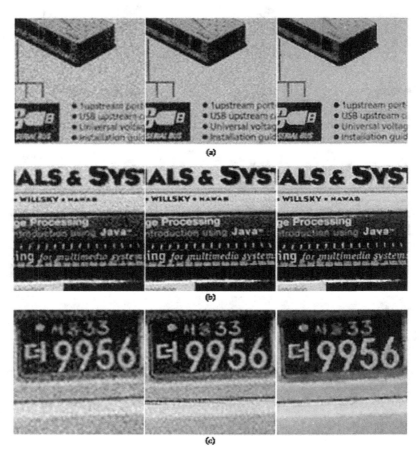

CONCLUSION

In this chapter, we propose a POCS-based SR algorithm of an ROI using multiple LR images of the same scene. We show that the feature-based ME method for the affine model is more efficient than the conventional method in terms of the computational load. Note that the ROIs extracted from similar images are well described by the simple global motion and ME is not performed in the iterative POCS algorithm. The proposed POCS-based method gives better results with a much lower computational load than the conventional POCS.

For noisy images, the conventional POCS method cannot reliably reconstruct important information. Thus, we apply the bilateral filter to noisy images in the pre-processing step, and demonstrate that the proposed POCS-based SR method reduces noise remarkably while efficiently preserving edges.

Future work will focus on the further reduction of the computational load while maintaining the HR image quality.

ACKNOWLEDGMENT

This work was supported in part by Samsung Electronics, Co., Ltd. and the Second Brain Korea 21 Project.

REFERENCES

Bergen, J., Burt, P., Hingorani, R., & Peleg, S. (1992). A three-frame algorithm for estimating two-component image motion. *IEEE Transactions on Pattern Analysis and Machine Intelligence, 14*(9), 886–896. doi:10.1109/34.161348.

Cao, B.-T., Tuan, D.-H., Thuong, L.-T., & Hoang, N.-D. (2011). Scene-based video super-resolution with minimum mean square error estimation. In *Proceedings of 2011 International Conference on Advanced Technologies for Communications (ATC)* (pp. 48-52). ATC.

Cetin, K., & Ari, F. (2012). Super-resolution image construction from video images based on block matching technique. In *Proceedings of 2012 20th Signal Processing and Communications Applications Conference (SIU)* (pp. 1-4). SIU.

Chai, Z., & Shi, J. (2011). Improving KLT in embedded systems by processing oversampling video sequence in real-time. In *Proceedings of 2011 International Conference Reconfigurable Computing and FPGAs (ReConFig)* (pp. 297-302). ReConFig.

Chang, S. G., Cvetkovic, Z., & Vetterli, M. (2006). Locally adaptive wavelet-based image interpolation. *IEEE Transactions on Image Processing, 15*(6), 1471–1485. doi:10.1109/TIP.2006.871162 PMID:16764272.

Chen, Z., Ye, Z., Wang, S., & Peng, G. (2009). Image magnification based on similarity analogy. *Chaos, Solitons, and Fractals, 40*(5), 2370–2375. doi:10.1016/j.chaos.2007.10.031.

Chung, J., Haber, E., & Nagy, J. (2006). Numerical methods for coupled super-resolution. *Inverse Problems, 22*, 1261–1272. doi:10.1088/0266-5611/22/4/009.

Eren, P. E., Sezan, M. I., & Tekalp, A. M. (1997). Robust, object-based high-resolution image reconstruction from low-resolution video. *IEEE Transactions on Image Processing, 6*(10), 1446–1451. doi:10.1109/83.624970 PMID:18282900.

Farsiu, S., Elad, M., & Milanfar, P. (2006). Multiframe demosaicing and super-resolution of color images. *IEEE Transactions on Image Processing, 15*(1), 141–159. doi:10.1109/TIP.2005.860336 PMID:16435545.

Farsiu, S., Robinson, M. D., Elad, M., & Milanfar, P. (2004). Fast and robust multiframe super resolution. *IEEE Transactions on Image Processing, 13*(10), 1327–1344. doi:10.1109/TIP.2004.834669 PMID:15462143.

Freeman, W. T., Jones, T. R., & Pasztor, E. C. (2002). Example-based super-resolution. *IEEE Computer Graphics and Applications, 22*(2), 56–65. doi:10.1109/38.988747.

Gonzalez, R. C., & Woods, R. E. (2010). *Digital image processing* (3rd ed.). Upper Saddle River, NJ: Pearson Education Inc..

Gunturk, B. K., Altunbasak, Y., & Mersereau, R. M. (2004). Super-resolution reconstruction of compressed video using transform-domain statistics. *IEEE Transactions on Image Processing, 13*(1), 33–43. doi:10.1109/TIP.2003.819221 PMID:15376955.

Haque, M. N., Biswas, M., Pickering, M. R., & Frater, M. R. (2012). A low-complexity image registration algorithm for global motion estimation. *IEEE Transactions on Circuits and Systems for Video Technology, 22*(3), 426–433. doi:10.1109/TCSVT.2011.2163983.

Hartley, R., & Zisserman, A. (2004). *Multiview geometry in computer vision* (2nd ed.). Cambridge, UK: Cambridge Press. doi:10.1017/CBO9780511811685.

Hong, S.-H., Park, R.-H., Yang, S., & Kim, J.-Y. (2008). Image interpolation using interpolative classified vector quantization. *Image and Vision Computing*, *26*(2), 228–239. doi:10.1016/j.imavis.2007.05.002.

Islam, M. M., Asari, V. K., Islam, M. N., & Karim, M. A. (2010). Super-resolution enhancement technique for low resolution video. *IEEE Transactions on Consumer Electronics*, *56*(2), 919–924. doi:10.1109/TCE.2010.5506020.

Islam, M. M., Islam, M. N., Asari, V. K., & Karim, M. A. (2012). Single image super-resolution in frequency domain. In *Proceedings of 2012 IEEE Southwest Symposium on Image Analysis and Interpretation (SSIAI)* (pp. 53-56). IEEE.

Jeon, B. W., Park, R.-H., & Yang, S. (2006). Resolution enhancement by prediction of the high-frequency image based on the Laplacian pyramid. *J. Applied Signal Processing. Article ID*, *72520*, 1–11.

Jianchao, Y., Wright, J., Huang, T. S., & Yi, M. (2010). Image super-resolution via sparse representation. *IEEE Transactions on Image Processing*, *19*(11), 2861–2873. doi:10.1109/TIP.2010.2050625.

Kim, S. H., Park, R.-H., & Yang, S. (2008). Superresolution of a region of interest using feature-based affine motion estimation. In *Proceedings of the Int. Conf. Consumer Electronics* (pp. 10.4-2:1-2). IEEE.

Leu, J. G. (2001). Sharpness preserving image enlargement based on a ramp edge model. *Signal Processing*, *34*(10), 1927–1938.

Li, F., Jia, X., & Fraser, D. (2009). Superresolution reconstruction of multispectral data for improved image classification. *IEEE Geoscience and Remote Sensing Letters*, *6*(4), 689–693. doi:10.1109/LGRS.2009.2023604.

Liu, J., & Wu, D. (2011). Joint POCS method with compressive sensing theory for super-resolution image reconstruction. In *Proceedings of 2011 3rd International Conference on Awareness Science and Technology (iCAST)* (pp. 99-102). iCAST.

Maymon, S., & Oppenheim, A. V. (2011). Sinc interpolation of nonuniform samples. *IEEE Transactions on Signal Processing*, *59*(10), 4745–4758. doi:10.1109/TSP.2011.2160054.

Meijering, E. (2002). A chronology of interpolation: From ancient astronomy to modern signal and image processing. *Proceedings of the IEEE*, *90*(3), 319–342. doi:10.1109/5.993400.

Molina, R., Vega, M., Abad, J., & Katsaggelos, A. K. (2003). Parameter estimation in Bayesian high-resolution image reconstruction with multisensors. *IEEE Transactions on Image Processing*, *12*(12), 1655–1667. doi:10.1109/TIP.2003.818117 PMID:18244719.

Panda, S. S., Prasad, M. S. R. S., & Jena, G. (2011). POCS-based super-resolution image reconstruction using an adaptive regularization parameter. *IJCSI International Journal of Computer Science Issues*, *8*(5-2), 155-158.

Paragios, N., & Deriche, R. (2005). Geodesic active regions and level set methods for motion estimation and tracking. *Computer Vision and Image Understanding*, *97*(3), 259–282. doi:10.1016/j.cviu.2003.04.001.

Park, S. C., Park, M. K., & Kang, M. G. (2003). Super-resolution image reconstruction. *IEEE Signal Processing Magazine*, *20*(3), 21–36. doi:10.1109/MSP.2003.1203207.

Patti, A. J., Sezan, M. I., & Tekalp, A. M. (1997). Superresolution video reconstruction with arbitrary sampling lattices and nonzero aperture time. *IEEE Transactions on Image Processing*, *6*(8), 1064–1076. doi:10.1109/83.605404 PMID:18282997.

Pizurica, A., Zlokolica, V., Schulte, S., Kerre, E., & Philips, W. (2007). Combined wavelet domain and motion compensated filtering compliant with video codecs. In *Proceedings of IEEE International Conference on Acoustics, Speech, and Signal Processing* (pp. I-765-I-768). IEEE.

Seong, Y., & Park, H. (2008). Superresolution technique for planar objects based on an isoplane transformation. *Optical Engineering (Redondo Beach, Calif.)*, *47*(5), 057007. doi:10.1117/1.2931461.

Shi, J., & Tomasi, C. (1994). Good features to track. In *Proceedings of IEEE Conference on Computer Vision and Pattern Recognition (CVPR)* (pp. 593-600). IEEE.

Song, H., He, X., Chen, W., & Sun, Y. (2010). An improved iterative back-projection algorithm for video super-resolution reconstruction. In *Proceedings of 2010 Symposium on Photonics and Optoelectronics* (pp. 1-4). IEEE.

Sun, J., Zheng, N.-N., Tao, H., & Shum, H.-Y. (2003). Image hallucination with primal sketch priors. In *Proceedings of 2003 IEEE International Conference Computer Vision and Pattern Recognition* (pp. 2-729-2-740). IEEE.

Suo, F., Hu, F., & Zhu, G. (2011). Robust super-resolution reconstruction based on adaptive regularization. In *Proceedings of 2011 International Conference on Wireless Communications and Signal Processing (WCSP)* (pp. 1-4). WCSP.

Takahashi, Y., & Taguchi, A. (2003). An arbitrary scale image enlargement method with the prediction of high-frequency components. *Electronics and Communications in Japan*, *86*(8), 41–51. doi:10.1002/ecjc.10018.

Tang, Z., Deng, M., Xiao, C., & Yu, J. (2011). Projection onto convex sets super-resolution image reconstruction based on wavelet bi-cubic interpolation. In *Proceedings of 2011 International Conference on Electronic and Mechanical Engineering and Information Technology (EMEIT)* (pp. 351-354). EMEIT.

Tom, B. C., & Katsaggelos, A. K. (2001). Resolution enhancement of monochrome and color video using motion compensation. *IEEE Transactions on Image Processing*, *10*(2), 278–287. doi:10.1109/83.902292 PMID:18249618.

Tomasi, C., & Manduchi, R. (1998). Bilateral filtering for gray and color images. In *Proceedings of 6th International Conference Computer Vision* (pp. 839-846). IEEE.

van Eekeren, A. W. M., Schutte, K., & van Vliet, L. J. (2010). Multiframe super-resolution reconstruction of small moving objects. *IEEE Transactions on Image Processing*, *19*(11), 2901–2912. doi:10.1109/TIP.2010.2068210 PMID:20729171.

Wang, Q., & Ward, R. (2003). A contour-preserving image interpolation method. In *Proceedings of IEEE International Conference Image Processing* (pp. 2-673-2-676). IEEE.

Ye, X., & Lu, X. (2011). A performance evaluation of image interpolation and superresolution algorithms. In *Proceedings of 2011 International Conference on Multimedia Technology (ICMT)* (pp. 4776-4779). ICMT.

Zhang, L., & Wu, X. (2006). An edge-guided image interpolation algorithm via directional filtering and data fusion. *IEEE Transactions on Image Processing*, *15*(8), 2226–2238. doi:10.1109/TIP.2006.877407 PMID:16900678.

ADDITIONAL READING

Biancardi, A., Cinque, L., & Lombardi, L. (2002). Improvements to image magnification. *Pattern Recognition, 35*(3), 677–688. doi:10.1016/S0031-3203(01)00034-6.

Carey, W. K., Chuang, D. B., & Hemami, S. S. (1999). Regularity-preserving image interpolation. *IEEE Transactions on Image Processing, 8*(9), 1293–1297. doi:10.1109/83.784441 PMID:18267546.

Clark, J. J., Palmer, M. R., & Lauence, P. D. (1985). A transformation method for the reconstruction of functions from nonuniformly spaced samples. *IEEE Transactions on Acoustics, Speech, and Signal Processing, 33*(4), 1151–1165. doi:10.1109/TASSP.1985.1164714.

Comaniciu, D., Ramesh, V., & Meer, P. (2003). Kernel-based object tracking. *IEEE Transactions on Pattern Analysis and Machine Intelligence, 25*(5), 564–575. doi:10.1109/TPAMI.2003.1195991.

Dufaux, F., & Konrad, J. (2000). Efficient, robust, and fast global motion estimation for video coding. *IEEE Transactions on Image Processing, 9*(9), 497–501. doi:10.1109/83.826785 PMID:18255419.

Figueiredo, M. A. T., Bioucas-Dias, J. M., & Nowak, R. D. (2007). Majorization-minimization algorithms for wavelet-based image restoration. *IEEE Transactions on Image Processing, 16*(12), 2980–2991. doi:10.1109/TIP.2007.909318 PMID:18092597.

Figueiredo, M. A. T., & Nowak, R. D. (2002). Image restoration under wavelet-domain priors: An expectation maximization approach. In *Proceedings of IEEE International Conference on Image Processing* (pp. 337-340). IEEE.

Gouet-Brunet, V., & Lameyre, B. (2008). Object recognition and segmentation in videos by connecting heterogeneous visual features. *Computer Vision and Image Understanding, 111*, 86–109. doi:10.1016/j.cviu.2007.10.004.

Jain, R., Kasturi, R., & Schunck, B. G. (1995). *Machine vision*. New York: McGraw-Hill.

Kim, C., & Hwang, J.-K. (2002). Fast and automatic video object segmentation and tracking for content-based applications. *IEEE Transactions on Circuits and Systems for Video Technology, 12*(2), 122–129. doi:10.1109/76.988659.

Kim, S. P., & Su, W. Y. (1993). Recursive high-resolution reconstruction of blurred multiframe images. *IEEE Transactions on Image Processing, 2*(4), 534–539. doi:10.1109/83.242363 PMID:18296238.

Lee, E. S., & Kang, M. G. (2003). Regularized adaptive high-resolution image reconstruction considering inaccurate subpixel registration. *IEEE Transactions on Image Processing, 12*(7), 826–837. doi:10.1109/TIP.2003.811488 PMID:18237957.

Li, X., & Orchard, T. (2001). New edge-directed interpolation. *IEEE Transactions on Image Processing, 10*(10), 1521–1527. doi:10.1109/83.951537 PMID:18255495.

Lowe, D. G. (2004). Distinctive image features from scale-invariant keypoints. *International Journal of Computer Vision, 60*(2), 91–110. doi:10.1023/B:VISI.0000029664.99615.94.

Segall, C. A., Katsaggelos, A. K., Molina, R., & Mateos, J. (2004). Bayesian resolution enhancement of compressed video. *IEEE Transactions on Image Processing, 13*(7), 898–911. doi:10.1109/TIP.2004.827230 PMID:15648857.

Shah, N. R., & Zakhor, A. (1999). Resolution enhancement of color video sequences. *IEEE Transactions on Image Processing*, *8*(6), 876–885. doi:10.1109/83.766865 PMID:18267501.

Sinha, A., & Wu, X. (2007). Fast generalized motion estimation and superresolution. In *Proceedings of IEEE International Conference on Image Processing* (pp. V-413-V-416). IEEE.

Tekalp, A. M. (1995). *Digital video processing.* Upper Saddle River, NJ: Prentice-Hall.

Tom, B. C., & Katsaggelos, A. K. (1996). Resolution enhancement of video sequences using motion compensation. In *Proceedings of 1996 IEEE International Conference on Image Processing* (pp. I-713-I-716). IEEE.

Waddell, J. P., & Brydon, N. (2003). Noise reduction preprocessing for MPEG-2 encoding. *SMPTE Motion Imaging Journal*, *112*(1), 17–23. doi:10.5594/J14123.

Zhang, D., & Lu, G. (2001). Segmentation of moving objects in image sequence: a review. *International Journal of Circuits, Systems, and Signal Processing*, *20*(2), 143–189. doi:10.1007/BF01201137.

Zibetti, M. V. W., & Mayer, J. (2007). A robust and computationally efficient simultaneous superresolution scheme for image sequences. *IEEE Transactions on Circuits and Systems for Video Technology*, *17*(10), 1288–1300. doi:10.1109/TCSVT.2007.903801.

KEY TERMS AND DEFINITIONS

Affine Transformation: Affine transformation is a geometric mapping that preserves straight lines. In two-dimensional (2-D) image plane, 2-D affine transformation is a linear mapping from 2-D coordinates to other coordinates. In motion estimation between two successive frames, an affine motion model represents the motion vector at each point in the image using six affine parameters (a linear mapping followed by a translation).

Features: Features are measurable or observable spectral, textural, or temporal attributes to describe an image or video in compact form, e.g., edges, corners, blobs, or motion vectors.

Image Resolution: Image resolution represents the measure of the amount of high-frequency or detail of an image. For example, it can be described in terms of the number of pixels in a digital image (pixel resolution), lines per inch (spatial resolution), or frames per second (temporal resolution).

Motion Estimation (ME): ME is to estimate motion vectors between two successive frames, which transform from the previous frame to the current frame. ME is classified into two classes: block-based ME and pixel-based ME.

Projection Onto Convex Sets (POCS): POCS is an iterative technique that effectively searches the solution in a unified set-theoretic framework, into which various constraints are mapped.

Region Of Interest (ROI): An ROI represents an area or region in a 2-D image for a particular interest, e.g., face, car, or object boundary in an image. ROI can be used in motion estimation, video coding, tracking, medical imaging, reconstruction, detection, segmentation, and so on.

Superresolution (SR): SR methods estimate one or a set of higher resolution images from a set of original low-resolution images by recovering image details or enhancing the resolution of an imaging system.

Chapter 7
Daubechies Complex Wavelet-Based Computer Vision Applications

Manish Khare
University of Allahabad, India

Rajneesh Kumar Srivastava
University of Allahabad, India

Ashish Khare
University of Allahabad, India

ABSTRACT

Many methods for computer vision applications have been developed using wavelet theory. Almost all of them are based on real-valued discrete wavelet transform. This chapter introduces two computer vision applications, namely moving object segmentation and moving shadow detection and removal, using Daubechies complex wavelet transform. Daubechies complex wavelet transform has advantages over discrete wavelet transform as it is approximately shift-invariant, has a better edge detection, and provides true phase information. Results after applying Daubechies complex wavelet transform on these two applications demonstrate that Daubechies complex wavelet transform-based methods provide better results than other real-valued wavelet transform-based methods, and it also demonstrates that Daubechies complex wavelet transform has the potential to be applied to other computer vision applications.

INTRODUCTION

In last two decades, many applications of wavelet theory have been emerged in the field of computer vision as an alternative to the well-known Fourier transform and its different variants. Wavelet transform was first introduced by Haar. The Haar

DOI: 10.4018/978-1-4666-4868-5.ch007

wavelet function has compact support and it is an integer function. After era of Haar wavelet, a lot of work towards development of theoretical concepts of wavelet and its applications has been done. Now, various popular forms of wavelet transform exists such as, Continuous wavelet transform, Discrete wavelet transform and its variants, Hyper analytic wavelet transform, Complex wavelet transform, Integer wavelet transform and many more. These forms of wavelet transforms have been successfully applied on various computer vision applications like Denoising, Deblurring, Object Tracking, Object Classification, Activity Recognition, Shadow detection and removal etc.

Wavelet transforms are useful in image and video applications due to following reasons:

1. Wavelet transform offers a simultaneous localization in time and frequency domain.
2. Wavelet transform is computationally faster than Fourier transform.
3. Wavelet transform is being able to separate fine details in an image.
4. Multiresolution property of wavelet transform is helpful to analyze an image or video at several scales.

The Discrete Wavelet Transform (DWT) is most commonly used form of wavelet transform due to its compact representation, but this form of wavelet transform have several limitations such as – shift sensitivity, poor directional selectivity, poor edge detection and no phase information. Shift sensitivity means small shifts in the input signal causes major variations in the distribution of energy between discrete wavelet transform coefficients at different scales (Selesnick et al., 2005). This is an undesirable property, making DWT not suitable for those applications where object is present in shifted from e.g. object tracking, moving object segmentation etc. Figure 1 illustrates the shift sensitivity problem of discrete wavelet transform. Figure 1(a) represents signal having 512 sample points, in which two sample points take value 1 and the remaining take the value 0. Figure 1(b) shows the detailed wavelet coefficients of signal at several scales using real valued discrete wavelet transform. Here db4 wavelet has been used. From the Figure 1, it is clear that nature of real valued discrete wavelet coefficients in shifted signal as well as at multiple scales does not remain same. Thus, effect of applying same

function will work in different way at different places and at difference scales.

In discrete wavelet transform, separable filtering along the rows and columns of an image produces four different images (*LL, LH, HL,* and *HH*) at each level. The *LH* subimage contains horizontal edges and *HL* subimage contains vertical edges, whereas *HH* subimage contains components from diagonal features. This means discrete wavelet transform has limited directional selectivity of four directions and due to this poor directionality, DWT have only limited directional edge detection characteristic.

Implementation of discrete wavelet transform uses real-valued wavelets and associated real filter-coefficients. Such a wavelet transform does not provide phase information. The information about the phase can be utilized in various image and signal processing applications, especially for certain class of coherent imaging systems. Amplitude-phase representation imparts greater robustness in signal and image processing applica-

Figure 1. (a) Original input signal, (b) detailed coefficients of signal at several levels using real wavelet transform

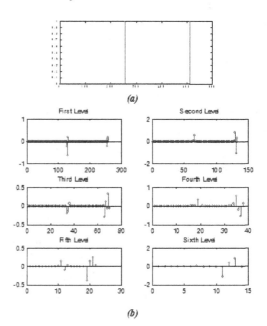

tions. Unfortunately, since discrete real wavelet transform does not provide phase information at all, so such type of robustness in computer vision applications can't be achieved using real valued discrete wavelet transform.

These limitations of real valued discrete wavelet transform can be overcomed by using complex wavelet transform. A review of the work in the domain of complex wavelet can be found in (Selesnick et al., 2005; Ville & Unser, 2008). Recent researches in the development of complex wavelet transform are mainly in two directions. One direction is redundant complex wavelet transform i.e. if the input signal has M Samples, then after transformation we will get N output wavelet coefficients with $N>M$. This class of transform relies on Dual-tree implementation. One famous example of this class of transform is Dual tree complex wavelet transform (Selesnick et al., 2005; Selesnick, 2004). Another direction of complex wavelet transform is non-redundant complex wavelet transform i.e. if the input signal has N Samples, then after transformation we get exactly N output wavelet coefficients. This non-redundancy is achieved by mapping the signal into a complex function space. Examples of such transforms are given in (Fernandes et al., 2003). One famous example of this class of transform is Daubechies complex wavelet transform (Lina & Mayrand, 1995).

In most of complex wavelet transforms, use of real filters makes them not a true complex wavelet transform (Jalobeanu et al., 2000) and due to the presence of redundancy, they are computationally costly as well. For avoiding redundancy and providing phase information, an approximate shift invariant Daubechies complex wavelet transform is used [Khare & Tiwary, 2006; Khare et al., 2010b], as proposed by Lina (Lina & Mayrand, 1995) and Lawton (Lawton, 1993). As Daubechies (Daubechies, 1992) has given real valued solution of wavelet equation, Lina (Lina & Mayrand, 1995) and Lawton (Lawton, 1993) have explored

the possibility of complex valued solution for the same wavelet equation and proved that the complex solutions do exist leading to complex Daubechies wavelet transform. Hence Daubechies complex wavelet transform is a natural extension of concept of Daubechies real valued wavelet transform. The Daubechies complex wavelet transform is a true sense complex wavelet transform as well.

In this chapter, we have discussed two computer vision applications namely moving object segmentation and moving shadow detection and removal using Daubechies complex wavelet transform. The basic algorithms have already been developed using real valued wavelet transform (Huang & Hsieh, 2003; Guan, 2010). Here we have shown that use of Daubechies complex wavelet transform on moving object segmentation and shadow detection gives better results than use of real valued wavelet transform.

DAUBECHIES COMPLEX WAVELET TRANSFORM

This section explores the advantages and construction of Daubechies complex wavelet transform, which provides the basic framework for development of adaptive techniques for computer vision applications. The Daubechies complex wavelet transform is a true sense complex wavelet transform, as it uses complex filters. The Daubechies complex wavelet can be made symmetric, thus leading to symmetric Daubechies complex wavelet transform, as it is more useful for imaging applications.

Advantages of Symmetric Daubechies Complex Wavelet Transform

Symmetric Daubechies complex wavelet transform is useful for imaging applications as it owns the following advantages:

1.   It is approximate shift invariant.
2.   It has perfect reconstruction property.
3.   It provides true phase information.
4.   No redundancy: other popular low-redundant complex wavelet transform like Dual tree complex wavelet transform (Selesnick et al., 2005) has a redundancy of $2^m{:}1$ for m-D signal, while Daubechies complex wavelet transform has no such redundancy.
5.   Number of computations in Daubechies complex wavelet transform (although it involves complex calculations) is same as that of Discrete wavelet transform, while other complex wavelet transform like Dual tree complex wavelet transform has 2^m times computations as that of Discrete wavelet transform for m-D signals.

Construction of Daubechies Complex Wavelet Transform

The basic equation of Multiresolution theory (Daubechies, 1992) is the scaling equation

$$\phi(t) = 2\sum_i a_i \, \phi(2t - n) \qquad (1)$$

where, $\phi(t)$ is scaling function and a_i s are the coefficients. The a_i s can be real as well as complex valued and $\sum a_i = 1$. Daubechies wavelet bases $\{\psi_{j,k}(t)\}$ in one dimension are defined through the above scaling function and multiresolution analysis of $L_2(R)$ (Daubechies, 1992). One can define the Laurent series expansion on the unit circle:

$$F(Z) = \sum_{i=-L}^{L+1} a_i \, z^i, \text{ with F(1) = 1 and } |z| = 1. \qquad (2)$$

For $\phi(t)$ to be Daubechies scaling function the following conditions must be satisfied:

1.   Compact support of ϕ: ϕ should be compactly support inside the interval $[-L, L+1]$ for some integer L that is $a_i \neq 0$, for $i = -L$, $-L+1, \ldots\ldots\ldots, L, L+1$.
2.   Othogonality of the ϕ: this condition defines in a large sense the Daubechies wavelets. The orthonormality of the set $\{\phi_{0,i}(x), k \in Z\}$ can be stated through the following identity

$$P(z) - P(-z) = z \qquad (3)$$

where the polynomial P(z) is defined as

$$P(z) = zF(z)\overline{F(z)} \qquad (4)$$

3.   Accuracy of the approximation: To maximize the regularity of the functions generated by the scaling function ϕ, we require the vanishing of the first L moments of the wavelet or terms of the polynomial Equation (2).

$$F'(-1) = F''(-1) = \ldots\ldots = F^{(L)}(-1) = 0 \qquad (5)$$

4. $\phi(t)$ should satisfy the multiresolution property: A multiresolution analysis (MRA) in $L^2(R)$ consists of the nested linear vector spaces $\ldots \subset V_1 \subset V_0 \subset V_{-1} \subset \ldots$ such that:

a.   The union of these subspaces is dense in the space of square integrable functions $L^2(R)$ i.e. $\overline{\underset{j}{\cup} V_j} = L^2(R)$.

b.   The intersection of these subspaces is a singleton set containing the all-zero function or zero vector i.e. $\underset{j}{\cap} V_j = \{0\}$.

c.   If $g(t) \in V_k$ then $g(2t) \in V_{k-1}$ and vice-versa.

d.   There exists a function (called a scaling function $\phi(t)$) s.t. $\{\phi(t-k), k \in \mathbb{Z}\}$ is a basis for V_0.

Daubechies (Daubechies, 1992) has given the general solution as follows:

Let $h(z) = \frac{1}{2}(1+z)$. Consider the following polynomial:

$$p_L(z) = \sum_{k=0}^{L} (-1)^k \binom{2L+1}{k} h(z)^{2L-2k} h(-z)^{2k} \tag{6}$$

that satisfies, $p_L(z) - p_L(-z) = z$.

If we denote Z_n, n = 1,2,........L, the set of roots of $p_L(z)$ inside the unit circle $\left(|Z_n| < 1\right)$, any selection R among the roots of $p_L(z)$ defines an admissible trigonometric polynomial

$$F(z) =$$
$$h(z)^{1+L} \prod_{m \in R}\left(\frac{z^{-1}-Z_m}{1-Z_m}\right) \times \prod_{n \notin R}\left(\frac{z^{-1}-\overline{Z_n}^{-1}}{1-\overline{Z_n}^{-1}}\right) \tag{7}$$

that satisfies the above four constraints. The solution of Equations (6) and (7) will lead to Daubechies scaling functions. During the formulation of general solution Daubechies considered a_i to be real-valued only. Relaxing the condition for a_i to be only real-valued will lead to the Daubechies complex scaling function and this leads to Daubechies complex wavelet transform.

The construction of Daubechies wavelet is done as described in (Lawton, 1993). The orthogonal wavelet basis $\{\psi_{j,k}(t), j \in \mathbb{Z}, k \in \mathbb{Z}\}$ and generating wavelet $\psi(t)$ are given by,

$$\psi(t) = 2\sum_n (-1)^n \overline{a_{1-n}} \; \phi(2t - n) \tag{8}$$

$\psi(t)$ and $\phi(t)$ share the same compact support [-L, L+1].

Lina (Lina & Mayrand, 1995) investigated first few solutions as follows:

1. L = 0
$$F(z) = h(z).$$
This corresponds to Haar solution.

2. L = 1
The polynomial $p_1(z)$ has two roots $Z_1=2-\sqrt{3}$ and Z_1^{-1}. The unique solution is
$$F(z) = \left(\frac{1+z}{2}\right)^2 \left(\frac{z^{-1}-Z_1}{1-Z_1}\right)$$
and this corresponds to db2 scaling function.

3. L=2
The polynomial $p_2(z)$ has four roots:
$$Z_1 = \frac{3}{2} - i\sqrt{\frac{5}{12}} - \frac{1}{2}\sqrt{\frac{10}{3}-2i\sqrt{15}},$$
$$Z_2 = \frac{3}{2} - i\sqrt{\frac{5}{12}} + \frac{1}{2}\sqrt{\frac{10}{3}-2i\sqrt{15}}$$
$$\overline{Z_1}^{-1},$$
and
$$\overline{Z_2}^{-1}$$

Now two distinct cases have been found for this case:

a. Selection of $R = \{1,2\}$ leads to polynomial:
$$F(z) = \left(\frac{1+z}{2}\right)^3 \left(\frac{z^{-1}-Z_1}{1-Z_1}\right)\left(\frac{z^{-1}-Z_2}{1-Z_2}\right)$$
and this corresponds to usual db3 scaling function.

b. Selection of $R = \{1\}$ leads to
$$F(z) = \left(\frac{1+z}{2}\right)^3 \left(\frac{z^{-1}-Z_1}{1-Z_1}\right)\left(\frac{z^{-1}-\overline{Z_2}^{-1}}{1-\overline{Z_2}^{-1}}\right)$$

This solution leads to symmetric but complex scaling function.

The filter bank is defined s.t. $h_i = \sqrt{2}a_i$. In this case we have the following solutions:

$$a_2 = a_3 = \frac{15 + i\sqrt{15}}{32},$$

$$a_1 = a_4 = \frac{5 - i\sqrt{15}}{64}$$

and

$$a_0 = a_5 = -\frac{3 + i\sqrt{15}}{64}$$

The complex solutions exist for all values of $L \geq 2$. Symmetry is only possible with even L (Lina & Mayrand, 1995).

Any function $f(t)$ can be decomposed into complex scaling function and wavelet function as:

$$f(t) = \sum_k c_k^{j_0} \, \phi_{j_0,k}(t) + \sum_{j=j_0}^{j_{max}-1} d_k^j \, \psi_{j,k}(t) \qquad (9)$$

where, j_0 is a given low resolution level, $\{c_k^{j_0}\}$ is called approximation coefficient and $\{d_k^j\}$ is known as detail coefficient.

PROPERTIES OF DAUBECHIES COMPLEX WAVELET TRANSFORM

In this section, we have shown different important properties of Daubechies complex wavelet transform which are useful in imaging applications. All the important properties of real Daubechies wavelet bases are derived from the amplitude $|F(z)|^2 = z^{-1} p_L(z)$ (Daubechies, 1992). Thus those properties do not depend on the particular factorization of $p_L(z)$ and are maintained in complex solution. Different useful properties are described in following subsections.

Symmetricity and Linear Phase Property

The symmetry property of filter makes it easy to handle the boundary problems for finite length signals. Zhang et al. (1999) has given a method to achieve approximate linear phase symmetric Daubechies complex wavelet. The linear phase response of the filter precludes the non-linear phase distortion and keeps the shape of the signal, which is very important in imaging applications.

Multiscale Edge Information

Let $\phi(t) = l(t) + i.v(t)$ be a scaling function and $\psi(t) = k(t) + i.u(t)$ be a wavelet function. Let $\hat{v}(\omega)$ and $\hat{l}(\omega)$ are Fourier transform of $v(t)$ and $l(t)$. Consider the ratio

$$\alpha(\omega) = -\frac{\hat{v}(\omega)}{\hat{l}(\omega)} \qquad (10)$$

Clonda et al. (2004) observed that $\alpha(\omega)$ is strictly real-valued and behaves as ω^2 for $|\omega| < \pi$. This observation relates the imaginary and real components of scaling function as $v(t)$ accurately approximate another derivative $l(t)$, upto some constant factor. Similarly for wavelet function $\psi(t)$, the ratio is

$$\beta(\omega) = -\frac{\hat{u}(\omega)}{\hat{k}(\omega)} \qquad (11)$$

is also real valued.

From the above property and Equation (10) and(11)indicates $v(t) \approx \alpha\Delta l(t)$ and $u(t) \approx \beta\Delta k(t)$. This gives multi-projection as

$$\left\langle f(t), \phi_{j,k}(t) \right\rangle = \left\langle f(t), l_{j,k}(t) \right\rangle + i\left\langle f(t), v_{j,k}(t) \right\rangle$$

$$\approx \left\langle f(t), l_{j,k}(t) \right\rangle + i\alpha\left\langle f(t), l_{j,k}(t) \right\rangle \qquad (12)$$

$$\left\langle f(t), \psi_{j,k}(t) \right\rangle = \left\langle f(t), k_{j,k}(t) \right\rangle + i \left\langle f(t), u_{j,k}(t) \right\rangle$$

$$\approx \left\langle f(t), k_{j,k}(t) \right\rangle + i\beta \left\langle f(t), k_{j,k}^{\bullet}(t) \right\rangle \tag{13}$$

From Equation (12), it can be seen that the real component of complex scaling function carries averaging information and the imaginary component carries edge information (Laplacian). Similarly from Equation (13), it can be concluded that the imaginary component of complex wavelet function also carries edge information.

Daubechies complex wavelet transform acts as local edge detector because imaginary components of complex wavelet coefficients represent strong edges. This helps in preserving the edges and implementation of edge sensitive computer vision applications such as moving object segmentation, shadow detection and object tracking etc.

Reduced Shift-Sensitivity of Daubechies Complex Wavelet

A transform is said to shift sensitive if shift in input signal causes an unpredictable change in transform coefficients. In real valued discrete wavelet transform the shift sensitivity arises due to down-sampler in the implementation. Further shift variance results in loss of information at multilevel whereas with Daubechies complex wavelet transform, the information is not significantly lost at multilevel due to its properties of shift invariance. For performing a precise detection of any feature of object a transform should not miss the feature due to shift of object. Clonda et al. (2004) has introduced the metric of measurement for translational shift sensitivity of wavelets. To measure the positional uncertainty, let us define center of energy for a sequence *u(k)* as

$$c(u) = \frac{1}{\|u\|^2} k \sum_k \left| u(k) \right|^2 \tag{14}$$

Table 1. Values of c_h and d_h for first three Daubechies complex and real wavelets

Complex wavelet (Real wavelet)	c_h (c_h real)	d_h (d_h real)
N=0 (Haar)	0.50 (0.50)	0.00 (0.00)
N=2: SDW6 (DAUB6)	0.50 (1.16)	0.19 (0.23)
N=4: SDW10 (DAUB10)	0.50 (1.74)	0.32 (0.48)

The center of energy of filtered sequence $\sum_j h(j)\, u(2k-j)$ is

$$c(Hu) = \frac{c(u)}{2} + c_h + \gamma(u) \tag{15}$$

where, c_h is signal independent and shifts the scaled new center of energy by $\frac{1}{2}c(u)$. This is perturbed with a signal-dependent correction parameter $\gamma(u)$ (Wickerhauser, 1994). Let d_h be the upper bound of the deviation $\gamma(u)$. Values of c_h and d_h for first three symmetric complex Daubechies wavelets are given in Table 1 (Clonda et al. 2004). From the Table 1 it is clear that for symmetric Daubechies complex wavelet c_h have constant values, while the values of d_h in case of complex wavelet are less than their real counterparts.

To perform a good detection of any feature, a transform should not "miss" the feature due to such shifts. Figure 2 shows the sensitivity of different wavelet transform to shift of the input image. It shows an image shifted by 0, 1, and 2 pixels to its right and its Daubechies real and Daubechies complex wavelet based reconstruction at 2 levels. From the Figure 2 it is clear that complex wavelet transform coefficients are less sensitive to shift in input and do not miss the feature of image (Khare & Tiwary, 2007). Figure 2 also has a circular edge structure and as the circular edge structure moves through space, the recon-

Figure 2. (a) Image shifted by 0, 1, and 2 pixels to the right. Image reconstructed from 2 levels of wavelet coefficients using (b) real db6 wavelet and (c) complex SDW6 wavelet.

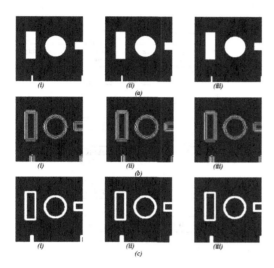

Figure 3. (a) An image, (b) imaginary component of wavelet coefficient upto three level of decomposition, (c) image reconstructed by the imaginary component only, and (d) the negative of image (c)

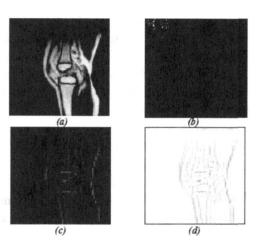

struction using real discrete wavelet transform coefficients changes erratically, while complex wavelet transform reconstructs all local shifts and orientation in the same manner. This indicates that complex wavelet transform in also rotation invariant. This rotation of object in different frames keep magnitude and energy of complex wavelet coefficients approximately same. This property is very much useful for detection of same object in different frames for video processing application of computer vision.

Phase Information in Daubechies Complex Wavelet

The phase of an image plays an important role in many different computer vision applications like medical imaging (Khare et al., 2009, 2010a), SAR imaging etc. The phase of complex wavelet coefficients represents the skeleton of the signal. The discrete wavelet transform does not provide any phase information. Phase and modulus of complex wavelet coefficients collaborate in a non-trivial

way to describe the data (Clonda et al. 2004). The phase encodes most of the coherent structure of the image while the modulus mostly encodes the strength of local information that could not be corrupted with the noise (Clonda et al. 2004). Khare et al. (Khare & Tiwary, 2007) observed that imaginary part of complex wavelet coefficients carries strong edge information. Figure 3 shows the imaginary part of Daubechies complex wavelet coefficients upto three levels and image reconstructed by only imaginary part of complex wavelet transform.

MOVING OBJECT SEGMENTATION

In this section, we have shown how Daubechies complex wavelet transform is useful for segmentation of moving object in comparison to other wavelet transform based methods. Motion segmentation is one of the important steps for development of any computer vision application. The objective of motion segmentation is to decompose a video in foreground objects and the background. Changing background, object occlusion, varying lighting condition, presence of noise etc. makes moving object segmentation a challenging task. Therefore, accurate and efficient moving object segmentation is a desirable task for vision applications. Though lots of literatures are available on image segmentation (Khare & Srivastava, 2012; Zhang et al. 2008; Peng et al. 2013), only few works have been reported on moving object segmentation. Wang et al. (2002) had reported four categories of moving object segmentation technique: motion information based method for segmentation of moving object (Huang & Hsieh, 2003), combination of motion information and spatial information based method for segmentation of moving object (Reza et al., 2009), edge detection based method for segmentation of moving object (Huang & Hsieh, 2003; Huang & Liao, 2001; Mansouri & Konard, 2003) and change detection based method for segmentation of moving object (Huang & Hsieh, 2003; Huang & Liao, 2001). All the methods mentioned above in different categories for segmentation of moving object are suffering from the problem of either slow speed or that of inaccurate segmentation of moving object due to non-removal of noise in consecutive frames.

The application of Daubechies complex wavelet transform in segmentation of moving objects in video frames is motivated by the fact that background removal part of this problem can be cast as a denoising problem. Motivated by this fact we have discussed here Daubechies complex wavelet transform based method for segmentation of moving object using single change detection. Single change detection is a method to obtain video object plane by interframe-difference of two consecutive frames and it provide automatic detection of appearances of new object. The aim here it to detect as many object edges as possible and at the same time suppress the noise by using denoising algorithm.

Figure 4. Block diagram of the Daubechies complex wavelet transform-based segmentation algorithm using single change detection approach

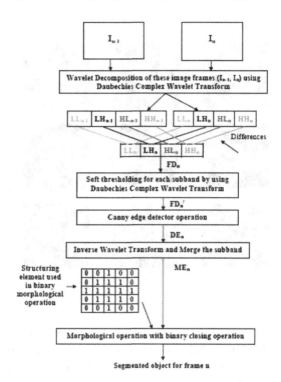

The block diagram of Daubechies complex wavelet based moving object segmentation using Single Change Detection (SCD) approach is shown in Figure 4. In single change detection approach proposed by Huang and Hsieh (2003), difference of two consecutive frames in terms of difference in values of pixel in *frame n* and *frame n-1* is computed by following rule.

```
FOR every (i,j) ∈ the co-ordinate of frame
    FD_n(i,j) = | I_n(i,j) - I_{n-1}(i,j) |
    IF FD_n(i,j) < P_thr  THEN FD_n(i,j) = 0
end FOR
```

In the proposed method, two sequential spatial domain frames I_{n-1} and I_n and are transformed into the Daubechies complex wavelet domain resulting in two images WI_{n-1} and WI_n with respective sub-bands. The frame difference in Daubechies complex wavelet domain are obtained by

$$\text{FD}_n(i,j) = \text{WI}_n(i,j) - WI_{n-1}(i,j) \qquad (16)$$

Generally, video data contains some noise due to camera system and due to non-uniform illumination. This noise is usually being random in nature. Therefore it gets enhanced by change detection process. Therefore change detection mask obtained by equation (16) can be expressed more accurately as follows

$$\text{FD}_n(i,j) = \text{FD}'_n(i,j) + \eta \qquad (17)$$

where, $\text{FD}'_n(i,j)$ is the frame difference without noise and η represents the noise as discussed above.

This noise is removed after application of soft thresholding together with the threshold function described in (Binh & Khare, 2010) in Daubechies complex wavelet domain to get noise free frame-difference $\text{FD}'_n(i,j)$.

Now canny edge detection operation is applied on $\{\text{FD}'_n(i,j)\}$, for detection of moving edge map of significant difference in all sub-bands i.e.

$$DE_n(i,j) = Canny(\text{FD}'_n(i,j)) \qquad (18)$$

After finding edge map $DE_n(i,j)$ in wavelet domain, next step is to achieve moving object edge map (ME_n) in spatial domain corresponding to frame n. Inverse wavelet transform of DE_n results in moving object edge map(ME_n). The point corresponding to the derived moving object edge map (ME_n) are not necessarily restricted to be on the boundary of moving object. Instead, these points may be part of interior of the boundary of the moving object.

After finding moving object edge map, the moving objects formed by the edges can be segmented from rest of the frame. There are some

disconnected edges which make it impossible to extract whole object. To overcome this problem of discontinuity, post processing is done on the moving object edge map (ME_n) using morphological operation. For this work, binary closing morphological operation as described by Gonzalez and Woods (Gonzalez & woods, 2008) has been chosen together with the structuring element as shown in Figure 4. We have tested the proposed moving object segmentation method on several video sequences and moving object segmentation results after applying the discussed method and some existing methods (Huang and Hsieh method (Huang & Hsieh, 2003), Reza et al. method (Reza et al., 2009) and Howe and Deschamps method (Howe & Deschamps, 2004)) for one representative Hall monitor video sequence are given in Figure 5.

For performance evaluation of the discussed algorithm and other algorithms (Huang & Hsieh, 2003; Reza et al., 2009; Howe & Deschamps, 2004), we have considered two performance metrics – one is Misclassification Penalty (MP) (Erdem et al., 2004) and another is Relative Position-based Measure (RPM) (Yang & Zhang, 2004).

Misclassification penalty have value in the range [0,1] and can be computed as (Erdem et al., 2004):

$$MP = \frac{\sum_{(\alpha,\beta)} I(\alpha,\beta).Chem_g(\alpha,\beta)}{\sum_{(\alpha,\beta)} Chem_g(\alpha,\beta)} \qquad (19)$$

where $Chem_g$ denotes the Chamfer distance transform of the boundary of ground-truth object. Indicator function I can be computed as

$$I(\alpha,\beta) = \begin{cases} 1, & if\ I_g(\alpha,\beta) \neq I_S(\alpha,\beta) \\ 0, & if\ I_g(\alpha,\beta) = I_S(\alpha,\beta) \end{cases} \qquad (20)$$

Figure 5. Segmentation result for hall monitor video sequence corresponding to (a) frame 25, (b) frame 75, (c) frame 125, (d) frame – 175 (i and ii – two sequential frames, iii – segmented frame obtained by the discussed method, iv – segmented frame obtained by the Huang and Hsieh method [Huang & Hsieh, 2003], v – segmented frame obtained by the Reza et al. method [Reza et al., 2009], vi – segmented frame obtained by the Howe and Deschamps method [Howe & Deschamps, 2004])

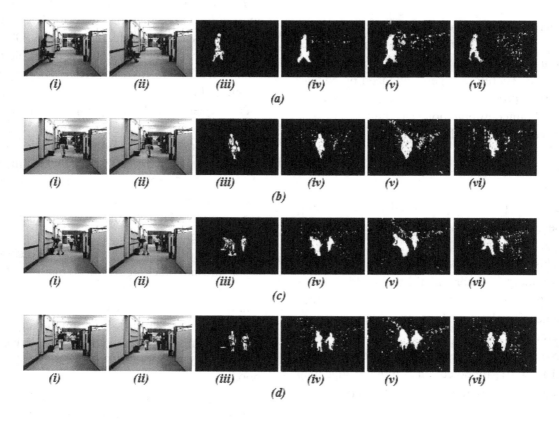

where $I_g(\alpha, \beta)$, $I_s(\alpha, \beta)$ are ground-truth and achieved segmented frames respectively with dimension $(\alpha \times \beta)$. Value of α and β are same in segmented frame as well as in ground-truth frame. Value of Misclassification penalty should be less for better segmentation.

Relative position based measure can be computed as (Yang & Zhang, 2004):

$$RPM = 1 - \frac{\| Centroid_{GT} - Centroid_{Seg} \|}{2\sqrt{\pi}.\sqrt{Area_{GT}}} \quad (21)$$

where $Centroid_{GT}$ and $Centroid_{Seg}$ are Centroids of object in ground-truth frame and achieved segmented frame respectively. $Area_{GT}$ is the area of object in ground-truth frame. $\|.\|$ is the Euclidean distance. Value of RPM will be 1 for a perfect segmentation and decreases with the centroid shift increases.

Performance table for the discussed algorithm and other algorithms (Huang & Hsieh, 2003; Reza et al., 2009; Howe & Deschamps, 2004) for Hall monitor video sequence are given in Table 2. From Figure 5 and Table 2, one can see that, use of Daubechies complex wavelet transform gives better result in segmentation of moving object

Table 2. Performance measures value for hall monitor video sequence

A–Misclassification Penalty				
Frame Number	The Discussed Method	Huang and Hsieh method (Huang & Hsieh, 2003)	Reza et al. method (Reza et al., 2009)	Howe and Deschamps method (Howe & Deschamps, 2004)
25	0.0190	0.1322	0.0821	0.1604
75	0.0418	0.0679	0.0281	0.0199
125	0.0079	0.0108	0.0382	0.0662
175	0.0061	0.0112	0.0170	0.0101
225	0.0035	0.0032	0.0093	0.0043
275	0.0037	0.0052	0.0063	0.0947
B–Relative Position Based Measure				
Frame Number	The Discussed Method	Huang and Hsieh method (Huang & Hsieh, 2003)	Reza et al. method (Reza et al., 2009)	Howe and Deschamps method (Howe & Deschamps, 2004)
25	0.9678	0.9185	0.7682	0.6152
75	0.8742	0.9116	0.8655	0.9064
125	0.9946	0.9561	0.8996	0.8701
175	0.9944	0.9529	0.8802	0.9676
225	0.9706	0.9408	0.9112	0.9625
275	0.9891	0.9761	0.8673	0.7137

in comparison to other wavelet domain method (Huang & Hsieh, 2003) as well as spatial domain methods (Reza et al., 2009; Howe & Deschamps, 2004).

SHADOW DETECTION AND REMOVAL

In this section, we have shown how Daubechies complex wavelet transform is useful for detection and removal of shadow from moving object. Presence of shadow reduces the performance of any computer vision system therefore shadow detection and removal is a challenging task for better performance of a vision system. Shadow of an object occurs when light from a light source cannot reach at certain portion of space due to obstruction by the object itself. Object part that is not illuminated by light is called self-shadow and projection of object on the background in the

Figure 6. Different types of shadow

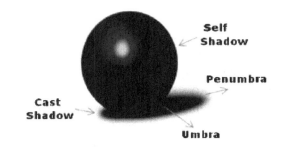

direction of light source is known as cast shadow. Cast shadow is divided into two parts: umbra and penumbra. Umbra is the darkest part of shadow where light source is completely occluded with object and penumbra is the portion where light source is obscured by the occluding body. It has been shown in Figure 6.

The real challenge for shadow detection problem is to distinguish object and its shadow as they share the same motion features. Main objectives of any shadow detection and removal algorithm is to locate shadow region, to distinguish shadow from foreground object, and then to remove it from scene. Various algorithms for shadow detection and removal exist for still images whereas only few algorithms have been developed for moving objects. Sanin et al. (2012) had reported four categories of shadow detection technique: physical method based shadow detection (Prati et al., 2003), geometry based shadow detection (Hsieh et al., 2003; Conaire et al., 2007), texture based shadow detection (Xu et al., 2005; Leone & Distante, 2007) and color based shadow detection (Guan, 2010; Cucchiara et al., 2003).

Physical method based shadow detection requires prior information of camera localization, geometry of observed objects, direction of light source etc. whereas geometry based shadow detection method have certain similarities with physical method based shadow detection as these method also require knowledge of ground surface, object geometry, etc. Principle behind texture based shadow detection is that the texture of foreground object is different from texture of background. One disadvantage of these types of methods is that they have limited capability to detect shadow from small region in frame. Color based shadow detection techniques are good in the sense that they does not require any pre analyzed parameter except color information and attempts to describe the color changes of shadow pixels and find the color features that are illumination invariant. Guan (2010) proposed a shadow detection and removal algorithm by using HSV color model and real valued discrete wavelet transform.

All the method mentioned above in different categories are suffering from the problem of either some algorithm fails to give accurate result in various lighting and environmental conditions or other algorithms are not able to detect shadow accurately in umbra and penumbra region. Motivated by these problem as well as work of Guan (2010),

Figure 7. Structuring element for morphological operation in the proposed method

0	1	0
1	1	1
0	1	0

which uses real valued wavelet transform, we have developed Daubechies complex wavelet transform based shadow detection and removal algorithm. The Daubechies complex wavelet transform have advantages of shift-invariance, better directional selectivity and strong edge information as compared to real valued wavelet transform.

We have used HSV color model, for detection of pixels, which have been changed due to moving object and its shadows, because this color model corresponds closely with the human perception of color and it easily separates chromaticity and luminosity. As Hue component of HSV changes quite dramatically depending on the strength of shadow, we have used value and saturation component of each frame for processing. In the developed method, the inputs are background (or reference) frame and a current frame with moving object. Value and saturation components of these images are further decomposed using Daubechies complex wavelet transform.

In the present approach, we have used Daubechies complex wavelet coefficients of value component of HSV to detect moving object with shadow and logical AND of complex wavelet coefficients of saturation component with complex wavelet coefficients of value component is used to remove shadow from detected moving object with shadow.

Let ΔV and ΔS be differences of current frame and background frame for value component and saturation component respectively. Let $DW_{\Delta V}$

and $DW_{\Delta S}$ be complex wavelet coefficients of ΔV and ΔS after wavelet decomposition using Daubechies complex wavelet transform respectively. Let $(\sigma)_{DW_{\Delta V}}$ and $(\sigma)_{DW_{\Delta S}}$ be standard deviation of $DW_{\Delta V}$ and $DW_{\Delta S}$ respectively. Here value of standard deviation is used as a threshold value.

Condition of shadow detection at each pixel (i,j) for foreground detected object with shadow is defined as:

$$SD = \begin{cases} 1, & if\, DW_{\Delta V} \geq (\sigma)_{DW_{\Delta V}} \\ 0, & otherwise \end{cases} \qquad (22)$$

Condition for detection of foreground object without shadow at each pixel (i,j) is defined as:

$$SR = \begin{cases} 1, & if\, DW_{\Delta V} \geq (\sigma)_{DW_{\Delta V}} \wedge DW_{\Delta S} \geq (\sigma)_{DW_{\Delta S}} \\ 0, & otherwise \end{cases}$$

$$(23)$$

Some shadow points are misclassified in detected object after shadow removal. Therefore to improve this problem some morphological operation is needed for better shape structure. For better shape structure we have used binary closing morphological operation as described by Gonzalez and Woods (Gonzalez & Woods, 2008) with structuring element given in Figure 7.

Figure 8. Shadow detection and removal results for highway video sequence corresponding to (a) frame 100, (b) frame 200, (c) frame 300, (d) frame 400 (i – current frame, ii – detected object after shadow detection using discussed method, iii – detected object after shadow detection using Guan method [Guan, 2010], iv – detected object after shadow removal using Discussed method, v – detected object after shadow removal using Guan method [Guan, 2010])

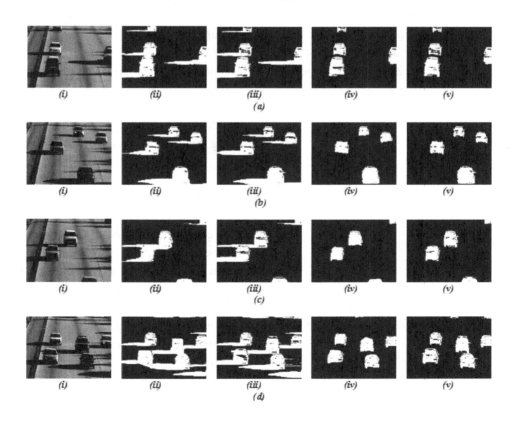

Table 3. Performance parameter value for highway video sequence

Methods Name	Shadow Detection Rate (η)	Shadow Discrimination Rate (ξ)
Discussed method	87.27	94.49
Guan method (Guan, 2010)	85.61	87.96

We have tested the proposed shadow detection and removal algorithm on a number of videos. Here shadow detection and removal result after applying the discussed method and Guan method (Guan, 2010) for one representative Highway video sequence are given in Figure 8.

From Figure 8, one can see that, result of the discussed method performs better than result of Guan method (Guan, 2010) for all frames of Highway video sequence. It can also be observed that the discussed method works well in low contrast between object and background as well as in case of poor shadow in comparison to Guan method (Guan, 2010).

For quantitative performance evaluation of the discussed method and Guan method (Guan, 2010), we have considered two performance parameters: Shadow detection rate (η) and Shadow discrimination rate (ξ) (Prati et al., 2003). Shadow detection and Shadow discrimination rates are computed as below (Prati et al., 2003).

$$\eta = \frac{TP_S}{TP_S + FN_S} \qquad (24)$$

and

$$\xi = \frac{\overline{TP_F}}{TP_F + FN_F} \qquad (25)$$

where TP is True positive and FN is False negative, subscript S and F stands for frame with shadow and frame without shadow, respectively.

Performance value of these two parameters for the discussed method and Guan method (Guan, 2010) are given in Table 3.

CONCLUSION

In this chapter, we have provided an overview of Daubechies complex wavelet transform based computer vision applications of moving object segmentation and shadow detection and removal. We have shown construction and different properties of Daubechies complex wavelet transform. Daubechies complex wavelet transform is beneficial than other real valued wavelet transform because real valued wavelet transform coefficients are shift dependent, have poor directional selectivity and sensitive for edges whereas Daubechies complex wavelet transform is approximate shift-invariance, have better directional selectivity and have better edge detection. Hopefully, the reader of this chapter will find that Daubechies complex wavelet transform is an active wavelet transform, which can be applied on several other computer vision applications. Here two applications—moving object segmentation and shadow detection and removal—have been discussed by using this transform.

FUTURE RESEARCH DIRECTIONS

This chapter is an attempt to demonstrate use of Daubechies complex wavelet transform for two applications. Yet many other computer vision applications remain exist on which Daubechies complex wavelet transform can be applied like denoising, deblurring, shape identification, image matching, rendering, face recognition, and activity recognition, etc.

ACKNOWLEDGMENT

This work was supported in part by the Department of Science and Technology, New Delhi, India, under grant no. SR/FTP/ETA-023/2009, and the University Grants Commission, New Delhi, India, under grant no. 36-246/2008(SR).

REFERENCES

Binh, N. T., & Khare, A. (2010). Multilevel threshold based image denoising in curvelet domain. *Journal of Computer Science and Technology*, *25*(3), 632–640. doi:10.1007/s11390-010-9352-y.

Clonda, D., Lina, J.-M., & Goulard, B. (2004). Complex Daubechies wavelets: Properties and statistical image modeling. *Signal Processing*, *84*, 1–23. doi:10.1016/j.sigpro.2003.06.001.

Conaire, C. O., Connor, N. E. O., & Smeaton, A. (2007). Detector adaptation by maximising agreement between independent data sources. In *Proceedings of the IEEE Conference on Computer Vision and Pattern Recognition* (pp. 1-6). IEEE.

Cucchiara, R., Grana, C., Piccardi, M., & Prati, A. (2003). Detecting moving objects, ghosts and shadows in video streams. *IEEE Transactions on Pattern Analysis and Machine Intelligence*, *25*(10), 1337–1342. doi:10.1109/TPAMI.2003.1233909.

Daubechies, I. (1992). *Ten lectures on wavelets*. Society for Industrial and Applied Mathematics. doi:10.1137/1.9781611970104.

Erdem, C. E., Sankur, B., & Tekalp, A. M. (2004). Performance measures for video object segmentation and tracking. *IEEE Transactions on Image Processing*, *13*(7), 937–951. doi:10.1109/TIP.2004.828427 PMID:15648860.

Fernandes, F. C. A., Spaendonck, R. L. C. V., & Burrus, C. S. (2003). A new framework for complex wavelet transforms. *IEEE Transactions on Signal Processing*, *51*(7), 1825–1837. doi:10.1109/TSP.2003.812841.

Gonzalez, R. C., & Woods, R. E. (2008). *Digital image processing* (2nd ed.). Englewood Cliffs, NJ: Prentice Hall Publications.

Guan, Y. P. (2010). Spatio-temporal motion-based foreground segmentation and shadow suppression. *IET Computer Vision*, *4*(1), 50–60. doi:10.1049/iet-cvi.2008.0016.

Howe, N. R., & Deschamps, A. (2004). *Better foreground segmentation through graph cuts* (Technical Report). Smith College. Retrieved January 31, 2013, from http://arxiv.org/abs/cs.CV/0401017

Hsieh, J. W., Hu, W. F., Chang, C. J., & Chen, Y. H. (2003). Shadow elimination for effective moving object detection by Gaussian shadow modeling. *Image and Vision Computing*, *21*(6), 505–516. doi:10.1016/S0262-8856(03)00030-1.

Huang, C. L., & Liao, B. Y. (2001). A robust scene-change detection method for video segmentation. *IEEE Transactions on Circuits and Systems for Video Technology*, *11*(12), 1281–1288. doi:10.1109/76.974682.

Huang, J. C., & Hsieh, W. S. (2003). Wavelet based moving object segmentation. *Electronics Letters*, *39*(19), 1380–1382. doi:10.1049/el:20030909.

Jalobeanu, A., Feraud, L.-B., & Zerubia, J. (2000). *Satellite image deconvolution using complex wavelets packets*. INRIA Report No. 3955.

Khare, A., Khare, M., Jeong, Y. Y., Kim H., & Jeon, M., (2010a). Despeckling of medical ultrasound images using Daubechies complex wavelet transform. *Signal Processing*, *90*(2), 428-439. doi:10.1016/j.sigpro.2009.07.008.

Khare, A., & Tiwary, U. S. (2006). Symmetric Daubechies complex wavelet transform and its application to denoising and deblurring. *WSEAS Transactions on Signal Processing, 2*(5), 738–745.

Khare, A., & Tiwary, U. S. (2007). Daubechies complex wavelet transform based technique for denoising of medical images. *International Journal of Image and Graphics. World Scientific Publications, 7*(4), 663–687.

Khare, A., Tiwary, U. S., & Jeon, M. (2009). Daubechies complex wavelet transform based multilevel shrinkage for deblurring of medical images in presence of noise. *International Journal of Wavelets, Multresolution, and Information Processing, 7*(5), 587–604. doi:10.1142/S0219691309003100.

Khare, A., Tiwary, U. S., Pedrycz, W., & Jeon, M. (2010b). Multilevel adaptive thresholding and shrinkage technique for denoising using Daubechies complex wavelet transform. *The Imaging Science Journal, 58*(6), 340–358. doi:10.1179/136821910X12750339175826.

Khare, M., & Srivastava, R. K. (2012). Level set method for segmentation of medical images without reinitialization. *Journal of Medical Imaging and Health Informatics, 2*(2), 158–167. doi:10.1166/jmihi.2012.1079.

Lawton, W. (1993). Applications of complex valued wavelet transform in subband decomposition. *IEEE Transactions on Signal Processing, 41*(12), 3566–3568. doi:10.1109/78.258098.

Leone, A., & Distante, C. (2007). Shadow detection for moving objects based on texture analysis. *Pattern Recognition, 40*(4), 1222–1233. doi:10.1016/j.patcog.2006.09.017.

Lina, J.-M., & Mayrand, M. (1995). Complex Daubechies wavelets. *Journal of Applied and Computational Harmonic Analysis, 2*, 219–229. doi:10.1006/acha.1995.1015.

Mansouri, A. R., & Konrad, J. (2003). Multiple motion segmentation with level sets. *IEEE Transactions on Image Processing, 12*(2), 201–220. doi:10.1109/TIP.2002.807582 PMID:18237901.

Peng, B., Zhang, L., & Zhang, D. (2013). A survey of graph theoretical approaches to image segmentation. *Pattern Recognition, 46*(3), 1020–1038. doi:10.1016/j.patcog.2012.09.015.

Prati, A., Mikic, I., Trivedi, M. M., & Cucchiara, R. (2003). Detecting moving shadows: Algorithms and evaluation. *IEEE Transactions on Pattern Analysis and Machine Intelligence, 25*(7), 918–923. doi:10.1109/TPAMI.2003.1206520.

Reza, H., Broojeni, S., & Charkari, N. M. (2009). A new background subtraction method in video sequences based on temporal motion windows. *International Journal of the Computer, the Internet and Management, 17*(SP1), 25.1-25.7.

Sanin, A., Sanderson, C., & Lovell, B. C. (2012). Shadow detection: A survey and comparative evaluation of recent methods. *Pattern Recognition, 45*(2), 1684–1695. doi:10.1016/j.patcog.2011.10.001.

Selesnick, I. W. (2004). The double-density dual-tree DWT. *IEEE Transactions on Signal Processing, 52*(5), 1304–1314. doi:10.1109/TSP.2004.826174.

Selesnick, I. W., Baraniuk, R. G., & Kingsbury, N. G. (2005). The dual-tree complex wavelet transform. *IEEE Signal Processing Magazine, 22*(6), 123–151. doi:10.1109/MSP.2005.1550194.

Ville, D. V. D., & Unser, M. (2008). Complex wavelet bases, steerability, and the Marr-like pyramid. *IEEE Transactions on Image Processing, 17*(11), 2063–2080. doi:10.1109/TIP.2008.2004797 PMID:18972650.

Wang, L., Hu, W., & Tan, T. (2002). Recent developments in human motion analysis. *Pattern Recognition*, *36*(3), 585–601. doi:10.1016/S0031-3203(02)00100-0.

Wickerhauser, M. V. (1994). *Adapted wavelet analysis from theory to software*. AK Peters Ltd..

Xu, D., Li, X., Liu, Z., & Yuan, Y. (2005). Cast shadow detection in video segmentation. *Pattern Recognition Letters*, *26*(1), 91–99. doi:10.1016/j.patrec.2004.09.005.

Yang, G. B., & Zhang, Z. Y. (2004). Objective performance evaluation of video segmentation algorithms with ground-truth. *Journal of Shanghai University*, *8*(1), 70–74. doi:10.1007/s11741-004-0015-5.

Zhang, H., Fritts, J. E., & Goldman, S. A. (2008). Image segmentation evaluation: A survey of unsupervised methods. *Computer Vision and Image Understanding*, *110*(2), 260–280. doi:10.1016/j.cviu.2007.08.003.

Zhang, X.-P., Desai, M. D., & Peng, Y.-N. (1999). Orthogonal complex filter banks and wavelets: Some properties and design. *IEEE Transactions on Signal Processing*, *47*(4), 1039–1048. doi:10.1109/78.752601.

KEY TERMS AND DEFINITIONS

Computer Vision: A branch of image processing with computer processing of images from the real world.

Daubechies Complex Wavelet Transform: The Daubechies complex wavelet transform is a special case of the Discrete wavelet transform that uses complex valued Daubechies wavelet as basis function.

Discrete Wavelet Transform: The Discrete wavelet transform is a special case of the wavelet transform that provides a compact representation of a signal in time and frequency that can be computed efficiently.

Moving Object Segmentation: Segmentation of object from video frames is known as moving object segmentation.

Shadow Detection: Detection of object with its associated shadow is known as shadow detection.

Shadow Removal: Detection of object without its associated shadow after shadow detection is known as shadow removal.

Shift-Invariance: A transform having shift-invariance property if input signal shift causes same effect on transform coefficients.

Single Change Detection: Difference of two consecutive frames in video is known as single change detection.

Chapter 8
Application of Computer Vision Techniques for Exploiting New Video Coding Mechanisms

Artur Miguel Arsenio

Nokia Siemens Networks SA, Portugal[1] & Universidade Tecnica de Lisboa, Portugal

ABSTRACT

One of the main concerns for current multimedia platforms is the provisioning of content that provides a good Quality of Experience to end-users. This can be achieved through new interactive, personalized content applications, as well by improving the image quality delivered to the end-user. This chapter addresses these issues by describing mechanisms for changing content consumption. The aim is to give Application Service Providers (ASPs) new ways to allow users to configure contents according to their personal tastes while also improving their Quality of Experience, and to possibly charge users for such functionalities. The authors propose to employ computer vision techniques to produce extra object information, which further expands the range of video personalization possibilities on the presence of new video coding mechanisms.

DOI: 10.4018/978-1-4666-4868-5.ch008

INTRODUCTION

Telecommunication operators need to deliver their clients not only new profitable services, but also good quality, personalized and interactive content. This chapter addresses mechanisms for transforming image content on videos (video clips, video stream), in the form of objects, into other objects as selected by end-users using the à priori availability of 3D models of objects (which we denote content impersonation). The chapter presents possible objects representations, according to a set of transmission parameters, so that it is transmitted not only information concerning image content, but also information concerning how objects in such image (within a video stream) can be transformed. We also address the efficient transmission of such content over a multimedia distribution network, describing a methodology that exploits new object-oriented video coding mechanisms.

Another important factor driving users' quality of experience, besides multimedia content personalization and interactivity, is the transparent reception of multimedia content over fixed-mobile convergent networks. Nowadays, terminal devices have different processing capabilities – often, home devices have considerable processing power and higher display resolution, while mobile terminals, such as mobile phones, have smaller displays. For content recording, mobile phones often produce video streams of lower resolution than the desirable ones to see on a large home set. So, it is desirable to increase resolution to specific image objects in order to better view the later in larger displays with higher resolution. We will further show how computer vision techniques can be employed to improve video consumers' Quality of Experience on a multimedia distribution network, while simultaneously expanding the content generation possibilities from users' mobile devices, and the correspondent content consumption. Such techniques support the convergence of mobile and fixed content, increasing objects' reso-

lution, and recovering from transmission errors in order to provide the end-user a better service. Therefore, we not only exploit object based coding on new video coding mechanisms, but also scalable video coding allowing the end-device to select among a set of scales the resolution that best fits its capabilities.

Current solutions are appropriate for merging video segments from different sources (in slices), or by removing segments (such as advertisement segments), or even replacing some segments by others. The other main application of current solutions is to respond to events on a video stream (e.g. upon appearance of a certain object, to display information concerning this object).

The closest solutions already in the market include Content Management Systems, used either for simply managing content provided by external entities or to provide some removal operations such as advertisement removal for videos. These solutions have the disadvantages that they are not able to adapt video content to users, by merging other data to create new content or transforming existing one – their power rely mostly on the removal of features and on adding descriptive texts (e.g. Biography of a soccer player on soccer games, which may be event triggered, such as the push of a button by a user).

This chapter describes solutions that allow ASPs to provide users automatic ways to adapt and configure the (online, live) content to their tastes—and even more—to manipulate the content of live (or offline) video streams (in a way that PhotoShop did for images or AdobePremiere, into a certain extent, to offline videos).

Indeed, a telecommunication provider or operator delivers to its client various services according to different quality of Service guarantees, sometimes dependent on the bandwidth available in the respective communication network. The objective of the approach provided in this chapter is in particular to enable an operator or application service provider to offer additional applications and/or services to a user that are of high interest for this user and allows a high degree of personalization to adjust the content to his or her individual taste. In order to overcome this problem, a method for processing a data stream is provided comprising the steps of: 1) identifying at least one object within a data stream that is tagged as transformable; 2) transformation of object within such stream. This new approach allows an Application Service Provider (ASP) to provide users with the possibility to adapt and/ or configure a data stream, e.g., a TV-broadcast, a video on demand, an online or live content to their particular preferences and in particular to further manipulate the content thereof.

This approach in particular relates to content manipulation of data streams comprising in audio and/or video content. The data stream may be provided in or via a network (such network nay comprise for instance an IP network). The user is connected to such IP network via any access network, comprising, e.g., a Digital Subscriber Line (DSL), a Radio Access Network (RAN), cable network, or the like.

Personalization, Interactivity, and Quality of Experience

Nowadays Television and Internet are a deep part of our society. Most people rely on those two mediums as primary sources of information. New TV related technologies and recent progresses on others, such as SmartTVs set-top boxes are pushing those two technologies together. However, TV broadcasting is still controlled by a few companies who define the information being delivered to their clients. New technologies such as Mobile TV (TV in the cellphone) and Over-the-top TV (OTTtv) (TV on desktop computers) are also arising, yet, they share the same principle as standard TV solutions, a broadcaster company controls the broadcast programs and information. On the other end, in the Internet, solutions are appearing (e.g. QiK) where any individual can start and broadcast live video to other users.

Said individual is responsible for controlling and choosing all the information shown in his virtual channel. User created content becomes therefore possible with the appearance of new Websites that allow live videos and shows. Any person can, with few resources when compared to huge broadcasting companies, start to host live programs and events like it already happened on television networks. With the advancement of mobile phones and wireless technologies new innovative applications are also being deployed. Technological advances allowed most phones to have video cameras, 4G network access and GPS technology. Technology is getting more integrated into everyday life. Another wide phenomenon is the concept of Lifecasting. Basically, Lifecasting is the continual broadcast of one's personal life thorough wearable cameras that shows the user's everyday life from his point of view.

The consumer becomes therefore the producer (prosumer) of multimedia content. Armed with a video camera any person can start transmitting live events (Rosa & Arsenio, 2010), whether news for a small town, sporting events or even accidents or natural disasters. Therefore, a main challenge for multimedia applications arises from the need for creating personal, interactive multimedia applications providing new levels of Quality of Experience to the end user. Equally important are the challenges brought by a diverse set of video acquisition and consumption terminals, for which the end-users should get delivered sufficient video quality. We propose to exploit computer vision techniques, combining them with new multimedia transmission protocols, and video coding mechanisms, in order to address such challenges.

Additionally, following the prosumer model, the real-time, dynamic annotation and transformation of multimedia content brings as well further opportunities, since a large number of versions of the original multimedia content produced by large companies, will be produced by end-users from transformations applied to the original broadcasted content.

Our approach enables an object based network mechanism to transform video content as chosen or selected by a user. The user can in particular select transformable objects within a video content (e.g., video broadcast, VoD, TV-broadcast) and configure a type of transformation, which may comprise a replacement of at least one object by at another object or changing a shape of (or transforming) an existing object. The object to be selected by the user is advantageously provided by a database as a template, which may be hierarchically structured and/or modelled. Such templates may comprise video as well as audio content. If, e.g., a person (or a portion thereof like his or her face) in a video content is identified, the person can be replaced by a video template showing a different person or an artificial person (e.g., a drawing) as well as by an audio template replacing the voice of said original person. Each template, video or audio, may be provided as a model that can be rather simple or very complex.

Additionally, new business models become possible based on user content generation, since transformed content is as such new content that can be sold as well by the application service provider (ASP) to other users. ASPs may charge users to view such content and give credits or a proportion of the profit to users that created such content.

New Possibilities Arising from Object-Based Video Coding

With new versions of MPEG-4, the images on a video will come decomposed as tagged objects. Hence, it will become easier to implement the object based video encoding solutions proposed in this chapter, since objects will not have to be detected and tracked in real-time on the video image. The user selects the feature to be replaced, which is already isolated on the image (e.g. instead of employing face detection, image faces might already come tagged as face objects on the MPEG-4 video stream). With new coding mechanisms, the solution might run completely in cheaper home hardware. Hence, new coding and transmission protocols become possible.

A video stream is usually made up of images at a fixed resolution, which are transmitted in different formats according to the video coding protocol employed. With the Improvement solutions proposed in this chapter, it becomes possible to specify video coding protocols in which an image is transmitted as high-resolution and low resolution objects, i.e., not all objects in an image have the same resolution, has is the case nowadays. This will require new video coding protocols (besides MPEG4 and MPEG7 which are targeting coding by objects – but of equal resolution).

Chapter Organization

This introduction started by presenting the problems addressed by this chapter, as well the main motivation behind our work. The next section presents the challenges brought by several new scenarios for applying computer vision techniques in multimedia solutions. It will also address the potential impact of new video content mechanisms for content creation and distribution.

We will discuss afterwards a new object oriented coding mechanism especially appropriate for image object processing, and for tagging such objects for transformations that can be applied anywhere on a distribution network.

We will also address the potential impact brought from computer vision techniques into applications employing scalable video coding techniques. In order to stream audio/ video over the network, the data is usually split into segments which are then encapsulated into packets with special headers appropriate for audio/ video transmissions, and we will discuss how intra-image adaptive techniques can be employed in order to provide different transmission quality levels to diverse video stream objects.

Finally, the chapter concludes with a discussion on the main benefits brought by the proposed approaches.

COMPUTER VISION VS. VIDEO CODING

This section reviews briefly main scenarios where computer vision techniques are potentially very useful for content adaptation, describing several use-cases demonstrating the potential for the usage of such techniques.

Various methods for data and/or object processing are known, e.g. object and/or face detection and recognition, 3D modelling of objects, deformable contours, multi-feature tracking, head gaze inference estimation, eye detection and eye tracking, image perspective projections (Arsenio, 2004). Furthermore, methods are known to track lips or movements in video contents.

Computer Vision for Image Processing on Multimedia Applications

It is beneficial importing computer vision techniques, traditionally employed on machine vision, into multimedia applications, such as object/face detection and recognition, 3D modeling, or deformable contours. We address several motivational use-cases enabled by applying computer vision techniques for exploiting new coding mechanisms.

As a possible scenario, consider an actor in a movie, and a set of end-user photos. Using computer graphics techniques (B-Splines or other Deformable Contours, image perspective transformations, Image correspondence techniques – a wide spectrum of technologies are now available) the movie can be changed dynamically and adapted to the end-user wishes. For instance, the actor's face can be replaced by the end-user face, and the later become suddenly the movie hero. Other people face, or an animation character head, can also be employed to replace the real face (or the all personage body) instead. And as the actor speaks on the real movie, so does the new hero on the new transformed movie.

This is currently not new for voice – new audio is added to a stream of images to avoid the use of subtitles in foreign countries to the movie maker. There are indeed currently some Content Management Systems on the market which are used for instance to remove advertisements from videos. But we want to go much further, and to create a Content Customization / Transformation System, which is a novelty.

Hence, merging received content with ones' own content turns possible changing a story with customizable actors. And this can be applied as well to change the person that delivers the night news, or the weather channel. The software required for this procedure can be deployed on a home STB or distributed on the network – the goal is to create a totally personalized Home Entertainment system.

Impersonate

Impersonate corresponds to making a person taking the place of another one (let's say, "face cloning"), by merging new content into streamed content, according to the illustration in Figure 1.

The figure presents two examples for content impersonation (Arsenio, 2009):

- Replacing a person's face on a news show by another person, such as a US president face. This is done by extracting from the video the face contours of the target, his leaps position, and possibly other features, such as emotional state from face image (Maglogiannis et al, 2009) or from voice content (Breazeal & Aryananda, 2002). A 3D model of the US president is then deformed according to this input so that the final view is used to replace the original content. The final image might then be filtered for better quality.
- Replacing a person's face on the news show by a synthetic creature, which requires a simpler operation than the previous, since

Figure 1. Illustration scenario for impersonation using both 3D models of real people and of synthetic characters. The flow works as follows: (1) the end-user selects the feature (from a set of available features, obtained from face detection, for instance) on a video stream (received from a TV channel selection) that he wants to be replaced, as well the new desired features; (2) a 3D model of the new feature, with the appearance build from face images from different views, and according to the model of the detected feature is created; (3) the new model is adapted to the original model (leaps position, emotional state, gazing direction, etc.), being the final view used to replace the original face (4). (2',3') presents a similar flow but in which a 3D model of a synthetic, artificial creature is used.

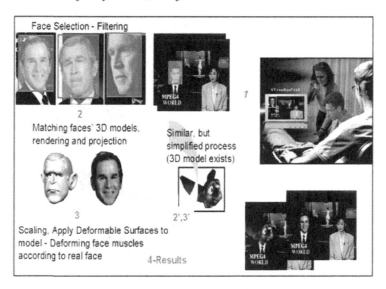

these models are easier to manipulate than ones built from real people images.

The user configures his/her content merging / transformation solution in order to replace all faces, during a given time interval, by a given category of faces. Or else, after a user configures the news shows for one time, it sets the system to apply the some configuration everyday at that time. For instance, this will require additionally face recognition in a multi-face image in order for the system to be able to determine which face should be replaced by a given new face. Hence, on the user's settings, it will be saved a set of features that describe uniquely the video people face (or set of faces) to be detected and replaced (standard face recognition schemes can be used, such as eigenfaces (Arsenio, 2004), face templates, etc.).

Stretch

Stretch corresponds to transforming a feature on a video so that the same feature appears stretched thereafter (Arsenio, 2009), as shown by Figure 2. Stretch is an example among a larger set of operations that may be performed on a collection of features (scaling, skewing, etc.) in order to personalize the content received.

Next Generation "Karaoke"

Karaoke is nowadays very common, corresponding to a performer trying to mimic a singer (or a movie actor) in order to match their voices as good as possible. Several karaoke systems are now available on the market, including solutions, which are offered by telecommunication operators on their IPTV packages.

Figure 2. Illustration scenario for stretching. This figure presents an embodiment for stretching a feature on a video. For instance, the user might want to stretch vertically or horizontally a face, so that people on a news show might appear as from another world. The flow works as follows: (1) the end-user selects the feature (from a set of available features, obtained from face detection, for instance) on a video stream (received from a TV channel selection, for instance) that he wants to be replaced, (2) a 2D model of the selected feature is built, and extended, (3) the 2D model is scaled according to the user's input, being the final view used to replace the original face (4).

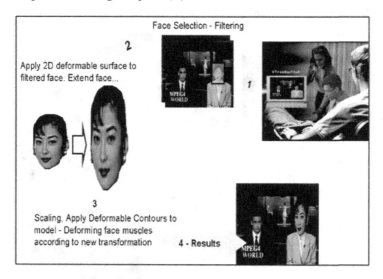

Movieoke is another form of entertainment in which a performer tries to mimic physically an actor, being place in front of a video-projection of the movie – the goal here is on matching as good as possible the gestures of the movie actor.

Next Generation Karaoke consists on mimicking both voice and gestures (at least face appearance and expression, as well as leap gestures and eye direction, for instance). This can be accomplished by placing the performer's image on the movie (instead of in front of it as it happens for Movieoke). This last step can be made according different levels of difficulty for the end-user to play the game (being the difficulty level selected with a scrollbar, for example), providing this way a differentiation factor in interactive karaoke: difficult level – performer's video is projected as it is on original video; medium level – the performer's face or body on the performer's video is projected to the original video according to the original actor's

pose; easy level – a 3D model of the performer's face is build, and projected to the original video as a face cloning in the Impersonate embodiment (Arsenio, 2009).

QoE Improvement

In another scenario, a video stream, as recorded by a mobile device, appears with a low resolution – not proper to be viewed on a plasma TV. But after additional processing a person's face on the video becomes clear and with a sharp contrast as if it were recorded with a higher resolution device (as illustrated by Figure 3). Notice that remaining non-processed video objects maintain the original quality. We will also address other techniques such as hallucinating objects (namely hallucinating faces (Baker & Kanade, 2000), described later in this chapter), which combine computer vision with machine learning mechanisms.

Figure 3. This figure presents the flow for increasing the resolution of image objects for improving overall mage quality and end-user quality of experience

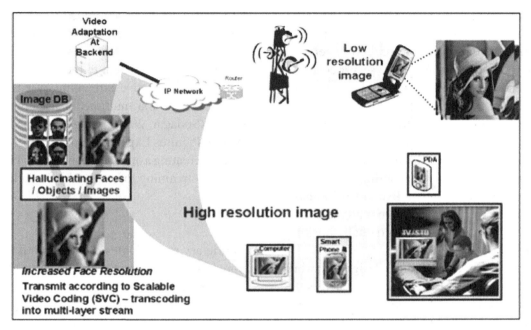

A database of faces represented at the target resolution is employed in order to increase the resolution of an image's object (a face) into such a target resolution. The global properties of a face as encoded on the Database are used to complement the face local properties on the low-resolution image, allowing to recover high resolution details of it.

After conversion, the video might be encoded again and streamed to multiple devices – according to new MPEG standard SVC, this streaming might be done on a multy-layer structure in order to match the resolution of multiple end-devices.

As another related scenario, let's consider an image object which, due to network packet losses, appears on a video stream with several "black" pixels (lost information), but after additional processing, appears again within a very good quality image. This processing consists of a mechanism for improving the image content quality on a video stream (degraded for instance due to packet loss, low-resolution source devices), based on object

manipulation in an image segmented into a set of objects. The solution uses information in a database of objects in order to compensate for the loss of information in image's detected objects. Such kind of scenarios as recovering from errors and increasing images resolutions are increasingly important, as in the near future MobileTV and IPTV solutions are converging, especially on content compatibility for both solutions.

New network planning and services delivery possibilities arise. According to the characteristics of an access networks, there are some links and / or network elements more prone than others to cause transmission errors. A possibility introduced by this solution is the configuration of a network considering multimedia improvement modules for error recovering at specific network points.

Streaming Technologies

In this section, we present the most commonly used video codecs and formats.

HTTP Streaming

HTTP Streaming works over TCP, and is becoming a trend in the industry. It allows the transmission of multimedia data from ordinary Web servers. This way, companies can reduce server costs – a media server is more expensive than a standard Web browser. Regarding live HTTP streaming, multiple companies have already launched their versions of adaptive bitrate streaming – a technology that allows the video bitrate to adapt according to the end user hardware capabilities. Additionally, using this technique, a live video can have a fast start by starting the stream with the lowest bitrate and then increasing it gradually, making for a higher quality video.

Adaptive bitrate streaming is designed to work efficiently over large HTTP networks such as the Internet. It works by monitoring the user's device bandwidth and CPU available capacity and arranges the video quality and bitrate in accordance to the available resources (Akhshabi & Begen, 2011). This way, in congested networks, the user can still receive video but with relative bad quality and when the network becomes unclogged, the video quality gets progressively better. This allows for little buffering, fast start-time and seek-time in both high and low quality networks.

Apple HTTP Live Streaming, Microsoft Smooth Streaming and Adobe's HTTP Dynamic Streaming are examples of adaptive bitrate streaming implementations. HTTP Live Streaming (HLS) is a protocol implemented by Apple that allows to stream live or previously recorded video over HTTP from an ordinary Web server to multiple types of devices such as Android and iOS mobile devices, and desktop computers. Since it only uses HTTP packets, unlike other protocols like RTP and RTSP, HTTP Live Streaming is capable of traversing any firewall. Other companies, such as *Akamai* and *Wowza* are also already streaming HLS. Microsoft Smooth Streaming is a IIS Media Services extensions that allows live and VOD adaptive streaming over HTTP. IIS Media

Services allows the Smooth Streaming of H.264 videos to be repacked into the HLS format and delivered to the devices supplied by HLS. Netflix is a provider of on-demand Internet streaming video that uses Microsoft Smooth Streaming to deliver the media content to the end-users.

Dynamic Adaptive Streaming over HTTP or MPEG DASH is a multimedia streaming technology (Sodagar, 2011) being developed by the Moving Pictures Expert Group (MPEG) with the intent of creating a open standard for HTTP-based adaptive streaming to be used by the industry.

HTML5

Proprietary technologies provided until recently more functionality than Web standards, allowing the creation of richer Internet applications. Some examples of these proprietary technologies are: Flash from Adobe, Quicktime from Apple and Silverlight from Microsoft. Despite the functionalities provided by proprietary technologies, they also tend to lock in users to these specific technologies (Vanghan-Nichols, 2010). HTML5 offers users and developers a standard with enhanced functionality with no need for proprietary technologies. With HTML5 it is possible to develop richer Web pages and Web based applications, so that proprietary plugins, which installation used to be required, are no longer necessary.

An example of one of the most important features of HTML5 is the canvas tags, which enable the creation and incorporation of 2-Dimensional (2D) shapes and bitmap images through JavaScript or Application Programming Interfaces (APIs). Canvas is a drawable region and using JavaScript drawing functions it is possible to access that region, allowing the dynamic generation of graphics. Some possible uses for canvas are: animations, games and image composition (Vanghan-Nichols, 2010).

HTML5 also has specific tags for video which inform that the information associated is to be handled as HTML5 video stream, which makes easier to embed video in a Web page with no need for a specific video player and decoder (Vanghan-Nichols, 2010).

Video Codecs

ITU-T H.263 (Wiegand et al., 2003) is a video compression scheme originally designed as a low-bitrate compressed format for videoconferencing. Much of the Web flash video content used to be encoded in a incomplete implementation of H.263.

Motion JPEG or MJPEG is composed of sequential JPEG compressed images (On-Net Surveillance Systems Inc, 2006). Since there is no dependency between frames, a Motion JPEG video is robust, and thus a frame can be dropped without affecting the quality of the remaining video frames.

MJPEG can also provide streaming over HTTP (Berc & Fenner, 1998). Each image is encapsulated into an HTTP packet and then RTP Streaming creates packets of a sequence of JPEG images, which can then be played by some Web browsers and video players such as VLC.

Its main disadvantage is its lack of efficiency, since it does not use any video compression techniques to reduce the overall data size. The end result is that is has a high bit rate for the delivered quality when compared to most recent compression standards such as H.264, resulting in high bandwidth usage and high storage requirements. However, the lack of any encoding and decoding, results in low latency, making it appropriate for live video. Motion JPEG is still vastly used in portable devices, such as Mobile Phones, Handheld consoles and digital cameras.

Hereafter, some of the MPEG Group standards will be overviewed.

The MPEG-4 is an ISO/IEC standard that adopts the object-based model and its main purpose is to offer users a new level of interactivity providing technology to view, access and manipulate audiovisual objects. The object-based model provides a representation of an audiovisual scene as a composition of audio, visual or audiovisual content called media objects integrating them, allowing the re-utilization of this kind of content and creating interactivity with the objects and its descriptions (Ebrahimi & Horne, 2000).

With MPEG-4 standard the user can now have an active role while is watching video content, like a TV program by interacting with the objects that compose a scene. Each MPEG-4 visual scene has one or more media objects and each of them is characterized by temporal and spatial information. A MPEG-4 scene has a hierarchical structure, where each node is a media object.

A Visual Object Sequence (VS) corresponds to the entire MPEG-4 scene that can contain multiple objects and its layers. A Video Object (VO) corresponds to a specific object in the scene. Each VO is sampled in time providing time samples that are called Video Object Plane (VOP), these time samples can be grouped to form a Group of Video Object Planes (GOV). To simplify, a VOP can be seen as a single image in a sequence of images, and the VO is the sequence of images itself.

Similar to standards like MPEG-1 and MPEG-2 that do not specify how a video sequence is created, the MPEG-4 does not standardize how a video object is generated.

The systems part of the MPEG-4 specifies the description of the relationship between the audiovisual components that constitute a scene. The Binary Format For Scenes (BIFS) describes the spatial and temporal behaviour of the objects as well as their interactivity characteristics; BIFS instructions can be used to insert new objects into a scene or to change characteristics of a specific object within a scene. BIFS provides support for coding individual MPEG-4 objects and provides tools to compose those objects into a scene (Pereira & Ebrahimi, 2002). The necessary information about scene composition is the scene description and is coded and transmitted with the media objects.

The scene descriptions are coded independently from streams related to primitive media objects (e.g., a fixed background, a person or a music), in order to make easier the development of authoring, manipulation and interaction tools. It is necessary to identify the parameters that belong to the scene description this is done through the differentiation of parameters that are used to improve coding from those that are used as modifiers of an object. Since MPEG-4 allow the modification of an object, those parameters related to modifiers are placed in the scene description and not in primitive media objects, so it is not necessary to decode the primitive media to access those parameters.

XMT is a Extensible Markup Language (XML) based framework for representing MPEG-4 scene description using a textual syntax. The XMT allows content authors to exchange information with other authors, tools or service providers. The XMT framework consists of two levels of textual format: the XMT-A and the XMT-O.

The XMT-A is the low level description and is based on XML, describes each audiovisual element using MPEG-4 specific features The XMT-A provides an one-to-one mapping between the textual and binary formats. The XMT-O is a high-level abstraction of MPEG-4 features and is extended from Synchronized Multimedia Integration Language (SMIL),which is a XML-based language that allows authors to create interactive multimedia content. The XMT-O provides content authors with an escape mechanism from O to A so they can preserve the original semantic information.

The interaction between users and content can be separated into two categories: client-side interaction and server-side interaction.

- Client-side involves content manipulation that is handled on the user device and can take several forms like changing objects from one side to another and can be implemented through the interpretation of user events. A user event can be for example, a mouse click.

- Server-side interaction requires content manipulation on the transmission end, it is initiated by an user action and requires a reserve channel to transmit to the server the user intention.

The MP4 File Format or MPEG-4 Part 14 is a multimedia container format standard specified as a part of MPEG-4. It is used to store the media information of a MPEG-4 presentation in a flexible, extensible format, which aims to facilitate interchange, management, edition and presentation of the correspondent media. The format allows streaming over the Internet. It is commonly used to stored video and audio streams, such as those specified by MPEG, but can also be used to store subtitles. The MP4 file format is also as streamable format, opposed to a streaming format. That is, metadata in the file provide instructions in how to deliver the media data over the network.

The MPEG-4 standard defines a compressed mechanism for audio and visual objects. In the system part of the MPEG-4 it is specified how these objects are decoded and presented. MPEG-4 also defines a Java application engine that specifies how applications are received, decoded, and executed at the client terminal, this part is called MPEG-J (Swaminathan & Bourges-Sevenier, 2010).

MPEG-J defines a set of Java APIs to access and control the MPEG-4 terminal that plays a MPEG-4 audiovisual session. A MPEG-J application is called MPEGlet and can be embedded in the content as a MPEG-J elementary stream similar to what is done for the audio and video streams. A delivery mechanism is defined in MPEG-J to carry the Java byte code and Java objects that constitute a MPEG-J application.

With the MPEG-J APIs, the applications have programmatic access to the scene, network, and decoder resources. MPEG-J offers enhanced interactivity with users adding value to it, responding to users actions, which results in intelligent responses to user interactions. Some examples of the application of MPEGlets are: adaptive rich media content for wireless devices, enhanced interactive Electronic Program Guide (EPG), enriched interactive digital TV and content personalization.

The MPEG-7 standard, formally called Multimedia Content Description Interface, is a standard that allow the description of audiovisual data content. The main objective of MPEG-7 is to specify a standard way of describing various types of multimedia information to facilitate the identification of interesting and relevant information and to manage that information efficiently (Martinez, 2010).

The audiovisual data content that can benefit from MPEG-7 are: pictures, graphics, 3-Dimensional (3D) models, audio, speech, video, and composition information about how these elements are combined in a multimedia scenario. If the material is encoded using MPEG-4, the MPEG-7 can attach descriptions to the MPEG-4 objects within the scene (Martinez, 2010).

Video Coding Mechanisms

Computer vision techniques are often employed in order to support video coding. We exploit the reverse direction: how to exploit coding mechanisms in order to augment the potential of computer vision applications. This section presents related state of the art work on video coding techniques, such as Scalable Video Coding (H.264). We will also address object-based video coding brought by MPEG4 part10.

Advanced Video Coding

H.264/MPEG-4 Part 10 Advanced Video Coding (AVC) (Wiegand et al., 2003) is an industry standard for video compression, and is actually one of the most commonly used formats for the distribution of high quality video. It is widely used for Internet streaming on Websites such as YouTube and on Web plugins such as Adobe Flash and Microsoft Silverlight. One of the biggest advantage of H.264 over other standards is

its compression performance, which can provide better image quality at the same compression bitrate or a lower compression bitrate for the same quality. However, this performance comes at a cost of a greater computational cost.

In H.264/AVC the input video signal is predicted using a concept based on differences between the current frame and the previous one, besides that of absolute pixel information. The former prediction is based on information in other frames (motion-compensated predictor). The later is denoted Intra-picture predictive coding (I-slice), which codes a full picture and is used to reduce the spatial redundancy within it, and so it does not require data from other pictures - temporal redundancy - for decoding. The prediction error is usually compressed with a transform coder operating on a block-by-block basis (Wiegand et al., 2003).

Layered Coding (Scalable Video Coding)

H.264/AVC success led to a scalable extension of this protocol, denominated H.264/SVC (Schwarz et al., 2007), based on layered coding. This protocol aims to support the transmission of several layers of video quality, including different levels of temporal frame rate (i.e., pictures per second), image spatial resolution (i.e., number of encoded pixels per image) and quality (i.e., image fidelity) in a progressive, scalable manner. This chapter will focus on the application of image processing techniques in order to further exploit spatial resolution and quality layers for augmented QoE. As such, we will hereafter briefly overview main SVC features (Monteiro, 2009).

Temporal Scalability

The main concepts of temporal scalability were already included in H.264/AVC. In SVC, hierarchical B-pictures/slices are usually employed for implementing temporal scalability (Monteiro, 2009).

Spatial Scalability

SVC enables as well several image resolutions ratios. Spatial scalability employs both motion-compensated and intra-prediction techniques within the same spatial layer. It uses as well an inter-layer prediction mechanism to reduce the spatial redundancy between these layers. The interlayer prediction prevents the decoder from decoding the base layer if the goal is the decoding at a higher definition. It reduces therefore the complexity of the decoding process by propagating the information of the coded motion vectors, mode information and residual data, from the lower spatial layers to the next higher resolution layers.

Quality Scalability

Similarly to spatial scalability, picture sizes vary between base and enhancement layers. It relies on both Coarse-Grain quality Scalable (CGS) and Medium-Grain quality Scalable (MGS) coding. In CGS the encoding of the transform coefficients are performed in a non-scalable way, as they may only be decoded as a whole. In MGS, which is a variation of CGS, fragments of transform coefficients are split into several units, enabling a definition of up to 16 MGS layers, and increasing the rate granularity for adaption purposes.

MGS defines pictures from the temporal base layer as key pictures, for which SVC sets the motion parameters equal between the base and enhancement layers, which enables a single-loop decoding of these pictures, similar to the one used in spatial scalability. Regarding the remaining pictures, it is up to the encoder to decide whether to use the reconstructed base layer or the enhancement layer to compute the motion parameters. However, it is usually employed the highest available quality for motion estimation and compensation.

Combined Scalability Structure

The aforementioned three scalability levels can be combined with each other within one bit stream, which is denoted as Combined Scalability. It allows for extraction of different operation points of the video bit stream, where each point is characterized by a certain level of spatial, temporal and SNR quality definitions (as illustrated in Figure 4).

SVC Profiles and Flexibility

The SVC amendment of H.264/AVC specifies three profiles for SVC: Scalable Baseline, Scalable High and Scalable High Intra profile. The Scalable Baseline profile is mainly targeted for applications that require a low decoding complexity. This profile has restrictions on the types of spatial scalability ratios and on cropping. Scalable High profile was designed for broadcast services (including IPTV), streaming, and storage applications, and supports spatial scalable coding with different resolution ratios and parameters. The Scalable High Intra profile was designed for professional applications and solely contains a specific type of pictures (IDR) for all layers.

A scalable coded video offers a trade-off between bitrate and subjective quality. Discarding parts of the video bit stream does not compromises the final result, which still represents a valid video sequence. A layered structure for several layers of quality was therefore required for the coded video in order to distinguish between basic information (base layer) from more refined details of the base layer quality (enhancement layers). The base layer of an encoded H.264/SVC bit stream is compatible with H.264/AVC, enabling backward compatibility with legacy equipment.

A bit stream can be partitioned into several other sub-streams by simply cutting parts of its data. This is important for rate adaptation purposes, since it may be performed in intermediate network elements without requiring computation-

Figure 4. SVC in combined scalability (S-spatial, T-temporal, Q-quality), as described by Moscoso et al. (2011)

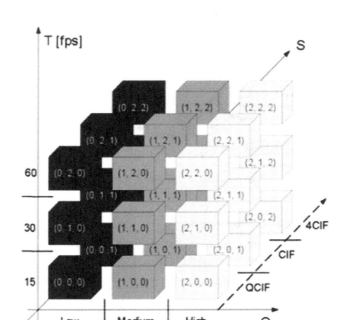

ally intensive mechanisms, like video transcoding does. Highly compressed bit-streams with different bitrates, video resolutions, and frame rates is thus possible. Furthermore, such streams can be adapted to end-users' devices capabilities and network conditions.

ENABLING USER CONTENT CUSTOMIZATION AND AUGMENTATION

This section addresses the challenge of allowing the end-user to transform the content according to its personal tastes. It starts by presenting an interactive approach for the identification of interesting objects to be replaced on a video stream.

It then addresses the topic of replacing natural characters, such as people, on a video stream, by synthetic characters (avatar-like). Thereafter it is described methodologies for objects' transforma-

tion and a new protocol enabling such transformations of multimedia content.

Content Impersonation

The solution here described, named Impersonate, consists of a mechanism for transforming image content on videos (video clips, video stream), in the form of objects, into other objects as selected by the end-users. This is done using the à priori availability of 3D models of objects. The procedure uses techniques for replacing objects representing people on a video stream, by rendering 3D models of other objects (such as 3D models of other people's faces) into the stream. This solution proposes a representation of objects according to a set of transmission parameters, so that it is transmitted not only information concerning image content, but also information concerning how objects in such image can be transformed.

A working example, according to a network architecture solution, is presented in Figure 5,

Figure 5. This figure presents an overall implementation for the content merging/transformation system. A user, using standard interfaces first subscribes a content merging / transformation service, selects options for service package, billing, etc. Once the service is subscribed and available, user is able to enter a front-end for configuration (provided by the content transformation server). Here the user can create and/or store templates (and select them at later times), or just select already available templates.

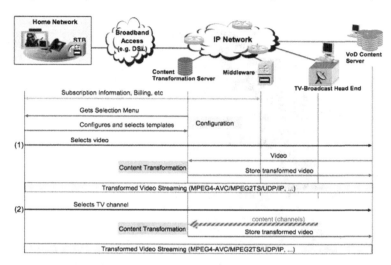

whether the solution components are contained on the machine denominated Content Transformation Server. It works as follows:

- User, using standard interfaces, subscribes a content merging/transformation service, selects options for service package, billing, etc.

- Once the service is subscribed and available, user is able to enter a front-end for configuration (provided by the Content Transformation Server). Here the user can create and/or store templates (and select them at later times), or just select already available templates.

- On the first task, upon choice of a video (e.g. from the information available on a Video on Demand—VoD—server, for a VoD subscriber), the video is transferred from the VoD content server to the Content Transformation Server. On the front-end, the user selects a set of movie features (from the ones available) she/he wants to

transform (replace a face, enlarge a face, etc.), selecting as well the temporal window, among other options. The video is then transformed so that the à-priori selected template replaces the selected movie features. The transformed video is then stored on the VoD content server as a new video (a new content to be offered) or else as an attachment to a category of contents associated to a main content (the original video). Depending on the user type of subscription and settings chosen, the transformed content might become available for view to only the user, a subset of users or all users. The video is then streamed to the user for viewing.

- On a second task, represented as well in Figure 5, the user now selects a TV channel to view (e.g. news), the features on the channel stream content to be changed, as well as the operation to be done (merge, transformation) and the new content. The video is then modified on the Content

Transformed Server and stored on the VoD content server, which streams the modified video to the end-user (optionally, the modified video could be streamed to the end-user using other transmission mechanisms).

On the first task (1), upon choice of a video (e.g. from the information available on a VoD server, for a VoD subscriber), the video is transferred from the VoD content server to the content transformation server. On the front-end, the user selects the movie features s/he wants to transform, and the temporal window for these changes, among other options. The video is then transformed so that the selected movie features are replaced by the à-priori chosen template. The transformed video is then stored on the VoD content server as a new video or else stored as an attachment to a category of contents associated to a main content (the original video). The video is then streamed to the user for viewing. On a second task (2), the user now selects a TV channel to view, the features on the channel stream content to be changed, as well as the operation to be done, and the new content. The video is then modified on the content transformed server and stored on the VoD content server, which streams the modified video to the end-user (optionally, the modified video could be streamed to the end-user using other transmission mechanisms).

Content Adaptation Through Synthetic Characters

Let's further extend the approach to introduce artificial personages into a video stream, which replaces and behaves as the original one. With such aim, we present a new means to transform content. The solution proposed is a Network Mechanism for Content Personalization and Transformation, consisting of:

- A client interface module, which includes a configuration component, as shown

Figure 6. This module builds an object model from a sequence of images, or else provides synthetic models (or other models downloaded from somewhere else) which are then added to a database of object models. The client interface allows the user to create, modify and select object models to be used.

- A content merging/transformation module, composed by several components:
  - The object detection component is used to extract features from a sequence of images, which may be selected by an user to be replaced or else transformed;
  - The Merge Objects component replaces the original object by a projection of the new object model.
  - The last component Applies Features of Tracked Object to the new object, so that the new object behaves as the original one.
- An optional client module, depending on the type of solution: networked or home-centered. Networked solutions are appropriate for limited capacity client hardware (e.g. STBs), so that the high processing consuming merge module is placed on the network, on an operator's backend infrastructure. For the networked type of solution, the client impersonate module implements the interface that enables the configuration / selection of objects which are stored and managed outside the home platform (these list of à-priori objects might even be shared by multiple users).

Content Merging/Transformation

The content merging/transformation system may be completely located on a networked server or on a home platform (such as a STB), or it even

Figure 6. a) Configuration module, which builds an object model from a sequence of images, or else provides synthetic models (or other models downloaded from somewhere else) which are then added to a database of object models (an object might be a face, an advertisement, a car, etc.). The model might be very complex (e.g. 3D geometry and appearance, leaps and eyes model, voice model for speech synthesis, etc.); b) content merging / transformation module, composed by an object detection component to detect objects of interests on images; an extraction of object features component, to extract additional information on the object. The object is also tracked on the video over time, so that the new object replaces the original in all frames. If the object disappears from the image, it will still be replaced in the future by object recognition whenever it reappears on the image; and acting on both the object features and the new object model, the merge objects component replaces the original object by a projection of the new object model, and the last component applies features of tracked object to the new object, so that the new object behaves as the original one. Alternatively, the transform object component modifies the object instead of replacing it.

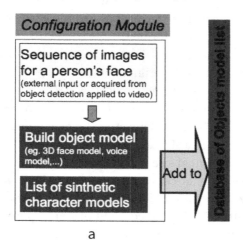

a

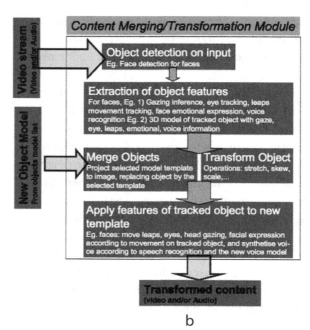

b

can have both home and networked components. Two different approaches are possible:

1. **Networked Impersonate:** This is the type of solution implementation that may be preferred by a telecommunications operator: it works with cheaper home hardware, and it is harder for an user to use the service without permission (see Figure 7).

2. **Client Impersonate:** This type of solution implementation is possible whenever the home platform (STB, PC-client, etc.) has enough processing power to support the system. For certain types of applications (such as the Next Generation Karaoke, as described before), the processing requirements on the home platform are not so strong, and hence this type of implementation might be appropriate (see Figure 8).

Figure 7. Networked impersonate solution. For this type of solution, the content merging / transformation module is completely located on the network (on a network server). The flow works as follows: (1) user access front-end, (2) user selects or configures object templates on the front-end (since the object templates are stored on the network, a client impersonate module implements the necessary interface), (3) video and 3D templates are merged, so that video features are replaced by the later (for stretching a feature, 3D templates are not required), (4) modified video is stored on video server and/or streamed to the end-user.

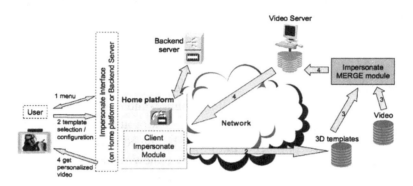

Figure 8. Client Impersonate solution. For this type of solution, the content merging/transformation module is completely located on the home platform. The flow works as follows: (1) user access front-end, (2) user selects or configures object templates on the front-end, (3) a video stream from the video server and 3D templates are merged on the home platform, so that video features are replaced by the later (for stretching a feature, 3D templates are not required), (4) modified video is then sent to the end-user TV set (the modified video can as well be stored on the home-platform or else on the video server).

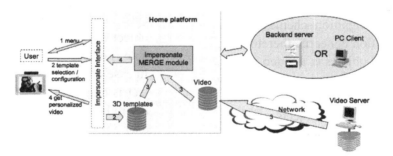

Implementations

One first implementation detail is the addition of a parameter to a video stream to tag it as Transformable (or not). The mechanism should then be only applied to compatible (transformable) video streams, and to transformable objects within each image of the video stream.

Active Object Detection

Object detection is applied to all object categories that are represented on the object database. If necessary, object detection and recognition might be applied not only to detect an object but also to recognize its category. Several approaches are referred on the literature for solving the face /

object detection problem (Arsenio, 2004; Viola & Jones, 2001). Another component, the Extraction of Object Features component, extracts additional information on the object. The object is also tracked on the video over time, so that the new object replaces the original in all frames. If the video object disappears from the image, it will be still replaced on the future by object recognition whenever reappears on the image (following the process described on (Arsenio, 2004).

Passive Object Detection

Most of the video-streams of interest, such as movies, advertisements, etc., are produced in studios in well-controlled environments. Some movies, for example, include special effects scenes in which objects are carefully merged into a scene in order to create, for instance, "physically impossible" actions (this merge is somehow the opposite step of object segmentation in active object detection). Hence, using new video coding formats (e.g. MPEG4, MPEG7), content producers and advertisers have all the conditions to tag appropriately objects in images, so that no active object detection and recognition schemes are necessary. Passive detection concerns therefore the use of à-priori tagged objects in a video stream. But this requires the definition of a protocol to tag objects for transformation (as it will be described thereafter), in such a way that objects are easily segmented from an image, relevant parameters are extracted from the objects (such as object scale, orientation), so that the 3D model of the replacing object can be transformed according to the same parameters.

Hybrid Active/Passive Object Detection

Another alternative implementation corresponds to use active detection mechanisms at the video content production source, in order to create object features (e.g. object segmentation with location and contours, object orientation). The video might then be transformed in a later stage using passively these object features. For instance, for live content, active detection techniques might be applied at the source, because careful video production in a studio is not possible in such a case.

The Protocol

The protocol for transmitting the Object Parameters structure is represented on the following figure, and described hereafter (see Figure 9).

The protocol requires objects on a video stream to be tagged as Transformable or not. In the former case, new metadata per object includes a set of parameters for tagging an object (including optional features). The parameters, their possible values and an according description are provided hereinafter, according to Table 1.

Transformable object means that the object can be transformed into an equivalent one:

- In case of active object detection, an object detection mechanism is available for that class of objects, and thus the output of the object detection algorithm provides a reliable result.
- In case of passive object detection, the object is tagged as transformable, and hence it will be available and/or accessible to the user interface for the user to select and change its appearance. Objects that are not tagged may preferably as such not be displayed to the user, thereby making them inaccessible for the user for transformation and/or replacement purposes. An identity ID of, e.g., "0" or "-1" may indicate whether or not an object is transformable, while An ID of "1" may indicate that a boost in object quality is possible (as discussed in section 4).

Figure 9. Protocol for transmitting the object parameters structure

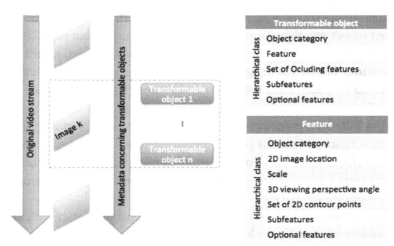

Table 1. Protocol parameters and values

Parameter:	Value:
Transformable Object	ID
Object Category	Name
2D image location	(x,y)
Scale	Real value s
3D viewing perspective angle	(ρ, φ, θ)
Set of 2D contour points	Collection of pairs of points, which define the boundaries of an object. $((x1,y1),..., (xn,yn))$
Set of occluding features	(name 1, ..., name n)
Subfeatures	Structure (see previous figure)
Optional Features	Any kind of values

The category name specifies the class of objects into which an object may be transformed. For example, a face can be transformed into another face, but is cannot be transformed into an object belonging to a car category.

- In case of active object detection, the category name assigned to an object corresponds to the class assigned or provided by an object recognition mechanism.
- In case of passive object detection, the category name is introduced by the content

producer or by any other encoding entity. Depending on the actual content, the scope of the class may be restricted in various ways. For instance, if only a person's face appears, the content producer may tag it to a face class (generic scope). But if the person's skin is visible in greater detail, the content producer may further classify the object as a "Caucasian face," narrowing the set of transformable objects into faces with Caucasian like skin-color.

The field 2D image location specifies a location provided by two-dimensional coordinates of the center of mass of the object template.

Scale indicates a scaling factor (in pixels) from which a real object appears downsized. For virtual objects, a reference measure can be used. Such reference may be applied for all virtual objects created. The scale value may be determined by a ratio between the object distance to the camera's focal center and the distance between the camera projection plane and the focal center.

The 3D angle parameter refers to a 3D-orientation of the object relative to a reference. It indicates to what extent a 3D-model is rotated along roll, pitch and yaw angles in order to be projected into the image, replacing another object appearing at the same orientation. A reference value (0°, 0°, 0°) can be set to a front view of the object. A transformed object can then projected into the image accordingly.

The Set of 2D contour points originates an object template provided by a set of 2D contour points. A repetition of a point may indicate that the contour is closed. A following point indicates a starting point of a next contour. Contour points may be sorted in a clockwise direction so that points to the contour's right hand side are inside of the object.

The set of occluding features parameter indicates which objects are at least partially occluding the current object.

The Subfeatures parameter is used to tag complex objects, i.e., objects comprising various features (e.g., wheels of a car).

Optional features comprise a field to indicate additional parameters that may be used to optimize the transformation, although not required. Such additional parameters may be:

- Color
- Information required to make two different classes compatible with one another, e.g.:
  - How to deform one class into the other;
  - How to scale up or down compatible classes of real objects, but of different dimensions (e.g., real sport cars and miniature sport cars);
- Additional transformations (e.g., change of texture).

Compatible Category Classes

It would be reductionist to solely allow an object to be replaced by objects within the same category class. Broader transformations are also possible for groups of compatible classes. This can be implemented according to the following strategies:

- Requesting information from a centralized Internet server, or more generally from the cloud, so that requests can be placed to the server concerning the compatibility of two object classes, or even requesting the group of classes compatible to one object class.
- Adding another parameter to the protocol (lets say "Compatible Categories"), that contains a list of compatible classes to the one of the represented object given by the object Category parameter.

Compatible classes shall therefore be composed by objects of similar category (e.g. people's faces), and mostly of similar geometry. The constraint of similar size is not mandatory, but additional information (introduction of an Optional Feature) is needed in order to correct for the scaling factor.

Object Transformation

After end-user's objects selection and objects image detection, objects are manipulated according to the process depicted in Figure 10.

For each image k of a video stream, the set of objects O is identified during detection, assigning a class to each of them, according to two methods:

- Actively, through object detection mechanisms. O is obtained by, for each object D_k in the database, applying an Object D_k detection algorithm, if such is available.
- Or passively, by extracting the object classes from the video coding objects tags. O corresponds then to all tagged objects for a given image.

From this set O of objects, T, the set of Impersonate (transformable) objects, is then determined, according to the process already described. At a certain point in time, the end-user selects one or more objects to be transformed, which are represented by S, which is a subset of T. For instance, the end-user first freezes an image (k), being showed

Figure 10. Architecture for object transformation on a video stream

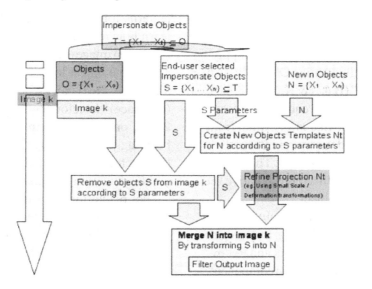

on the user-interface all the transformable objects T. Upon selection of a subset of n objects, the end-user then selects the a group of N new objects from a group of available 3D models of objects.

Using S parameters and the image k, S objects' templates are then removed from the image. New image templates N_t are created by projection of the N new objects into image coordinates according to a perspective transformation given by the S parameters of the objects S to be replaced. So, N_1 is projected according to S_1, and N_n is projected according to S_n. The projection is then refined upon a tolerance margin (e.g. 5%) so that all image pixels are filled and the contours of the projected image objects do not differ significantly (e.g. more than the tolerance factor) than the original S object's contours (otherwise transformation might be cancelled for that particular object). Small transformations, such as small scaling and/ or deformations might be applied within small margins just to optimize the fit of the new objects N_t contours to the S old ones.

The algorithm to perform the perspective transformation given S parameters can be one of several image-processing methods available for performing perspective transformations (Faugeras, 1993).

On a last step, filtering is applied to points in the neighborhood of the new object contours, to smooth any large edges over these regions.

CONTENT AUGMENTATION THROUGH HALLUCINATING APPROACHES

ASPs need nowadays to offer new services to their clients, meeting the growing demand for quality, namely image resolution for video streaming. And this is even more important in convergent scenarios, in which, for instance, videos from low-resolution mobile devices need to be displayed on 55" TVs. In addition, ASPs need to reduce as well OPEX, and hence the need to develop automatic mechanisms for recovering from network packet loss, which degrades signal quality.

This section addresses the application of hallucinating approaches for recovering image information or increasing image resolution on a video stream, therefore allowing providing different objects within a video stream with various levels of quality.

Object Transformation Tagging

The integration of image processing with video coding tagging mechanisms is achieved by applying the technique of "Hallucinating Objects" (such as "Hallucinating faces" (Baker & Kanade, 2000), as shown in Figure 11). This requires the usage of a database of objects, so that information from the object database is used to recover information about the object on the video image. The Object database is built à-priori with a representative set of template images of the object.

The problem of improving the quality of content is thus solved by employing a Network Mechanism for Content Improvement and Recovery, consisting of a Low QoE detection component, which is responsible for triggering the system to improve image quality, upon detection of loss of image quality. Such problem may occur from network packet losses, or from low-resolution video sources.

The method is illustrated in Figure 12, and works as follows. Upon triggering, and using such a database of objects, such as of people faces, and given a person face image (low-resolution or damaged), the algorithm extracts common patterns for faces from the database in order to learn how to extrapolate face pixels into a larger resolution image (or to recover from image errors). The image object location and contours (such as a person's face) can be detected using an object (e.g. face) detector algorithm (Viola & Jones, 2001), or else video stream objects might have been tagged à-priori by the content producer, so that such image information is already available and no detection is required.

For resolution increase, the object resolution is increased into a target value (e.g. 4x, 16x). This is only possible if the database contains images for that object class at the target resolution. This algorithm might be applied in a sequential manner, i.e. first error recovery and then resolution increase, vice versa, and even both simultaneously. Of notice that resolution is not increased for all image, but only for a particular set of image objects for which there is a database representation.

Figure 11. This figure illustrates some of the early results from the literature in Baker and Kanade (2000) for face error recovery and increasing resolution, using a technique named "hallucinating faces." Image resolution is increased as much as 64 times.

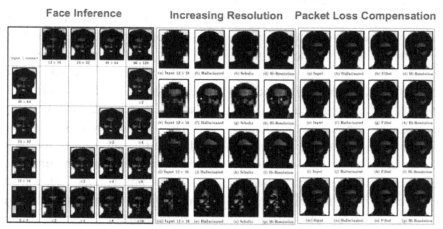

Results/images taken from Baker & Kanade – "Hallucinating Faces"

Figure 12. Architecture for improving quality of video quality content. It consists of 6 components: low QoE detector, a database of objects, object detection (in order to extract its image location and contours), hallucinating object algorithm, augmenting image component, and optionally, as described thereafter, H.264/SVC encoding component of the augmented stream.

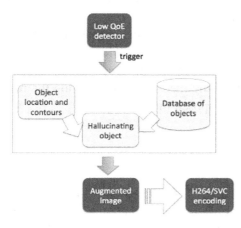

Object Augmentation Tagging

and Scalable Coding

This section further extends the previous section to exploit scalable video coding in order to provide new multimedia applications. It refers to the optional last step of previous Figure 12, in which the augmented and improved content is inserted again into the network for distribution. Exploiting the H.264/SVC protocol, such augmented content can be efficiently distributed. For instance, devices that do not support higher resolutions might not download the augmented content, while other device might get as well such extra information.

Figure 13 illustrates an encoding structure that uses a combined quality and spatial encoding. It is illustrated a dyadic spatial scalability, where the spatial base layer (or reference layer) is represented by a Quarter Common Intermediate Format (QCIF) sequence and the enhancement layer by a Common Intermediate Format (CIF) sequence. Although in that figure there are only two spatial layers, the encoder supports multiple spatial scalability layers combined with temporal

Figure 13. This figure illustrates the integration of frame image improvement on a video stream using hallucinating objects technique, and how such enhancement can be used to create additional H.264/SVC quality and spatial layers.

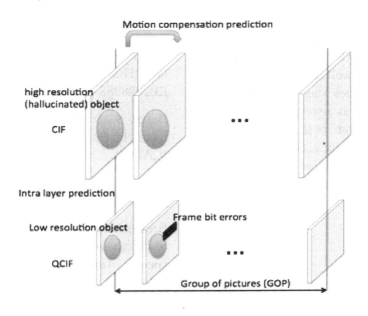

and/or quality layers. Using our approach, better quality layers with bit error correction techniques based on hallucinating objects become possible along the quality dimension. On the other hand, along the spatial resolution dimension, higher resolution layers can also be obtained for the original video stream. Afterwards, both the original video stream, as the base layer, as well as the improved quality and resolution layers, can be encoded using H.264/SVC and streamed to other users to consume the content.

CONCLUSION

This chapter presented new network mechanisms either to transform (and personalize) video content, as well as to improve its quality, using an object-based approach, applied to each transformable object in a video stream frame. In order to effectively represent such information on a video stream, a novel object tagging protocol was also proposed, in which: 1) video streams are tagged as transformable (or not); 2) objects are equally tagged as transformable, being further optional details introduced to optimize the content quality improvement; and 3) introduction of hierarchy tagging structures. Our solution for transforming video stream objects based on image processing techniques, supports, and benefits, from the future MPEG-4 and MPEG-7 tagging mechanisms. Additionally, it is very well suited for usage with coding adaptive schemes such as H.264/SVC. Flexible deployment was also considered, since benefits can result from both applying these techniques near the user (e.g. Set-Top-Box), or else near the content distribution source. As such, we described several possible implementations exploiting such scenarios.

FUTURE DIRECTIONS FOR RESEARCH

Such solution has a wide range of applications. Besides personalization of multimedia content, it allows consumers of broadcast content to change the consumed content, and to distribute adapted versions of such content to other users, becoming multimedia prosumers.

Future research directions include the replacement of objects with complex features on a video stream, as well as the specification of a video compressing mechanism integrating the mechanisms proposed in this chapter.

REFERENCES

Akhshabi, C., & Begen, A. (2011). An experimental evaluation of rate-adaptation algorithms in adaptive streaming over HTTP. In *Proceedings of the Second Annual ACM Conference on Multimedia Systems*, (pp. 157-168). ACM.

Arsenio, A. (2004). Object recognition from multiple percepts. In *Proceedings of the IEEE RAS/RSJ International Conference on Humanoid Robots*. IEEE.

Arsenio, A. (2009). *Method and device for processing a data stream and system comprising such device*. Applicants: Nokia Siemens Networks GMBH & CO. KG. International Patent Number: EP2098988-A1.

Baker, S., & Kanade, T. (2000). Hallucinating faces. In *Proceedings of the Fourth ICAFGR*. ICAFGR.

Berc, R., & Fenner, W. (1998). *RTP payload format for JPEG-compressed video*.

Breazeal, C., & Aryananda, L. (2002). Recognition of affective communicative intent in robot-directed speech. *Autonomous Robots*, *12*(1), 83–104. doi:10.1023/A:1013215010749.

Ebrahimi, T., & Horne, C. (2000). MPEG-4 natural video coding - An overview. *Signal Processing Image Communication*, *15*(4-5), 365–385. doi:10.1016/S0923-5965(99)00054-5.

Faugeras, O. (1993). *Three - dimensional computer vision: A geometric viewpoint*. Cambridge, MA: MIT Press.

Maglogiannis, I., Vouyioukas, D., & Aggelopoulos, C. (2009). Face detection and recognition of natural human emotion using Markov random fields. *Personal and Ubiquitous Computing*, *13*(1), 95–101. doi:10.1007/s00779-007-0165-0.

Martinez, J. (2010). *MPEG-7 overview*.

Monteiro, J. (2009). *Quality assurance solutions for multipoint scalable video distribution over wireless IP networks*. (Ph.D. Dissertation). Instituto Superior Tecnico - Universidade Tecnica de Lisboa, Lisbon, Portugal.

Moscoso, P., Cruz, R., & Nunes, M. (2011). Internet TV architecture based on scalable video coding. In *Proceedings of the 9th European Interactive TV Conference Workshop on Quality of Experience for Multimedia Content Sharing: Ubiquitous QoE Assessment and Support, QoEMCS'11*. QoEMCS.

On-Net Surveillance Systems Inc. (2006). *MJPEG vs MPEG4 - Understanding the differences, advantages and disadvantages of each compression technique* (White Paper). Author.

Pereira, F., & Ebrahimi, T. (2002). *The MPEG-4 book*. Upper Saddle River, NJ: Prentice Hall PTR.

Rosa, C., & Arsenio, A. (2010). *ASK4Stream - Location based mobile live video streaming on request*. Paper presented at the 10th National Conference on Computer Networks. Lisbon, Portugal.

Schwarz, H., Marpe, D., & Wiegand, T. (2007). Overview of the scalable video coding extension of the H.264/AVC Standard. *IEEE Transactions on Circuits and Systems for Video Technology*, *17*(9). doi:10.1109/TCSVT.2007.905532.

Sodagar, I. (2011). *Overview of dynamic adaptive streaming over HTTP (DASH)* (white-paper).

Swaminathan, V., & Bourges-Sevenier, M. (2010). *MPEG-J* (White Paper).

Vaughan-Nichols, S. (2010). Will HTML 5 restandardize the web? *Computer*, *43*(4), 13–15. doi:10.1109/MC.2010.119.

Viola, P., & Jones, M. (2001). *Robust real-time object detection (Technical report)*. Cambridge, MA: COMPAQ Cambridge Research Laboratory.

Wiegand, S., Sullivan, G., & Luthra, A. (2003). *Overview of the H.264/AVC video coding standard*.

KEY TERMS AND DEFINITIONS

Hallucinating Objects: Techniques for recovering or augmenting information concerning an object by using features extracted from other objects of the same category.

Impersonate: Technique for replacing an object on a video stream by a different object.

Interactive Multimedia Content Distribution: Methods and Infrastructure for the delivery of multimedia content allowing bidirectional communications between the content source and the viewer, so that the multimedia content consumed by the viewer depends on its own interactive choices while consuming the content.

Multimedia Content Adaptation: Modification of multimedia content in order to meet different criteria, such as the viewers personal tastes, a mobile device's resolution capability, a geographic target or quality of service requirements.

Networking Applications: Applications that are distributed over one or more networks, making use of communication channels and several distributed machines.

Personalized Content: Customization of content targeting a specific user or community of users.

Scalable Coding: Technique for coding multimedia video streams that compress the content according to scalable levels of quality.

ENDNOTES

[1] This work was developed at Nokia Siemens Networks (NSN) by the author. The author is no longer with NSN.

Chapter 9
Recognition of Humans and Their Activities for Video Surveillance

Alok Kumar Singh Kushwaha
Indian Institute of Technology (BHU), India

Rajeev Srivastava
Indian Institute of Technology (BHU), India

ABSTRACT

Human Activity Recognition is an active area of research in computer vision with wide-scale applications in video surveillance, motion analysis, virtual reality interfaces, robot navigation and recognition, video indexing, browsing, HCI, choreography, sports video analysis, etc. The analysis of vision-based human activities in videos is an area with increasingly important consequences from security and surveillance to public place and personal archiving. Several challenges at various levels of processing-robustness against errors in low-level processing, view and rate-invariant representations at mid-level processing, and semantic representation of human activities at higher-level processing make this problem hard to solve. The task is challenging due to variations in motion performance, recording settings, and inter-personal differences. In this chapter, the authors explicitly address these challenges. They present a survey of existing work and describe some of the more well-known methods in these areas. They also describe their own research and outline future possibilities. Detailed overviews of current advances in the field are provided. Image representations and the subsequent classification processes are discussed separately to focus on the novelties of recent research. Moreover, the authors discuss the limitations of the state of the art and outline promising directions of research.

DOI: 10.4018/978-1-4666-4868-5.ch009

INTRODUCTION

Human activity recognition is a popular area of research in the field of computer vision. It is the basis of applications in many areas such as security, surveillance, clinical applications, biomechanical applications, human robot interaction, entertainment, education, training, digital libraries and video or image annotations as well as in video conferencing and model based coding. Recognition of human actions and activities provides important cue for human behavior analysis techniques.

In this chapter, we first provide the motivation for Human Activity Recognition then the challenges and different steps in Activity Recognition. Then we categorize the activity classification approaches according to our taxonomy. We give the motivation behind our approach, following by that we provide a brief review of the previous related work and situate our work in the context of existing techniques.

MOTIVATION FOR HUMAN ACTIVITY RECOGNITION

The 9/11 event in USA and 26/11 event in Mumbai, India have demonstrated that there is a strong need for analysis and understanding of human activity in public areas in order to prevent terrorist activities. Now the aim is to analyze the video sequences, which include detection and tracking of moving human objects, and to analyze their activity and behavior. This analysis becomes the basis of applications in many areas such as security and surveillance, clinical applications, biomechanical applications, human robot interaction, entertainment and education etc. Security is depending on the CCTV cameras but the problem with CCTV camera based visual surveillance is that the human intervention is required for operation and decisions have to be taken by human operators. Today, video surveillance networks have a greater number of CCTV cameras. For large infrastructures, such as a mass transit system, over a thousand surveillance CCTV cameras may be deployed. These installations represent a huge amount of video to transmit, view and archive, making it impossible for a human monitor to analyze all of these video recordings in order to detect suspicious activity or events. This is especially true since security control centre personnel are also required to manage other tasks, such as access control, issuance of badges/keys/permits, handling emergency calls, following up on fire alarms, radio communications control, etc. Several studies show the limits of human surveillance. After only 20 minutes of looking at and analyzing video surveillance screens, the attention of most people falls below an acceptable level(Hampapur et al. 2003). A monitor cannot attentively follow 9 to 12 cameras for over 15 minutes (Hampapur et al. 2003). Certain studies report that the ratio between the number of screens and the number of cameras can be between 1:4 and 1:78 in certain video surveillance networks (Dee et al. 2008). The probability of reacting immediately to an event captured by a surveillance camera network is estimated at 1 out of 1,000 (Hampapur et al. 2003). That is why, historically, CCTV based video surveillance is mainly a post-event investigation tool. It is difficult and man power intensive to monitor the data collected from various cameras continuously and this gives rise to the necessity for automatic understanding of human actions and building a higher level knowledge of the events occurring in the scene by the computer vision system. Analysis in surveillance scenarios often requires the detection of abnormal human actions. Most of the normal human activities are periodic like walking, running etc. Lack of periodicity is therefore an important cue of an activity being deviant from the normal. Consider for example a typical event of surveillance interest: exchange of brief cases by two agents. The scene essentially consists of an agent walking across the scene who then bends to lift up or leave the briefcase. This event can be described as concatenation of walk-bend, walk actions, where bend is deviant from normal behavior. However abnormal events and therefore abnormal human activities are context dependent and may vary for different situations. For example, in a shopping mall where people normally walk from one counter to another, running could be defined as an abnormal action and could be an event of interest for surveillance purposes. This calls for a need of unified frame work for detecting and recognizing both periodic and non periodic human actions.

LITERATURE REVIEW OF RECOGNITION ALGORITHMS

An activity is a sequence of movements generated during performance of a task. Activity recognition is a difficult task because the shape of the different actors performing an activity can be different and the speed and style in which an activity is performed can vary from person to person. Although the approaches to solve the activity recognition problem are few and far between, but the activity recognition methods available in literature can broadly be categorized into two groups: sensor based activity recognition and vision based activity recognition. In sensor based activity recognition methods some smart sensory device is used to capture various activity signals for activity recognition. Vision based activity recognition methods use the spatial or temporal structure of an activity in order to recognize it. A recent survey on vision-based action representation and recognition methods can be found in (Weinland et al. 2011). Machine learning based and template based methods are popular vision based approaches for human activity recognition in videos. The machine learning based approaches for activity recognition generally solve the problem of activity recognition as a classification problem and classify an activity into one of known activity classes. For training such classifiers a number of feature types (Schmidt-Rohr et al. 2007) and

methods are used, but the drawbacks of machine learning based methods are the long training time, slow operation, constrained accuracy and it is difficult to include a new activity as well. Template based methods are good options for activity recognition in video and can be easily used because of their simplicity and robustness. Weinland et al. (2011) divide the template-based activity recognition methods into three groups: body template based methods (Gavrila and Davis 1995; Yacoob and Black 1998), image template based methods (Bobick and Davis 2001; Weinland et al. 2006; Laptev and Perez 2007; Fathi and Mori 2008; Souvenir and Babbs 2008; Farhadi and Tabrizi 2008) and feature template based methods (Laptevand and Lindeberg 2003; Ke et al. 2007a). Image models are simpler than the body models and can be computed efficiently. Motion energy images and motion history images can be used to compute 'where' and 'how' motion in the scene is taking place which helps in figuring out the location and type of activity in the scene (Bobick and Davis 2001). The chamfer distance (Weinland and Boyer 2008) or shape context descriptors (Lv and Nevatia et al. 2007) are used in contexts where background segmentation is difficult. Motion Energy Images (MEI) and Motion History Images (MHI) can be used for describing 'where' and 'how' in a video scene. 'Where' represents the location of an action in image and MHI records the steps of action i.e. 'how'. Bobick et al. (2001) use motion templates for recognizing the activities in an aerobic exercise. They used only motion information for constructing the MHIs in a view-specific environment and for obtaining segmented foreground they used MEIs, which does not give good activity recognition accuracy in outdoor environment. Moreover, their technique is capable of only identifying one activity in the scene with one actor at a time.

Bremond and Thonnat (1997) investigated the use of contextual information in activity recognition. The use of declarative models for activity recognition from video sequences was described in (Rota and Thonnat 2002). Each activity was represented by a set of conditions between different objects in the scene. This translated into a constraint satisfaction problem for recognizing activity. In a more recent work, an activity recognition algorithm using dynamic instants was proposed (Rao et al. 2002). In (Parameswaran and Chellappa 2002; Parameswaran and Chellappa 2003), each human action was represented by a set of 3D curves, which are quasi-invariant to the viewing direction. The various methods can be classified as either 2D or 3D approaches. Two-dimensional approaches are effective for applications where precise pose recovery is not needed or possible due to low image resolution (e.g. tracking pedestrians in a surveillance setting). However, it is unlikely that they will perform well in applications that require a high level of discrimination between various unconstrained and complex human movements (e.g. humans making gestures while walking, social interactions, dancing etc.). In such applications, 3D approaches are preferred because they can recover body pose, which allows better prediction and handling of occlusion and collision. Also, many researchers used different model for human activity recognition i.e. model based approach and non-model based approach. Model-based approaches generally follow the postulation by Johansson (1975) that human perception of activity depends on structural information. The structural Approach to recognition is implemented as stick figures (Akita 1984), cardboard models (Haritaoglu et al. 2000), volumetric models (Bottino and Laurentini 2001), and hybrid models that track both edges and regions (Green and Guan 2004). Other model-based approaches to activity recognition include hidden Markov models (HMMs) (Cuntoor et al. 2003; Ivanov and Bobick 2000; Sun et al. 2002) and multidimensional indexing (BenArie et al. 2002). All model-based approaches, however, are faced with the challenge of matching model parameters of varying complexity to a human image. On the other hand, Non-model-based systems

recognize human activity by nonstructural means using global shape of motion features (Boyd and Little 1997). Periodicity of human locomotion is one such motion feature that has often been used as a recognition criterion. Polana et al. (Polana and Nelson 1997) exploit periodicity and use the spatio-temporal motion magnitude template as a basis for recognition of activities such as walking, running and swinging. However, template matching fails when sufficient normalization cannot be carried out and is computationally more expensive.

MOTIVATION OF OUR APPROACH AND OTHER RELATED WORK

Motivation

The existing methods of human activity often require special markers attached with the objects being tracked, which prevent the widespread applications The human activity systems has inherited difficult challenges in computer vision application, e.g. illumination variation, viewpoint variation, scale (view distance) variation, and orientation variation. Other problems with the existing activity system are

1. They depend on data from limited field of view, i.e., fixed camera with limited view.
2. Human operators are required to monitor activities
3. Require a lot of human intervention to track the same object in case the multiple cameras are used
4. Lack of human activity & behavior prediction and anomaly detection.
5. The present algorithms for performing various tasks in video surveillance face many challenges like: critical lighting conditions, movement of cameras, occlusion, clutter, etc.

Our Approach

In this approach, we are using the spatio-temporal template to recognize the activities using rotation, scale and translation invariant. Firstly, we performed training of actions in different views of activity. For each view of each action a statistical model of the moments using variance and covariance is generated for MHIs. The 7 moment invariants (Hu 1962) are used as activity descriptors. To recognize an input action, a mahalanobis distance is calculated between the moment description of the input and each of the known actions. The distance matrix so obtained is analyzed in terms of separation distances for different actions.

The proposed algorithm for different human activity recognition is given below:

Step 1: The background in the video is modeled by learning the pixel variance and covariance in frames accumulated over a period of time. Let R denote statistical background model of the scene constructed for background segmentation and V $(v_1, v_2, v_3...v_k)$ is the video frame sequence.

For each v_i in V do

1. $F_i(u,v) = | v_i (u,v) - R(u,v) |$ (1)
2. Perform thresholding on the resultant foreground segmented image F_i (x,y)

$$F_i(u,v) = \begin{cases} 0 & \text{if } F_i(u,v) < T \\ 1 & otherwise \end{cases} \quad (2)$$

where T represents the threshold value.

3. Update reference image using following condition

$$R_{new}(u,v) = S \times R(u,v) + (1-S) \times F(u,v) \quad (3)$$

where, R(u,v) is the old background model and $R_{new}(u,v)$ is the updated background model, F(u,v) denotes the current frame of the video at which updation occurs and S is the updation speed. To obtain the binary image the threshold can be applied as given in Equation (2). The updation of background model is done only when there is variation in lighting conditions and background.

Step 2: The spatio-temporal activity templates can be constructed using MHIs collections of each activity performed on the segmented video frames obtained from step1. The MHIs are used for creating spatio-temporal templates for each activity in activity set A $(a_1, a_2, a_3...a_k)$ and can be constructed in the following manner:

For each a_i in A do

1. Initialize the motion history image MHI for activity a_i with the initial pose of the actor in order to include spatial information in MHI.
2. Measure the minimum and maximum durations, τ_{min} τ_{max} that a movement may take.
3. At each time step, a new MHI, $H_\tau(u,v,t)$ is computed setting $\tau = \tau_{max}$, where τ_{max} is the longest time window we want the system to consider. We choose

$$\Delta\tau = \frac{(\tau_{max} - \tau_{min})}{(n-1)},$$

where $\Delta\tau$ is the time difference, and n is the number of temporal integration windows to be considered. A simple thresholding of MHI values less than $(\tau - \Delta\tau)$ generates $H_{(\tau-\Delta\tau)}$ as below:

$$H_{\tau-\Delta\tau}(u,v,t) = \begin{cases} (H_\tau(u,v,t) - \Delta\tau) & H_\tau(u,v,t) > \Delta\tau \\ 0 & otherwise \end{cases}$$

(4)

where $H_{\tau-\Delta\tau}$ defines the MHI values for time duration $\tau - \Delta\tau$. We store the MHI values for each activity in order to match them against the actual actions.

4. The direction of motion in video, is computed using the gradient orientation. Gradients of the MHI can be calculated by convolution with separable Sobel filters in the X and Y directions which yields $F_x(x,y)$ and $F_y(x,y)$. Where, $F_x(x,y)$ and $F_y(x,y)$ represent the derivatives in x and y directions. At each pixel, gradient orientation, $\phi(x,y)$ can be calculated as follows:

$$\phi(x,y) = \arctan\frac{F_y(x,y)}{F_x(x,y)} \quad (5)$$

The gradient orientation is calculated only for the pixels inside the MHI, where the intensity values for these pixels are non-zero.

Step 3: For matching the spatio-temporal templates for various activities created in step 2.

1. We use the similar moment invariants for scale, translation and rotation as used in (Bobick and Davis 2001).
2. Mahalanobis distance is calculated for matching the input action with the stored templates trained in step 2.

$$mahal(p) = (p-m)^T K^{-1}(p-m) \quad (6)$$

where p is a moment feature vector, m is the mean value of vector p and K^{-1} represents the inverse covariance matrix of the feature vectors.

If more than one match is found for an activity then the match with the smaller mahalanobis distance is chosen.

Comparison to Related Work and Results

In this topic, we am comparing our method to Bobick et al. (2001). In our approach considers the shape information along with the motion history for performing an activity. For obtaining the accurate foreground segmentation a robust statistical background model is constructed. The technique can recognize the static activities like standing and sleeping as well as dynamic activities like walking, jogging, etc. In the proposed approach, covariance based matching is applied to recognize static activities and moment invariants (Bobick and Davis 2001; Hu 1962) are used to recognize dynamic activities. The proposed technique has two advantages over the technique described in (Bobick and Davis 2001). One is that the background segmentation is obtained using a robust statistical model which can better adapt the changes in lighting conditions whereas in (Bobick and Davis 2001) simple frame differencing is not adaptive to these changes. Secondly, the proposed method uses motion as well as object shape information to construct the MHIs while on contrary Bobick et al. (Bobick and Davis 2001) used only motion to construct the MHIs. So the proposed method can accurately recognize the activities with very less motion such as standing and sleeping.

In Figure 1 and Figure 2, we are creating the formation of MHIs in Bobick's method (Bobick and Davis 2001) and in proposed method, respectively. It is clear from Figure 2 that in the proposed method MHI is initialized with the spatial pose of the actor in frame 0 unlike Bobick's method (Bobick and Davis 2001) which uses only motion and therefore frame no. 0 is empty. Figure 3 shows the MHIs for different activities constructed using the proposed method for different activities including boxing, clapping, hand waving, running, and walking. We tested the proposed method for activity recognition with our own activity database as well as with standard KTH database.

Figure 1. MEI-based activity template formation during the sitting activity performed by a human object in Bobick and Davis (2001). Only motion information is used for constructing activity templates.

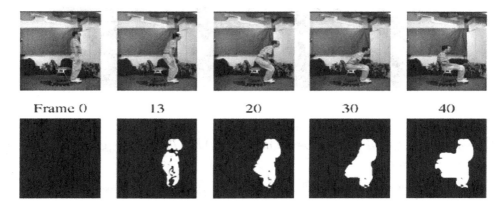

Figure 2. The spatio-temporal MHI based template formation of the sitting activity by the proposed technique. Background segmentation is achieved using statistical background model.

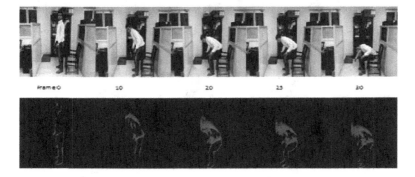

In Figure 4, we have shown results for our own created database. This database contains four static human activities namely, sitting, sleeping, standing, bending and two dynamic activities namely, walking and jogging. These videos are taken in real outdoor environment. From the observation of this figure, it is clear that the proposed method is well capable of recognizing these static and dynamic activities. Moreover, there is some little movement in each activity, i.e. pose of human object does not remain still for all the time. Direction of each human object also changes in different frames. Therefore, the proposed method is pose invariant and frontal view is not necessary for recognition of objects and suits for

recognition of objects with frontal as well as side view. In addition to this activities (a,c,d,e,f) are performed in outdoor environment whereas activity (b) is performed in indoor environment. But in both scenarios, the proposed method is capable of recognizing these activities. Shadow is also present in scene, but it does not impose any restriction on recognition accuracy.

In Figure 5, we have shown activity recognition with standard KTH database. This database includes six activities like boxing, handclapping, hand waving, jogging, running and walking. For this database also, the proposed method performs well. Moreover, this database not only contains activities involving leg motion (like jogging, run-

Figure 3. MHIs of different activities by the proposed method: (a) boxing, (b) clapping, (c) hand waving, (d) running, and (e) walking

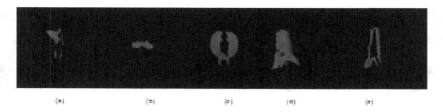

Figure 4. Recognition of activities in our own database: (a) bending, (b) jogging, (c) sitting, (d) sleeping, (e) standing, and (f) walking

ning and walking) but it also contains activities involving hand motion (like boxing, handclapping and hand waving).

Table 1 presents confusion matrix for the proposed method in performing different activities. Total 10 different activities have been considered. We take 50 instances of each activity for experiment and confusion matrix shows that how these instances are recognized. The average recognition accuracy of the proposed method is revealed as 86.52%.

In this chapter, we are comparing the abilities of the space-time approaches for human activity recognition methods. We have collected the per-

formance statistics of the techniques from (Aggarwal and Ryoo 2011). Space-time approaches are suitable for human recognition of periodic actions and gestures, and many have been tested on public datasets such as the KTH dataset (Schuldt et al. 2004) and the Weizmann dataset (Blank et al. 2005). Fundamental approaches using space-time volumes provide a straight-forward solution, but often have difficulties handling speed and motion variations inherently. Recognition approaches using space-time trajectories are able to perform detailed-level analysis and are view-invariant in most cases. However, 3-D modeling of body parts from videos, which still is an un-

Figure 5. Recognition of activities with KTH database: (a) walking, (b) running, (c) jogging, (d) hand clapping, (e) hand waving, (f) boxing

Table 1. Confusion matrix of the proposed method for activity recognition considering 50 instances of each activity

Recognized Instances	Boxing	Hand Clapping	Hand Waving	Jogging	Running	Walking	Sitting	Sleeping	Standing	Bending
Total Instances										
Boxing (50)	43	3	1	1	0	0	0	0	1	1
Hand Clapping (50)	1	42	2	2	1	1	0	0	1	0
Hand Waving (50)	2	1	42	2	1	1	0	0	1	0
Jogging (50)	1	0	0	44	2	2	1	0	0	0
Running (50)	0	0	0	4	44	1	0	0	1	0
Walking (50)	0	0	0	2	3	44	0	0	1	0
Sitting (50)	0	0	0	0	0	0	48	0	1	1
Sleeping (50)	0	0	0	0	0	0	0	43	6	1
Standing (50)	1	0	0	1	1	0	0	4	43	0
Bending (50)	0	0	0	0	0	0	2	1	1	46

solved problem, is required for a trajectory-based approach to be applied.

The spatio-temporal local feature-based approaches are getting an increasing amount of attention because of their reliability under noise and illumination changes. Furthermore, many approaches (Niebles et al. 2006; Ryoo et al. 2009) are able to recognize multiple human activities without background subtraction. The major limitation of the space-time feature-based approaches is that they are not suitable for modeling more complex activities (see Table 2).

CONCLUSION AND DISCUSSION

Human activity recognition is a popular area of research in the field of computer vision with applications in many diverse fields. The application to surveillance is natural in today's environment, where the single or multiple tracking and monitoring of different people are becoming an integral part of everyday activities. Many other applications include human-computer interaction, biometrics based on gait or face, and hand and face gesture recognition. In this chapter, we have provided an overview of the current approaches to human activity recognition. In this chapter, we have summarized the methodologies that have previously been explored for the recognition of human activities, and discussed advantages and disadvantages of those approaches.

Further, today's environment for human activity recognition is significantly different from the scenario at the end of the last decade. The cameras were mostly fixed cameras and without pan-tilt-zoom adjustments. Today's cameras may be mounted on several types of moving platforms ranging from a moving car or a truck to an Unmanned Aerial Vehicle (UAV). A global positioning system may be attached to the camera system to pinpoint its location. The recognition of activity from a moving platform poses many more challenges. Noise, tracking, and segmentation

Table 2. Comparing the abilities of the important space-time approaches

Approach Type	Author	Required low level	Structural Consideration	Scale Invariant	Localization	View Invariant	Multiple Activities
Space-time volume	Bobick and Davis (2001)	Background	Volume-based	Templates needed	√		
	Shechtman and Irani (2005)	None	Volume-based	Scaling required	√		
	Ke et al. (2007b)	None	Volume-based	Templates needed	√		
	Rodriguez et al. (2008)	None	Volume-based	√	√		
Space-time trajectories	Campbell and Bobick (1995)	Body-part estimation		√	√	√	
	Rao and Shah (2001)	Skin detection	Ordering only	√	√	√	
	Sheikh et al. (2005)	Body-part estimation	Ordering only	√	√	√	
Space-time features	Chomat and Crowley (1999)	None		√	√		
	Zalnik-Manor and Irani (2001)	None		√			
	Laptev and Lindeberg (2003)	None		√	√		
	Shuldt et al. (2004)	None		√			
	Dollar et al. (2005)	None		√			
	Yilmaz and Shah (2005)	Background	Ordering only	√	√	√	
	Blank et al. (2005)	Background		√	√	√	
	Niebles et al. (2006)	None		√	√		√
	Wong et al. (2007)	None	√	√	√		
	Savarese et al. (2008)	None	Proximity-based	√	√		√
	Liu and Shah (2008)	None	Co-occur only	√			
	Laptev et al. (2008)	None	Grid-based	√			
	Ryoo and Aggarwal (2009)	None	√	√	√		√

issues arising out of stabilization of video add to the difficulty of the problem of the recognition of activities. Tracking is a difficult problem though animals and human do it almost effortlessly. If the tracking algorithm does not extract the object of the focus of attention, recognition of the activity being performed becomes enormously more difficult. Designing an activity recognition system which is able to compensate for such low-level failures in those environments (i.e. moving platforms) is an extremely challenging task. In 1999, human activity recognition was in its infancy as (Aggarwal and Cai 1999) pointed out. A significant amount of progress on human activity recognition has been made at the end of the last 10 year decade, but it is still far from being an off the shelf technology. We are at a stage where experimental systems are deployed at airports and other public places for human safety. It is likely that more and more, such systems will be deployed. There is a strong interaction between the surveillance-authorities and computer vision researchers for deployed intelligent video surveillance system in public place.

FUTURE RESEARCH DIRECTIONS

The future direction of research is obviously encouraged and dictated by applications. The pressing applications are the surveillance and monitoring of public facilities like train stations, underground subways or airports, monitoring patients in a hospital environment or other health care facilities, monitoring activities in the context of UAV surveillance, and other similar applications. All of these applications are trying to understand the activities of an individual or the activities of a crowd as a whole and as subgroups. These problems will occupy us for a number of years and several generations of graduate students.

There are a number of other innovative approaches being explored. One such approach is exploiting the fact that images, high dimensional signals, are possibly residing in low dimensional

manifolds. Several researchers are pursuing issues relating to characterizing the manifolds and exploring the relationships of the manifolds of different activities of the same person or the same activity of different persons (Veeraraghavan et al. 2006). The temporal segmentation of activities and gestures is still a difficult issue. The inability to simultaneously register rigid and non-rigid parts of a face (in general parts of the human body) contributes to this difficulty. In certain activities, parts of the body move fairly rigidly whereas other parts undergo non-rigid motion, for example, the movement of the head or face. Shape deformations may be modeled as a linear combination of unknown shape bases (La Torre Frade et al. 2007), providing another approach to the recognition of facial expressions.

REFERENCES

Aggarwal, J. K., & Cai, Q. (1999). Human motion analysis: A review. *Computer Vision and Image Understanding*, *73*(3), 428–440. doi:10.1006/cviu.1998.0744.

Aggarwal, J. K., & Ryoo, M. S. (2011). Human activity analysis: A review. *J. of ACM Comp. Sur*, *43*(3).

Akita, K. (1984). Image sequence analysis of real world human motion. *Pattern Recognition*, *17*(1), 73–83. doi:10.1016/0031-3203(84)90036-0.

BenArie, J., Wang, Z., Pandit, P., & Rajaram, S. (2002). Human activity recognition using multidimensional indexing. *IEEE Transactions on Pattern Analysis and Machine Intelligence*, *24*(8), 1091–1104. doi:10.1109/TPAMI.2002.1023805.

Blank, M., Gorelick, L., Shechtman, E., Irani, M., & Basri, R. (2005). Actions as space-time shapes. In *Proceedings of the IEEE International Conference on Computer Vision (ICCV), Perspectives on Motivation* (pp. 1395-1402). IEEE.

Bobick, A. F., & Davis, J. W. (2001). The recognition of human movement using temporal templates. *IEEE Transactions on Pattern Analysis and Machine Intelligence*, *23*(3), 257–267. doi:10.1109/34.910878.

Bottino, A., & Laurentini, A. (2001). A silhouette based technique for the reconstruction of human movement. *Comput. Vis. Image Under-standing*, *83*, 79–95. doi:10.1006/cviu.2001.0918.

Boyd, J. E., & Little, J. J. (1997). Global versus structured interpretation of motion: Moving light displays. In *Proc. IEEE Workshop Motion Non-Rigid and Articulated Objects: Perspectives on Motivation* (pp. 18–25). IEEE.

Bremond, B. F., & Thonnat, M. (1997). Analysis of human activities described by image sequences. In *Proc. Int. Florida AI Research Symp*. IEEE.

Campbell, L. W., & Bobick, A. F. (1995). Recognition of human body motion using phase space constraints. In *Proceedings of the IEEE International Conference on Computer Vision (ICCV), Perspectives on Motivation* (pp. 624–630). IEEE.

Chomat, O., & Crowley, J. (1999). Probabilistic recognition of activity using local appearance. In *Proceedings of the IEEE Conference on Computer Vision and Pattern Recognition (CVPR)*. IEEE.

Cuntoor, N., Kale, A., & Chellappa, R. (2003). Combining multiple evidences for gait recognition. In *Proc. ICASSP: Vol. 3 Perspectives on Motivation* (pp. 33–36). IEEE.

Dee, H. M., & Velastin, S. A. (2008). How close are we to solving the problem of automated visual surveillance? A review of real-world surveillance, scientific progress and evaluative mechanisms. *International journal of Machine Vision and Applications, 19*, 329-343.

Dollar, P., Rabaud, V., Cottrell, G., & Belongie, S. (2005). Behavior recognition via sparse spatio-temporal features. In *Proceedings of the 2nd Joint IEEE International Workshop on Visual Surveillance and Performance Evaluation of Tracking and Surveillance (VS-PETS), Perspectives on Motivation* (pp. 65-72). IEEE.

Farhadi, A., & Tabrizi, M. K. (2008). Learning to recognize activities from the wrong view point. In *Proc. European Conference on Computer Vision: Perspectives on Motivation* (pp. 154-166). IEEE.

Fathi, A., & Mori, G. (2008). Action recognition by learning mid-level motion features. In *Proc. Conference on Computer Vision and Pattern Recognition: Perspectives on Motivation* (pp. 1-8). IEEE.

Gavrila, D., & Davis, L. (1995). Towards 3-D model-based tracking and recognition of human movement. In *Proceedings of the Int. Workshop on Face and Gesture Recognition: Perspectives on Motivation* (pp. 272–277). IEEE.

Green, R. D., & Guan, L. (2004). Quantifying and recognizing human movement patterns from monocular video images—Part I: A new frame-work for modeling human motion. *IEEE Transactions on Circuits and Systems for Video Technology, 14*(2), 179–189. doi:10.1109/TCSVT.2003.821976.

Hampapur, A., Brown, L., Connell, J., Pankanti, S., Senior, A., & Tian, Y. (2003). Smart surveillance: Applications, technologies and implications. In *Proceedings of the Fourth International Conference on Information, Communications & Signal Processing and Fourth Pacific-Rim Conference on Multimedia*, (Vol. 2, pp. 1133-1138). IEEE.

Haritaoglu, I., Harwood, D., & Davis, L. S. (2000). W4: Real-time surveillance of people and their activities. *IEEE Transactions on Pattern Analysis and Machine Intelligence, 22*(8), 809–830. doi:10.1109/34.868683.

Hu, M. (1962). Visual pattern recognition by moment invariants. *I.R.E. Transactions on Information Theory*, 8(2), 179–187. doi:10.1109/TIT.1962.1057692.

Ivanov, Y. A., & Bobick, A. F. (2000). Recognition of visual activities and interactions by stochastic parsing. *IEEE Transactions on Pattern Analysis and Machine Intelligence*, 22(8), 852–872. doi:10.1109/34.868686.

Johansson, G. (1975). Visual motion perception. *Scientif. Amer.*, 76–88.

Ke, Y., Sukthankar, R., & Hebert, M. (2007a). Event detection in crowded videos. In *Proc. International Conference on Computer Vision: Perspectives on Motivation* (pp. 1-8). IEEE.

Ke, Y., Sukthankar, R., & Hebert, M. (2007b). Spatio-temporal shape and flow correlation for action recognition. In *Proceedings of the IEEE Conference on Computer Vision and Pattern Recognition (CVPR)*. IEEE.

KTH Research Project Activity Database. (n.d.). Retrieved from http://www.nada.kth.se/cvap/actions/

La Torre Frade, F. D., Campoy, J., Cohn, J., & Kanade, T. (2007). Simultaneous registration and clustering for temporal segmentation. In *Proceedings of the International Conference on Computer Vision Theory and Applications: Perspectives on Motivation* (pp. 110-115). IEEE.

Laptev, I., & Lindeberg, T. (2003). Space-time interest points. In P*roc. International Conference on Computer Vision: Vol. 1, Perspectives on Motivation* (pp. 432-439). IEEE.

Laptev, I., Marszalek, M., Schmid, C., & Rozenfeld, B. (2008). Learning realistic human ac-tions from movies. In *Proceedings of the IEEE Conference on Computer Vision and Pattern Recognition (CVPR)*. IEEE.

Laptev, I., & Perez, P. (2007). Retrieving actions in movies. In *Proc. of Int. Conference on Computer Vision: Perspectives on Motivation* (pp. 1-8). IEEE.

Liu, J., & Shah, M. (2008). Learning human actions via information maximization. In *Proceedings of the IEEE Conference on Computer Vision and Pattern Recognition (CVPR)*. IEEE.

Lv, F., & Nevatia, R. (2007). Single view human action recognition using key pose matching and viterbi path searching. In *Proc. Conference on Computer Vision and Pattern Recognition: Perspectives on Motivation* (pp. 1-8). IEEE.

Niebles, J. C., Wang, H., & Fei-Fei, L. (2006). Unsupervised learning of human action cate-gories using spatial-temporal words. In *Proceedings of the British Machine Vision Conference (BMVC)*. BMVC.

Parameswaran, V., & Chellappa, R. (2002). Quasi-invariants for human action representation and recognition. In *Proc. Int. Conf. Pattern Recogn: Perspectives on Motivation* (pp. 307–310). IEEE.

Parmeswaran, V., & Chellappa, R. (2003). View invariants for human action recognition. In *Proc. IEEE Comput. Soc. Conf. Comput. Vis. Pattern Recogn.: Perspectives on Motivation* (pp. 613–619). IEEE.

Polana, R., & Nelson, R. (1997). Detection and recognition of periodic, non-rigid motion. *Comput. Vis.*, 23, 261–282. doi:10.1023/A:1007975200487.

Rao, C., & Shah, M. (2001). View-invariance in action recognition. In *Proceedings of the IEEE Conference on Computer Vision and Pattern Recognition (CVPR)*. IEEE.

Rao, C., Yilmaz, A., & Shah, M. (2002). View-invariant representation and recognition of actions. *International Journal of Computer Vision*, 50(2), 203–226. doi:10.1023/A:1020350100748.

Rodriguez, M. D., Ahmed, J., & Shah, M. (2008). Action MACH: A spatio-temporal maximum average correlation height filter for action recognition. In *Proceedings of the IEEE Conference on Computer Vision and Pattern Recognition (CVPR)*. IEEE.

Rota, N., & Thonnat, M. (2002). Activity recognition from video sequence using declarative models. In *Proceedings of the Eur. Conf. Artif. Intell: Perspectives on Motivation* (pp. 673-680). IEEE.

Ryoo, M. S., & Aggarwal, J. K. (2009). Spatiotemporal relationship match: Video structure comparison for recognition of complex human activities. In *Proceedings of the IEEE International Conference on Computer Vision (ICCV)*. IEEE.

Savarese, S., DelPozo, A., Niebles, J., & Fei-Fei, L. (2008). Spatial-temporal correlations for unsupervised action classification. In *Proceedings of the IEEE Workshop on Motion and Video Computing (WMVC)*. IEEE.

Schmidt-Rohr, S., Knoop, S., Vacek, S., & Dillmann, R. (2007). Feature set selection and optimal classifier for human activity recognition. In *Proc. 16th IEEE International Conference on Robot & Human Interactive Communication: Perspectives on Motivation* (pp. 1022-1027). IEEE.

Schuldt, C., Laptev, I., & Caputo, B. (2004). Recognizing human actions: A local SVM approach. In *Proceedings of the International Conference on Pattern Recognition (ICPR), Vol. 3: Perspectives on Motivation* (pp. 32–36). IEEE.

Shechtman, E., & Irani, M. (2005). Space-time behavior based correlation. In *Proceedings of the IEEE Conference on Computer Vision and Pattern Recognition (CVPR), Vol. 1: Perspectives on Motivation* (pp. 405–412). IEEE.

Sheikh, Y., Sheikh, M., & Shah, M. (2005). Exploring the space of a human action. In *Proceedings of the IEEE International Conference on Computer Vision (ICCV): Vol. 1: Perspectives on Motivation* (pp. 144–149). IEEE.

Souvenir, R., & Babbs, J. (2008). Learning the viewpoint manifold for action recognition. In *Proc. Conference on Computer Vision and Pattern Recognition: Perspectives on Motivation* (pp. 118-125). IEEE.

Sun, X., Chen, C. W., & Manjunath, B. S. (2002). Probabilistic motion parameter models for human activity recognition. In *Proc. ICPR: Vol. 1, Perspectives on Motivation* (pp. 443–446). IEEE.

Veeraraghavan, A., Chellappa, R., & Roy-Chowdhury, A. (2006). The function space of an activity. In *Proceedings of the IEEE Conference on Computer Vision and Pattern Recognition (CVPR), Vol. 1: Perspectives on Motivation* (pp. 959-968). IEEE.

Weinland, D., & Boyer, E. (2008). Action recognition using exemplar-based embedding. In *Proc. Conference on Computer Vision and Pattern Recognition: Perspectives on Motivation* (pp. 1-7). IEEE.

Weinland, D., & Ronfard, R. (2011). A survey of vision based methods for action representation, segmentation and recognition. *International Journal of Computer Vision and Image Understanding, 115*, 221–241.

Weinland, D., Ronfard, R., & Boyer, E. (2006). Free viewpoint action recognition using motion history volumes. *Int. Journal Computer Vision and Image Understanding, 104*(2), 249–257. doi:10.1016/j.cviu.2006.07.013.

Wong, S.-F., Kim, T.-K., & Cipolla, R. (2007). Learning motion categories using both semantic and structural information. In *Proceedings of the IEEE Conference on Computer Vision and Pattern Recognition (CVPR)*. IEEE.

Yacoob, Y., & Black, M. (1998). Parameterized modeling and recognition of activities. In *Proc. Int. Conference on Computer Vision: Perspectives on Motivation* (pp.120-127). IEEE.

Yilmaz, A., & Shah, M. (2005). Actions sketch: A novel action representation. In *Proceedings of the IEEE Conference on Computer Vision and Pattern Recognition (CVPR), Vol. 1: Perspectives on Motivation* (pp. 984-989). IEEE.

Zelnik-Manor, L., & Irani, M. (2001). Event-based analysis of video. In *Proceedings of the IEEE Conference on Computer Vision and Pattern Recognition (CVPR)*. IEEE.

KEY TERMS AND DEFINITIONS

Computer Vision: Computer vision is concerned with modeling and replicating human vision using computer software and hardware. It combines knowledge in computer science, electrical engineering, mathematics, physiology, biology, and cognitive science. It needs knowledge from all these fields in order to understanding simulate the operation of the human vision system.

Human Activity: Human activity aims to recognize the human actions and goals of one or more agents from a series of observations on the agents' actions and the environmental conditions.

Motion Analysis: The motion analysis processing can in the simplest case be to detect motion, i.e., find the points in the image where something is moving.

Robot Navigation: Robot navigation includes different interrelated activities such as perception – obtaining and interpreting sensory information; exploration – the strategy that guides the robot to select the next direction to go; etc.

Video Surveillance: Closed-Circuit Television (CCTV) is the use of video cameras to transmit a signal to a specific place, on a limited set of monitors.

Chapter 10
Video Authentication:
An Intelligent Approach

Saurabh Upadhyay
Saffrony Institute of Technology, India

Shrikant Tiwari
Indian Institute of Technology (BHU), India

Shalabh Parashar
HCL Technologies, India

ABSTRACT

With the growing innovations and emerging developments in sophisticated video editing technology, it is becoming highly desirable to assure the credibility and integrity of video information. Today digital videos are also increasingly transmitted over non-secure channels such as the Internet. Therefore, in surveillance, medical, and various other fields, video contents must be protected against attempts to manipulate them. Video authentication has gained much attention in recent years. However, many existing authentication techniques have their own advantages and obvious drawbacks. The authors propose a novel authentication technique that uses an intelligent approach for video authentication. This chapter presents an intelligent video authentication algorithm for raw videos using a support vector machine, which is a non-linear classifier, and its applications. It covers both kinds of tampering attacks, spatial and temporal. It uses a database of more than 2000 tampered and non-tampered videos and gives excellent results with 98.38% classification accuracy. The authors also discuss a vast diversity of tampering attacks, which can be possible for video sequences. Their algorithm gives good results for almost all kinds of tampering attacks.

DOI: 10.4018/978-1-4666-4868-5.ch010

INTRODUCTION

With the rapid development and innovation in digital information technologies, video applications are infiltrating into our daily lives at breakneck speed, from traditional television broadcasting to Internet/Intranet, wireless communication and consumer products such as VCD/DVDs and smart phones. Though this immense development in digital information technology has brought us in the new era of powerful information, we are having some severe challenging issues related with the information. One of them is credibility of the information. Today, editing or modifying the content of a digital video can be done efficiently and seamlessly, and the credibility of the digital data decreases significantly (Friedman, 1993). To ensure the trustworthiness, authentication techniques (Lin & Chang, 2001; Naor & Pinkas, 1997; Perrig, Canetti, Tygar, & Song, 2000) are needed for verifying the originality of video content and preventing the forgery. Building a mechanism that enables media authenticity verification, is basically needed in court of law where digital media might be used as evidence against potential criminals. A possible scenario that justifies the need of such a mechanism is a case where a defendant claims that an incriminated media was fabricated.

So the video authentication is a process which ascertains that the content in a given video is authentic and exactly same as when captured. For verifying the originality of received video content, and to detect malicious tampering and preventing various types of forgeries, performed on video data, video authentication techniques are used.

These techniques also detect the types and locations of malicious tampering. In fact a wide range of powerful digital video processing tools are available in the market that allow extensive access, manipulations and reuse of visual materials (Hauzia & Noumeir, 2007). Since different video recording devices and close circuit television camera system become more convenient and af-

fordable option in the private and public sectors, there is a corresponding increase in the frequency in which they are encountered in criminal investigations[1]. The video evidences have significant role in criminal investigations due to their ability to obtain detailed information from their own. And they have tremendous potential to assist in investigations. Therefore, it would be necessary to take utmost care to make sure that the given video evidence, presented in the court, is authentic.

MOTIVATION BEHIND VIDEO AUTHENTICATION

In some applications the authenticity of the video data is of paramount interest such as in video surveillance, forensic investigations, law enforcement and content ownership (Upadhyay, Singh, Vatsa, & Singh, 2007). For example, in court of law, it is important to establish the trustworthiness of any video that is used as evidence. As in another scenario, for example, suppose a stationary video recorder for surveillance purpose, is positioned on the pillar of a railway platform to survey every activity on that platform along a side. It would be fairly simple to remove a certain activity, people or even an event by simply removing a handful of frames from this type of video sequences. On the other hand it would also be feasible to insert, into this video, certain objects and people, taken from different cameras and in different time. A video clip can be doctored in a specific way to defame an individual. In the recent years, several cases have been reported where the eminent personalities of the society were caught in illegal activities in the video recordings made by so called journalists. However in the absence of foolproof techniques to authenticate the video it is difficult to trust on such reports. On the other hand criminals get free from being punished because the video (used as evidence), showing their crime cannot be proved conclusively in the court of law. In the case of surveillance systems, it is difficult to assure that the digital video produced as evidence, is the same as it was actually shot by camera. In another scenario, a news maker cannot prove that the video played by a news channel is trustworthy; while a video viewer who receives the video through a communication channel cannot ensure that video being viewed is really the one that was transmitted (Pradeep, et. al., n.d.). In the scenario of sensitive cases where a video is produced as a witness in the court of law, even a small modification may not be acceptable. However there are some scenarios where editing also may be allowed while keeping intact the authenticity of the video. For example after shooting the video, a journalist may need to perform some editing before broadcasting it on a news channel. In such a case a video authentication system should be able to allow editing on the video up to a certain level ensuring the authenticity of the video (Pradeep, Atrey, El Saddik, & Kankanhalli, 2009). Now a day an ordinary person can easily make unauthorized copies of digital video data and manipulate them in such a way that may lead to severe financial and social losses. These are the instances where malicious modifications cannot be tolerated. Therefore, there is a compelling need for video authentication. Although traditional data authentication technology for message integrity was mature, video authentication is still in its early development stage and many fundamental questions remain open (Han & Chu, 2010). For example, for a number of different authentication algorithm developed over the past few years, it is difficult to affirm which approach seems most suitable for ensuring the integrity adapted to videos (Han & Chu, 2010). For verifying the credibility of received video content, and to detect malicious tampering attacks and preventing various types of forgeries, performed on video data, video authentication techniques are used.

CHALLENGING SCENARIOS FOR VIDEO AUTHENTICATION

In some of the surveillance systems storage and transmission costs are the important issues. In order to reduce the storage and transmission cost only those video clips, containing objects of interest, are required to be sent and stored. Moreover in most of the surveillance applications background object changes very slowly in comparison to foreground objects. A possible efficient solution in these scenarios is that only the objects of interest (mostly foreground objects) are sent out frame by frame in real time while the background object is sent once in a long time interval. In such surveillance applications, it becomes very important to protect the authenticity of the video: the authenticity against malicious alterations and the authenticity for the identity of the transmission source (i.e. identify the video source).

In event based surveillance systems, the video sequences are captured when there is any kind of change in the scene (existence of an event) which would be captured by the camera. If there is uniformity in the scene in such a way that there is not any change in the scene then the surveillance camera does not capture any video sequence. This kind of surveillance system is used in military system for border security purpose. Authenticity for this kind of video sequences is a challenging issue because there is no proper time sequence in video sequences which are captured by surveillance camera.

In another scenario where a surveillance camera is recording the postmortem activity of a human body in postmortem house, any kind of disturbance in recording (due to electricity problem or some other hardware problem) would be resulted in frame dropping. This would be a severe issue since some important activities may have happened during frame dropping and these activities may be missed to be recorded by surveillance camera. Authentication of this kind of video sequence is also a very challenging task because we are not in the condition of detecting all the positions where and how many frames have been dropped.

In addition of these scenarios, there are some challenging conditions for video authentication. To assure the authenticity of the videos, captured in the following situations, would be fairly difficult.

- The videos recorded in the foggy and rainy weather condition
- The videos recorded in the hazardous condition.
- The videos recorded in a condition where the camera or the objects (recorded by the camera) or both are moving very rapidly.
- The videos recorded in the night vision mode.

These all are the different scenarios which poses considerable challenges for the authentication purpose.

VIDEO TAMPERING

A continuous video data $V_c(x, y, t)$ is a scalar real valued function of two spatial dimensions x and y and time t, usually observed in a rectangular spatial window W over some time interval T. If $M(x, y, t)$ is modification vector then the tampered video $B_c(x, y, t)$ would also be a scalar real valued function of spatial dimensions x and y and time t as follows:

$$B_c(x, y, t) = M(x, y, t) + V_c(x, y, t)$$

When the content of information, being produced by a given video data is maliciously altered, then it is called tampering of video data. It can be done for several purposes, for instance to manipulate the integrity of an individual or to deceive any one by producing fake information through tampered video. Since a wide range of

sophisticated and low cost video editing software are available in the market that makes it easy and less expensive to manipulate the video content information maliciously, it poses serious challenges to researchers to be solved.

VIDEO TAMPERING ATTACKS

There are several possible attacks that can be applied to modify the contents of a video data. Formally a wide range of authentication techniques have been proposed in the literature but most of them have been primarily focused on still images. However the basic task of video authentication system is to prove whether the given video is tampered or not but in several applications, due to large availability of information in video data, it may be more significant if the authentication system can tell where the modifications happened (It indicates the locality property of authentication) and how the video is tampered (Yin et al., n.d.). On considering these where and how, the video tampering attacks can have different classifications. A lot of works have been done that briefly address the classification based on where (Upadhyay, Singh, Vatsa, & Singh, 2007; Yin et al., n.d.). And some papers address the classification based on how (Dittman et al., 2000). In general finding where the video data is altered is more efficient than to find out how the how data is tampered. When a video is being recorded by a video recording device, it captures the scene which is in front of the camera lens, frame by frame, with respect to time. Number of frames being captured by video recording device in a second, depends on the hardware specification of the device. Thus a video can be viewed as a collection of consecutive frames with temporal dependency, in a three-dimensional plane, as shown in Figure 1.

It refers to the regional property of the video sequences. When a malicious modification is performed on a video, it either attacks on the

Figure 1. Three-dimensional view of video information

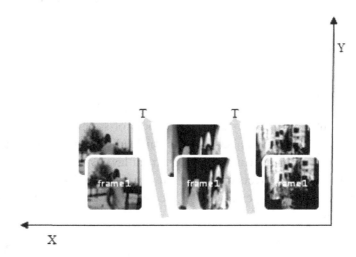

contents of the video (i.e. visual information presented by the frames of the video), or attacks on the temporal dependency between the frames of the video. Therefore based on the regional property of the video sequences, we can broadly classify the video tampering attacks into three categories: spatial tampering attacks, temporal tampering attacks and the combination of these two, spatio-temporal tampering attacks (Yin et al., n.d.). They can be further classified into their subcategories.

Spatial Tampering

In spatial tampering malicious alterations are performed on the content of the frames (X-Y axis). The operations which are performed as a tampering attack in spatial tampering are cropping and replacement, morphing, content (object) adding and removing, in the frames of the video, etc. (Yin et al., n.d.). These attacks can be efficiently performed with the help of any professional video editing software for example Photoshop, etc.

Temporal Tampering

In temporal tampering malicious manipulation is performed on the sequence of the video frames. The focus is on the temporal dependency of the video. Temporal tampering attacks are mainly affecting the time sequence of visual information, captured by video recording devices. The common attacks in temporal tampering are frame addition, frame removal and frame reordering or shuffling in the video.

Spatio-Temporal Tampering

Spatio-temporal tampering attacks are the combination of the both kinds of tampering attacks: spatial and temporal tampering attacks. Frame sequences are altered and also visual contents of the frames are modified in the same video. The authentication system should be able to identify both kinds of tampering attacks.

All these tampering are further classified into their subcategories. Spatial tampering can be in effect either at block level or at pixel level. In both the cases the objects of the frames of the video are altered.

Further the objects of the frames are classified into two categories: Foreground objects and Background objects. The foreground objects are those which are captured as individual elements, excluding the background, in a frame. And the background object is the background part of the frame excluding all of the foreground objects. The different pieces of visual information shown in the frames of the video are altered in spatial tampering. Basically the contents of the video frames are treated as objects. Based on these objects and their classification the spatial tampering can be further classified as shown in Figure 2.

OBJECT REMOVAL ATTACK

In object removal attack of the spatial tampering, the objects of the frames of the video are eliminated. This kind of tampering attack is commonly performed where a particular person wants to hide his/her presence in a certain sequence of frames. With this kind of attack he /she may disappear in a specific time domain, recorded in the video, and with the help of this, he/she can easily prove his/her absence in any event which has been recorded by video recording device, as shown in Figure 3.

OBJECT ADDITION ATTACK

An object or set of object is inserted in a frame or in a set of frames of the video in object addition attack of spatial tampering. In any video, which can be treated as evidence, an additional object can be pasted in a frame or set of frames, with the help of sophisticated video editing software to mislead the investigation agencies as well as court of law. With the help of this kind of attack, one can prove his/her presence in any event of the pre-recorded video, as shown in Figure 4.

OBJECT MODIFICATION ATTACK

In Object modification attack of the spatial tampering, an existing object of the frame(s) can be modified in such a way that the original identity of that object is lost, and a new object may be in appearance which is completely different from the original object. The object modification attacks can be existed in many prospects of the given video. For instance, the size and shape of any existing object may be changed, the color of the object may be changed or it may be discolored, and with the help of additional effect the nature of the object and it's relation with other objects also may be changed. It depends upon the intention. In

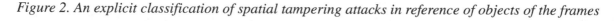

Figure 2. An explicit classification of spatial tampering attacks in reference of objects of the frames

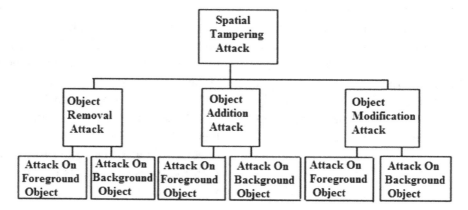

Figure 3. Example of object removal attack: (a) shows object removal attack with foreground object, where a small device is removed from the original frame in tampered frame, whereas (b) shows the object removal attack with background object

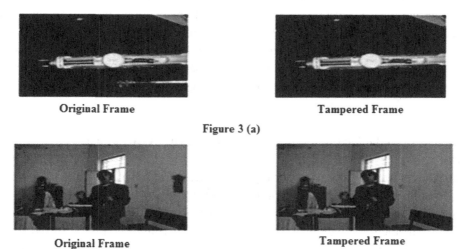

Original Frame   Tampered Frame

Figure 3 (a)

Original Frame   Tampered Frame

Figure 3 (b)

Figure 4. Example of object addition attack: in original frame (a) two persons are there as major fore-ground objects, while in tampered frame (a) an additional person as a foreground object is added. In tampered frame (b), not only a foreground object is added but also an additional wall as a background object in the middle of the frame is added

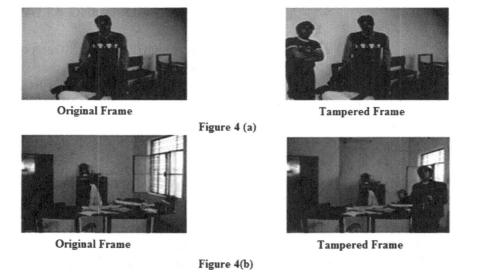

Original Frame   Tampered Frame

Figure 4 (a)

Original Frame   Tampered Frame

Figure 4(b)

fact it is very hard to detect and locate this kind of attack of spatial tampering for authentication systems, since these attacks are performed at pixel level. The authentication systems should also be robust enough to differentiate this kind of attack with the normal video processing operations. Figure 5 shows a typical example of object modification attack where the face of a person has been changed in such a way that the person's face, which is introduced in the altered frame, is completely different from the face of the person in original frame.

Besides spatial tampering, temporal tampering attacks have also sub classifications. Temporal tampering attacks are specific to video applications and can be performed at scene level, shot level and frame level, but the primary focus is on attacking the temporal dependency of the frames of the video. This kind of tampering attack basically affects the sequencing of video frames. We call it 'Third dimensional (dimension with respect to time) attack' on the video sequences. Therefore based on this third dimensional attack we can classify the temporal tampering attacks into following subcategories.

FRAME ADDITION ATTACK

In frame addition attack of temporal tampering, additional frames from another video, which has the same statistical (height and width of frames) and dimensional (number of frames per second) properties, are intentionally inserted at some random locations in a given video. This attack is intended to camouflage the actual content and provide incorrect information (Upadhyay, Singh, Vatsa, & Singh, 2007). A typical example of the frame addition attack is shown in Figure 6.

FRAME REMOVAL ATTACK

In frame removal attack of temporal tampering, the frames of the given video are intentionally eliminated. In this kind of tampering attack frames or set of frames can be removed from a specific location to a fixed location or can be removed from different locations. It depends upon the intention. Commonly this kind of tampering attack is performed on surveillance video where an intruder wants to remove his/her presence at all. Figure 7 shows a typical example of frame removal attack.

FRAME SHUFFLING ATTACK

In frame shuffling attack of temporal tampering, frames of a given video are shuffled or reordered in such a way that the correct frame sequence is intermingled and wrong information is produced by the video as compared to original recorded

Figure 5. Example of object modification attack: the face of the person in original frame is modified in tampered frame in such a way that the new face of the person cannot be identified as the same as in original frame

Original Frame

Tampered Frame

Figure 6. Example of frame addition attack: in first row the original frame sequence from frame 6 to frame 16 has been shown. After attack, the second row of the frames shows the altered frame sequence in which a new frame is inserted between frame 6 and frame 16.

Figure 7. Example of frame removal attack: the first row of this figure shows the original frame sequence with frame 14, frame 22, and frame 30. In second row of the frame sequence, which shows the tampered frame sequence with frame removal attack, frame 22 is eliminated from the video and hence frame 30 becomes frame 29.

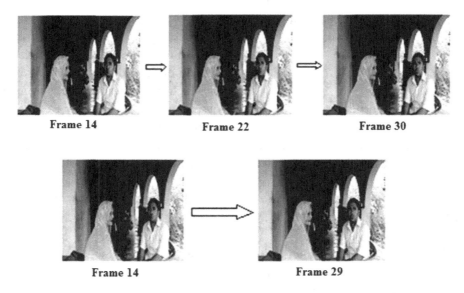

video. Figure 8 shows a typical example of frame shuffling attack where two frames are shuffled.

In addition to these types of tampering attacks, tampering can be done at different levels in video sequences.

Scene Level

When the tampering attacks are performed at scene level then a whole scene of the video sequence is manipulated in such a way that, not even the scene itself is modified but also in reference to

Figure 8. Example of frame shuffling attack: the first row of this figure shows the original frame sequence with frame 13, frame 20, and frame 26. After the frame shuffling attack, the original frame sequence is tampered as shown in second row of the figure where the positions of frame 13 and frame 26 have been changed.

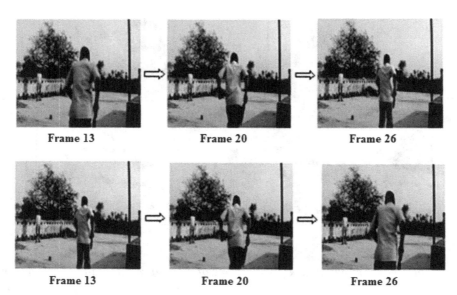

the given video the scene of that video is modified. It means spatial and temporal both kinds of tampering can be done at scene level.

Shot Level

In shot level tampering a particular shot of the given video is modified in reference to the given video. In shot level tampering a shot can be added or removed from the video. It can also be performed with all kinds of tampering attacks.

Frame Level

When frames of the given video are maliciously modified, then it is called tampering at frame level. Frame removal, frame inserting and frame shuffling are the common tampering attacks that can be performed at frame level. In other words, temporal tampering attacks are commonly performed at frame level.

Block Level

In block level tampering, tampering attacks are performed on the blocks of the video frames. The content of the video frames are treated as blocks on which the tampering attacks are applied. Blocks (a specified area on the frame of the video) can be cropped and replaced, morphed or modified in any way in block level tampering. Spatial tampering attacks are commonly performed at block level.

Pixel Level

In pixel level tampering contents of the video frames are modified at pixel level. This is the smallest level in video sequences at which tampering attacks can be performed. The video authentication system should be robust enough to differentiate the normal video processing operation and pixel level tampering, since many normal video processing operations are performed at pixel level. Spatial tampering attacks are commonly performed at pixel level.

All these levels of tampering show the different aspects of tampering.

AUTHENTICATION TECHNIQUES

By definition, authenticity means sometimes "as being in accordance with fact, as being true in substance," or "as being what it professes in origin or authorship, as being genuine" (Authenticity, 1989). Another definition of authentication is to prove that something is "actually coming from the alleged source or origin" (Authenticity, n.d.). A video authentication system ensures the integrity of digital video and verifies that whether the given video has been tampered or not. But in most of the cases, especially in the court of law, it may be more beneficial if the authentication system can tell where the tampering happens and how the video is tampered. A typical video authentication system is shown in Figure 9. For a given video, authentication process starts with feature extraction. After that, with a specific video authentication algorithm, the authentication data H is generated using the features f of the video. This authentication data H is encrypted and packaged with the video as a signature or alternatively

it can be embedded into the video content as a watermark. The video integrity is verified by computing new authentication data H` for the given video. The new authentication data H` is compared with decrypted original authentication data H. If both are matched, the video is treated as authentic else it is considered as tampered video.

An ideal video authentication system, to be effective, must support to the properties such as sensitivity to malicious alteration, localization and self-recovery of altered regions, robustness to normal video processing operations, tolerance against some loss of information, compactness of signature, sensitivity against false intimation and computational feasibility. In fact in addition to having robustness against benign operations, an ideal video authentication system must make a given video resistant against all possible attacks and must verify whether a given video is tampered or not. Benign operations are those video processing operations that do not modify its content semantically such as geometric transformations, image enhancements and compression. Once the verification is done for the given video, it would be useful to find where and how the tampering has been done.

However, based on the objectives of authentication, an authentication system can be categorized as complete verification and content verification.

Figure 9. A typical video authentication system

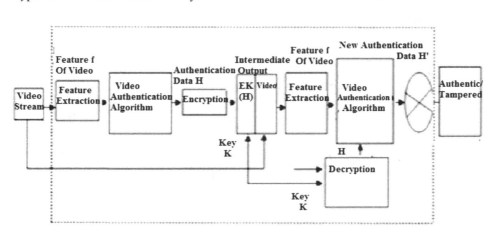

Techniques that are proposed for complete verification consider that the multimedia data, which have to be authenticated, have to be exactly the same as the original one. Content verification is a characteristic of multimedia data authentication.

CLASSIFICATION OF AUTHENTICATION TECHNIQUES

In past few years, watermarking and digital signatures have been widely used for the purpose of video authentication. Different techniques have their own advantages and shortcomings. In fact fragile watermarking and digital signatures are the two commonly used schemes for authentication.

Fragile watermarking embeds the authentication data into the primary multimedia sources, while digital signature stores the authentication data separately, either in user defined field, as like, in the header of MPEG sequence, or in a separate file (Yin et al., n.d.). Moreover there has also been worked on intelligent techniques for

video authentication (Upadhyay, Singh, Vatsa, & Singh, 2007; Singh, Vatsa, Singh, & Upadhyay, 2008). Intelligent authentication techniques use learning based techniques for authentication purpose. Apart from these digital signature, fragile watermarking and intelligent techniques, some other authentication techniques are also introduced by researchers, which are specifically designed for various cases of malicious attacks. Basically video authentication techniques are broadly classified into four categories: Digital signature based techniques, watermark based techniques, intelligent techniques, and other authentication techniques. Figure 10 represents a tree structure of authentication techniques which have been commonly proposed for the purpose of video/ image authentication.

Digital Signature

Integrity of multimedia data can be greatly verified by digital signature. For the authentication of multimedia data, it was first introduced by

Figure 10. Tree structure of authentication techniques

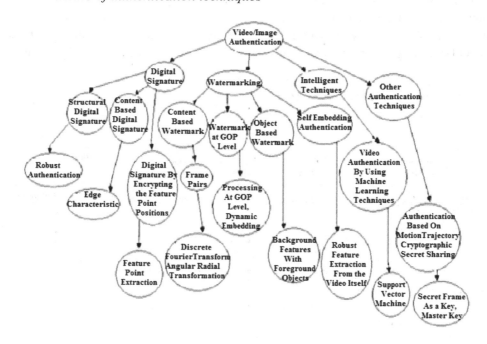

Diffie and Hellman in 1976 (Diffie & Hellman, 1976). For the purpose of authentication, digital signatures can be saved in two different ways. Either they can be saved in the header of the compressed source data, or it can be saved as an independent file. Further they can be produced for verification. In the prospective of robustness, since the digital signature remains unchanged when the pixel values of the images/videos are changed, they provide better results. In the digital signature authentication, the digital signature of the signer to the data depends on the content of data on some secret information which is only known to signer (Wohlmacher, 1998). Hence, the digital signature cannot be forged, and the end user can verify a received multimedia data by examining whether the contents of data match the information conveyed in the digital signature. In fact digital signature can be used to verify the integrity of multimedia data which is endorsed by the signer.

In Lin and Chang (1999), two types of robust digital signatures are used for video authentication in different kinds of situations. The first type of authentication signature is used in situation where the GOP (Group of Pictures) structure of the video is not modified, after transcoding or editing processes. The situation, where the GOP structure is modified and only the pixel values of picture will be preserved, a second type of digital signature is used.

In another work, video authentication is done by generating digital signatures for image blocks and using them as watermarks (Celik et al., 2002). In this approach localization packet, watermark insertion is done via LSB modification of pixel values. As compared to (Mobasseri & Evans, 2001) where video tampering is identified through an analysis of watermark sequencing, here (explicit) block ID's are used for this purpose.

The Johns Hopkins University Applied Physics Laboratory (APL) has developed a system for authentication of digital video (Johns Hopkins). The authentication system computes secure com-puter generated digital signatures for information recorded by a standard digital video camcorder. While recording, compressed digital video is simultaneously written to digital tape in the camcorder and broadcast from the camera into the Digital video authenticator. In this authentication system, video is separated into individual frames and three unique digital signatures are generated per frame—one each for video, audio, and (camcorder) control data—at the camcorder frame rate.

Here the key cryptography is used. One key, called a "private" key is used to generate the signatures and is destroyed when the recording is complete. The second a "public" key is used for verification. The signatures that are generated make it easy to recognize tampering. If a frame has been added it would not have a signature and will be instantly detected and if an original frame is tampered the signature would not match the new data and it will be detected in verification process.

In digital signature based video authentication schemes, different features are used for different applications. Dittman (Ditmann, Steinmetz, & Steinmetz, 1999) and Queluz (Queluz, 1998) used the edge /corner of the image as the feature to generate the digital signature. They claimed this feature is robust against high quality compression and scaling but the problem is that the signature generated based on the edge is too long, and the consistency of the edge itself is also a problem. Formally digital signature based authentication techniques are able to detect regions that have been tampered, but often they are too fragile to resist incidental manipulations. For this type of incidental manipulations structural digital signature (Lu & Liao, 2003) can be used for image authentication. This approach makes use of an image's content to construct a Structural Digital Signature (SDS) for image authentication. The characteristic of the SDS is that it can tolerate content preserving modifications while detecting content changing modifications. In this approach (Lu & Liao, 2003), many incidental manipulations which can be detected as malicious modifications in other digital signature verifications or fragile watermarking schemes, can be ignored.

In the scenario of a station streaming video over network, it is significant for the audiences to have guarantees that the video stream they are watching is indeed from the station. Schemes that are used for this purpose can prevent the malicious parties from injecting commercials or offensive materials into the video streams. Actually, this problem has been covered in information security called streaming signing (Gennaro & Rohatgi, 1997; Park, Chong, & Siegel, 2002), which is an extension from message signing by digital signature schemes which are able to both protect the integrity of the message and prevent the signer's repudiation.

In another technique, a separate authentication code is written in (Su, Chen, & Chang, 2009) from the blocks of the video frames. Here the authors Po-Chyi Su, Chun Chieh Chen and Hong Min Chang use the approach of scalar/vector quantization on the reliable features. Once the authentication code is written, it is transmitted along with the video. Thus, the authenticity of the given video content can be checked by matching the extracted feature with the transmitted authentication code. The authentication code chosen by authors is sensitive to malicious modifications of video data. The proposed work also considers two classical false detection tests. These are false alarms and misses. In the situation of former false detection test the authentication scheme wrongly signals a happening of tampering while the normal video processing operations are there. In the later situation, false detections are related to misses of detection after an actual tampering on video content has been performed. This work is resilient to lossy compression procedures, while the tampered regions on the video frames can be located if malicious attacks were applied (Su, Chen, & Chang, 2009).

Navjit Saikia and Prabin K. Bora present a scheme for video authentication in (Saikia & Bora, 2007) that generates the Message Authentication Code (MAC) for a Group Of Frames (GOF) using coefficients from the last but one high pass band at full level of temporal wavelet decomposition. This digital signature based scheme uses temporal wavelet transform for the generation of message authentication code. After the extraction of GOFs from the video, these GOFs are recursively decomposed into high pass band up to a certain level using temporal wavelet transform (Chuk, Jayant, & Farrardin, 1995). At this level the high pass band consists of two frames. In the signature generation process, these frames are divided into some blocks of fixed sizes. These blocks are randomly mapped on to a set of groups, using a mapping key in such a way that each group contains equal number of blocks. With the transform coefficients and these groups of blocks, a set of linear combination values is evaluated for each frame in the high pass band. And with these sets of linear combination values, message authentication code (MAC) is obtained for the GOF. In the signature verification process, the distances d $(MAC_{i,1}, MAC`_{i,1})$ and $d(MAC_{i,2}, MAC`_{i,2})$ are calculated where d is any distance measure and $\{ MAC_{i,1}, MAC_{i,2} \}$ is the MAC of ith GOF of the original video and $\{MAC`_{i,1}, MAC`_{i,2}\}$ is the MAC of corresponding GOF calculated at receiver site. Here the GOF of the video would be authentic if these two distances are below some predefined threshold values, otherwise tampered. When all GOFs in it are found authentic then the given video is declared as authentic video. This authentication scheme would be advantageous for spatio-temporal manipulations, since it is effective for spatial tampering as well as for temporal tampering.

Watermarking

Watermarking always remains a significant issue for solving authentication problems regarding digital multimedia data, in past few years. A wide variety of watermark based authentication techniques have been proposed by various researchers in literature. However watermarking techniques can be used for authenticating various multimedia data, but most of the work has been done for image and video authentication. Based on the application areas, watermarking can be classified in different categories (Dittman et al., 2000). Beside to ensure the integrity of the digital data and recognizing the malicious manipulations, watermarking can be used for the authentication of the author or producer of the content. Watermarks can be embedded with the multimedia data, without changing the meaning of the content of the data. The advantageous feature with the watermarks is that, they can be embedded without degrading the quality of multimedia data too much. Since the watermarks are embedded in the content of video data, once the data is manipulated, these watermarks will also be modified such that the authentication system can examine them to verify the integrity of data. In (Guerrini, Leonardi, & Migliorati, 2004), authors describe the use of video authentication template, which uses a bubble random sampling approach applied for synchronization and content verification in the context of video watermarking. The authentication template is introduced in order to ensure temporal synchronization and to prevent content tampering in video sequences (Guerrini, Leonardi, & Migliorati, 2004).

Basically in past few years, an increasing use of digital information in our society and availability of very sophisticated and low cost video editing software creates problems associated with copyright protection and authentication. One of the main advantage of digital world is that here perfect copying is performed easily. That causes severe security related issues. The owners or producers of information resources are being worried of releasing proprietary information to an environment that appears to be lacking in security (Queluz, 2001). On the other hand with the help of powerful video editing software one can challenge the trustworthiness of digital information.

In (Queluz, 2001), M. P. Queluz presents the generic models with labeling and watermarking approaches for content authentication, in which existing techniques for content authentication are described and compared. In labeling based approach authentication data are written in separate file (Queluz, 2001), while in watermarking based approach the authentication information is embedded in the frames. In this labeling-based authentication system, features C and C` are extracted from the original and modified pictures respectively as according:

$$C = f_c \left(I \right),$$

$$C' = f_c(\hat{I})$$

In order to assure the authenticity of the label content, it is signed in a trustworthy way, that is, the label is encrypted with a private key (K_{pr}). The label content is produced as:

$$L = EKpr(C, \; C_I)$$

where C_I is optional information, say Complementary Information, about the frame and its author, assigned by an author society. Besides image-dependent features, the label can also convey this information. In the authentication system the corresponding public key Kpu is used to decrypt the label, producing:

$$C, \; C_I = EKpu(L)$$

Moreover in (Queluz, 2001), M. P. Queluz presents two classical image features for image/video content authentication. The first image feature is concerned with second order image moments. It has a less computational requirement with small memory which makes it more advantageous computational feature. The second feature relies on image edges and it takes the problem of image/video authentication from a semantic, higher level point of view (Queluz, 2001). In image moments feature, for a two dimensional continuous function f(x, y), the moments of order $(p + q)$ is defined as

$$m_{pq} = \int\limits_{-\infty}^{+\infty}\int\limits_{-\infty}^{+\infty} x^p y^q \ f(x,y) \, dx dy \, for \ p, \ q = 0, 1, 2, \ldots\ldots\ldots$$

For a digital image the above equation would be as follows:

$$m_{pq} = \sum_i \sum_j i^p j^q \ f(i, \ j)$$

where $f(i, \ j)$ represents image color values at pixel site (i, j). Moments are usually normalized dividing it by the image total mass, defined as $\sum_i \sum_j f(i,j)$. He also presents a brief comparison of labeling approach with watermarking for tamper detection, which is independent of applications where they can specifically be implemented. The video authentication techniques using the watermarking approach have wide dimension in the literature.

In (Liang, Li, & Niu, 2007), Chang-yin Liang, Ang Li and Xia-mu Nin proposed a video authentication system which is robust enough to separate the malicious attack from natural video processing operations with the cloud watermark. The authentication system in (Liang, Li, & Niu, 2007) first of all splits the video sequence into shots and extracts the feature vector from each shot. Then the extracted feature is used to generate watermark cloud drops with a cloud generator (Liang, Li, & Niu, 2007). Here, for robustness, a con tent based and semi fragile watermark is used for authentication. In this authentication technique DCT coefficients are evaluated firstly by partially decoding the given video. After watermarking the video is encoded again (Liang, Li, & Niu, 2007). Invariable features of the video are selected for content based watermarking. The watermarks are then embedded back into DCT coefficients of the video. The extracted watermarks are compared with the features derived from the received video, to check the authenticity of the given video.

However attacks on watermarks may not necessarily remove the watermark (Johnson, n.d.), but can disable its readability. Image/video processing operations and transforms are commonly employed to create and apply watermarks on the multimedia data. These techniques can also be used to disable or overwrite watermarks. Multiple watermarks can be placed in an image and one cannot determine which one is valid (Craver, Memon, Yeo, & Yeung, 1998).

In (Mobasseri & Evans, 2001), the proposed algorithm explains the frame-pair concept where one video frame would watermark another frame downstream based on a specific sequencing and a key. Basically in this approach three points are there: First the watermark is derived from the video itself, therefore cannot be pirated. Second if video frames are taken out, it is possible to identify their locations by simply monitoring the breaks in authentication key sequence. And third, video frames that are removed could actually be recovered because frame pairs contain copies of other frames disguised as watermarks. In this approach unless both frames are removed, frame restoration is possible. Watermarking can also be used for the authentication of compressed video (Cross & Mobasseri, 2002). Here the watermarking of compressed video (Cross & Mobasseri, 2002) is done by identifying label carrying VLCs in MPEG-2 bit stream. In this approach every bit in the watermark payload is compared with the LSB of the current label carrying VLC. If they are the same, the VLC remains unchanged, if they are not, the LSB is replaced by the watermark bit. The embedded watermark may be used for the authentication of video and protection against tampering.

For the authentication of MPEG video, authentication data can be embedded at the Group Of Pictures (GOP) level (Yin et al., n.d.). Since it is almost infeasible to embed information in all pictures of a video clip or embed all the information for each picture in a video clip, Dynamic Embedding for each picture in a digital video can be adopted (Yin et al., n.d.). In this approach current GOP's authentication data (bits) are embedded into next GOP. Basically this approach has three advantageous features. First, by making each watermarked GOP dependent upon other GOP, the problem of watermark counterfeiting becomes computationally impossible and thus reduces the chances of success for the attackers. Second, for MPEG video, if watermark is added in I picture in a GOP, it results in drift errors for the following P or B pictures in the same GOP. If the video quality requirement is in demand, the drift errors should be corrected, the correction could cause the changes of the authentication bits and thus need to re-add the watermark in I picture. This will cause dead loop. Therefore it would be advantageous to embed the authentication data at the GOP level. Third this operation is causal and saves much memory to store a GOP's data.

For the investigation of the authenticity of uncompressed video signal, the quality of digitization process is considered significantly (Geradts & Bijhold, n.d.). The way the A/D conversion is done is important for the result. For this purpose the histogram of gray values can be checked. Previously Lin et al (Lin & Chang, 1999) and Peng et al (Peng, 2002) have worked on compressed domain schemes that are robust against transcoding and editing operations. For computing the signature Lin (Lin & Chang, 1999) used the difference in DCT coefficients of frame pairs. Since the value of DCT coefficients can be modified keeping their relationship preserved, it is vulnerable to counterfeiting attacks. Peng (Peng, 2002) used DC-DCT coefficients as features to build watermark.

An object based watermarking scheme for video authentication is proposed by Dajun et al (He, Sun, & Tian, 2003). They use background features to embed the watermark into foreground objects to establish a relation between background and the foreground of a video. Here the raw video is segmented into foreground objects and background video the watermark is generated by using the features extracted from both the foreground and background. The watermark is then embedded into foreground objects, so that a secure link between foreground objects and the back ground is created. At the receiving end integrity between the foreground objects and the background can be verified by comparing two sets of codes: one is the watermark extracted from the objects and the other is regenerated from both the received object and the background. If these two sets of codes are the same, then the video is claimed as authentic.

A more robust authentication scheme for scalable video streaming by employing Error Correction Coding (ECC) in different ways (Sun, He, Zhang, & Tian, 2003) has also been produced. This scheme achieves an end - to-end authentication independent of specific streaming infrastructure. Actually this scheme is an extension from (Sun, Chang, & Maeno, 2002) where a semi fragile authentication framework, for images in terms of ECC and public key infrastructure, is used.

In another work, a semi fragile object based authentication solution is produced for MPEG 4 video (He, Sun, & Tian, 2003). To protect the integrity of the video objects/sequences, a content based watermark is embedded into each frame in the Discrete Fourier Transform domain before the MPEG 4 encoding. A set of Angular Radial Transformation (ART) coefficients are selected as the robust features of the video objects. Error Correction Coding (ECC) is used for watermark generation and embedding. The main difference between the frame based video application and the object based video application lies in the utilization of the shape information.

In a self-embedding authentication system (Martinian, Wornell, & Chen, n.d.), a robust and important feature of the video is extracted and embedded in to the video at the sending site; the detector retrieves this original feature from the watermark and compares it with the feature extracted from the received video to determine the authenticity of the video. If the difference exceeds a threshold, the received video will be claimed as un-authentic video.

INTELLIGENT TECHNIQUES

Intelligent techniques for video authentication use database of video sequences. The database comprises authentic video clips as well as tampered video clips. As in (Upadhyay, Singh, Vatsa, & Singh, 2007), the authors proposed an intelligent technique for video authentication which uses inherent video information for authentication, thus making it useful for real world applications. The proposed algorithm in (Upadhyay, Singh, Vatsa, & Singh, 2007) is validated using a database of 795 tampered and non-tampered videos and the results of algorithm show a classification accuracy of 99.92%. The main advantage of intelligent techniques is that they do not require the computation and storage of secret key or embedding of watermark. The algorithm in (Upadhyay, Singh, Vatsa, & Singh, 2007) computes the local relative correlation information and classifies the video as tampered or non-tampered. Performance of this algorithm is not affected by acceptable video processing operations such as compression and scaling. Here the algorithm uses Support Vector Machine (SVM) for the classification of the tampered and authentic videos. SVM (Vapnik, 1995) is a powerful methodology for solving problems in nonlinear classification, function estimation and density estimation (Singh, Vatsa, & Noore, 2006). In fact SVM is a nonlinear classifier that performs classification tasks by constructing hyper planes in a multi-dimensional space and separates the data points in different classes. This algorithm (Upadhyay, Singh, Vatsa, &

Singh, 2007) is performed in two stages: (1) SVM training and (2) Tamper detection and classification, using SVM. In SVM training, the algorithm trains the SVM by using a manually labeled training video database, if the video in the training data is tampered, then it is assigned the label -1 otherwise the label is +1 (for the authentic video). From the training videos, relative correlation information between two adjacent frames of the video is computed, with the help of corner detection algorithm (Kovesi, 1999). Then relative correlation information RC is computed for all adjacent frames of the video with the help of

$$RC = \frac{1}{m} \sum_{i=1}^{m} L_i$$

where Li is local correlation between two frames for i=1,2,...m. and m is the number of corresponding corner points in the two frames. The local correlation information RC is computed for each video and the RC with the label information of all the training video data are provided as input to the SVM. With this information of all the video in video database the SVM (Vapnik, 1995) is trained to classify the tampered and non-tampered video data. Output of SVM training is a trained hyper plane with classified tampered and non-tampered video data. In (Singh, Vatsa, Singh, & Upadhyay, 2008), authors integrate the learning based support vector machine classification (for tampered and non-tampered video) with singular value decomposition watermarking. This algorithm is independent of the choice of watermark and does not require any key to store. This intelligent authentication technique embeds the inherent video information in frames using SVD watermarking and uses it for classification by projecting them into a nonlinear SVM hyper plane. This technique can detect multiple tampering attacks.

OTHER AUTHENTICATION TECHNIQUES

Apart from digital signature, watermarking and intelligent techniques, various other techniques are there for authentication purpose of digital video in the literature. In (Yan & Kankanhalli, 2003), an authentication scheme for digital video is introduced which is based on motion trajectory and cryptographic secret sharing (Yan & Kankanhalli, 2003). In this scheme, the given video is firstly segmented into shots then all the frames of the video shots are mapped to a trajectory in the feature space by which the key frames of the video shot are computed. Once the key frames are evaluated, a secret frame is computed from the key frames information of the video shot. These secret frames are used to construct a hierarchical structure and after that final master key is obtained. This master key is used to identify the authenticity of the video. Any modification in a shot or in the important content of a shot will be reflected as changes in the computed master key. Here trajectory is constructed, using the histogram energy of the frames of the video shot. For a particular video shot, in Figure 11, vertical axis indicates the histogram energy of each frame of the shot and the horizontal axis marks the frame number in the shot. A polyline belonging to the video shot is drawn which is a motion trajectory. This figure also shows the process of key frames extraction from the video shot. The starting frame S and the last frame E of the trajectory are connected to each other. Then a distance d between each frame point and this line is computed by using:

$$d = \frac{\left| Ax + By + C \right|}{\sqrt{A^2 + B^2}}$$

where d is the distance from a point (x, y) to the straight line $Ax + By + C = 0$.

After that the point at the maximum distance from the line is chosen and the corresponding frame is declared as one of the key frames in this shot. Once the key frames are computed these are utilized to compute the secret frame by extrapolation. Now an interpolating polynomial $f(x)$ is computed by using key frames as follows.

$$f\left(x\right) = \sum_{j=1}^{n+1} \prod_{i=1}^{n+1} \frac{x - x_i}{x_j - x_i} I_j$$

This is Lagrange interpolation formulation where the x_i position refers to each key frame and I_i is the pixel value of the key frames. By using this equation and extrapolation a frame at $x = 0$ is computed, which is regarded as the secret key. Considering the set of secret keys as another set of shares, the master key frame is computed for that particular video. With this scheme any video can be authenticated by comparing its computed master key with the original master key. This comparison can be performed by using the general cosine correlation measure given by:

$$sim = \frac{I_O \cdot I_N}{\left| I_O \cdot I_N \right|}$$

where I_O and I_N are the original master key and the new master key considered as vectors. The similarity value would be in the range [0, 1] and if sim = 1, the two master keys would be the same, however if sim = 0, the two master keys would be different. Here the authors also claim that if the similarity value is high then the video has undergone benign transformations. But if the similarity value is low, then the video must have undergone some significant tampering. In (Latechi, Wildt, & Hu, n.d.), the key frames are selected by deleting the most predictable frame. In the approach of reference (Zhao, Qi, Li, Yang, & Zhang, 2000), the key frames are extracted from a video shot based on the nearest feature line. The work in (Quisquater, 1997) authenticates a video by guaranteeing the edited video to be the subse-

Figure 11. Frames with their histogram energy for a video shot

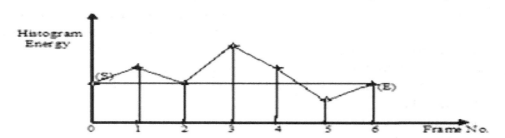

quence of the original video using a special hash function. The MPEG video standard is one of the most popular video standards in today's digital era. In (Wang & Farid, 2007) Weihong Wang and Hany Farid have been worked on MPEG video standard (MPEG-1 and MPEG-2) in this paper they specifically show how a doubly compressed MPEG video sequence introduces specific static and temporal statistical perturbations whose presence can be used as evidence of tampering. In a MPEG video sequence, there are three types of frames: I-frame, P-frame and B-frame. Each with different level of compression occurs in a periodic sequence in the MPEG video. Amidst all the frames I-frames are the highest quality frames of the video sequence, which are usually encoded by standard JPEG compression scheme. In the I-frame, compression is achieved at spatial level by reducing spatial redundancies within a single frame (Wang & Farid, 2007). Temporal redundancies are concerned with P-frames arcos the frames of video sequence. For achieving double MPEG compression, I-frames of the MPEG video sequence are compressed twice. For this purpose when the frames are double quantized with different step size, there is a significant difference in their histogram. When the step size decreases in image quantization, some bins in the histogram are empty while in greater step size some bins of the histogram contain more samples than their neighboring bins (Wang & Farid, 2007). In both cases of double quantization, periodicity of the artifacts is introduced in to histograms. This artifact would be used as evidence of double compression and hence tampering. In temporal analysis, addition or deletion of frames from a video sequence and re-encoding the resulting sequence, results in a large motion error between consecutive P-frames of the video, since they originated from different GOPs. Moreover this increased motion error would be periodic, occurring throughout each of the group of pictures following the frame deletion or addition. Periodic spikes in the motion error indicate tampering (Wang & Farid, 2007).

In (Farid, 2006), Hany Farid describes three techniques to expose digital forgeries in which the approach is to first understand how a specific form of tampering disturbs certain statistical properties of an image and then to develop a mathematical algorithm to detect this perturbation. These are Cloning, Lighting and Retouching. In Cloning, a digital image is first partitioned into small blocks of the regions. The blocks are then reordered so that they are placed a distance to each other that is proportional to the differences in their pixel colors (Farid, 2006). Since it is statistically unlikely to find identical and spatially coherent regions in an image, therefore their presence can be used as evidence of tampering. In lighting approach the direction of an illuminating light source for each object or person in an image is automatically evaluated by some mathematical techniques. The retouching technique exploits the technology by which a digital camera sensor records an image, for detecting a specific form of tampering.

A robust video authentication system should tolerate the incidental distortion, which may be introduced by normal video processing such as compression, resolution conversion and geometric transformation, while being capable of detecting the intentional distortion, which may be introduced by malicious attack. There has also been some work for scene change detection of video sequences in the literature.

LIMITATIONS OF EXISTING VIDEO AUTHENTICATION TECHNIQUES

There are different challenges with the existing watermark and digital signature based video authentication approaches. However there is no issue related with the size of authentication code in digital signature based video authentication techniques, but if the location where digital signature is stored is compromised then it is easy to deceive the authentication system. On the other hand fragile watermarking algorithms perform better than algorithm based on conventional cryptography (Hauzia & Noumeir, 2007). Fragile and semi fragile algorithms show good results for detecting and locating any malicious manipulations but often they are too fragile to resist incidental manipulations. Moreover embedding the watermark may change the content of video which is not permissible in court of law (Upadhyay, Singh, Vatsa, & Singh, 2007).In other techniques, most of the authentication techniques are established for specific attacks. Moreover existing algorithms are also affected by compression and scaling operations.

PROPOSED METHODOLOGY

Keeping in mind all those limitations, we are going to propose an intelligent video authentication

technique, which does not require computation and storage of any key or embedding of any secret information in the video data. We have designed our algorithm especially for raw videos (videos captured and given in any situation or condition), which suited best for surveillance videos. Our proposed video authentication algorithm computes the statistical local features information in digital video frames and establishes a relationship among the frames. A Support Vector Machine (SVM) (Vapnik, 1995) based learning algorithm is then used to classify the video as tampered or non-tampered. The proposed algorithm uses inherent video information for authentication, thus making it useful for real world applications.

SUPPORT VECTOR MACHINE

Support Vector Machine, pioneered by Vapnik (Vapnik, 1995), is a powerful methodology for solving problems in nonlinear classification, function estimation and density estimation (Singh, Vatsa, & Noore, 2006). The main idea of a support vector machine is to construct a hyper plane as the decision surface in such a way that the margin of separation between two classes of examples is maximized. It performs the classification task by constructing hyper planes in a multidimensional space and separates the data points into different classes. SVM uses an iterative training algorithm to maximize the margin between two classes (Upadhyay, Singh, Vatsa, & Singh, 2007; Singh, Vatsa, & Noore, 2006). The mathematical formulation of SVM is as follows:

Let $\left\{(x_i, d_i)\right\}_{i=1}^{N}$ be the training sample of N data vectors, where x_i is the input pattern for the ith example and d_i is the corresponding desired response. It is assumed that the pattern (class) represented by the subset $d_i = +1$ and the pattern represented by the subset $d_i = -1$, are linearly separable. The equation of generalized decision function can be written as:

$$f\left(x\right) = \sum_{i=1}^{N} w_i \varphi_i \left(x\right) + b = \quad W\overline{\varphi}\left(x\right) + b$$

where $\varphi_i \left(x\right)$ is a nonlinear function representing hidden nodes and

$$\overline{\varphi}\left(x\right) = \left[\varphi_1 \left(x\right), \quad \varphi_2 \left(x\right), \ldots \varphi_N (x)\right]^T,$$

and b is a bias. To obtain a non linear decision boundary which enhances the discrimination power, the above equation can be rewritten as:

$$f\left(x\right) = \sum_{i=1}^{N} d_i \propto_i K\left(x, x_i\right) + b$$

Here $K\left(x, x_i\right)$ is the nonlinear kernel that enhances the discrimination power and $\propto_i$ is the Lagrangian multiplier (Upadhyay, Singh, Vatsa, & Singh, 2007). Basically a nonlinear SVM uses a kernel function $K\left(x, x_i\right)$ to map the input space to the feature space so that the mapped data becomes linearly separable. One example of such kernel is the RBF kernel

$$K\left(x, x_i\right) = exp\left(-\gamma x - x_i^2\right), \quad \gamma > 0$$

where x and x_i represent the input vectors and γ is the RBF parameter (Upadhyay, Singh, Vatsa, & Singh, 2007). Additional details of SVM can be found in (Vapnik, 1995).

PROPOSED VIDEO AUTHENTICATION ALGORITHM

As mentioned above the common tampering attacks on a video data are spatial and temporal tampering attacks which include object addition, object removal, object modification, frame removal, frame addition, and frame shuffling. Our proposed algorithm gives excellent results for temporal and spatial, both types of tampering attacks. In this chapter, we have focused on the three kinds of tampering attacks, frame addition attacks, frame removal attacks and spatial tampering attacks. However the proposed algorithm can handle all kinds of malicious attacks. Since we are using SVM based learning and classification technique, it can also differentiate between attack and acceptable operations.

The concept of the proposed algorithm is shown in Figure 12. The proposed video authentication algorithm computes the statistical local features information between two consecutive video frames.

Here we take the absolute difference of every two consecutive video frames. The average object area and entropy of difference frames are used as statistical local features information. They are worked here as the basis for SVM learning. This information is computed locally using statistical tools and then classification is performed using support vector machine (Vapnik, 1995). Based on the functionality, the proposed algorithm is divided into two stages: (1) SVM Learning and (2) tamper detection and classification using SVM.

SVM LEARNING

SVM learning is the first step of the proposed algorithm. For this purpose a database of 50 tampered and non-tampered video clips is used, and the hyper planes are trained for frame addition, frame removal and spatial tampering attacks, separately. Training is performed using manually labeled training videos of the video database. For each of the video of the video database, if the video in the training data is tampered then it is assigned the label 0 otherwise (if it is not tampered) the label is 1. From the training videos, statistical local information (average object area and entropy) are extracted. This labeled information, together with the statistical local information (SL), is then used as input to the SVM which

Figure 12. Block diagram of the proposed video authentication algorithm

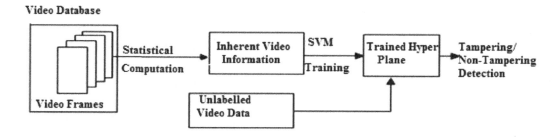

performs learning and generates a non-linear hyper plane that can classify the video as tampered and non-tampered. All these steps involved in the training of the kernel are performed for the video database and are explained in the learning algorithm.

Learning Algorithm

- **Input:** Labeled training video frames.
- **Output:** Trained SVM with a non-linear hyper plane to classify tampered and non-tampered video data.
- **Algorithm:**
  - Individual frames are obtained from the different tampered and non tampered video data.
  - The difference frames of all the video data are obtained by taking absolute difference between every two consecutive frames. In absolute difference, we subtract each pixel value in second frame from the corresponding pixel value in the first frame.
  - All these difference frames are converted into binary frames.
  - The total number of objects in first binary difference frame and their area are calculated. Then the average object area and the entropy of the first binary difference frame are computed statistically.

If the area of an object in a binary frame is a_i then the average object area of the binary frame A would be

$$A = \frac{1}{N}\sum_{i=1}^{N} a_i$$

where N is the total number of objects.

If the average object area and entropy of a binary frame are A_i and E_i then the statistical local information of a video of the video database would be defined as

$$SL = \sum_{i=1}^{m}\left[A_i, E_i\right]$$

This statistical local information is a column vector of size $\left[(m-1)\times 2\right]$ where m is the total number of binary difference frames extracted from all the tampered and non tampered video of the video database.

Steps 1-6 are performed on all the labelled training videos and the statistical local information SL is computed for each video of the video database.

- Statistical local information and labels of all the training videos are given as input to the Support Vector Machine.
- In the learning process the SVM kernel (Vapnik, 1995) is trained to classify the tam-

pered and non tampered video data. Output of this training is a trained hyper plain with classified tampered and non tampered video data.

TAMPER DETECTION AND CLASSIFICATION

We now explain the proposed tamper detection and classification algorithm. Input to this classification algorithm is a video data of which authenticity needs to be established. As performed in SVM learning algorithm, statistical local information of all the binary frames of the given video is computed and the trained SVM is used to classify the video. The proposed algorithm uses the dynamically adoptive threshold value to decide whether the given video frame is tampered or not. It automatically selects a threshold value with the help of learning database, for declaring any binary difference frame as a tampered frame. If the SVM classifies the input video as tampered then the location of tampering is computed. The tamper detection and classification algorithm is described below.

Tamper Detection and Classification

- **Input:** Unlabelled video frames.
- **Output:** Classification result as tampered and non-tampered video data.
- **Algorithm:**
  1. Using steps 1-7 of the SVM learning algorithm, the statistical local information SL for the input video is computed.
  2. This statistical local information of the input video data is projected into the SVM hyper plane to classify the video as tampered or non-tampered. If the output of SVM is one for all of the difference frames of the input video then the given video is authentic otherwise it is tampered.

  3. If any of the frame of given video is classified as tampered then we determine the particular frames of the video that have been tampered.
  4. Plot the statistical local information SL (average object area and entropy) of difference frames of all the adjacent frames of the video.
  5. Local values showing the maximum deviation in the plot are the values corresponding to the tampered frames.
  6. Plot the trained SVM classifier which shows the support vectors for the training video data

EXPERIMENTAL RESULTS AND DISCUSSION

The proposed algorithm shows very good results for all the three kinds of attacks, frame addition attacks, frame removal attacks and spatial tampering attacks. We have shown the results for all kinds of tampering attacks of temporal tampering and also for spatial tampering.

RESULTS FOR FRAME REMOVAL ATTACK

Figure 13 shows the plot of average object area values as statistical local information (SL) for 120 tampered videos, 120 non-tampered videos and 100 videos for validation process in the database, subjected to frame removal attack. Here 120 tampered and 120 non-tampered videos of the database are used for the learning process of SVM. The average object area (SL) values of all the non-tampered videos are below than almost all the SL values of tampered videos. However some of the SL values of tampered videos are below than some of the SL values of non-tampered videos. This is because; some of the videos in database have normally greater difference in consecutive frames than the difference due to malicious modifications, in consecutive frames.

Here we are using 100 testing videos for the validation of our algorithm. The testing video, which has the SL value lower than the highest SL value of non-tampered videos and also lower than or equal to lowest SL value of tampered videos, would definitely be a non-tampered video. In the same way the testing video, which has the SL value higher than the highest SL value of non-tampered videos and the lowest SL value of tampered videos, would be detected as tampered video. For the SL values which are below than the highest SL value of non-tampered videos but are above than the lowest SL value of tampered videos, the testing videos may be detected as either tampered or non-tampered videos. In that case videos with the lower SL values would be treated as non-tampered videos and the videos with the higher SL values would be detected as

tampered videos. These boundaries for tampered and non-tampered videos are automatically defined by our algorithm once the learning process completes and highest and lowest SL values of learning videos work as a threshold for testing videos. As shown in the graph of Figure 13, the SL values of almost all the testing videos are higher than the highest SL value (which is the threshold value) of non-tampered videos except one. It means that here our algorithm misclassifies only one tampered video as a non-tampered video, and correctly classifies 99 videos as tampered video.

RESULTS FOR FRAME ADDITION ATTACK

In frame addition attack, since the consecutive frames at the tampered positions in the videos

Figure 13. Plot of average object area as statistical local information of 120 tampered, 120 non-tampered, and 100 testing videos of the database, in which our algorithm correctly classifies 99 videos and misclassifies one video subjected to frame removal attack

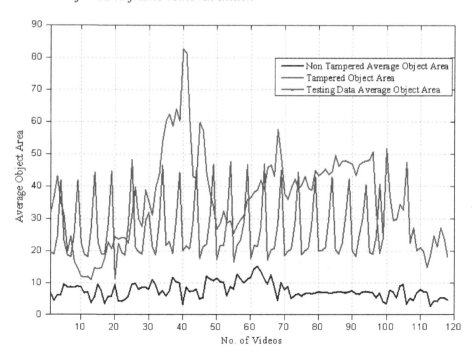

have much difference (compared to each other), our algorithm gives better results for frame addition attack. Figure 14 shows the plot for average object area values as SL values for 96 tampered videos, 96 non-tampered videos and 100 testing videos of the database, subjected to frame addition attack. Here in this figure, the SL values of all the tampered videos are much higher than the SL values of all the non-tampered videos. So the learning is performed well. Our algorithm dynamically adopts the highest SL value of non-tampered videos as a threshold value. For the validation process we have taken 100 tampered videos. Our algorithm successfully classifies all the 100 videos as tampered videos, as not a single testing video has a SL value lower than or equal to the SL values of any non-tampered video.

RESULTS FOR SPATIAL TAMPERING ATTACKS

For spatial tampering, we have modified the spatial content of the frames of the video with the help of professional software and created the tampered videos for our video database. These tampered videos include almost all kinds of spatial tampering attack. In spatial tampering attacks, we basically consider the object addition and object removal attacks. In spatial tampering, sometimes changes, due to tampered objects, in consecutive frames are small enough to be ignored as compared to normal changes in consecutive frames. It depends upon the size and movement of the tampered objects in the frames. It also depends upon the size and movement of other non-tampered objects in the frames of the video.

Figure 14. Plot of average object area as statistical local information of 96 tampered, 96 non-tampered, and 100 testing videos of the database in which the algorithm correctly classifies all the tampered videos subjected to frame addition attack

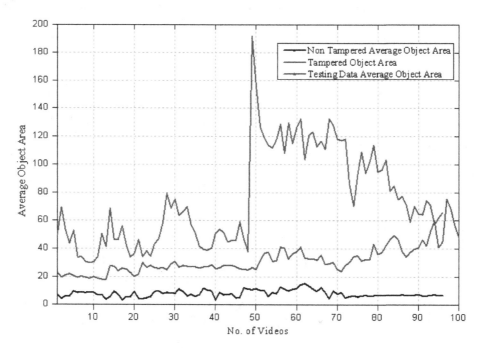

Here the tampered object is referred to as an object which is either removed from some frames or pasted to some frames additionally. If the tampered object is small in size and less in movement as compared to other non-tampered objects of the frames, then it creates small enough changes in consecutive frames, to be ignored and it cannot be detected as a malicious attack. While on the other hand if a non-tampered object, big in size (total area of all the pixels covered by it), moves very rapidly then it creates big enough changes in consecutive frames to be detected as a malicious attack. Therefore the proposed algorithm, sometimes, does not give very good results for spatial tampering attacks. However, since our algorithm is a learning based algorithm, it gives overall good results for spatial tampering attacks. In Figure 15, the SL values of testing videos are much higher than the SL values of learning videos. We have taken 96 non-tampered and 96 tampered videos for learning purpose. Here the SL value line of tampered videos touches the SL value line of non-tampered videos at several points in x-axis. It means some of the tampered and non-tampered videos have same SL values. Therefore, the adoptive threshold value would be changed for the points, in x-axis, where the SL value lines of tampered and non-tampered videos touch each other. For these points, the highest SL value of tampered videos would be adoptive threshold value for testing videos.

Thus here two adoptive threshold value works, one for the points, in x-axis, where the SL value lines of tampered and non-tampered videos touch each other and another for the points, in x-axis, where the SL values of tampered videos are

Figure 15. Plot of average object area as statistical local information of 96 tampered, 96 non-tampered, and 103 testing videos of the database in which our algorithm misclassifies 12 videos subjected to spatial tampering attack

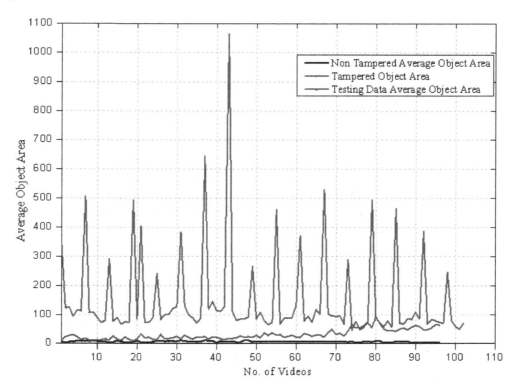

greater than the SL values of non-tampered videos. The highest SL value of non-tampered videos would be the adoptive threshold value for the later one. For the validation process we took 103 tampered videos. In the Figure 15, it can be seen that our algorithm misclassifies 12 videos out of 103 videos with a false acceptance rate of 11. 65% and correctly classifies 91 videos.

VALIDATION OF PROPOSED ALGORITHM

The proposed tamper detection algorithm is validated by using a video database which contains fifty videos. Our video database contains 50 originally recorded non-tampered videos with 2000 frames, each captured at 24 fps. The frame size of each video clip is 720×576. This video data is used as the ground truth. Each video of the database is further split into 10 equal sized video of 200 frames. For each of the 50 ground truth videos of the video database, different tampered copies are created by subjecting them to different video tampering attacks Experimental protocols for validation process are as follows:

1. For each video, 10 copies are created with frame removal attack in which 1to 20frames have been dropped at random positions. For the frame addition attack, an additional video other than the 50 videos in the database is chosen. Frames of this additional video are inserted at random positions in the database videos to generate 10 tampered copies of each groundtruth videos. For spatial tampering attacks we used professional software. With the help of this software we altered the contents of the frames of each ground truth video. This alteration is performed in various aspects, such as, object addition and object removal from the frames. Ten copies of each video of the video database are created, subjected to spatial tampering attacks.

We, thus have total 50 ground truth videos with 500 non-tampered videos, 500 videos with frame addition attack, 500 videos with frame removal attack and 500 videos with spatial tampering attacks.

2. 624 videos from the video database are used to train the support vector machine, for frame removal, frame addition and spatial tampering attacks. This SVM training is performed for each kinds of attack separately with different tampered and non-tampered videos.

3. The remaining videos of the video database are used as the probe database to determine the performance of the proposed algorithm.

The performance of the proposed video authentication algorithm is evaluated with this experimental protocol.

All of the computations are performed using the hardware configuration of Pentium ® Dual-Core CPU 2.20 GHz computer with 2 GB RAM under MATLAB programming environment. The RBF parameter used in the proposed algorithm is computed empirically using the training video frames. The best suited value of RBF parameter (γ) among 1 to 5 is 3. The value of $\gamma = 3$, gives the maximum classification accuracy. We therefore used $\gamma = 3$ for classification on the probe data.

The results given in Table 1 summarize the performance of the proposed video authentication algorithm. For authentic videos and videos subjected to the frame addition attack of temporal tampering, our algorithm gives the result with maximum accuracy and yields 100% correct classification. For frame removal attack, a classification accuracy of 99% is obtained. For frame removal attack our algorithm misclassified one tampered video out of 100 tampered videos, because the object movements in the binary difference frames were very small. For spatial tampering attacks, the proposed algorithm gives the result with 88.35% accuracy and misclassifies twelve tampered videos out of 103 tampered videos. Thus the overall classification accuracy of the proposed algorithm is 98.38%.

According to steps 3-5 of our tamper detection algorithm, the SL values, obtained from video frames, are analyzed. This analysis gives the specific frames that have been altered. These results show the efficacy of our proposed video authentication algorithm for all kinds of tampering attack of temporal tampering and spatial tampering.

We also compared the performance of the proposed video authentication algorithm with the motion trajectory based video authentication algorithm (Yan & Kankanhalli, 2003), proposed by Wei-Qi Yan et al. Table 2 depicts a theoretical comparison of both algorithms. Motion trajectory based algorithm (Yan & Kankanhalli, 2003) is fast and simple but unable to detect spatial tampering attacks (object addition, removal and modification in a frame). It also gives poor results in frame removal attacks of temporal tampering, when only three or four frames are dropped (in case of twenty-frame removal). It also gives unsatisfactory results in frame removal attack of temporal tampering, when object movements within consecutive frames of the video, are very less.

On the other hand, our proposed algorithm uses an intelligent technique, namely SVM classification which is able to detect both kinds of attack, spatial as well as temporal. Thus our proposed algorithm covers a wide range of tampering attacks with good classification accuracy and a minor increase in computational time.

Table 1. Classification results of the proposed video authentication algorithm for tampered and non tampered video frames

Tampering Attacks	Total Number of Videos	Number of Correctly Classified Videos	Classification Accuracy (%)
Non-tampered	500	500	100
Frame Addition	100	100	100
Frame Removal	100	99	99
Spatial Tampering	103	91	88.35
Total	803	790	98.38

Table 2. Theoretical comparison of the proposed video authentication algorithm with the motion trajectory-based video authentication algorithm (Yan & Kankanhalli, 2003)

Category	Motion Trajectory based Video Authentication (Yan & Kankanhalli, 2003)	Proposed Video Authentication Algorithm
Basic Concept	Master Key computation based on motion trajectory	Statistical Local Information is computed from video frames.
Classification	Using empirical threshold values and cosine correlation measure	Using Non-linear Support Vector Machine for classification
Advantage	Simple algorithm, It handles frame addition and frame removal attack	In addition of frame addition and frame removal attack, it handles frame alteration attack (Spatial Tampering).
Disadvantage	It cannot handle frame alteration and other attacks	Computationally expensive and a little bit slow algorithm due to the use of SVM and a video database.

CONCLUSION AND FUTURE RESEARCH DIRECTIONS

From entertainment to court decision, from broadcasting to surveillance, and from investigation agencies to smart classes, video applications have already infiltrated into many aspects of our lives. In the past decade, video based industry has flourished at an unparalleled speed. However, as a spin-off of this exciting development, many security issues have inevitably emerged. In video industry, in contrast to the copyright issue, which only concerns the video content providers, the issue of video content integrity or authenticity concerns not only the content provider, but also the content receiver. Thus, the issue of video content authenticity, sooner or later, will bottleneck video industry if it is not solved properly. Most of the existing video authentication algorithms use watermarking or digital signature based algorithms. Digital signature based algorithm can be deceived, if the location where digital signature is stored is compromised and watermarking based algorithms are not acceptable in court of law because they may alter the content of video during watermark embedding and extraction. To address these issues we have proposed an efficient intelligent video authentication algorithm which can detect multiple video tampering attacks. Our proposed algorithm computes the statistical local information of all of the binary difference frames of the given video and projects them into a non-linear SVM hyper plane to determine if the video is tampered or not. Our algorithm dynamically adopts the threshold values for the statistical local information of tampered video frames. It automatically opts the best suited threshold value for declaring the binary difference frames as tampered frames. The algorithm is validated on an extensive video database containing 1500 tampered and 500 non-tampered videos. The results show that the proposed algorithm yields a classification accuracy of 98.38%. In future we would like to expand our video database, which would cover some more critical conditions for

video recording, like the videos captured in different light conditions such as in day light and night vision systems, and in a situation where the camera and objects are moving very fast, videos in critical weather conditions and the videos captured in hazardous condition, and apply the intelligent authentication algorithms for obtaining the results regarding all kinds of tampering attacks.

REFERENCES

Authenticity. (1989). *The Oxford English dictionary* (2nd Ed.). Oxford, UK: Oxford University Press.

Authenticity. (n.d.). *The Webster's new 20th century dictionary*. New York: Webster.

Celik, M. V. et al. (2002). Video authentication with self recovery. In *Proc. Security and Watermarking of Multimedia Contents IV* (Vol. 4314, pp. 531–541). IEEE. doi:10.1117/12.465311.

Craver, S., Memon, N., Yeo, B., & Yeung, N. M. (1998). Resolving rightful ownerships with invisible watermarking techniques: Limitations, attacks, and implications. *IEEE Journal on Selected Areas in Communications*, 16(4), 573–586. doi:10.1109/49.668979.

Cross, D., & Mobasseri, B. G. (2002). Water marking for self authentication of compressed video. In *Proc. IEEE International Conference on Image Processing*. Rochester, NY: IEEE.

Diffie, W., & Hellman, M. E. (1976). New directions in cryptography. *IEEE Transactions on Information Theory*, 22(6), 644–654. doi:10.1109/TIT.1976.1055638.

Ditmann, J., Steinmetz, A., & Steinmetz, R. (1999). Content based digital signature for motion pictures authentication and content fragile watermarking. []. IEEE.]. *Proceedings of Multimedia Computing and Systems*, 2, 209–213.

Dittman, J., Mukharjee, A., & Steinbach, M. (2000). Media independent watermarking classification and the need for combining digital video and audio watermarking for media authentication. In *Proceedings of the International Conference on Information Technology: Coding and Computing*. IEEE.

Farid, H. (2006). Digital doctoring: How to tell the real from fake. *Significance, 3*(4), 162–166. doi:10.1111/j.1740-9713.2006.00197.x.

Friedman, G. L. (1993). The trustworthy digital camera: restoring credibility to the photographic image. *IEEE Transactions on Consumer Electronics, 39*, 905–910. doi:10.1109/30.267415.

Gennaro, R., & Rohatgi, P. (1997). How to sign digital stream. [ACM.]. *Proceedings of Crypto, 97*, 180–197.

Geradts, Z. J., & Bijhold, J. (n.d.). Forensic video investigation with real time digitized uncompressed video image sequences. *Investigation and Forensic Science Technologies.*.

Guerrini, F., Leonardi, R., & Migliorati, P. (2004). A new video authentication template based on bubble random sampling. In *Proceedings of the European Signal Processing Conference*. IEEE.

Han, S.-H., & Chu, C.-H. (2010). Content based image authentication: current status, issues, and challenges. *Int. J. Inf. Security, 9*, 19-32. DOI 10.1007/s 10207-009-0093-2

Hauzia, A., & Noumeir, R. (2007). Methods for image authentication: A survey. In *Proceedings of the Multimedia Tools Appl*. DOI 10.1007/s11042-007-0154-3

He, D., Sun, O., & Tian, Q. (2003). A semi fragile object based video authentication system. In *Proceedings of IEEE ISCAS*. Bangkok, Thailand: IEEE.

Johns Hopkins. (n.d.). *APL creates system to detect digital video tampering*. Retrieved from http://www.jhu.edu/

Johnson, N.F. (n.d.). *An introduction to watermark recovery from images*. Fairfax, VA: Center for Secure Information System, George Mason University.

Kovesi, P. D. (1999). Image features from phase congruency. *Videre: Journal of Computer Vision Research, 1*(3).

Latechi, L. Wildt, D., & Hu, J. (n.d.). *Extraction of key frames from videos by optimal colour composition matching and polygon*.

Liang, C.-Y., Li, A., & Niu, X.-M. (2007). Video authentication and tamper detection based on cloud model. In *Proceedings of the Third International Conference on International Information Hiding and Multimedia Signal Processing (IIH-MSP 2007)*, (pp. 225-228). IIH-MSP.

Lin, C., & Chang, S. (2001). Authentication procedures-The procedures and integration working group. In *Proceedings of CME'2001*. Tokyo, Japan: CME.

Lin, C.-Y., & Chang, S.-F. (1999). Issues and solutions for authenticating MPEG video. In *Proceedings of SPIE Electronic Imaging*. San Jose, CA: SPIE.

Lu, C.-S., & Liao, H. Y. M. (2003). Structural digital signature for image authentication: An incidental distortion resistant scheme. *IEEE Transactions on Multimedia, 5*(2), 161–173. doi:10.1109/TMM.2003.811621.

Martinian, E., Wornell, G. W., & Chen, B. (n.d.). Authentication with distortion criteria. *IEEE Transactions on Information Theory*.

Mobasseri, B. G., & Evans, A. E. (2001). Content dependent video authentication by self water marking in color space. [). IEEE.]. *Proceedings of Security and Watermarking of Multimedia Contents III, 4314,* 35–46. doi:10.1117/12.435437.

Naor, M., & Pinkas, B. (1997). Visual authentication and identification. *LNCS, 1294.*

Park, J. M., Chong, E. K. P., & Siegel, H. J. (2002). Efficient multicast packet authentication using signature amortization. In *Proceedings of the IEEE Symposium on Security and Privacy,* (pp. 227-240). IEEE.

Peng, H. (2002). *A semi fragile water marking system for MPEG video authentication.* Paper presented at ICASSP. Orlando, FL.

Perrig, A., Canetti, R., Tygar, J., & Song, D. (2000). Efficient authentication and signing of multicast streams over lossy channels. In *Proceedings IEEE Symposium on Security and Privacy.* IEEE.

Podil Chuk, C. I., Jayant, N. S., & Farrardin, N. (1995). Three dimensional sub band coding of video. *IEEE Transactions on Image Processing, 4*(2), 125–139. doi:10.1109/83.342187.

Pradeep, K. A., El Saddik, A., & Kankanhalli, M. (2009). *Digital video authentication.* Hershey, PA: IGI Global.

Pradeep, K. A., Yan, W.-Q., Chang, E.-C., & Kankanhalli, M.S. (n.d.). *A hierarchical signature scheme for robust video authentication using secret sharing.*

Queluz, M. P. (1998). Toward robust, content based techniques for image authentication. In *Proceedings of Multimedia Signal Processing.* IEEE. doi:10.1109/MMSP.1998.738950.

Queluz, M. P. (2001). Authentication of digital images and video: Generic models and a new contribution. *Signal Processing Image Communication, 16,* 461–475. doi:10.1016/S0923-5965(00)00010-2.

Quisquater, J. (1997). Authentication of sequences with the SL2 hash function application to video sequences. *Journal of Computer Security, 5*(3), 213–223.

Saikia, N., & Bora, P. K. (2007). Video authentication using temporal wavelet transform. In *Proceedings of the 15th International Conference on Advanced Computing and Communications (ADCOM 2007).* ADCOM.

Singh, R., Vatsa, M., & Noore, A. (2006). Intelligent biometric information fusion using support vector machine. In *Soft Computing in Image Processing: Recent Advances.* Berlin: Springer Verlag.

Singh, R., Vatsa, M., Singh, S. K., & Upadhyay, S. (2008). *Integrating SVM classification with SVD watermarking for intelligent video authentication.* Telecommunication Systems Journal. doi:10.1007/s11235-008-9141-x.

Su, P.-Y., Chen, C.-C., & Chang, H. M. (2009). Towards effective content authentication for digital videos by employing feature extraction and quantization. *IEEE Transactions on Circuits and Systems for Video Technology, 19*(5), 668–677. doi:10.1109/TCSVT.2009.2017404.

Sun, Q., Chang, S.-F., & Maeno, K. (2002). A new semi fragile image authentication framework combining ECC and PKI infrastructure. Paper presented in ISCAS. Phoenix, AZ.

Sun, Q., He, D., Zhang, Z., & Tian, Q. (2003). *A secure and robust approach to scalable video authentication.* ICME.

Upadhyay, S., Singh, S. K., Vatsa, M., & Singh, R. (2007). Video authentication using relative correlation information and SVM. In A. E. Hassanien, J. Kacprzyk, & A. Abraham (Eds.), *Computational Intelligence in Multimedia Processing: Recent Advances.* Berlin: Springer Verlag.

Vapnik, V. N. (1995). *The nature of statistical learning theory*. Berlin: Springer Verlag. doi:10.1007/978-1-4757-2440-0.

Wang, W., & Farid, H. (2007). Exposing digital forgeries in video by detecting duplication. In *Proceedings of the 9th Workshop on Multimedia & Security*. IEEE.

Wohlmacher, P. (1998). Requirements and mechanism of IT-security including aspects of multimedia security. In *Proceedings of the Multimedia and Security Workshop at ACM Multimedia 98*. Bristol, UK: ACM.

Yan, W.-Q., & Kankanhalli, M. S. (2003). Motion trajectory based video authentication. *ISCAS, 3*, 810–813.

Yin, P., & Yu, H. H. (n.d.). Classification of video tampering methods and countermeasures using digital watermarking. In *Proceedings of SPIE* (Vol. 4518, pp. 239–246). SPIE.

Zhao, L., Qi, W., Li, S., Yang, S., & Zhang, H. (2000). Key frame extraction and shot retrieval using nearest feature line (NFL). In *Proceedings of ACM Multimedia*. ACM.

KEY TERMS AND DEFINITIONS

Digital Signature: Digital signatures can be used for the purpose of authentication.

Fragile Watermarking: Fragile watermarking can be used for the authentication of the author or producer of the content.

Intelligent Techniques: Intelligent techniques use machine learning approach to solve the problems.

Support Vector Machine: Support Vector Machine, is a powerful methodology for solving problems in nonlinear classification, function estimation and density estimation.

Video Authentication: Video authentication is a process, which ascertains that the content in a given video is authentic and exactly same as when captured.

Video Database: A database which contains the videos is called video database.

Video Tampering Attacks: Video tampering attacks can be applied to modify the contents of a video data.

ENDNOTES

[1] Law Enforcement/Emergence Services Video Association (LEWA).

Compilation of References

Acosta, E., Torres, L., Albiol, A., & Delp, E. J. (2002). An automatic face detection and recognition system for video indexing applications. In *Proceedings of the IEEE International Conference on Acoustics, Speech and Signal Processing*, (Vol. 4, pp. 3644-3647). Orlando, FL: IEEE.

Aggarwal, J. K., & Cai, Q. (1999). Human motion analysis: A review. *Computer Vision and Image Understanding*, *73*(3), 428–440. doi:10.1006/cviu.1998.0744.

Aggarwal, J. K., & Ryoo, M. S. (2011). Human activity analysis: A review. *J. of ACM Comp. Sur*, *43*(3).

Aguilar, J. F. (2006). *Adapted fusion schemes for multimodal biometric authentication*. Ph.D. Thesis.

Ahonen, T., Hadid, A., & Pietikainen, M. (2006). Face description with local binary patterns: Application to face recognition. *IEEE Transactions on Pattern Analysis and Machine Intelligence*, *28*(12), 2037–2041. doi:10.1109/TPAMI.2006.244 PMID:17108377.

Akhloufi, M. A., & Bendada, A. (2008). *Infrared face recognition using distance transform*. World Academy of Science, Engineering and Technology.

Akhshabi, C., & Begen, A. (2011). An experimental evaluation of rate-adaptation algorithms in adaptive streaming over HTTP. In *Proceedings of the Second Annual ACM Conference on Multimedia Systems*, (pp. 157-168). ACM.

Akita, K. (1984). Image sequence analysis of real world human motion. *Pattern Recognition*, *17*(1), 73–83. doi:10.1016/0031-3203(84)90036-0.

Amiri, S. H., & Jamzad, M. (2009). A robust image watermarking method in wavelet domain using genetic algorithm. In *Proceedings of the International Conference on Availability, Reliability and Security* (ARES, 2009), (pp. 612-617). ARES.

Arnaud, E. (2004). *PhD Thesis: Methods de filtrage pour du Suivi des sequences d'images - application au suivi de Points Caracteristiques*. France: Universite de Rennes I.

Arsenio, A. (2004). Object recognition from multiple percepts. In *Proceedings of the IEEE RAS/RSJ International Conference on Humanoid Robots*. IEEE.

Arsenio, A. (2009). *Method and device for processing a data stream and system comprising such device*. Applicants: Nokia Siemens Networks GMBH & CO. KG. International Patent Number: EP2098988-A1.

Arun, A., Ross, K., Nandakumar, A., & Jain, K. (2006). *Handbook of multibiometrics*. Berlin: Springer.

Aslantas, V., Ozer, S., & Ozturk, S. (2008). A novel fragile watermarking based on particle swarm optimization. In *Proceedings of the International Conference on Multimedia and Expo* (ICME 2008), (pp. 268-272). ICME.

Aslantas, V., Ozer, S., & Ozturk, S. (2009). Improving the performance of DCT based fragile watermarking using intelligent optimization algorithms. *Optics Communications*, *282*, 2806–2817. doi:10.1016/j.optcom.2009.04.034.

Aswani Kumar, C., & Srinivas, S. (2006). Latent semantic indexing using eigen value analysis for efficient information retrieval. *International Journal of Applied Mathematics and Computer Science*, *16*(4), 551–558.

Authenticity. (1989). *The Oxford English dictionary* (2nd Ed.). Oxford, UK: Oxford University Press.

Authenticity. (n.d.). *The Webster's new 20th century dictionary*. New York: Webster.

Baker, S., & Kanade, T. (2000). Hallucinating faces. In *Proceedings of the Fourth ICAFGR*. ICAFGR.

Balci, K., & Atalay, V. (2002). PCA for gender estimation: Which eigenvectors contribute? In *Proceedings of the Sixteenth International Conference on Pattern Recognition*, (Vol. 3, pp. 363-366). Quebec City, Canada: IEEE.

Banks, J. E., Bennamoun, M., Kubik, K., & Corke, P. (1997). *A Taxonomy of image matching techniques for Stere Vision*. Brisbane: Queensland University of Technology.

Bansal, R., Sehgal, P., & Bedi, P. (2012). Securing fingerprint images through PSO based robust facial watermarking. *International Journal of Information Security and Privacy*, *6*(2), 34–52. doi:10.4018/jisp.2012040103.

Bartlett, M. S., Movellan, J. R., & Sejnowski, T. J. (2002). Face recognition by independent component analysis. *IEEE Transactions on Neural Networks*, *13*, 1450–1464. doi:10.1109/TNN.2002.804287 PMID:18244540.

Bay, H., Ess, A., Tuytelaars, T., & Gool, L. V. (2008). Surf: Speeded up robust features. *Computer Vision and Image Understanding*, *110*(3), 346–359. doi:10.1016/j.cviu.2007.09.014.

Beaulieu, J., & Goldberg, M. (1989). Hierarchy in picture image segmentation.[IEEE.]. *IEEE Transactions on Pattern Analysis and Machine Intelligence*, *11*, 150–163. doi:10.1109/34.16711.

Belhumeur, P. N., Hespanha, J. P., & Kriegman, D. J. (1997). Eigenfaces vs. fisherfaces: Recognition using class specific linear projection. *IEEE TPAMI*, *19*, 711–720. doi:10.1109/34.598228.

BenArie, J., Wang, Z., Pandit, P., & Rajaram, S. (2002). Human activity recognition using multidimensional indexing. *IEEE Transactions on Pattern Analysis and Machine Intelligence*, *24*(8), 1091–1104. doi:10.1109/TPAMI.2002.1023805.

Bender, W., Gruhl, D., & Morimoto, N. (1996). Techniques for data hiding. *IBM Systems Journal*, *45*(3-4), 313–336. doi:10.1147/sj.353.0313.

Berc, R., & Fenner, W. (1998). *RTP payload format for JPEG-compressed video*.

Bergen, J., Burt, P., Hingorani, R., & Peleg, S. (1992). A three-frame algorithm for estimating two-component image motion. *IEEE Transactions on Pattern Analysis and Machine Intelligence*, *14*(9), 886–896. doi:10.1109/34.161348.

Beymer, D. (2000). Person Counting using Stereo. *Proceedings of Workshop on Human Motion*, (pp. 628 - 635).

Bhatnagar, G., & Balasubramanian, R. (2009). A new robust reference watermarking schemebsed on DWT-SVD. *Computer Standards & Interfaces*, *31*, 1002–1013. doi:10.1016/j.csi.2008.09.031.

Bhattacharjee, D. Seal, A. Ganguly, S., Nasipuri, M., & Basu, D. K. (2012). A comparative study of human thermal face recognition based on Haar wavelet transform (HWT) and local binary pattern (LBP). *Computational Intelligence and Neuroscience*. doi: doi:10.1155/2012/261089.

Bhowmik, M. K., Bhattacharjee, D., Nasipuri, M., Basu, D. K., & Kundu, M. (2008). Classification of polar-thermal eigenfaces using multilayer perceptron for human face recognition. In *Proceedings of the 3rd IEEE Conference on Industrial and Information Systems* (ICIIS-2008). IEEE.

Bhowmik, M. K., Saha, K., Majumder, S., Majumder, G., Saha, A., & Sarma, A. N. … Nasipuri, M. (2011). Thermal infrared face recognition – A biometric identification technique for robust security system. In P. M. Corcoran (Ed.), Reviews, refinements and new ideas in face recognition. Vienna, Austria: InTech Open Access Publisher.

Binh, N. T., & Khare, A. (2010). Multilevel threshold based image denoising in curvelet domain. *Journal of Computer Science and Technology*, *25*(3), 632–640. doi:10.1007/s11390-010-9352-y.

Birchfield, S. (1998). Elliptical head tracking using intensity gradients and color histograms. *IEEE Conference on Computer Vision and Pattern Recognition (CVPR)* (pp. 232 - 237). IEEE.

Black, M., & Jepson, A. (1998). Eigentracking: Robust matching and tracking of articulated objects using a view-based representation. *International Journal of Computer Vision*, *26*(1), 63–84. doi:10.1023/A:1007939232436.

Blank, M., Gorelick, L., Shechtman, E., Irani, M., & Basri, R. (2005). Actions as space-time shapes. In *Proceedings of the IEEE International Conference on Computer Vision (ICCV), Perspectives on Motivation* (pp. 1395-1402). IEEE.

Blatteis, C. M. (1998). *Physiology and pathophysiology of temperature regulation*. World Scientific Publishing Co. doi:10.1142/3507.

Blum, A., & Mitchell, T. (1998). Combining labeled and unlabeled data with co-training. *11th Annual Conference on Computational Learning Theory*, (pp. 92 - 100).

Bobick, A. F., & Davis, J. W. (2001). The recognition of human movement using temporal templates. *IEEE Transactions on Pattern Analysis and Machine Intelligence*, *23*(3), 257–267. doi:10.1109/34.910878.

Bolle, R. M., Connell, J. H., Panakanti, S., Ratha, N. K., & Senior, A. W. (2003). *Guide to biometrics*. New York: Springer.

Bolle, R., Connell, J., Pankanti, S., Ratha, N., & Senior, A. (2003). *Guide to biometrics*. Berlin: Springer Verlag.

Bottino, A., & Laurentini, A. (2001). A silhouette based technique for the reconstruction of human movement. *Comput. Vis. Image Under-standing*, *83*, 79–95. doi:10.1006/cviu.2001.0918.

Bourel, F., Chibelushi, C. C., & Low, A. A. (2000). Robust facial feature tracking. In *Proceedings of the British Machine Vision Conference*, (pp. 232-241). Bristol, UK: IEEE.

Boyd, J. E., & Little, J. J. (1997). Global versus structured interpretation of motion: Moving light displays. In *Proc. IEEE Workshop Motion Non-Rigid and Articulated Objects: Perspectives on Motivation* (pp. 18–25). IEEE.

Breazeal, C., & Aryananda, L. (2002). Recognition of affective communicative intent in robot-directed speech. *Autonomous Robots*, *12*(1), 83–104. doi:10.1023/A:1013215010749.

Bremond, B. F., & Thonnat, M. (1997). Analysis of human activities described by image sequences. In *Proc. Int. Florida AI Research Symp*. IEEE.

Brunelli, R., & Poggio, T. (1992). HyperBF networks for gender classification. In *Proceedings of the DARPA Image Understanding Workshop*, (pp. 311-314). DARPA.

Brunelli, R., & Falavigna, D. (1995). Person identification using multiple cues. *IEEE Transactions on Pattern Analysis and Machine Intelligence*, *17*(10), 955–966. doi:10.1109/34.464560.

Bruyelle, J. (1994). *PhD Thesis:Conception et Realisation d'un Dispotif de prise de vue Stereoscopique Lineaire - application a la Detection d' obstacles a l'avant des vehicules Routiers*. France: universite des sciences et technologies de Lille.

Bubeck, U. M., & Sanchez, D. (2003). *Biometric authentication: Technology and evaluation (Technical Report)*. San Diego, CA: San Diego State University.

Buddharaju, P., Pavlidis, I., & Kakadiaris, I. (2004). Face recognition in the thermal infrared spectrum. In *Proceedings of the 2004 IEEE Computer Society Conference on Computer Vision and Pattern Recognition Workshops (CVPRW'04)*. IEEE.

Burie, J., Bruyelle, J., & Postaire, J. (1995). Detecting and localising Obstacles in front of a moving Vehicle using linear Stereo Vision. *Mathematical and Computer Modelling*, *22*(4-7), 235–246. doi:10.1016/0895-7177(95)00135-O.

Burrus, C., Gopinath, R., & Guo, H. (1998). *Introduction to wavelets and wavelet transforms*. Upper Saddle River, NJ: Prentice Hall.

Burton, A. (1935). Human calorimetry: The average temperature of the tissues of the body. *The Journal of Nutrition*, *9*, 261–280.

Campbell, L. W., & Bobick, A. F. (1995). Recognition of human body motion using phase space constraints. In *Proceedings of the IEEE International Conference on Computer Vision (ICCV), Perspectives on Motivation* (pp. 624–630). IEEE.

Cao, B.-T., Tuan, D.-H., Thuong, L.-T., & Hoang, N.-D. (2011). Scene-based video super-resolution with minimum mean square error estimation. In *Proceedings of 2011 International Conference on Advanced Technologies for Communications (ATC)* (pp. 48-52). ATC.

Caselles, V., Kimmel, R., & Sapiro, G. (1995). Geodesic active contours. *IEEE International Conference on Computer Vision (ICCV)* (pp. 694 - 699). IEEE ICCV.

Celik, M. V. et al. (2002). Video authentication with self recovery. In *Proc. Security and Watermarking of Multimedia Contents IV* (Vol. 4314, pp. 531–541). IEEE. doi:10.1117/12.465311.

Cetin, K., & Ari, F. (2012). Super-resolution image construction from video images based on block matching technique. In *Proceedings of 2012 20ᵗʰ Signal Processing and Communications Applications Conference (SIU)* (pp. 1-4). SIU.

Chai, Z., & Shi, J. (2011). Improving KLT in embedded systems by processing oversampling video sequence in real-time. In *Proceedings of 2011 International Conference Reconfigurable Computing and FPGAs (ReConFig)* (pp. 297-302). ReConFig.

Chang, C. C., Tsai, P., & Lin, C. C. (2005). SVD based digital watermarking scheme. *Pattern Recognition Letters*, *26*, 1577–1586. doi:10.1016/j.patrec.2005.01.004.

Chang, K. I., Bowyer, K. W., & Flynn, P. J. (2005). An evaluation of multimodal 2D+3D face biometrics. *IEEE Transactions on Pattern Analysis and Machine Intelligence*, *27*(4), 619–624. doi:10.1109/TPAMI.2005.70 PMID:15794165.

Chang, S. G., Cvetkovic, Z., & Vetterli, M. (2006). Locally adaptive wavelet-based image interpolation. *IEEE Transactions on Image Processing*, *15*(6), 1471–1485. doi:10.1109/TIP.2006.871162 PMID:16764272.

Cheddad, A., Condell, J., Curran, K., & Mc Kevitt, P. (2010). Digital image steganography - Survey and analysis of current methods. *J Signal Processing*, *90*(3), 752–776.

Chen, X., Flynn, P. J., & Bowyer, K. W. (2003). PCA-based face recognition in infrared imagery: Baseline and comparative studies. In *Proceedings of the IEEE International Workshop on Analysis and Modeling of Faces and Gestures* (AMFG'03). IEEE.

Chen, Y., Rui, Y., & Huang, T. (2001). Jpdaf based HMM for real - time contour tracking. *IEEE Conference on Computer Vision and Pattern Recognition (CVPR)* (pp. 543 - 550). IEEE.

Chen, L. F., Mark Liao, H. Y., Ko, M. T., & Yu, G. J. (2000). A new LDA-based face recognition system which can solve the small size problem. *Pattern Recognition*, *33*(10), 1713–1726. doi:10.1016/S0031-3203(99)00139-9.

Chen, X., Flynn, P. J., & Bowyer, K. W. (2005). IR and visible light face recognition. *Computer Vision and Image Understanding*, *99*(3), 332–358. doi:10.1016/j.cviu.2005.03.001.

Chen, Y., & Wang, M. (2002). Human face recognition using thermal image. *Journal of Medical and Biological Engineering*, *22*(2).

Chen, Z., Ye, Z., Wang, S., & Peng, G. (2009). Image magnification based on similarity analogy. *Chaos, Solitons, and Fractals*, *40*(5), 2370–2375. doi:10.1016/j.chaos.2007.10.031.

Chomat, O., & Crowley, J. (1999). Probabilistic recognition of activity using local appearance. In *Proceedings of the IEEE Conference on Computer Vision and Pattern Recognition (CVPR)*. IEEE.

Choras, M. (2005). Ear biometrics based on geometrical features extraction. *Electron. Lett. Comput. Vis. Image Anal.*, *5*(3), 84–95.

Choras, M., & Choras, R. S. (2006). Geometrical algorithms of ear contour shape representation and feature extraction. In *Proceedings of Intelligent Systems Design and Applications (ISDA)*. IEEE. doi:10.1109/ISDA.2006.253879.

Choudhry, T., Clarkson, B., Jebara, T., & Pentland, A. (1999). Multimodal person recognition using unconstrained audio and video. In *Proceedings of the International Conference on Audio and Video-Based Person Authentication*, (pp. 176-181). IEEE.

Chung, J., Haber, E., & Nagy, J. (2006). Numerical methods for coupled super-resolution. *Inverse Problems*, *22*, 1261–1272. doi:10.1088/0266-5611/22/4/009.

Clonda, D., Lina, J.-M., & Goulard, B. (2004). Complex Daubechies wavelets: Properties and statistical image modeling. *Signal Processing*, *84*, 1–23. doi:10.1016/j.sigpro.2003.06.001.

Collins, R., Lipton, A., Fujiyoshi, H., & Kanade, T. (2001). Algorithms for cooperative multisensor surveillance.[IEEE.]. *Proceedings of the IEEE*, 1456–1477. doi:10.1109/5.959341.

Colmenarez, A., Frey, B. J., & Huang, T. S. (1999). A probabilistic framework for embedded face and facial expression recognition. In *Proceedings of the IEEE Conference on Computer Vision and Pattern Recognition*, (Vol. 1, pp. 1592-1597). Ft. Collins, CO: IEEE.

Comaniciu, D., & Meer, P. (2002). Mean shift: A robust approach toward feature space analysis.[IEEE.]. *IEEE Transactions on Pattern Analysis and Machine Intelligence*,603–619. doi:10.1109/34.1000236.

Comaniciu, D., Ramesh, V., & Andmeer, P. (2003). Kernel based object tracking.[IEEE.]. *IEEE Transactions on Pattern Analysis and Machine Intelligence*, 25, 564–575. doi:10.1109/TPAMI.2003.1195991.

Conaire, C. O., Connor, N. E. O., & Smeaton, A. (2007). Detector adaptation by maximising agreement between independent data sources. In *Proceedings of the IEEE Conference on Computer Vision and Pattern Recognition* (pp. 1-6). IEEE.

Condensation Algorithm on Wikipedia. (n.d.). Retrieved from Wikipedia: http://en.wikipedia.org/wiki/condensationalgorithm

Cox, I. J., Kilian, J., Leighton, F. T., & Shamoon, T. (1997). Secure spread spectrum watermarking for multimedia. *IEEE Transactions on Image Processing*, 6(12), 1673–1687. doi:10.1109/83.650120 PMID:18285237.

Craver, S., Memon, N., Yeo, B., & Yeung, N. M. (1998). Resolving rightful ownerships with invisible watermarking techniques: Limitations, attacks, and implications. *IEEE Journal on Selected Areas in Communications*, 16(4), 573–586. doi:10.1109/49.668979.

Cremers, D., & Schnorr, C. (2005). Statistical shape knowledge in variational motion segmentation I.Srael Nent. Cap. J. 21. *International Journal of Computer Vision, 54:2003.2005. ICCV 2005*, 1492 - 1499.

Crisan, S., Tarnovan, I. G., & Crisan, T. E. (2010). Radiation optimization and image processing algorithms in the identification of hand vein patterns. *International Journal of Computer Standards and Interfaces*, 32(3), 130–140. doi:10.1016/j.csi.2009.11.008.

Cross, D., & Mobasseri, B. G. (2002). Water marking for self authentication of compressed video. In *Proc. IEEE International Conference on Image Processing*. Rochester, NY: IEEE.

Cross, J. M., & Smith, C. L. (1995). Thermo graphic imaging of the subcutaneous vascular network of the back of the hand for biometric identification. In *Proceedings of the IEEE 29th International Carnahan Conference on Security Technology* (pp. 20–35). IEEE.

Cucchiara, R., Grana, C., Piccardi, M., & Prati, A. (2003). Detecting moving objects, ghosts and shadows in video streams. *IEEE Transactions on Pattern Analysis and Machine Intelligence*, 25(10), 1337–1342. doi:10.1109/TPAMI.2003.1233909.

Cuntoor, N., Kale, A., & Chellappa, R. (2003). Combining multiple evidences for gait recognition. In *Proc. ICASSP: Vol. 3 Perspectives on Motivation* (pp. 33–36). IEEE.

Cutler, R. (1996). *Face recognition using infrared images and eigenfaces.* Retrieved from http://citeseer.ist.psu.edu/cutler96face.html

Darwish, A., Abd Elghafar, R., & Fawzi Ali, A. (2009). Multimodal face and ear images. *Journal of Computer Science*, 5(5), 374–379. doi:10.3844/jcssp.2009.374.379.

Daubechies, I. (1992). *Ten lectures on wavelets.* Society for Industrial and Applied Mathematics. doi:10.1137/1.9781611970104.

Daugman, J. (2007). New methods in iris recognition. *IEEE Transactions on Systems. Man and Cybernetics B*, 37(5), 1167–1175. doi:10.1109/TSMCB.2007.903540.

Davis, J., & Keck, M. (2005). A twostage approach to person detection in thermal imagery. In *Proceedings of the Workshop on Applications of Computer Vision*. IEEE.

Dee, H. M., & Velastin, S. A. (2008). How close are we to solving the problem of automated visual surveillance? A review of real-world surveillance, scientific progress and evaluative mechanisms. *International journal of Machine Vision and Applications, 19*, 329-343.

Diffie, W., & Hellman, M. E. (1976). New directions in cryptography. *IEEE Transactions on Information Theory*, 22(6), 644–654. doi:10.1109/TIT.1976.1055638.

Ding, Y., Zhuang, D., & Wang, K. (2005). A study of hand vein recognition method. In *Proceedings of IEEE International Conference on Mechatronics & Automation* (pp. 2106–2110). Niagara Falls, Canada: IEEE.

Ditmann, J., Steinmetz, A., & Steinmetz, R. (1999). Content based digital signature for motion pictures authentication and content fragile watermarking.[). IEEE.]. *Proceedings of Multimedia Computing and Systems, 2*, 209–213.

Dittman, J., Mukharjee, A., & Steinbach, M. (2000). Media independent watermarking classification and the need for combining digital video and audio watermarking for media authentication. In *Proceedings of the International Conference on Information Technology: Coding and Computing*. IEEE.

Dollar, P., Rabaud, V., Cottrell, G., & Belongie, S. (2005). Behavior recognition via sparse spatio-temporal features. In *Proceedings of the 2nd Joint IEEE International Workshop on Visual Surveillance and Performance Evaluation of Tracking and Surveillance (VS-PETS), Perspectives on Motivation* (pp. 65-72). IEEE.

Ebrahimi, T., & Horne, C. (2000). MPEG-4 natural video coding - An overview. *Signal Processing Image Communication*, *15*(4-5), 365–385. doi:10.1016/S0923-5965(99)00054-5.

Elgammal, A., Hardwood, D., & Davis, L. (2000). Non - parametric model for background subtraction. *European Conference on Computer Vision (ECCV)* (pp. 751 - 767). ECCV.

Engelbrecht, A. P. (2005). *Fundamentals of computational swarm intelligence*. Hoboken, NJ: John Wiley& Sons.

Erdem, C. E., Sankur, B., & Tekalp, A. M. (2004). Performance measures for video object segmentation and tracking. *IEEE Transactions on Image Processing*, *13*(7), 937–951. doi:10.1109/TIP.2004.828427 PMID:15648860.

Eren, P. E., Sezan, M. I., & Tekalp, A. M. (1997). Robust, object-based high-resolution image reconstruction from low-resolution video. *IEEE Transactions on Image Processing*, *6*(10), 1446–1451. doi:10.1109/83.624970 PMID:18282900.

Farhadi, A., & Tabrizi, M. K. (2008). Learning to recognize activities from the wrong view point. In *Proc. European Conference on Computer Vision: Perspectives on Motivation* (pp. 154-166). IEEE.

Farid, H. (2006). Digital doctoring: How to tell the real from fake. *Significance*, *3*(4), 162–166. doi:10.1111/j.1740-9713.2006.00197.x.

Farsiu, S., Elad, M., & Milanfar, P. (2006). Multiframe demosaicing and super-resolution of color images. *IEEE Transactions on Image Processing*, *15*(1), 141–159. doi:10.1109/TIP.2005.860336 PMID:16435545.

Farsiu, S., Robinson, M. D., Elad, M., & Milanfar, P. (2004). Fast and robust multiframe super resolution. *IEEE Transactions on Image Processing*, *13*(10), 1327–1344. doi:10.1109/TIP.2004.834669 PMID:15462143.

Fathi, A., & Mori, G. (2008). Action recognition by learning mid-level motion features. In *Proc. Conference on Computer Vision and Pattern Recognition: Perspectives on Motivation* (pp. 1-8). IEEE.

Faugeras, O. (1993). Three-dimensional computer vision: a geometric viewpoint. MA, USA: Cambridge.

Fernandes, F. C. A., Spaendonck, R. L. C. V., & Burrus, C. S. (2003). A new framework for complex wavelet transforms. *IEEE Transactions on Signal Processing*, *51*(7), 1825–1837. doi:10.1109/TSP.2003.812841.

Fernandez, F.A. (2008). *Biometric sample quality and its application to multimodal authentication systems*.

Fieguth, P., & Terzoupoulos, D. (1997). Color-based tracking of heads and other mobile objects at video frame rates. *IEEE Conference on Computer Vision and Pattern Recognition (CVPR)* (pp. 21 - 27). IEEE.

Fields, C., Hugh, C. F., Warren, C. P., & Zimberoff, M. (1960). The ear of the newborn as an identification constant. *Journal of Obstetrics & Gynaecology*, *16*, 98–101. PMID:13822693.

Forsyth, D. A., & Ponce, J. (2002). *Computer Vision: A Modern Approach*. Upper Saddle River, NJ, USA: Prentice Hall.

Freeman, W. T., Jones, T. R., & Pasztor, E. C. (2002). Example-based super-resolution. *IEEE Computer Graphics and Applications*, *22*(2), 56–65. doi:10.1109/38.988747.

Friedman, G. L. (1993). The trustworthy digital camera: restoring credibility to the photographic image. *IEEE Transactions on Consumer Electronics*, *39*, 905–910. doi:10.1109/30.267415.

Galton, F. (1899). *Finger prints of young children*. London: British Association for the Advancement of Science.

Ganong, W. F. (2001). *Review of medical physiology* (20th ed.). New York: McGraw-Hill Medical Publishing Division.

Gao, X., Boult, T., Coetzee, F., & Ramesh, V. (2000). Error analysis of background adaption. *IEEE Conference on Computer Vision and Pattern Recognition (CVPR)* (pp. 503 - 510). IEEE CVPR.

Gavrila, D., & Davis, L. (1995). Towards 3-D model-based tracking and recognition of human movement. In *Proceedings of the Int. Workshop on Face and Gesture Recognition: Perspectives on Motivation* (pp. 272–277). IEEE.

Gennaro, R., & Rohatgi, P. (1997). How to sign digital stream.[ACM.]. *Proceedings of Crypto, 97*, 180–197.

Geradts, Z. J., & Bijhold, J. (n.d.). Forensic video investigation with real time digitized uncompressed video image sequences. *Investigation and Forensic Science Technologies.*.

Gong, M., & Yee-Hong, Y. (2005b). Near real-time reliable stereo matching using programmable graphics hardware. *Proceedings of IEEE Computer Society Conference on Computer Vision and Pattern Recognition* (pp. 924 - 931). IEEE.

Gong, M., & Yee-Hong, Y. (2005a). Fast unambiguous stereo matching using reliability-based dynamic programming.[IEEE.]. *IEEE Transactions on Pattern Analysis and Machine Intelligence, 27*(6), 998–1003. doi:10.1109/TPAMI.2005.120 PMID:15943431.

Gonzalez, R. C., & Woods, R. E. (2008). *Digital image processing* (2nd ed.). Englewood Cliffs, NJ: Prentice Hall Publications.

Gonzalez, R. C., & Woods, R. E. (2010). *Digital image processing* (3rd ed.). Upper Saddle River, NJ: Pearson Education Inc..

Gray, J. E., Suresh, G., Ursprung, R., Edwards, W. H., Nickerson, J., & Shinno, P. H. (2006). Patient misidentification in the neonatal intensive careunit: Quantification of risk. *Pediatrics, 117*, e46–e47. doi:10.1542/peds.2005-0291 PMID:16396847.

Green, R. D., & Guan, L. (2004). Quantifying and recognizing human movement patterns from monocular video images—Part I: A new frame-work for modeling human motion. *IEEE Transactions on Circuits and Systems for Video Technology, 14*(2), 179–189. doi:10.1109/TCSVT.2003.821976.

Grewe, L., & Kak, A. (1995). Interactive learning of a multi-attribute hash table classfier for fast object recogniiton. *Computer Vision Image UNderstand., 61*, 3.

Guan, Y. P. (2010). Spatio-temporal motion-based foreground segmentation and shadow suppression. *IET Computer Vision, 4*(1), 50–60. doi:10.1049/iet-cvi.2008.0016.

Guerrini, F., Leonardi, R., & Migliorati, P. (2004). A new video authentication template based on bubble random sampling. In *Proceedings of the European Signal Processing Conference*. IEEE.

Gunturk, B. K., Altunbasak, Y., & Mersereau, R. M. (2004). Super-resolution reconstruction of compressed video using transform-domain statistics. *IEEE Transactions on Image Processing, 13*(1), 33–43. doi:10.1109/TIP.2003.819221 PMID:15376955.

Guyton, A. C., & Hall, J. E. (1996). *Textbook of medical physiology* (9th ed.). Philadelphia: W.B. Saunders Company.

Haddadnia, J., Faez, K., & Ahmadi, M. (2003). An effcient human face recognition system using pseudo zernike moment invari- ant and radial basis function neural network. *International Journal of Pattern Recognition and Artificial Intelligence, 17*(1), 41–62. doi:10.1142/S0218001403002265.

Hampapur, A., Brown, L., Connell, J., Pankanti, S., Senior, A., & Tian, Y. (2003). Smart surveillance: Applications, technologies and implications. In *Proceedings of the Fourth International Conference on Information, Communications & Signal Processing and Fourth Pacific-Rim Conference on Multimedia*, (Vol. 2, pp. 1133-1138). IEEE.

Han, S.-H., & Chu, C.-H. (2010). Content based image authentication: current status, issues, and challenges. *Int. J. Inf. Security, 9*, 19-32. DOI 10.1007/s 10207-009-0093-2

Haque, M. N., Biswas, M., Pickering, M. R., & Frater, M. R. (2012). A low-complexity image registration algorithm for global motion estimation. *IEEE Transactions on Circuits and Systems for Video Technology*, 22(3), 426–433. doi:10.1109/TCSVT.2011.2163983.

Haritaoglu, I., Harwood, D., & Davis, L. (2000). W4: real-time surveillance of people and their activities. *IEEE Transactions Pattern Analysis Mach. Intell. 22, 8* (pp. 809 - 830). IEEE.

Haritaoglu, I., Harwood, D., & Davis, L. S. (2000). W4: Real-time surveillance of people and their activities. *IEEE Transactions on Pattern Analysis and Machine Intelligence*, 22(8), 809–830. doi:10.1109/34.868683.

Harris, C., & Stephens, M. (1988). A combined corner and edge detector. In *Proceedings of the Fourth Alvey Vision Conference*, (pp. 146-151). IEEE.

Hartley, R., & Zisserman, A. (2004). *Multiview geometry in computer vision* (2nd ed.). Cambridge, UK: Cambridge Press. doi:10.1017/CBO9780511811685.

Hartung, F., & Kutter, M. (1999). Multimedia watermarking techniques. *Proceedings of the IEEE*, 87(7), 1085–1103. doi:10.1109/5.771066.

Harville, M. (2004). Stereo person tracking with adaptive plan-view templates of height and occupancy statistics. IVC, 22(2).

Hauzia, A., & Noumeir, R. (2007). Methods for image authentication: A survey. In *Proceedings of the Multimedia Tools Appl.* DOI 10.1007/s11042-007-0154-3

Hawkes, P. L., & Clayden, D. O. (1993). Veincheck research for automatic identification of people. In *Proceedings of Seminar on hand and fingerprint*. NPL.

Hayashi, K., Hashimoto, M., Sumi, K., & Sasakawa, K. (2004). Multiple-person tracker with a fixed slanting stereo camera. *Proceedings of the Sixth IEEE International Conference on Automatic Face and Gesture Recognition (FGR' 04)* (pp. 681 - 686). IEEE.

He, D., Sun, O., & Tian, Q. (2003). A semi fragile object based video authentication system. In *Proceedings of IEEE ISCAS*. Bangkok, Thailand: IEEE.

Hearn, D., & Baker, M. P. (1996). *Computer graphics C version* (2nd ed.). Englewood Cliffs, NJ: Prentice Hall.

Hermosilla, G., Loncomilla, P., & Ruiz-del-Solar, J. (2010). Thermal face recognition using local interest points and descriptors for HRI applications. In *Proceedings of the Computer Vision and Pattern Recognition Workshops (CVPRW)*. IEEE.

Holt, S. B. (1973). The significance of dermatoglyphics in medicine. *Clinical Pediatrics*, 12(8), 471–484. doi:10.1177/000992287301200904 PMID:4579966.

Hong, S.-H., Park, R.-H., Yang, S., & Kim, J.-Y. (2008). Image interpolation using interpolative classified vector quantization. *Image and Vision Computing*, 26(2), 228–239. doi:10.1016/j.imavis.2007.05.002.

Horn, B. (1977). Understanding image intensities. *Artificial Intelligence*, 1–31.

Horn, B., & Sjoberg, R. (1979). Calculating the reflectance map. *Applied Optics*, 18, 1770–1779. doi:10.1364/AO.18.001770 PMID:20212547.

Howe, N. R., & Deschamps, A. (2004). *Better foreground segmentation through graph cuts* (Technical Report). Smith College. Retrieved January 31, 2013, from http://arxiv.org/abs/cs.CV/0401017

Hsieh, J. W., Hu, W. F., Chang, C. J., & Chen, Y. H. (2003). Shadow elimination for effective moving object detection by Gaussian shadow modeling. *Image and Vision Computing*, 21(6), 505–516. doi:10.1016/S0262-8856(03)00030-1.

Huang, C. L., & Liao, B. Y. (2001). A robust scene-change detection method for video segmentation. *IEEE Transactions on Circuits and Systems for Video Technology*, 11(12), 1281–1288. doi:10.1109/76.974682.

Huang, J. C., & Hsieh, W. S. (2003). Wavelet based moving object segmentation. *Electronics Letters*, 39(19), 1380–1382. doi:10.1049/el:20030909.

Hu, M. (1962). Visual pattern recognition by moment invariants. *I.R.E. Transactions on Information Theory*, 8(2), 179–187. doi:10.1109/TIT.1962.1057692.

Huttenlocher, D., Noh, J., & Rucklidge, W. (1993). Tracking non - rigid objects in complex scenes. *IEEE International Conference on Computer Vision (ICCv)* (pp. 93 - 101). IEEE ICCV.

Iain, M., Takahiro, I., & Baker, S. (2003). The template update problem.[IEEE.]. *IEEE Transactions on Pattern Analysis and Machine Intelligence*, *26*, 810–815. PMID:18579941.

Intille, S., Davis, J., & Andbobicka, A. (1997). Real-time closed-world tracking. *IEEE Conference on Computer Vision and Pattern Recognition (CVPR)* (pp. 697 - 703). IEEE CVPR.

Irani, M., & Anandan, P. (1998). Video indexing based on mosaic representations. *IEEE Transactions Pattern Analysis Mach. Intell. 20, 6* (pp. 577 - 589). IEEE.

Isard, M., & MacCormick, J. (2001). Bramble: A bayesian multiple-blob tracker. *IEEE International Conference on Computer Vision (ICCv)* (pp. 34 - 41). IEEE.

Isard, M., & Blake, A. (1998). Condensation conditional density propagation for visual tracking. *International Journal of Computer Vision*,5–28. doi:10.1023/A:1008078328650.

Islam, M. M., Islam, M. N., Asari, V. K., & Karim, M. A. (2012). Single image super-resolution in frequency domain. In *Proceedings of 2012 IEEE Southwest Symposium on Image Analysis and Interpretation (SSIAI)* (pp. 53-56). IEEE.

Islam, M. M., Asari, V. K., Islam, M. N., & Karim, M. A. (2010). Super-resolution enhancement technique for low resolution video. *IEEE Transactions on Consumer Electronics*,*56*(2), 919–924. doi:10.1109/TCE.2010.5506020.

Islam, S. M. S., Davies, R., Mian, A., & Bennamoun, M. (2008). A fast and fully automatic ear recognition approach based on 3D local surface features.[ACIVS]. *Proceedings of Advanced Concepts for Intelligent Vision Systems*, *5259*, 1081–1092. doi:10.1007/978-3-540-88458-3_98.

Ivanov, Y. A., & Bobick, A. F. (2000). Recognition of visual activities and interactions by stochastic parsing. *IEEE Transactions on Pattern Analysis and Machine Intelligence*, *22*(8), 852–872. doi:10.1109/34.868686.

Jain, A. K., & Lu, X. (2004). Ethnicity identification from face images. In *Proceedings of SPIE International Symposium on Defense and Security: Biometric Technology for Human Identification*. SPIE.

Jain, A. K., Nandakumar, K., Lu, X., & Park, U. (2004). Integrating faces, fingerprints and soft biometric traits for user recognition. In *Proceedings of Biometric Authentication Workshop* (LNCS), (vol. 3087, pp. 259–269). Prague, Czech Republic: Springer.

Jain, A. K., Ross, A., & Prabhakar, S. (2001). Fingerprint matching using minutiae and texture features. In *Proceedings of the International Conference on Image Processing (ICIP 2001)*, (pp. 282-285). ICIP.

Jain, R., & Nagel, H. (1979). On the analysis of accumulative difference pictures from image sequences of real world scenes. *IEEE Trans. Pattern Analysis Mach. Intell.1, 2* (pp. 206 - 214). IEEE.

Jain, V., & Mukherjee, A. (2002). *The Indian face database*. Retrieved from http://vis-www.cs.umass.edu/~vidit/IndianFaceDatabase/

A. K. Jain, R. Bolle, & S. Pankanti (Eds.). (1999). *Biometrics: Personal identification in networked society* (pp. 87–102). London: Kluwer Academic Publishers.

Jain, A. K., Flynn, P., & Ross, A. (2007). *Handbook of biometrics*. New York: Springer.

Jain, A. K., Hong, L., Pankati, S., & Bolle, R. (1997). An identity authentication system using fingerprints. *Proceedings of the IEEE*, *85*(9), 1365–1388. doi:10.1109/5.628674.

Jain, A. K., & Pankanti, S. (2000). Fingerprint classification and recognition. In A. Bovik (Ed.), *The Image and Video Processing Handbook*. New York: Academic Press.

Jain, A. K., Ross, A., & Prabhakar, S. (2004). An introduction to biometric recognition. *IEEE Transactions on Circuits and Systems for Video Technology*, *14*(1), 4–20. doi:10.1109/TCSVT.2003.818349.

Jalobeanu, A., Feraud, L.-B., & Zerubia, J. (2000). *Satellite image deconvolution using complex wavelets packets*. INRIA Report No. 3955.

Jarno, M. (2006). LSB matching revisited. *IEEE Signal Processing Letters*, *13*(5), 285–287. doi:10.1109/LSP.2006.870357.

Jeon, B. W., Park, R.-H., & Yang, S. (2006). Resolution enhancement by prediction of the high-frequency image based on the Laplacian pyramid. *J. Applied Signal Processing. Article ID*, *72520*, 1–11.

Jia, W., Cai, H., Gui, J., et al. (2011). Newborn footprint recognition using orientation feature. *Journal of Neural Computing & Applications*.

Jianchao, Y., Wright, J., Huang, T. S., & Yi, M. (2010). Image super-resolution via sparse representation. *IEEE Transactions on Image Processing*, *19*(11), 2861–2873. doi:10.1109/TIP.2010.2050625.

Jiang, G., & Kang, L. (2007). Character analysis of facial expression thermal image. In *Proceedings of the IEEE/ICME International Conference on Complex Medical Engineering*. IEEE.

Jiang, G., Song, X., Zheng, F., Wang, P., & Omer, A. M. (2005). Facial expression recognition using thermal. In *Proceedings of the 27th Annual Conference on IEEE Engineering in Medicine and Biology*. IEEE.

Johansson, G. (1975). Visual motion perception. *Scientif. Amer.*, 76–88.

Johns Hopkins. (n.d.). *APL creates system to detect digital video tampering*. Retrieved from http://www.jhu.edu/

Johnson, N.F. (n.d.). *An introduction to watermark recovery from images*. Fairfax, VA: Center for Secure Information System, George Mason University.

Kalman filter on Wikipedia. (n.d.). Retrieved from Wikipedia: http://en.wikipedia.org/wiki/kalmanfilter

Kanade, T., Collins, R., Lipton, A., Burt, P., & Wixson, L. (1998). Advances in cooperative multi - sensor video surveillance. *Darpa IU Workshop* (pp. 3 - 24). Darpa IU.

Kang, J., Cohen, I., & Medioni, G. (2004). Object re-acquisition using geometric invariant apperance model. *International Conference on Pattern Recognition (ICPR)* (pp. 759 - 762). ICPR.

Kass, M., Witkin, A., & Terzopoulos, D. (1988). Snakes: active contour models. *International Journal of Computer Vision*, *1*, 321–332. doi:10.1007/BF00133570.

Katzenbeisser, S., & Petitcolas, F. A. P. (2002). *Information hiding techniques for steganography and digital watermarking*. New York: Artech House.

Ke, Y., Sukthankar, R., & Hebert, M. (2007a). Event detection in crowded videos. In *Proc. International Conference on Computer Vision: Perspectives on Motivation* (pp. 1-8). IEEE.

Ke, Y., Sukthankar, R., & Hebert, M. (2007b). Spatio-temporal shape and flow correlation for action recognition. In *Proceedings of the IEEE Conference on Computer Vision and Pattern Recognition (CVPR)*. IEEE.

Khare, A., Khare, M., Jeong, Y. Y., Kim H., & Jeon, M., (2010). Despeckling of medical ultrasound images using Daubechies complex wavelet transform. *Signal Processing*, *90*(2), 428-439. doi:10.1016/j.sigpro.2009.07.008.

Khare, A., & Tiwary, U. S. (2006). Symmetric Daubechies complex wavelet transform and its application to denoising and deblurring. *WSEAS Transactions on Signal Processing*, *2*(5), 738–745.

Khare, A., & Tiwary, U. S. (2007). Daubechies complex wavelet transform based technique for denoising of medical images. *International Journal of Image and Graphics. World Scientific Publications*, *7*(4), 663–687.

Khare, A., Tiwary, U. S., & Jeon, M. (2009). Daubechies complex wavelet transform based multilevel shrinkage for deblurring of medical images in presence of noise. *International Journal of Wavelets, Multresolution, and Information Processing*, *7*(5), 587–604. doi:10.1142/S0219691309003100.

Khare, A., Tiwary, U. S., Pedrycz, W., & Jeon, M. (2010b). Multilevel adaptive thresholding and shrinkage technique for denoising using Daubechies complex wavelet transform. *The Imaging Science Journal*, *58*(6), 340–358. doi:10.1179/136821910X12750339175826.

Khare, M., & Srivastava, R. K. (2012). Level set method for segmentation of medical images without reinitialization. *Journal of Medical Imaging and Health Informatics*, *2*(2), 158–167. doi:10.1166/jmihi.2012.1079.

Kim, K. (2005). Intelligent immigration control system by using passport recognition and face verification. In *Proceedings of the International Symposium on Neural Networks*, (pp. 147-156). Chongqing, China: IEEE.

Kim, S. H., Park, R.-H., & Yang, S. (2008). Superresolution of a region of interest using feature-based affine motion estimation. In *Proceedings of the Int. Conf. Consumer Electronics* (pp. 10.4-2:1-2). IEEE.

Kishore, V., Sivasankar, A., & Ramashri, T., & Hari-Krishna, K. (2010). Robust image watermarking using particle swarm optimization. *Advances in Computational Sciences and Technology*, *3*(3), 397–406.

Kockelkorn, M., Luneburg, A., & Scheffer, T. (2003). Using transduction and multiview learning to answer emails. *European Conference on Principle and Practise of Knowledge Discovery in Databases*, (pp. 266 - 277).

Kong, S. G., Heo, J., Abidi, B. R., Paik, J., & Abidi, M. A. (2005). Recent advances in visual and infrared face recognition - A review. *Computer Vision and Image Understanding*, 97(1), 103–135. doi:10.1016/j.cviu.2004.04.001.

Kovesi, P. D. (1999). Image features from phase congruency. *Videre: Journal of Computer Vision Research, 1*(3).

KTH Research Project Activity Database. (n.d.). Retrieved from http://www.nada.kth.se/cvap/actions/

Kucken, M., & Newell, A. C. (2005). Fingerprint formation. *Journal of Theoretical Biology, 235*, 71–83. doi:10.1016/j.jtbi.2004.12.020 PMID:15833314.

Kuhn, H. (1955). The Hungarian method for solving the assignment problem. *Naval Research Logistics Quart., 2*, 83–97. doi:10.1002/nav.3800020109.

Kumar, A., & Prathyusha, K. V. (2009). Personal authentication using hand vein triangulation and knuckle shape. *IEEE Transactions on Image Processing, 18*(9), 2127–2136. doi:10.1109/TIP.2009.2023153 PMID:19447728.

Kurita, T., & Taguchi, T. (n.d.). *A modification of kernel-based Fisher discriminant analysis for face detection.*

La Torre Frade, F. D., Campoy, J., Cohn, J., & Kanade, T. (2007). Simultaneous registration and clustering for temporal segmentation. In *Proceedings of the International Conference on Computer Vision Theory and Applications: Perspectives on Motivation* (pp. 110-115). IEEE.

Lam, L., Lee, S. W., & Suen, C. Y. (1992). Thinning methodologies: A comprehensive survey. *IEEE Transactions on Pattern Analysis and Machine Intelligence, 14*(9), 869–885. doi:10.1109/34.161346.

Laptev, I., & Lindeberg, T. (2003). Space-time interest points. In P*roc. International Conference on Computer Vision: Vol. 1, Perspectives on Motivation* (pp. 432-439). IEEE.

Laptev, I., & Perez, P. (2007). Retrieving actions in movies. In *Proc. of Int. Conference on Computer Vision: Perspectives on Motivation* (pp. 1-8). IEEE.

Laptev, I., Marszalek, M., Schmid, C., & Rozenfeld, B. (2008). Learning realistic human ac-tions from movies. In *Proceedings of the IEEE Conference on Computer Vision and Pattern Recognition (CVPR)*. IEEE.

Latechi, L. Wildt, D., & Hu, J. (n.d.). *Extraction of key frames from videos by optimal colour composition matching and polygon.*

Lawton, W. (1993). Applications of complex valued wavelet transform in subband decomposition. *IEEE Transactions on Signal Processing, 41*(12), 3566–3568. doi:10.1109/78.258098.

Lee, J. H., & Kim, W. Y. (2004). Video summarization and retrieval system using face recognition and MPEG-7 descriptors.[LNCS]. *Proceedings of Image and Video Retrieval, 3115*, 179–188.

Leone, A., & Distante, C. (2007). Shadow detection for moving objects based on texture analysis. *Pattern Recognition, 40*(4), 1222–1233. doi:10.1016/j.patcog.2006.09.017.

Leu, J. G. (2001). Sharpness preserving image enlargement based on a ramp edge model. *Signal Processing, 34*(10), 1927–1938.

Levin, A., Viola, P., & Fruend, Y. (2003). Unsupervised improvement of visual detectors using co-training. *IEEE International Conference on Computer Vision (ICCV)* (pp. 626 - 633). IEEE ICCV.

Li, Q., Yuan, C., & Zong, Y. Z. (2007). Adaptive DWT-SVD domain image watermarking using human visual model. In *Proceedings of ICACT*, (pp. 1947-1951). ICACT.

Li, Y. (2006). *Study on some key issues in ear recognition.* (PhD thesis). University of Science and Technology Beijing, Beijing, China.

Liang, C.-Y., Li, A., & Niu, X.-M. (2007). Video authentication and tamper detection based on cloud model. In *Proceedings of the Third International Conference on International Information Hiding and Multimedia Signal Processing (IIH-MSP 2007)*, (pp. 225-228). IIH-MSP.

Li, B., Chellappa, R., Zheng, Q., & Der, S. (2001). Model - based temporal object verification using video.[IEEE.]. *IEEE Transactions on Image Processing*, 897–908.

Lienhart, R., & Maydt, J. (2002). An extended set of Haar-like features for rapid object detection. In *Proceedings of IEEE International Conference on Image Processing*, (pp. 900–903). IEEE.

Li, F., Jia, X., & Fraser, D. (2009). Superresolution reconstruction of multispectral data for improved image classification. *IEEE Geoscience and Remote Sensing Letters*, *6*(4), 689–693. doi:10.1109/LGRS.2009.2023604.

Li, J., Hao, P., Zhang, C., & Dou, M. (2008). Hallucinating faces from thermal infrared images. In *Proceedings of Image Processing*. IEEE.

Li, L., He-Huan, X., Chin-Chen, C., & Ying-Ying, M. (2011). A novel image watermarking in redistributed invariant wavelet domain. *Journal of Systems and Software*, *84*, 923–929. doi:10.1016/j.jss.2011.01.025.

Lim, E., Jiang, X., & Yau, W. (2002). Fingerprint quality and validity analysis. In *Proceedings of the International Conference on Image Processing* (ICIP, 2002), (pp. 469-472). ICIP.

Lin & Lee. (1996). *Neural fuzzy systems*. Beijing, China: Prentice Hall International.

Lin, C., & Chang, S. (2001). Authentication procedures-The procedures and integration working group. In *Proceedings of CME'2001*. Tokyo, Japan: CME.

Lin, C.-Y., & Chang, S.-F. (1999). Issues and solutions for authenticating MPEG video. In *Proceedings of SPIE Electronic Imaging*. San Jose, CA: SPIE.

Lina, J.-M., & Mayrand, M. (1995). Complex Daubechies wavelets. *Journal of Applied and Computational Harmonic Analysis*, *2*, 219–229. doi:10.1006/acha.1995.1015.

Lin, C. L., & Fan, K. C. (2004). Biometric verification using thermal images of palm-dorsa vein patterns. *IEEE Transactions on Circuits and Systems for Video Technology*, *14*(2), 199–213. doi:10.1109/TCSVT.2003.821975.

Liu, J., & Shah, M. (2008). Learning human actions via information maximization. In *Proceedings of the IEEE Conference on Computer Vision and Pattern Recognition (CVPR)*. IEEE.

Liu, J., & Wu, D. (2011). Joint POCS method with compressive sensing theory for super-resolution image reconstruction. In *Proceedings of 2011 3rd International Conference on Awareness Science and Technology (iCAST)* (pp. 99-102). iCAST.

Liu, W., Wang, Y., Li, S. Z., & Tan, T. (2004). Space approach of fisher discriminant analysis for face recognition. In *Proceeding of ECCV Workshop on Biometric Authentication*, (pp. 32-44). ECCV.

Liu, J. N. K., Wang, M., & Feng, B. (2005). iBotGuard: An internet-based intelligent robot security system using invariant face recognition against intruder. *IEEE Transactions on Systems, Man and Cybernetics. Part C, Applications and Reviews*, *35*, 97–105. doi:10.1109/TSMCC.2004.840051.

Liyuan, L., & Maylor, L. (2002). Integrating intensity and texture differences for robust change detection. *IEEE Transactions Image Process. 11, 2* (pp. 105 - 112). IEEE.

Lowe, D. (2004). Distinctive image features from scale-invariant keypoints. *International Journal of Computer Vision*, *60*(2), 91–110. doi:10.1023/B:VISI.0000029664.99615.94.

Lu, C.-S., & Liao, H. Y. M. (2003). Structural digital signature for image authentication: An incidental distortion resistant scheme. *IEEE Transactions on Multimedia*, *5*(2), 161–173. doi:10.1109/TMM.2003.811621.

Lv, F., & Nevatia, R. (2007). Single view human action recognition using key pose matching and viterbi path searching. In *Proc. Conference on Computer Vision and Pattern Recognition: Perspectives on Motivation* (pp. 1-8). IEEE.

MacGregor, R., & Welford, R. (1991). Veincheck: Imaging for security and personal identification. *Advanced Imaging (Woodbury, N.Y.)*, *6*(7), 52–56.

Maglogiannis, I., Vouyioukas, D., & Aggelopoulos, C. (2009). Face detection and recognition of natural human emotion using Markov random fields. *Personal and Ubiquitous Computing*, *13*(1), 95–101. doi:10.1007/s00779-007-0165-0.

Maltoni, D., Maio, D., Jain, A. K., & Prabhakar, S. (2003). *Handbook of fingerprint recognition*. New York: Springer.

Mansouri, A. (2002). Region tracking via level set pdes without motion computation. *IEEE Trans. Patt. Analy. Mach. Intell. 24, 7* (pp. 947 - 961). 947 - 961.

Mansouri, A. R., & Konrad, J. (2003). Multiple motion segmentation with level sets. *IEEE Transactions on Image Processing*, *12*(2), 201–220. doi:10.1109/TIP.2002.807582 PMID:18237901.

Martinez, B., Binefa, X., & Pantic, M. (2010). Facial component detection in thermal imagery. In *Proceedings of IEEE Computer Society Conference on Computer Vision and Pattern Recognition workshops*(CVPRW), (pp. 48-52). IEEE.

Martinez, J. (2010). *MPEG-7 overview*.

Martinian, E., Wornell, G. W., & Chen, B. (n.d.). Authentication with distortion criteria. *IEEE Transactions on Information Theory*.

Matthies, L., Szeliski, R., & Kanade, T. (1989). Kalman filter based algorithms for estimating depth from image sequences. *International Journal of Computer Vision*, *3*(3), 209–238. doi:10.1007/BF00133032.

Maymon, S., & Oppenheim, A. V. (2011). Sinc interpolation of nonuniform samples. *IEEE Transactions on Signal Processing*, *59*(10), 4745–4758. doi:10.1109/TSP.2011.2160054.

Meijering, E. (2002). A chronology of interpolation: From ancient astronomy to modern signal and image processing. *Proceedings of the IEEE*, *90*(3), 319–342. doi:10.1109/5.993400.

Metaxas, D. N., Venkataraman, S., & Vogler, C. (2004). Image-based stress recognition using a model- based dynamic face tracking system. In *Proceedings of the International Conference on Computational Science*, (pp. 813-821). IEEE.

Middendorf, C., & Bowyer, K. W. (2008). Multibiometrics using face and ear. In *Handbook of Biometrics* (pp. 315–341). Berlin: Springer. doi:10.1007/978-0-387-71041-9_16.

Mikolajczyk, K., & Schmid, C. (2003). A performance evaluation of local descriptors. *IEEE Conference on Computer Vision and Pattern Recognition (CVPR)* (pp. 1615 - 1630). IEEE.

Miura, N., Nagasaka, A., & Miyatake, T. (2004). Feature extraction of finger-vein patterns based on repeated line tracking and its application to personal identification. *Machine Vision and Applications*, *15*(4), 194–203. doi:10.1007/s00138-004-0149-2.

Miura, N., Nagasaka, A., & Miyatake, T. (2007). Extraction of finger-vein patterns using maximum curvature points in image profiles. *IEICE Transactions on Information and Systems*, *E90-D*(8), 1185–1194. doi:10.1093/ietisy/e90-d.8.1185.

Mobasseri, B. G., & Evans, A. E. (2001). Content dependent video authentication by self water marking in color space.[). IEEE.]. *Proceedings of Security and Watermarking of Multimedia Contents III*, *4314*, 35–46. doi:10.1117/12.435437.

Moghaddam, B., & Yang, M. H. (2002). Learning gender with support faces. *IEEE Transactions on Pattern Analysis and Machine Intelligence*, *24*, 707–711. doi:10.1109/34.1000244.

Molina, R., Vega, M., Abad, J., & Katsaggelos, A. K. (2003). Parameter estimation in Bayesian high-resolution image reconstruction with multisensors. *IEEE Transactions on Image Processing*, *12*(12), 1655–1667. doi:10.1109/TIP.2003.818117 PMID:18244719.

Monnet, A., Mittal, A., Paragios, N., & Ramesh, V. (2003). Background modeling and subtraction of dynamic scenes. *IEEE International Conference on Computer Vision (ICCV)* (pp. 1305 - 1312). IEEE ICCV.

Monteiro, J. (2009). *Quality assurance solutions for multipoint scalable video distribution over wireless IP networks*. (Ph.D. Dissertation). Instituto Superior Tecnico - Universidade Tecnica de Lisboa, Lisbon, Portugal.

Moon, H. (2004). Biometrics person authentication using projection-based face recognition system in verification scenario. In *Proceedings of the International Conference on Bioinformatics and its Applications*, (pp. 207-213). Hong Kong, China: IEEE.

Moravec, H. (1979). Visual mapping by a robot rover. *In Proceedings of the International Joint Conference on Artificial Intelligence* (pp. 598 - 600). IJCAI.

Morgan, L. E., & Pauls, F. (1939). Palm prints for infant identification. *The American Journal of Nursing, 39*(8), 866–868.

Morik, K., Brockhausen, P., & Joachims, T. (1999). Combining statistical learning with a knowledge-based approach -- A case study in intensive care monitoring. In *Proceedings of the 16th International Conference on Machine Learning* (ICML-99). San Francisco, CA: Morgan Kaufmann.

Morse, B.S. (1998-2004). *Image processing review, neighbors, connected components, and distance.*

Mosby. (2009). *Medical dictionary* (8th Ed.). London: Elsevier.

Moscoso, P., Cruz, R., & Nunes, M. (2011). Internet TV architecture based on scalable video coding. In *Proceedings of the 9th European Interactive TV Conference Workshop on Quality of Experience for Multimedia Content Sharing: Ubiquitous QoE Assessment and Support, QoEMCS'11.* QoEMCS.

Munoz-Slinas, R., Aguirre, E., & Miguel, G.-S. (2007). People detection and tracking using stereo vision and color. *Image and Vision Computing, 25*(6), 995–1007. doi:10.1016/j.imavis.2006.07.012.

Naik, A. K., & Holambe, R. S. (2010). A blind DCT domain digital watermarking for biometric authentication. *International Journal of Computers and Applications, 1*(16), 11–15.

Nalpantidis, L., Georgios, C., & Antonios, G. (2008). Review of Stereo Vision Algorithms: From Software to Hardware. *International Journal of Optomechatronics, 2,* 435–462. doi:10.1080/15599610802438680.

Nandakumar, K. (2008). *Multibiometric systems: Fusion strategies and template security.* (Ph.D. Thesis).

Nanni, L., & Lumini, A. (2007). A multi-matcher for ear authentication. *Pattern Recognition Letters, 28*(16), 2219–2226. doi:10.1016/j.patrec.2007.07.004.

Naor, M., & Pinkas, B. (1997). Visual authentication and identification. *LNCS, 1294.*

Niebles, J. C., Wang, H., & Fei-Fei, L. (2006). Unsupervised learning of human action cate-gories using spatial-temporal words. In *Proceedings of the British Machine Vision Conference (BMVC).* BMVC.

Ojala, T., Pietikainen, M., & Maenpaa, T. (2002). Multiresolution gray-scale and rotation invariant texture classification with local binary patterns. *IEEE Transactions on Pattern Analysis and Machine Intelligence, 24*(7), 971–987. doi:10.1109/TPAMI.2002.1017623.

Oliver, N., Rosario, B., & Pentland, A. (2000). A bayesian computer vision system for modeling human interactions. *IEEE Transactions Pattern Analysis Mach. Intell 22, 8* (pp. 831 - 843). IEEE.

On-Net Surveillance Systems Inc. (2006). *MJPEG vs MPEG4 - Understanding the differences, advantages and disadvantages of each compression technique* (White Paper). Author.

Panda, S. S., Prasad, M. S. R. S., & Jena, G. (2011). POCS-based super-resolution image reconstruction using an adaptive regularization parameter. *IJCSI International Journal of Computer Science Issues, 8*(5-2), 155-158.

Papageorgiou, C., Oren, M., & Poggio, T. (1998). A general framework for object detection. *IEEE International Conference on Computer Vision (ICCV)* (pp. 555 - 562). IEEE ICCV.

Paragios, N., & Deriche, R. (2005). Geodesic active regions and level set methods for motion estimation and tracking. *Computer Vision and Image Understanding, 97*(3), 259–282. doi:10.1016/j.cviu.2003.04.001.

Paragois, N., & Deriche, R. (2000). Geodesic active contours and level sets for the detection and tracking of moving objects. *IEEE Transactions. Pattern Analysis Mach. Intell. 22, 3* (pp. 266 - 280). IEEE.

Paragois, N., & Deriche, R. (2002). Geodesic active regions and level set methods for supervised yexture segmentation. *International Journal of Computer Vision, 46*(3), 223–247. doi:10.1023/A:1014080923068.

Parameswaran, V., & Chellappa, R. (2002). Quasi-invariants for human action representation and recognition. In *Proc. Int. Conf. Pattern Recogn: Perspectives on Motivation* (pp. 307–310). IEEE.

Parameswaran, L., & Anbumani, K. (2007). A semi-fragile image watermarking using wavelet inter coefficient relations. *International Journal of Information Security and Privacy*, *1*(3), 61–75. doi:10.4018/jisp.2007070105.

Park, J. M., Chong, E. K. P., & Siegel, H. J. (2002). Efficient multicast packet authentication using signature amortization. In *Proceedings of the IEEE Symposium on Security and Privacy*, (pp. 227-240). IEEE.

Park, S. C., Park, M. K., & Kang, M. G. (2003). Super-resolution image reconstruction. *IEEE Signal Processing Magazine*, *20*(3), 21–36. doi:10.1109/MSP.2003.1203207.

Parmeswaran, V., & Chellappa, R. (2003). View invariants for human action recognition. In *Proc. IEEE Comput. Soc. Conf. Comput. Vis. Pattern Recogn.: Perspectives on Motivation* (pp. 613–619). IEEE.

Patti, A. J., Sezan, M. I., & Tekalp, A. M. (1997). Super-resolution video reconstruction with arbitrary sampling lattices and nonzero aperture time. *IEEE Transactions on Image Processing*, *6*(8), 1064–1076. doi:10.1109/83.605404 PMID:18282997.

Pel'a, N. T. R., Mamede, M. V., & Tavares, M. S. G. (1975). Article. *Revista Brasileira de Enfermagem*, *29*, 100–105.

Peng, H. (2002). *A semi fragile water marking system for MPEG video authentication*. Paper presented at ICASSP. Orlando, FL.

Peng, B., Zhang, L., & Zhang, D. (2013). A survey of graph theoretical approaches to image segmentation. *Pattern Recognition*, *46*(3), 1020–1038. doi:10.1016/j.patcog.2012.09.015.

Pereira, F., & Ebrahimi, T. (2002). *The MPEG-4 book*. Upper Saddle River, NJ: Prentice Hall PTR.

Perrig, A., Canetti, R., Tygar, J., & Song, D. (2000). Efficient authentication and signing of multicast streams over lossy channels. In *Proceedings IEEE Symposium on Security and Privacy*. IEEE.

Ping, Y., & Bowyer, K. W. (2005). Empirical evaluation of advanced ear biometrics. In *Proceedings of Empirical Evaluation Methods in Computer Vision*. San Diego, CA: IEEE.

Pittner, S., & Kamarthi, S. V. (1999). Feature extraction from wavelet coefficients for pattern recognition tasks. *IEEE Transactions on Pattern Analysis and Machine Intelligence*, *21*(1). doi:10.1109/34.745739.

Pizurica, A., Zlokolica, V., Schulte, S., Kerre, E., & Philips, W. (2007). Combined wavelet domain and motion compensated filtering compliant with video codecs. In *Proceedings of IEEE International Conference on Acoustics, Speech, and Signal Processing* (pp. I-765-I-768). IEEE.

Podil Chuk, C. I., Jayant, N. S., & Farrardin, N. (1995). Three dimensional sub band coding of video. *IEEE Transactions on Image Processing*, *4*(2), 125–139. doi:10.1109/83.342187.

Polana, R., & Nelson, R. (1997). Detection and recognition of periodic, non-rigid motion. *Comput. Vis.*, *23*, 261–282. doi:10.1023/A:1007975200487.

Potdar, V. M., Han, S., & Chang, E. (2005). A survey of digital image watermarking techniques. In *Proceedings of the 3rd International Conference on Industrial Informatics*, (pp. 709-716). IEEE.

Prabhakar, S., Pankanti, S., & Jain, A. K. (2003). Biometric recognition: security and privacy concerns. *IEEE Security and Privacy*, *1*(2), 33–42. doi:10.1109/MSECP.2003.1193209.

Pradeep, K. A., Yan, W.-Q., Chang, E.-C., & Kankanhalli, M. S. (n.d.). *A hierarchical signature scheme for robust video authentication using secret sharing*.

Pradeep, K. A., El Saddik, A., & Kankanhalli, M. (2009). *Digital video authentication*. Hershey, PA: IGI Global.

Prati, A., Mikic, I., Trivedi, M. M., & Cucchiara, R. (2003). Detecting moving shadows: Algorithms and evaluation. *IEEE Transactions on Pattern Analysis and Machine Intelligence*, *25*(7), 918–923. doi:10.1109/TPAMI.2003.1206520.

Prokoski, F. (2000). History, current status, and future of infrared identification. In *Proceedings of the IEEE Workshop Computer Vision Beyond Visible Spectrum: Methods and Applications*, (pp. 5–14). IEEE.

Prokoski, F. J., Riedel, R. B., & Coffin, J. S. (1992). Identification of individuals by means of facial thermography. In *Proceedings of the IEEE International Carnahan Conference on Security Technology: Crime Countermeasures*, (pp. 120-125). Atlanta, GA: IEEE.

Queluz, M. P. (1998). Toward robust, content based techniques for image authentication. In *Proceedings of Multimedia Signal Processing*. IEEE. doi:10.1109/MMSP.1998.738950.

Queluz, M. P. (2001). Authentication of digital images and video: Generic models and a new contribution. *Signal Processing Image Communication*, *16*, 461–475. doi:10.1016/S0923-5965(00)00010-2.

Quisquater, J. (1997). Authentication of sequences with the SL2 hash function application to video sequences. *Journal of Computer Security*, *5*(3), 213–223.

Rafigh, M., & Moghaddam, M. E. (2010). A robust evolutionary based digital image watermarking technique in DCT domain. In *Proceedings of the Seventh International Conference on Computer Graphics, Imaging and Visualization (CGIV) 2010*, (pp. 105-109). CGIV.

Rangarajan, K., & Shah, M. (1991). Establishing motion correspondence.[IEEE.]. *Conference Vision Graphics Image Process*, *54*, 56–73.

Rao, C., & Shah, M. (2001). View-invariance in action recognition. In *Proceedings of the IEEE Conference on Computer Vision and Pattern Recognition (CVPR)*. IEEE.

Rao, C., Yilmaz, A., & Shah, M. (2002). View-invariant representation and recognition of actions. *International Journal of Computer Vision*, *50*(2), 203–226. doi:10.1023/A:1020350100748.

Reza, H., Broojeni, S., & Charkari, N. M. (2009). A new background subtraction method in video sequences based on temporal motion windows. *International Journal of the Computer, the Internet and Management*, *17*(SP1), 25.1-25.7.

Rittscher, J., Kato, J., Joga, S., & Blake, A. (2000). A probabilistic background model for tracking. *European Conference on Computer Vision (ECCV) Vol.2* (pp. 336 - 350). ECCV.

Rodriguez, M. D., Ahmed, J., & Shah, M. (2008). Action MACH: A spatio-temporal maximum average correlation height filter for action recognition. In *Proceedings of the IEEE Conference on Computer Vision and Pattern Recognition (CVPR)*. IEEE.

Rohani, M., & Avanaki, A. N. (2009). A watermarking method based on optimizing SSIM index using PSO in DCT domain.[CSICC.]. *Proceedings of CSICC, 2009*, 418–422.

Ronfard, R. (1994). Region based strategies for active contour models. *International Journal of Computer Vision*, *13*(2), 229–251. doi:10.1007/BF01427153.

Rosa, C., & Arsenio, A. (2010). *ASK4Stream - Location based mobile live video streaming on request*. Paper presented at the 10th National Conference on Computer Networks. Lisbon, Portugal.

Rota, N., & Thonnat, M. (2002). Activity recognition from video sequence using declarative models. In *Proceedings of the Eur. Conf. Artif. Intell: Perspectives on Motivation* (pp. 673-680). IEEE.

Rowe, S., & Blake, A. (1996). Statistical mosaics for tracking. *Israel Verj. Cap. j. 14*, 549 - 564.

Rowley, H., Baluja, S., & Andkanade, T. (1998). Neural network-based face detection. *IEEE Transactions. Pattern Analysis Mach. Intell. 20, 1* (pp. 23 - 38). IEEE.

Rubisley, P., Lemes, O. R., Bellon, P., Silva, L., & Jain, A. K. (2011). Biometric recognition of newborns: Identification using palmprints. In *Proceedings of the International Joint Conference on Biometrics*. Washington, DC: IEEE.

Ruichek, Y., Hariti, M., & Issa, H. (2007). Global techniques for Edge based Stereo Matching. In R. S. (Ed), Scene reconstruction pose estimation and tracking (pp. 383-410). Austria: I-tech education and publishing.

Ryoo, M. S., & Aggarwal, J. K. (2009). Spatio-temporal relationship match: Video structure comparison for recognition of complex human activities. In *Proceedings of the IEEE International Conference on Computer Vision (ICCV)*. IEEE.

Saikia, N., & Bora, P. K. (2007). Video authentication using temporal wavelet transform. In *Proceedings of the 15th International Conference on Advanced Computing and Communications (ADCOM 2007)*. ADCOM.

Salari, V., & Sethi, I. K. (1990). Feature point correspondence in the presence of occlusion.[IEEE.]. *IEEE Transactions on Pattern Analysis and Machine Intelligence*, 87–91. doi:10.1109/34.41387.

Sanin, A., Sanderson, C., & Lovell, B. C. (2012). Shadow detection: A survey and comparative evaluation of recent methods. *Pattern Recognition*, 45(2), 1684–1695. doi:10.1016/j.patcog.2011.10.001.

Savarese, S., DelPozo, A., Niebles, J., & Fei-Fei, L. (2008). Spatial-temporal correlations for unsupervised action classification. In *Proceedings of the IEEE Workshop on Motion and Video Computing (WMVC)*. IEEE.

Schmidt-Rohr, S., Knoop, S., Vacek, S., & Dillmann, R. (2007). Feature set selection and optimal classifier for human activity recognition. In *Proc. 16th IEEE International Conference on Robot & Human Interactive Communication: Perspectives on Motivation* (pp. 1022-1027). IEEE.

Schuldt, C., Laptev, I., & Caputo, B. (2004). Recognizing human actions: A local SVM approach. In *Proceedings of the International Conference on Pattern Recognition (ICPR), Vol. 3: Perspectives on Motivation* (pp. 32–36). IEEE.

Schwarz, H., Marpe, D., & Wiegand, T. (2007). Overview of the scalable video coding extension of the H.264/AVC Standard. *IEEE Transactions on Circuits and Systems for Video Technology*, 17(9). doi:10.1109/TCSVT.2007.905532.

Schweitzer, H., Bell, J., & Wu, F. (2002). Very fast template matching. *European Conference on Computer Vision (ECCV)* (pp. 358 - 372). IEEE.

Seal, A., Bhattacharjee, D., Nasipuri, M., & Basu, D. K. (2011a). Minutiae based thermal face recognition using blood perfusion data. In *Proceedings of the IEEE International Conference on Image Information Processing*. IEEE.

Seal, A., Bhattacharjee, D., Nasipuri, M., & Basu, D. K. (2011b). Minutiae from bit-plane sliced thermal images for human face recognition. In *Proceedings of the Springer International Conference on Soft Computing for Problem Solving*. Roorkee, India: Springer.

Seal, A., Bhattacharjee, D., Nasipuri, M., & Basu, D. K. (2012). Minutiae based thermal human face recognition using label connected component algorithm. In *Proceedings of the Elsevier International Conference on Computer, Communication, Control and Information Technology*. Elsevier.

Selesnick, I. W. (2004). The double-density dual-tree DWT. *IEEE Transactions on Signal Processing*, 52(5), 1304–1314. doi:10.1109/TSP.2004.826174.

Selesnick, I. W., Baraniuk, R. G., & Kingsbury, N. G. (2005). The dual-tree complex wavelet transform. *IEEE Signal Processing Magazine*, 22(6), 123–151. doi:10.1109/MSP.2005.1550194.

Seong, Y., & Park, H. (2008). Superresolution technique for planar objects based on an isoplane transformation. *Optical Engineering (Redondo Beach, Calif.)*, 47(5), 057007. doi:10.1117/1.2931461.

Sethi, I., & Jain, R. (1987). Finding trajectories of feature points in a monocular image sequence.[IEEE.]. *IEEE Transactions on Pattern Analysis and Machine Intelligence*, 56–73. doi:10.1109/TPAMI.1987.4767872 PMID:21869377.

Shafique, K., & Shah, M. (2003). A non-iterative greedy algorithm for multi-frame point correspondence. *IEEE International Conference on Computer Vision (ICCV)* (pp. 110 - 115). IEEE.

Shechtman, E., & Irani, M. (2005). Space-time behavior based correlation. In *Proceedings of the IEEE Conference on Computer Vision and Pattern Recognition (CVPR), Vol. 1: Perspectives on Motivation* (pp. 405–412). IEEE.

Sheikh, Y., Sheikh, M., & Shah, M. (2005). Exploring the space of a human action. In *Proceedings of the IEEE International Conference on Computer Vision (ICCV): Vol. 1: Perspectives on Motivation* (pp. 144–149). IEEE.

Shepard, K. S., Erickson, T., & Fromm, H. (1966). Limitations of footprinting as a means of infant identification. *Pediatrics*, 37(1). PMID:5948147.

Shi, J., & Malik, J. (2000). Normalized cuts and image segmentation. *IEEE Transactions Pattern Analysis Mach. Intell. 22, 8* (pp. 888 - 905). IEEE.

Shi, J., & Tomasi, C. (1994). Good features to track. In *Proceedings of IEEE Conference on Computer Vision and Pattern Recognition (CVPR)* (pp. 593-600). IEEE.

Shinfeng, D. L., Shie, S. C., & Guo, J. Y. (2010). Improving the robustness of DCT-based image watermarking against JPEG compression. *Computer Standards & Interfaces, 32*, 60–66.

Shinohara, Y., & Otsu, N. (2004). Facial expression recognition using Fisher weight maps. In *Proceedings of the IEEE International Conference on Automatic Face and Gesture Recognition*, (Vol. 100, pp. 499-504). IEEE.

Shiqian, W., Fang, Z. J., Xie, Z. H., & Liang, W. (2008). *Blood perfusion models for infrared face recognition*. Jiangxi, China: Jiangxi University of Finance and Economics.

Siddiqui, R., Sher, M., & Rashid, K. (2004). *Face identification based on biological trait using infrared images after cold effect enhancement and sunglasses filtering*. Retrieved from http://wscg.zcu.cz/wscg2004/Papers_2004_Poster/E97.pdf

Siegal, R., & Howell, J. (1981). *Thermal radiation heat transfer*. New York: McGraw-Hill.

Sim, T., Sukthankar, R., Mullin, M., & Baluja, S. (2000). Memory-based face recognition for visitor identification. In *Proceedings of the IEEE International Conference on Automatic Face and Gesture Recognition* (pp. 214-220). IEEE.

Singh, R., Vatsa, M., & Noore, A. (2006). Intelligent biometric information fusion using support vector machine. In *Soft Computing in Image Processing: Recent Advances*. Berlin: Springer Verlag.

Singh, R., Vatsa, M., Singh, S. K., & Upadhyay, S. (2008). *Integrating SVM classification with SVD watermarking for intelligent video authentication*. Telecommunication Systems Journal. doi:10.1007/s11235-008-9141-x.

Singh, S., & Papanikolopoulos, N. (1997). *Vision-based detection of driver fatigue (technical report)*. Minneapolis, MN: Department of Computer Science, University of Minnesota.

Socolinsky, D. A., & Selinger, A. (2004A). Thermal face recognition in an operational scenario. In *Proceedings of IEEE Conference on Computer Vision and Pattern Recognition*, (pp. 1012-1019). Washington, DC: IEEE.

Socolinsky, D., Wolff, L., Neuheisel, J., & Eveland, C. (2001). Illumination invariant face recognition using thermal infrared imagery. In *Proceedings of the IEEE Computer Society International Conference on Computer Vision and Pattern Recognition*, (Vol. 1, pp. 527-534). Kauai, HI: IEEE.

Sodagar, I. (2011). *Overview of dynamic adaptive streaming over HTTP (DASH)* (white-paper).

Song, H., He, X., Chen, W., & Sun, Y. (2010). An improved iterative back-projection algorithm for video super-resolution reconstruction. In *Proceedings of 2010 Symposium on Photonics and Optoelectronics* (pp. 1-4). IEEE.

Song, Y.-J., Kim, Y.-G., Kim, N., & Ahn, J.-H. (n.d.). Face recognition using both geometric features and PCA/LDA. In *Proceedings of the Sixth International Conference on Advanced Language Processing and Web Information Technology*. IEEE.

Souvenir, R., & Babbs, J. (2008). Learning the viewpoint manifold for action recognition. In *Proc. Conference on Computer Vision and Pattern Recognition: Perspectives on Motivation* (pp. 118-125). IEEE.

Stapleton, M.E. (1999). Best foot forward: Infant footprints for personal identification. *Law Enforcement Bulletin, 63*.

Stauffer, C., & Grimson, W. (2000). Learning patterns of activity using real time tracking. *IEEE Transactions Pattern Analysis Mach. Intell. 22, 8* (pp. 747 - 767). IEEE.

Stenger, B., Ramesh, V., Paragois, N., Coetzee, F., & Buhmann, J. (2001). Topology free hidden markov models: Application to background modeling. *IEEE International Conference on Computer Vision (ICCV)* (pp. 294 - 301). IEEE ICCV.

Sun, J., Zheng, N.-N., Tao, H., & Shum, H.-Y. (2003). Image hallucination with primal sketch priors. In *Proceedings of 2003 IEEE International Conference Computer Vision and Pattern Recognition* (pp. 2-729-2-740). IEEE.

Sun, Q., Chang, S.-F., & Maeno, K. (2002). A new semi fragile image authentication framework combining ECC and PKI infrastructure. Paper presented in ISCAS. Phoenix, AZ.

Sun, X., Chen, C. W., & Manjunath, B. S. (2002). Probabilistic motion parameter models for human activity recognition. In *Proc. ICPR: Vol. 1, Perspectives on Motivation* (pp. 443–446). IEEE.

Sun, Q., He, D., Zhang, Z., & Tian, Q. (2003). *A secure and robust approach to scalable video authentication*. ICME.

Suo, F., Hu, F., & Zhu, G. (2011). Robust super-resolution reconstruction based on adaptive regularization. In *Proceedings of 2011 International Conference on Wireless Communications and Signal Processing (WCSP)* (pp. 1-4). WCSP.

Su, P.-Y., Chen, C.-C., & Chang, H. M. (2009). Towards effective content authentication for digital videos by employing feature extraction and quantization. *IEEE Transactions on Circuits and Systems for Video Technology, 19*(5), 668–677. doi:10.1109/TCSVT.2009.2017404.

Swaminathan, V., & Bourges-Sevenier, M. (2010). *MPEG-J* (White Paper).

Takahashi, Y., & Taguchi, A. (2003). An arbitrary scale image enlargement method with the prediction of high-frequency components. *Electronics and Communications in Japan, 86*(8), 41–51. doi:10.1002/ecjc.10018.

Tanaka, T., & Kubo, N. (2004). Biometric authentication by hand vein patterns. In *Proceedings of SICE Annual Conference* (pp.249–253). Okayama, Japan: SICE.

Tang, Z., Deng, M., Xiao, C., & Yu, J. (2011). Projection onto convex sets super-resolution image reconstruction based on wavelet bi-cubic interpolation. In *Proceedings of 2011 International Conference on Electronic and Mechanical Engineering and Information Technology (EMEIT)* (pp. 351-354). EMEIT.

Tao, H., Sawhney, H., & Kumar, R. (2002). Object Tracking with Bayesian estimation of dynamic layer representations. *IEEE Trans. Patt. Analy. Mach. Intell. 24, 1* (pp. 75 - 89). IEEE.

Terzopoulos, D., & Szeliski, R. (1992). Tracking with kalman snakes. In A. V. Yuille (Ed.), *A. Blake, & A.* MIT Press.

Thompson, J. E., Clark, D. A., Salisbury, B., & Cahill, J. (1981). Footprinting the infant: Not cost-effective. *The Journal of Pediatrics, 99*, 797–798. doi:10.1016/S0022-3476(81)80415-5 PMID:6795326.

Tiwari, S., Singh, A., & Singh, S. K. (2011). Newborn's ear recognition: Can it be done? In *Proceedings of IEEE, International Conference on Image Information Processing*. IEEE.

Tiwari, S., Singh, A., & Singh, S. K. (2012a). Can ear and soft-biometric traits assist in recognition of newborn? In *Proceedings of International Conference on Computer Science, Engineering and Applications*. Berlin: Springer. DOI:10.1007/978-3-642-30157-5

Tiwari, S., Singh, A., & Singh, S. K. (2012b). Can face and soft-biometric traits assist in recognition of newborn? In *Proceedings of IEEE, International Conference on Recent Advanced in Information Technology*. IEEE.

Tiwari, S., Singh, A., & Singh, S. K. (2012c). Fusion of ear and soft-biometrics for recognition of newborn. *Signal & Image Processing: An International Journal, 3*(3), 103–116. doi:10.5121/sipij.2012.3309.

Tiwari, S., Singh, A., & Singh, S. K. (2012d). Integrating faces and soft-biometrics for newborn recognition. *International Journal of Advanced Computer Engineering & Architecture, 2*(2), 201–209.

Tiwary, R. K., & Sahoo, G. (2011). A novel methodology for data hiding in PDF files. *Information Security Journal: A Global Perspective, 20*(1), 45-57.

Toh, K., Eng, A. H. L., Choo, Y. S., Cha, Y. L., Yau, W. Y., & Low, K. S. (2006). Identity verification through palm vein and crease texture. In *Proceedings of the IEEE International Conference on Advances in Biometrics* (pp. 546-553). Hong Kong, China: IEEE.

Tomasi, C., & Manduchi, R. (1998). Bilateral filtering for gray and color images. In *Proceedings of 6th International Conference Computer Vision* (pp. 839-846). IEEE.

Tom, B. C., & Katsaggelos, A. K. (2001). Resolution enhancement of monochrome and color video using motion compensation. *IEEE Transactions on Image Processing*, *10*(2), 278–287. doi:10.1109/83.902292 PMID:18249618.

Toth, B. (2005). *Biometric liveness detection*. Information Security Bulletin.

Toyoma, K., Krumm, J., & Meyers, B. (1999). Wallflower: Principles and practices of background maintenance. *IEEE International Conference on Computer Vision (ICCV)* (pp. 255 - 261). IEEE ICCV.

Tredoux, C. G., Rosenthal, Y., Costa, L. D., & Nunez, D. (1999). Face reconstruction using a configural, eigenface-based composite system. In *Proceedings of the 3rd Biennial Meeting of the Society for Applied Research in Memory and Cognition* (SARMAC). Boulder, CO: SARMAC.

Trujillo, L., Olague, G., Hammoud, R., & Hernandez, B. (2005). Automatic feature localization in thermal images for facial expression recognition. In *Proceedings of the 2005 IEEE Computer Society Conference on Computer Vision and Pattern Recognition* (CVPR'05). IEEE.

Turk, M., & Pentland, A. (1991). Eigenfaces for recognition. *Journal of Cognitive Neuroscience*, *3*, 71–86. doi:10.1162/jocn.1991.3.1.71 PMID:23964806.

Upadhyay, S., Singh, S. K., Vatsa, M., & Singh, R. (2007). Video authentication using relative correlation information and SVM. In A. E. Hassanien, J. Kacprzyk, & A. Abraham (Eds.), *Computational Intelligence in Multimedia Processing: Recent Advances*. Berlin: Springer Verlag.

van Eekeren, A. W. M., Schutte, K., & van Vliet, L. J. (2010). Multiframe super-resolution reconstruction of small moving objects. *IEEE Transactions on Image Processing*, *19*(11), 2901–2912. doi:10.1109/TIP.2010.2068210 PMID:20729171.

Vapnik, V. N. (1995). *The nature of statistical learning theory*. Berlin: Springer Verlag. doi:10.1007/978-1-4757-2440-0.

Vaswani, N., Roychowdhury, A., & Chellappa, R. (2003). Activity recognition using the dynamics of the configuration of interacting objects. *IEEE Conference on Computer Vision and Pattern Recognition (CVPR)* (pp. 633 - 640). IEEE.

Vatsa, M., Singh, R., Noore, A., Houck, M. M., & Morris, K. (2006). Robust biometric image watermarking for fingerprint and face template protection. *IEICE Electronics Express*, *3*(2), 23–28. doi:10.1587/elex.3.23.

Vaughan-Nichols, S. (2010). Will HTML 5 restandardize the web? *Computer*, *43*(4), 13–15. doi:10.1109/MC.2010.119.

Veenman, C., Reinders, M., & Backer, E. (2001). Resolving motion correspondence for densely moving points. [IEEE]. *IEEE Transactions on Pattern Analysis and Machine Intelligence*, 54–72. doi:10.1109/34.899946.

Veeraraghavan, A., Chellappa, R., & Roy-Chowdhury, A. (2006). The function space of an activity. In *Proceedings of the IEEE Conference on Computer Vision and Pattern Recognition (CVPR), Vol. 1: Perspectives on Motivation* (pp. 959-968). IEEE.

Veksler, O. (2002). Dense features for semi-dense stereo correspondence. *International Journal of Computer Vision* *47(1 - 3)*, 247 - 260.

Veksler, O. (2003). Extracting dense features for visual correspondence with graph cuts. *Proceedings of IEEE Computer Society Conference on Computer Vision and Pattern Recognition* (pp. 689 - 694). IEEE.

Vellasques, E., Sabourin, R., & Granger, E. (2011). A high throughput system for intelligent watermarking of bi-tonal images. *Applied Soft Computing*, *11*, 5215–5229. doi:10.1016/j.asoc.2011.05.038.

Vermaak, J., Doucet, A., & Perez, P. (2003). Maintaining multimodality thorugh mixture tracking. *Ninth IEEE International Conference on Computer Vision* (pp. 1110 - 1116). IEEE.

Vermaak, J., Godsill, S., & Perez, P. (2005). Monte Carlo filtering for multi-target tracking and data association. [IEEE.]. *IEEE Transactions on Aerospace and Electronic Systems*, *41*, 309–332. doi:10.1109/TAES.2005.1413764.

Victor, B., Bowyer, K., & Sarkar, S. (2002). An evaluation of face and ear biometrics. In *Proceedings of the 16th International Conference on Pattern Recognition*. IEEE.

Ville, D. V. D., & Unser, M. (2008). Complex wavelet bases, steerability, and the Marr-like pyramid. *IEEE Transactions on Image Processing*, *17*(11), 2063–2080. doi:10.1109/TIP.2008.2004797 PMID:18972650.

Viola, P., & Jones, M. (2001). Rapid object detection using boosted cascade of simple features. In *Proceedings of IEEE Computer Vision and Pattern Recognition*. IEEE.

Viola, P., Jones, M., & Snow, D. (2003). Detecting pedestrians using patterns of motion and appearance. *IEEE International Conference on Computer Vision (ICCV)* (pp. 734 - 741). IEEE ICCV.

Viola, P., & Jones, M. (2004). Robust real-time face detection. *International Journal of Computer Vision, 57*(2), 137–154. doi:10.1023/B:VISI.0000013087.49260.fb.

Vyaghreswara, R. N., & Pandit Narahari, S. N. (2007). Multimedia digital rights protection using watermarking techniques. *Information Security Journal: A Global Perspective, 16*(2), 93-99.

Wang, K., & Zhang, Y. Yuan & Zhuang, D. (2006). Hand vein recognition based on multi supplemental features of multi-classifier fusion decision. In *Proceeding of the IEEE International Conference on Mechatronics and Automation* (pp. 1790-1795). Luoyang, Henan: IEEE.

Wang, Q., & Ward, R. (2003). A contour-preserving image interpolation method. In *Proceedings of IEEE International Conference Image Processing* (pp. 2-673-2-676). IEEE.

Wang, W., & Farid, H. (2007). Exposing digital forgeries in video by detecting duplication. In *Proceedings of the 9th Workshop on Multimedia & Security*. IEEE.

Wang, L., Hu, W., & Tan, T. (2002). Recent developments in human motion analysis. *Pattern Recognition, 36*(3), 585–601. doi:10.1016/S0031-3203(02)00100-0.

Wang, L., & Leedham, G. (2005). A thermal hand-vein pattern verification system. In S. Singh, M. Singh, C. Apte, & P. Perner (Eds.), *Pattern Recognition and Image Analysis (LNCS)* (Vol. 3687, pp. 58–65). New York: Springer. doi:10.1007/11552499_7.

Wang, L., Leedham, G., & Cho, D. S. Y. (2008). Minutiae feature analysis for infrared hand vein pattern biometrics. *Pattern Recognition, 41*(3), 920–929. doi:10.1016/j.patcog.2007.07.012.

Wang, Y., Lin, W., & Yang, L. (2011). An intelligent watermarking method based on particle swarm optimization. *Expert Systems with Applications, 38*, 8024–8029. doi:10.1016/j.eswa.2010.12.129.

Wang, Y., & Pearmain, A. (2004). Blind image data hiding based on self reference. *Pattern Recognition Letters, 25*, 1689–1697. doi:10.1016/j.patrec.2004.06.012.

Wang, Z., & Bovik, A. C. (2004). A universal image quality index. *IEEE Signal Processing Letters, 9*(3), 81–84. doi:10.1109/97.995823.

Wang, Z., Sun, X., & Zhang, D. (2007). A novel watermarking scheme based on PSO algorithm. *LNCS, 4688*, 309–314.

Watanabe, M., Endoh, T., Shiohara, M., & Sasaki, S. (2005). *Palm vein authentication technology and its applications*. Paper presented at the Biometric Consortium Conference. Arlington, VA.

Wayman, J. L., Jain, A. K., Maltoni, D., & Maio, D. (2005). *Biometric systems: Technology, design and performance evaluation*. Berlin: Springer.

Weingaertner, D., Bello, O., & Silva, L. (2008). Newborn's biometric identification: Can it be done? In *Proceedings of the VISAPP*. VISAPP.

Weinland, D., & Boyer, E. (2008). Action recognition using exemplar-based embedding. In *Proc. Conference on Computer Vision and Pattern Recognition: Perspectives on Motivation* (pp. 1-7). IEEE.

Weinland, D., & Ronfard, R. (2011). A survey of vision based methods for action representation, segmentation and recognition. *International Journal of Computer Vision and Image Understanding, 115*, 221–241.

Weinland, D., Ronfard, R., & Boyer, E. (2006). Free viewpoint action recognition using motion history volumes. *Int. Journal Computer Vision and Image Understanding, 104*(2), 249–257. doi:10.1016/j.cviu.2006.07.013.

Weiss, Y. (1999). Segmentation using Eigenvectors: a unifying view. *Proc. IEEE Internatinal Conference on Computer Vision* (pp. 975-982). IEEE Newspapers & Conf.

Wickerhauser, M. V. (1994). *Adapted wavelet analysis from theory to software*. AK Peters Ltd..

Wiegand, S., Sullivan, G., & Luthra, A. (2003). *Overview of the H.264/AVC video coding standard*.

Wierschem, J. (1965). Know them by their feet. *Medical Record News, 168*, 158–160.

Wijaya, S. L., Savvides, M., & Kumar, B. V. K. V. (2005). Illumination-tolerant face verification of low-bitrate JPEG2000 wavelet images with advanced correlation filters for handheld devices. *Applied Optics*, *44*, 655–665. doi:10.1364/AO.44.000655 PMID:15751847.

Wilder, J., Phillips, P., Jiang, C., & Wiener, S. (1996). Comparison of visible and infra-red imagery for face recognition. In *Proceedings of the IEEE International Conference on Automatic Face and Gesture Recognition (AFGR '96)*, (pp. 182-187). Killington, VT: IEEE.

Wilson, C. (2010). *Vein pattern recognition: A privacy-enhancing biometric*. Boca Raton, FL: CRC Press. doi:10.1201/9781439821381.

Windsor, O. (2007). *A statistical approach towards performance analysis of multimodal biometrics systems*. (Ph.D. Thesis).

Wohlmacher, P. (1998). Requirements and mechanism of IT-security including aspects of multimedia security. In *Proceedings of the Multimedia and Security Workshop at ACM Multimedia 98*. Bristol, UK: ACM.

Wong, S.-F., Kim, T.-K., & Cipolla, R. (2007). Learning motion categories using both semantic and structural information. In *Proceedings of the IEEE Conference on Computer Vision and Pattern Recognition (CVPR)*. IEEE.

Wren, C., Azarbayejani, A., & Pentland, A. (1997). Pfinder: Real-time tracking of the human body. *IEEE Transactions Pattern Analysis Mach. Intell. 19, 7* (pp. 780 - 785). IEEE.

Wu, S. Q., Gu, Z. H., Chia, K. A., & Ong, S. H. (2007). Infrared facial recognition using modified blood perfusion. In *Proceedings 6th Int. Conf. Inform., Comm., & Sign*. IEEE.

Wu, D. C., & Tsai, W. H. (2003). A steganographic method for images by pixel-value differencing. *J Pattern Recognition Letters*, *24*, 1626–1639.

Wu, J. D., & Ye, S. H. (2009). Driver identification using finger-vein patterns with Radon transform and neural network. *International Journal on Expert System with Applications*, *36*(3), 5793–5799. doi:10.1016/j.eswa.2008.07.042.

Wu, Z., & Leahy, R. (1993). An optimal graph theoretic approach to data clustering: Theory and its applications to image segmentation.[IEEE.]. *IEEE Transactions on Pattern Analysis and Machine Intelligence*, *11*, 1101–1113. doi:10.1109/34.244673.

Xiaolong, L., Yang, B., Cheng, D., & Zheng, T. (2009). A generalization of LSB matching. *IEEE Signal Processing Letters*, *16*(2), 69–72. doi:10.1109/LSP.2008.2008947.

Xu, N., & Ahuja, N. (2002). Object contour tracking using graph cuts based active contours. *IEEE International Conference on Image Processing (ICIP)* (pp. 277 - 280). IEEE ICIP.

Xu, D., Li, X., Liu, Z., & Yuan, Y. (2005). Cast shadow detection in video segmentation. *Pattern Recognition Letters*, *26*(1), 91–99. doi:10.1016/j.patrec.2004.09.005.

Yacoob, Y., & Black, M. (1998). Parameterized modeling and recognition of activities. In *Proc. Int. Conference on Computer Vision: Perspectives on Motivation* (pp.120-127). IEEE.

Yanagawa, T., Aoki, S., & Ohyama, T. (2007). *Human finger vein images are diverse and its patterns are useful for personal identification*. Kyushu University.

Yang, C. H., Weng, C. Y., Wang, S. J., & Sun, H. M. (2008). Adaptive data hiding in edge areas of pixels with spatial LSB domain systems. *IEEE Transactions on Information Forensics and Security*, *3*(3), 488–497. doi:10.1109/TIFS.2008.926097.

Yang, G. B., & Zhang, Z. Y. (2004). Objective performance evaluation of video segmentation algorithms with ground-truth. *Journal of Shanghai University*, *8*(1), 70–74. doi:10.1007/s11741-004-0015-5.

Yan, W.-Q., & Kankanhalli, M. S. (2003). Motion trajectory based video authentication. *ISCAS*, *3*, 810–813.

Ye, X., & Lu, X. (2011). A performance evaluation of image interpolation and superresolution algorithms. In *Proceedings of 2011 International Conference on Multimedia Technology (ICMT)* (pp. 4776-4779). ICMT.

Yilmaz, A., & Shah, M. (2005). Actions sketch: A novel action representation. In *Proceedings of the IEEE Conference on Computer Vision and Pattern Recognition (CVPR), Vol. 1: Perspectives on Motivation* (pp. 984-989). IEEE.

Yilmaz, A., Javed, O., & Shah, M. (2006). Object Tracking. *Survey (London, England)*.

Yin, M., & Narita, S. (2002). *Speedup method for real-time thinning algorithm*. Paper presented at Digital Image Computing Techniques and Applications. Melbourne, Australia.

Yin, P., & Yu, H. H. (n.d.). Classification of video tampering methods and countermeasures using digital watermarking. In *Proceedings of SPIE* (Vol. 4518, pp. 239–246). SPIE.

Yoshitomi, Y., Miyaura, T., Tomita, S., & Kimura, S. (1997). Face identification using thermal image processing. In *Proceedings of the IEEE Int. Workshop Robot Hum. Commun.*, (pp. 374–379). IEEE.

Zebbiche, K., Ghouti, L., Khelifi, F., & Bouridane, A. (2006). Protecting fingerprint data using watermarking. In *Proceedings of the First NASA/ESA Conference on Adaptive Hardware and Systems (AHS)*, (pp. 451-456). NASA/ESA.

Zebbiche, K., Khelifi, F., & Bouridane, A. (2008). An efficient watermarking technique for the protection of fingerprint images. *EURASIP Journal on Information Security*. Article Id 918601.

Zelnik-Manor, L., & Irani, M. (2001). Event-based analysis of video. In *Proceedings of the IEEE Conference on Computer Vision and Pattern Recognition (CVPR)*. IEEE.

Zhang, Y. B., Li, Q., You, J., & Bhattacharya, P. (2007). Palm vein extraction and matching for personal authentication. In *Proceedings of the 9th International Conference Advances in Visual Information Systems* (pp.154–164). Shanghai, China: IEEE.

Zhang, Z., Ma, S., & Han, X. (2006). Multiscale feature extraction of finger-vein patterns based on curvelets and local interconnection structure neural network. In *Proceedings of the 18th International Conference on Pattern Recognition* (pp. 145 – 148). Hong Kong, China: IEEE.

Zhang, H., Fritts, J. E., & Goldman, S. A. (2008). Image segmentation evaluation: A survey of unsupervised methods. *Computer Vision and Image Understanding*, *110*(2), 260–280. doi:10.1016/j.cviu.2007.08.003.

Zhang, L., & Wu, X. (2006). An edge-guided image interpolation algorithm via directional filtering and data fusion. *IEEE Transactions on Image Processing*, *15*(8), 2226–2238. doi:10.1109/TIP.2006.877407 PMID:16900678.

Zhang, T. Y., & Suen, C. Y. (1984). A fast parallel algorithm for thinning digital patterns. *Communications of the ACM*, *27*(3), 236–239. doi:10.1145/357994.358023.

Zhang, X.-P., Desai, M. D., & Peng, Y.-N. (1999). Orthogonal complex filter banks and wavelets: Some properties and design. *IEEE Transactions on Signal Processing*, *47*(4), 1039–1048. doi:10.1109/78.752601.

Zhao, L., Qi, W., Li, S., Yang, S., & Zhang, H. (2000). Key frame extraction and shot retrieval using nearest feature line (NFL). In *Proceedings of ACM Multimedia*. ACM.

Zhao, Q., Liu, F., Zhang, L., & Zhang, D. (2010). A comparative study on quality assessment of high resolution fingerprint images. In *Proceedings of the International Conference on Image Processing* (ICIP, 2010), (pp. 3089-3092). ICIP.

Zhong, J., & Sclaroff, S. (2003). Segmenting foreground objects from a dynamic textured background via a robust kalman filter. *IEEE International Conference on Computer Vision (ICCV)* (pp. 44 - 50). IEEE ICCV.

Zhou, S., Chellapa, R., & Moghadam, B. (2003). Adaptive visual tracking and recognition using particle filters. *IEEE International Conference on Multimedia and Expo (ICME)* (pp. 349 - 352). IEEE.

Zhou, R. W., Quek, C., & Ng, G. S. (1995). A novel single-pass thinning algorithm and an effective set of performance criteria. *Pattern Recognition Letters*, *16*(12), 1267–1275. doi:10.1016/0167-8655(95)00078-X.

About the Contributors

Rajeev Srivastava is currently working as an Associate Professor in the Dept. of Computer Engineering, Indian Institute of Technology (BHU), Varanasi, India, since November 2007. He received his Ph.D. degree in Computer Engineering from Faculty of Technology, University of Delhi, Delhi. He has around 15 years of teaching and research experience. He has around 50 research publications in refereed journals, conferences, in edited books as book chapters and two books published by an international publisher (Germany) to his credit. He is reviewer of many international journals and technical program committee member of many international conferences. He was awarded a project by the NMEICT, MHRD, Govt. of India in 2010 for the design and development of an interactive e-content for the subject digital image processing and machine vision. His biography was listed in *Marquis Who's Who is Science and Engineering*, USA, 11th edition, 2011-12 and "2000 Outstanding Intellectuals of the 21st Century-2011" by IBC, Cambridge, UK. He is the recipient of "2010 Publication Scholar Award" by IIT-BHU Global Alumni Association. He has delivered many invited talks in his research area. He was the coordinator and Organizing Secretary of a Refresher Course on ICT applications and a National conference on AI and Agents Applications, respectively. His research interests include image processing and computer vision, medical image processing, pattern recognition, video surveillance, and algorithms.

Sanjay K. Singh is Associate Professor in Department of Computer Engineering at Indian Institute of Technology (Banaras Hindu University), Varanasi, India. He is a certified Novel Engineer and Novel administrator. His research has been funded by UGC and AICTE. He has over 70 publications in refereed journals, book chapters, and conferences. His research interests include computational intelligence, biometrics, video authentication, pattern recognition, and machine learning. Dr. Singh is a member of IET, IEEE, ISTE, CSI.

K. K. Shukla is professor of Computer Engineering at Indian Institute of Technology, BHU, India. He has 30 years of research and teaching experience. Professor Shukla has published more than 120 research papers in reputed journals and conferences and has more than 100 citations. 15 Ph.D.s have been awarded under his supervision. Professor Shukla has to his credit many projects of national importance at BHU, Hindustan Aeronautics, and Smiths Aerospace, UK. Presently, he has research collaboration with Space Applications Center, ISRO, Tata Consultancy Services, Institut National de Recherche en Informatique et en Automatique (INRIA), France, and E´cole de Technologie Supe´rieure (ETS), Canada. He has written 4 books on neuro-computers, real time task scheduling, fuzzy modeling, and image compression, and has contributed chapters to 3 books published in the USA. Professor Shukla is a Fellow of the Institution of Engineers, Fellow of the Institution of Electronics and Telecommunications Engineers, Senior Member, ISTE, and the Senior Member, Computer Society of India.

* * *

Artur Arsénio is currently YDreams Robotics CEO, and an Assistant Professor in Computer Science and Computer Networks Engineering at Instituto Superior Técnico. He received his doctoral degree in Computer Science from the Massachusetts Institute of Technology (MIT) in Robotics and Artificial Intelligence in 2004, and his MSc and Engineering degree from Lisbon's Instituto Superior Técnico. In 2005, Artur Arsénio joined Siemens as a Solution Leader Architect on its IPTV and SmartHome projects, where he led several international teams and become the technical responsible for the SmartHome solution. From 2008 until May 2012, he headed Innovation at Nokia Siemens Networks Portugal S.A. (NSN). He has authored/co-authored over 90 papers in book chapters, journals, and conferences, and holds several international patent applications, acting as journal editor, session chairman, reviewer, and committee member for several international IEEE conferences and journals. He is co-founder and vice-chair of the ACM SIGCOMM chapter in Portugal. He is the recipient of several international scientific and innovation awards. He is a Fulbrighter, and the president of the MIT alumni association in Portugal.

Roli Bansal is currently pursuing Ph. D. under the joint supervision of Dr. Punam Bedi and Dr. Priti Sehgal from the Dept. of Computer Science, University of Delhi. She is working in the area of fingerprint image enhancement and watermarking. She completed her M.C.A. in 1997, and since then she has been working as Assistant Professor in Keshav College, University of Delhi.

Punam Bedi received her Ph.D. in Computer Science from the Department of Computer Science, University of Delhi, India in 1999 and her M.Tech. in Computer Science from IIT Delhi, India, in 1986. She is an Associate Professor in the Department of Computer Science, University of Delhi. She has about 25 years of teaching and research experience and has published about 120 papers in national/international journals/conferences. Dr. Bedi is a member of AAAI, ACM, senior member of IEEE, and life member of Computer Society of India. Her research interests include Web Intelligence, Soft Computing, Semantic Web, Multi-Agent Systems, Intelligent Information Systems, Intelligent Software Engineering, Intelligent User Interfaces, Requirement Engineering, Human Computer Interaction (HCI), Trust, Information Retrieval, and Personalization.

Seng Kah Phooi received the Bachelor of Engineering (1st class) and PhD in Engineering from University of Tasmania, Australia, in 1997 and 2001, respectively. She is currently an Adjunct Professor at Sunway University. She was a Professor and Head of Department of Computer Science & Networking in Sunway University. She was also the Director of Affective & Assistive Technologies (AAT) Research Centre in Sunway University. Prior to joining Sunway University, she was Associate Professor at School of Electrical and Electronic Engineering, Nottingham University. She and another colleague Dr Kenneth Li Minn Ang formed a research group called Visual Information Engineering Research (VIER) group in Nottingham University, Malaysia campus. She also worked in Monash University in Malaysia, Tasmania and Griffith Universities in Australia before joining Nottingham University. Her research interests include the fields of visual processing, multi-biometrics, artificial intelligence, affective computing and wireless visual sensor networks.

Ilaiah Kavati received B.Tech. and M.Tech. from JNTU Hyderabad, India. Currently pursuing Ph.D. from University of Hyderabad, India. His research interests include biometrics, pattern recognition, and image processing.

Ashish Khare received M.Sc. (Computer Science) and D. Phil. degree both from Department of Electronics and Communication, University of Allahabad, Allahabad, India, in 1999 and 2007, respectively. He did his post-doctoral research from Gwangju Institute of Science and Technology, Gwangju, South Korea, in 2007-2008. Presently, he is working as an Assistant Professor in Department of Electronics and Communication, University of Allahabad. His research interests include applications of wavelet transforms, computer vision, cyber security, and human behaviour understanding. He is working as Principal Investigator on research projects funded by UGC and DST. He has supervised a number of Ph.D. students and has published one book and more than 50 research papers.

Manish Khare is pursuing for his D.Phil. degree in Computer Science from University of Allahabad, Allahabad, India. Previously, he obtained M. Tech. degree in Computer Science and Engineering from School of IT, Centre for Development of Advanced Computing, Noida, India, in year 2009, and M. Sc. in Computer Science from University of Allahabad in year 2006. He is a student member of IEEE. His Research interests include Image and Video Processing, Computer Vision, and Wavelet Transforms. He has published more than 10 papers in International Journals, International and National Conferences.

Hwa-Young Kim was born in Busan, Korea, in 1983. She received the B.S. and M.S. degrees in electronic engineering from Sogang University, Seoul, Korea, in 2007 and 2009, respectively. She is currently working in Central Advanced Research & Engineering Institute, Hyundai Motor Company. Her current research interests are computer vision for preventing collisions and intelligent safety car.

Sung Hyun Kim was born in Seoul, Korea, in 1975. He received the B.S. and M.S. degrees in electronic engineering from Sogang University, Seoul, Korea, in 2002 and 2004, respectively. His current research interests are image enhancement and computer vision.

Yeong Lee Seng received the Masters of Engineering from the University of Nottingham in 2004. He is currently a lecturer and researcher at Sunway University. His current research interest includes visual processing, sensor networks and reconfigurable computing.

Ang Li-Minn received the Bachelor of Engineering (1ˢᵗ class) and PhD in Engineering from Edith Cowan University, Australia, in1996 and 2001, respectively. He is currently a research staff at School of Engineering, Edith Cowan University. Prior to joining Edith Cowan University, he was Associate Professor at School of Electrical and Electronic Engineering, Nottingham University. He was also the research group leader of research group called Visual Information Engineering Research (VIER) group in Nottingham University, Malaysia campus. He also worked in Monash University Malaysia before joining Nottingham University. His research interests include the fields of video compression, visual processing, wireless visual sensor networks, and reconfigurable computing.

Shalabh Parashar received his Master degree in computer application in 2007. He is currently working as Project Lead in HCL Technologies, Noida, India. He has been working for projects of Microsoft and GE. He is also the member of HCL gold club. Currently, he is involved in the development of a robust video authentication system that can identify different tampering attacks to determine the authenticity of the video. His current areas of interest include software development, pattern recognition, video and image processing, watermarking, and artificial intelligence.

Rae-Hong Park was born in Seoul, Korea, in 1954. He received the B.S. and M.S. degrees in electronics engineering from Seoul National University, Seoul, Korea, in 1976 and 1979, respectively, and the M.S. and Ph.D. degrees in electrical engineering from Stanford University, Stanford, CA, USA, in 1981 and 1984, respectively. In 1984, he joined the faculty of the Department of Electronic Engineering, Sogang University, Seoul, Korea, where he is currently a Professor. In 1990, he spent his sabbatical year as a Visiting Associate Professor with the Computer Vision Laboratory, Center for Automation Research, University of Maryland at College Park, USA. In 2001 and 2004, he spent sabbatical semesters at Digital Media Research and Development Center (DTV image/video enhancement), Samsung Electronics Co., Ltd., Suwon, Korea. In 2012, he spent a sabbatical year in Digital Imaging Business (R&D Team) and Visual Display Business (R&D Office), Samsung Electronics Co., Ltd., Suwon, Korea. His current research interests are video communication, computer vision, and pattern recognition. He served as Editor for the Korea Institute of Telematics and Electronics (KITE) *Journal of Electronics Engineering* from 1995 to 1996. Dr. Park was the recipient of a 1990 Post-Doctoral Fellowship presented by the Korea Science and Engineering Foundation (KOSEF), the 1987 Academic Award presented by the KITE, the 2000 Haedong Paper Award presented by the Institute of Electronics Engineers of Korea (IEEK), the 1997 First Sogang Academic Award, and the 1999 Professor Achievement Excellence Award presented by Sogang University. He is a co-recipient of the Best Student Paper Award of the IEEE Int. Symp. Multimedia (ISM 2006) and IEEE Int. Symp. Consumer Electronics (ISCE 2011).

Munaga V. N. K. Prasad received his Ph.D. from the Institute of Technology, Banaras Hindu University, India. He is currently working as Assistant professor in Institute for Development and Research in Banking Technology (IDRBT), Hyderabad. His research interests include biometrics, digital watermarking, and payment system technologies. Nearly 40 international journal and conference papers to his credit. He is a Member IEEE, Life Member IUPRAI.

Mohamed Saifuddin obtained his BSc (Hons) in Computer Science from the University of Nottingham in 2011. Since 2012, he has been pursuing MSc in Computer Science (by Research) from the Sunway University under the Sunway-Lancaster Masters Programme. His main topic of research is Stereo Vision.

Ayan Seal received the B.TECH degree from Jalpaiguri Government Engineering College in 2007 and M.TECH degree from N.I.T.T.T.R, Kolkata, in 2009. Now he is pursuing Ph.D. (Engg.) in the department of Computer Science and Engineering, Jadavpur University, India. He is DST INSPIRE Fellow. His current research interest is thermal face recognition for biometric security system.

Priti Sehgal received her Ph.D. in Computer Science from the Department of Computer Science, University of Delhi, India, in 2006, and her M. Sc. in Computer Science from DAVV, Indore, India, in 1994. She is an Associate Professor in the Department of Computer Science, Keshav Mahavidyalaya, University of Delhi. She has about 17 years of teaching and research experience and has published numerous papers in national/international journals/conferences. Dr. Sehgal has been a member of the program committee of the CGIV International Conference and is a life member of Computer Society of India. Her research interests include Computer Graphics, Image Processing, Biometrics, Visualization, and Image Retrieval.

Alok Kumar Singh Kushwaha received the B.Sc. degree in Maths and M.Sc. degree in Computer Science from University of Allahabad, Allahabad, India, in 2007 and 2009. He received the M.Tech degree in Computer Science (Specialization in Software Engineering) from the Devi Ahilya University, Indore, India, in 2011. He worked as Asst. Professor in GLA University, Mathura, India. He is a member of Computer Society of India. Currently, he is a Ph.D. Research Scholar in the Department of Computer Engineering at the Indian Institute of Technology (Banaras Hindu University), Varanasi (U.P.) India. He has been working on image processing and video processing. His research area includes video segmentation, classification, tracking, and human activity analysis in videos.

Rajneesh Kumar Srivastava has received his Ph.D. degree from University of Allahabad, Allahabad, India, in 2008. He received his M.Tech. degree from IT-BHU, Varanasi. Presently he is working as an Assistant Professor in Department of Electronics and Communication, University of Allahabad, India. Earlier he worked as research staff at CRL, BEL, Ghaziabad, India. His research interests include Photo Electrets, Mobile Communication, and Image Processing. He is also serving as Principal Investigator of research project sponsored by UGC. He has supervised a number of Ph.D. students and has published one book and more than 50 research papers.

Shrikant Tiwari received his M.Tech. degree in Computer Science and Technology from University of Mysore, India, in 2009. He is currently working toward the PhD degree at the Indian Institute of Technology (Banaras Hindu University), Varanasi, India. His research interests include Biometrics, Image Processing, and Pattern Recognition.

Saurabh Upadhyay received the B. Tech. degree in computer science and engineering in 2001 and is currently working toward the Ph.D. degree in computer science at U.P. Technical University, India. He is an Associate Professor in the Department of Computer Science and Engineering, Saffrony Institute of Technology, Gujarat, India. He is actively involved in the development of a robust video authentication system, which can identify tampering to determine the authenticity of the video. His current areas of interest include pattern recognition, video and image processing, watermarking, and artificial intelligence.

Seungjoon Yang received the B.S. degree from Seoul National University, Seoul, Korea, in 1990, and the M.S. and Ph.D. degrees from the University of Wisconsin-Madison, in 1993 and 2000, respectively, all in electrical engineering. He was with the Digital Media R&D Center at Samsung Electronics Co., Ltd. from September 2000 to August 2008. He is currently with the School of Electrical and Computer Engineering at the Ulsan National Institute of Science and Technology in Ulsan, Korea. His research interests are in image processing, estimation theory, and multi-rate systems. Professor Yang received the Samsung Award for the Best Technology Achievement of the Year in 2008 for his work in the premium digital television platform project.

Index

A

abnormal human actions 184
activity recognition algorithm 186
Application Service Provider (ASP) 157-159

B

basal metabolism 10
binarization 57, 64
binary closing morphological operation 147, 151
block matching algorithms (BMAs) 119

C

CCTV cameras 184
complex scaling function 142-144
Computationally Intelligent watermarking 67, 83
computer vision 2-3, 7-8, 13, 19-23, 33, 48, 50-51,
    88, 91-92, 96, 107, 112-117, 134-136, 138-140,
    144-145, 149, 152-153, 155-160, 162, 167,
    181, 183-184, 186, 192, 194-198, 229
condensation algorithm 107, 112
Content Management Systems 157, 160
core temperature 9
criminal investigations 200
Cumulative Match Curves (CMC) 34, 39, 45-46, 59,
    62

D

Daubechies complex wavelet transform 138, 140-
    146, 148-155
Decision Module 27
digital signatures 210-211, 231
digital watermarking 67, 69-70, 85-86, 88, 231
Discrete Wavelet Transform (DWT) 74, 77, 85, 138-
    141, 144-145, 150, 154-155

E

edge-stereo matching activity 96
Eigenface 11-12, 42

F

Face Detection 5, 8, 20, 26, 33, 49, 51, 115, 159-
    162, 181
facial thermograms 11
Far Infrared (FIR) 54, 59
Feature Extraction Module 27
fingerprint-based identification 65, 67
fragile watermarking 71, 77, 85, 199, 210, 212, 219,
    228, 231
frame addition attack 206-207, 223-224, 226
frame removal attack 206-207, 222-223, 226-227
frame shuffling attack 206-208

G

global thresholding algorithm 55
gradient descent method 125

H

Hand Geometry 3, 26, 32, 53, 66
hidden Markov models (HMMs) 186
HTML5 164
HTTP Streaming 164

I

Iris Pattern 26, 32

K

Kalman filters 107, 110, 113-114, 116
karaoke 161-162, 172

L

Least Significant Bits (LSB) Matching 72, 86-87
Lifecasting 158
Long-Wave Infrared (LWIR) imagery spectrum 12

M

machine learning 22, 162, 185, 231
Matching Module 27
Matching Pursuit Filters 11
media authenticity verification 200
Misclassification Penalty (MP) 147
Motion Energy Images (MEI) 185
Motion Estimation (ME) 59, 110, 118-129, 132-134, 136-137, 168
Motion History Images (MHI) 185
Motion JPEG (MJPEG)human activity recognition 165, 181
multi-modal biometrics 27

O

object based network mechanism 159
object detection 49, 51, 91-93, 100-101, 107, 110-111, 114, 117, 153, 171-176, 179, 181
object modification attack 204, 206
object removal attack 204-205

P

particle filters 107, 116
Particle Swarm Optimization (PSO) 75, 78, 89
patchwork techniques 72
Peak Signal to Noise Ratio (PSNR) 82-84, 127
Photoshop 157, 203
post-event investigation tool 184
predictive coding 73, 167
primary biometric disciplines 66
Projection Onto Convex Sets (POCS)-based method 118-123, 125-132, 134-135, 137
prosumer 158

Q

qualitative motion heuristics 105

R

Radiant emission 7
Relative Position-based Measure (RPM) 147
Resolution Enhancement (RE) 119

S

Scalability 167-169, 179
Sensor or Biometric Capture Module 27
shadow detection 138-140, 144, 149-152, 154-155
SIFT (Scale Invariant Feature Transform) technique 101
Signature Dynamics 26
spatial tampering attacks 203-204, 208, 220, 222, 224-227
spatio-temporal tampering attacks 203
spring model 109
steady-state conditions 9
stereo vision 91-94, 100, 105, 110-112, 114, 117
Super Resolution (SR) 118-123, 125-129, 131-133, 137, 153
Support Vector Machine 12, 108, 199, 216, 219-221, 226, 230-231
SVM learning 220, 222

T

temporal tampering attacks 203, 206, 208, 220
Texture Block Coding 73
Thermal emission 5-6, 8
thermoneutral environment 9
Transform Coding of Grey Scale Projections 11
Triangulation 63, 94-96

U

unimodal biometric system 27, 41, 43, 45
Unmanned Aerial Vehicle (UAV) 192

V

vein pattern authentication 52, 58
Video Codecs 126, 135, 163, 165

W

wavelet theory 138